The

ILLUSTRATED ENCYCLOPEDIA

of

Roses

The

ILLUSTRATED ENCYCLOPEDIA

of

Roses

GENERAL EDITOR

Mary Moody

CONSULTING EDITOR

Peter Harkness

Timber Press
Portland, Oregon

Contributing writers:

Gillian Appleton, Susan Barrett M.A.I.H., Kaye Healey,
Susan McAffer, Dr Judyth McLeod M.A.I.H.,
Mary Moody, Jennifer Rollins

Miniature rose Baby Darling

Published in North America and the United Kingdom by Timber Press, Inc.
The Haseltine Building
133 S.W. Second Avenue, Suite 450
Portland Oregon 97204, U.S.A.
1-800-327-5680 (U.S.A and Canada only)

First published 1992
Reprinted 1997, 1999
ISBN 0-88192-271-4

Published by Lansdowne Publishing Pty Ltd
Level 1, The Argyle Centre
18 Argyle Street, The Rocks NSW 2000 Australia

© Copyright: Lansdowne Publishing Pty Ltd 1992
© Copyright design: Lansdowne Publishing Pty Ltd

Project Coordinator: Deborah Nixon
Designer: Stan Lamond, Lamond Art & Design
Illustrator: Mike Gorman

Designed on Aldus Pagemaker
Set in 9.6 point ITC Garamond
Printed in Singapore by Kyodo Printing

Contents

Hybrid tea rose Golden Jubilee

Floribunda Hannah Gordon

Shrub rose Ferdinand Pichard

Floribunda Hakuun

Foreword

Flowers of all hue,
And without Thorn the Rose.

JOHN MILTON ON THE GARDEN OF EDEN,
PARADISE LOST

According to Milton we owe our prickly roses to the Fall of Man. This is an insight shared by others long before his time, for St Ambrose in the 4th century AD was equally sure that roses are smooth in Paradise, while the Zoroastrians of ancient Persia held that no thorns existed before Ahriman, the spirit of evil, came into the world.

Unappealing they may be, yet even prickles can be a pretty adornment, as anyone who has seen young shoots on the Wing Thorn rose will know. What these stories illustrate is the abiding fascination with roses that overrides boundaries of time and place, drawing people of many nations to write about roses, to grow them, to depict them in all sorts of ways, and above all to love them.

That love is easy to explain if we think of the qualities for which the rose is valued. Surely it is the most versatile of garden plants. We can crouch beside 'Wee Jock', inches from the ground and glance heavenwards where corymbs of 'Kiftsgate' wave gracefully against the sky, fifty feet above. There are roses for so many uses—for beds and borders, to plant in containers and troughs, for cutting to enjoy indoors or surprise our friends at shows, to grow under glass, to cover the ground or to form a hedge, to naturalise—with minimal attention—in wild gardens, or use to festoon almost any object we can think of—fence, wall, pillar, pergola, to conceal eyesores, to romanticise old ruins. Growth can be spiky, spreading, sprawling, weeping, compact, diffuse. The colour range is extraordinary, lacking only black and blue—and if current hopes are realised, the blue could soon be with us. As for fragrance, roses have been likened to everything from bananas to bedbugs, damask to disinfectant.

For this richness we must thank plant hunters and explorers who through centuries of time brought roses from distant lands, and gardeners and breeders who, with a blend of luck, skill and dedication, successfully combined the roses' genes, giving the ever increasing variety that exists today.

As fashions change, or plants improve, older types fade from view sometimes irretrievably. Nurseryman Thomas Rivers put it plainly in the 19th century, when repeat-flowering hybrid perpetuals were all the rage: 'Summer roses will soon be out of favour except a few of the very best.' In the century since, the hybrid perpetuals have themselves been for the most part lost, reduced from four thousand known varieties to the modest four score traceable today.

It is heartwarming to find in this book so many old varieties, those so meritorious—or fortunate—that they have survived for our enjoyment. It also embraces the cream of the new, selecting from a multitude those most worthy of inclusion. Rose lovers the world over will welcome such comprehensive treatment, and the many illustrations—quite apart from their pictorial beauty—will be a useful aid in helping identify those 'mystery' roses so often inherited in gardens.

PETER HARKNESS

Opposite: The mysterious and beautiful
R. rugosa scabrosa appeared in the Harkness
nursery from an unknown source, and was
introduced to the public in 1950.

Introduction

Roses have distinctive features that set them apart from other plants. These characteristics include thorny stems, the formation of hips and the way in which the leaves grow.

The genus *Rosa* is only found naturally occurring in the northern hemisphere, and the distribution of species is divided into four regions: Europe, America, Asia and the Middle East. It is believed that roses grew in the wild from prehistoric times, and fossils thought to be 20 million years old prove the existence of the rose in this phase of history. It is not possible, however, to prove a direct link to present-day wild roses, even though species are found growing in the same regions as the fossil traces.

The use of roses as ornamental garden plants may have started in China, where they were grown in the Imperial gardens as early as the 6th century BC. The bringing together of different species and varieties in these Chinese gardens led to a whole range of new forms, some of them very different in character from roses available in the West.

Roses in Europe and western Asia were probably cultivated not so much for ornamental as for practical use. Two in particular were valuable in an age of unhygienic smells: damask roses were used to make rose water, and their origin may go back to Arabia or Persia several centuries BC; and gallica roses also met cosmetic needs, because the dried petals retain fragrance for long periods. Gallicas may well have been 'farmed' 3000 years ago.

The rose has been called 'almost an index of civilisation', and through succeeding centuries in the East and West the range of varieties gradually evolved. When in the 18th century the Chinese garden roses were taken to other lands, the mingling of their genes with the European hybrids brought about a rose revolution, giving gardeners of the world a feast of new colour, new shapes, and an extended growing season.

The international nature of the rose is evidenced by the fact that three of the most important hybrids came from Italy, South Carolina and L'Ile de la Réunion in the Indian Ocean. During the 19th century a systematic attempt to collect all known roses in one garden was made by Empress Josephine, wife of Napoleon, and her patronage greatly helped the development of further new varieties. She was a vigorous promoter of the fashion for roses from 1799 until her death in 1844, and French growers continued to play a major role. One of the most famous was J.P. Vibert who established a nursery near Paris in 1815; some of his roses are still in cultivation today. To a later Frenchman, Guillot, we owe the earliest recognised hybrid tea and polyantha.

Standard roses combined with climbers and ramblers in a formal landscape

The modern shrub rose Prospero

The wild rose R. pimpinellifolia spinosissima

The Bourbon rose Mme Isaac Pereire

Botanical expeditions of the 19th century, notably to Asia Minor, China and the Himalayan regions, meant that by 1900 nearly all the world's species had been discovered. Most have been used by breeders, and the world looks forward to unbounded opportunities for future rose developments.

GENETIC ENGINEERING

No plant in history has been as admired and as manipulated as the rose. Although it is in the nature of the genus to interbreed, over the centuries this characteristic has been freely exploited, producing a seemingly unending stream of new varieties and new flower colours every season. Rose breeding has even evolved to the point of bio-technological genetic engineering. For example, an Australian company has isolated the blue gene in petunias and has developed, via tissue culture, a 'Delphinium Blue' rose.

This ability of the rose to interbreed has also made the tracing of rose ancestry very complex, indeed at times impossible. There is much speculation as to the ancestry of various groups, and unless genetic testing can be used in the future to determine the exact genes of individual species, some of the mysteries of the rose will remain forever unravelled.

The main problem with tracing the history of the rose is that much of the early plant material has been neglected and lost over the past two centuries. As breeders developed new and 'better' roses, the original

parents fell by the wayside. Now, fortunately, old-style roses have regained popularity, and this has led to the re-introduction of hundreds of roses into the marketplace.

MODERN VS OLD ROSES

There is a cross-over between modern and old roses. Hybrid tea roses, for example, are generally perceived as modern; however, the earliest example was produced in the 1860s by combining the elegance and perpetual flowering of the tea rose with the robustness and free-flowering nature of the hybrid perpetual. In general, groups such as gallica, damask, alba, moss, centifolia, Portland, China, tea, bourbon, rugosa, boursault, noisette and hybrid perpetual are considered to be 'old-fashioned roses'; while hybrid tea, floribunda, miniature and dwarf roses are considered to be 'modern'. Within those groups, however, are roses from both eras, and there can be no strict time division between 'old' and 'new'.

USING THIS BOOK

In this encyclopedia the roses have been alphabetically arranged into class groupings. These groups have then been arranged according to their ancestry, i.e. wild roses are positioned first, as they are the oldest known group. By grouping roses together this way we can see how the more modern groupings gradually emerged, and gain some understanding of the lineage.

The expectations of rose growers must vary from one country to another, from one climate zone to the next. In warmer areas roses will grow more vigorously than in cool to cold climates, and the height and spread of a mature plant will therefore be different. In warm and humid climates the risk of common rose problems, such as black spot, will also increase. In the coldest regions of England and the United States many rose varieties are only suited to cultivation under glass, and can produce different results from the same rose being grown in the open garden. Throughout the text the term 'continuously' has been applied to the flowering period of some varieties. Again, this intermittent flowering is more a feature of roses grown in warm climates. In this situation blooms appear in a flush, then a few emerge singly, followed by another flush. To encourage this flowering pattern keep dead-heading or picking flowers regularly.

The colour of roses blooms will also change according to the climate. Burning summer sun will fade the colour intensity considerably, and this is apparent in comparative photographs taken of the same rose grown in the northern and southern hemispheres.

The index cross references both botanical and common names, to make finding specific roses easier. A glossary of terms explains language used to describe the characteristics and cultivation of various species.

MARY MOODY

Care and Cultivation of Roses

Roses thrive in an open, sunny location in moderately rich, well-drained soil.

Summary

• Roses prefer full sun and an open position.
• Provide protection from strong winds.
• Allow sufficient space for the mature growth of each plant.

Roses require love and attention if they are to thrive. Although some varieties are more hardy and easier to cultivate than others, in general rose plants will not produce good results without some care and consideration.

LOCATION

Roses require an open, sunny position. Some varieties can tolerate semi-shaded conditions if the soil is good; however, all varieties prefer plenty of light and a sunny, open aspect. Roses grown in semi-shade have to compete with the roots of larger species for both moisture and nutrients. Roses in an open area, free from the shade of overhanging trees, will stand a much better chance of remaining healthy and producing beautiful blooms.

Most roses dislike strong wind and draughts, so precautions should be taken to provide shelter from fierce prevailing winds. A windbreak located at a suitable distance and not casting shade or shadows is ideal. Avoid growing roses down the side of a house where there is a wind tunnel effect between the house and fence.

In warm to hot climates some of the more sensitive rose varieties wilt and wither in the heat of the summer sun. In these climates select roses that are more robust and resilient to these climatic conditions.

Great success can be achieved by growing roses against a wall, especially the larger climbing or rambling varieties. If the wall or fence is in semi-shade, always plant taller-growing varieties that can grow upwards towards the sun. Remember that some ramblers and climbers grow very large indeed, so beware of locating them where they will block the light of windows or overwhelm adjoining species.

Certain varieties are tender and resent cold winters and frost. When growing these, provide a warm, sheltered position, or grow under glass for complete protection.

SOIL CONDITIONS

Although roses can be grown successfully in a wide range of soil types—clay, chalk, gravel or sand—ideally a rich, fertile and well-drained loam is preferred. Soils that are either too heavy in clay content, or too light and sandy, will have problems sustaining healthy, vigorous growth.

Light and sandy soil dries out very rapidly after rain or watering, and the nutrients are quickly leached away from the roots of the plants. On the other hand, moisture and nutrients find it very difficult to move through heavy, clay soil because of its density. Both these soil types benefit from the addition of organic matter to improve moisture-holding capacity and to allow free air circulation. Organic matter should be added prior to planting, to ensure that the best possible growing conditions are available from the start.

Roses appreciate well-mulched roots and plenty of air circulation at their base.

The best organic matter to improve the soil texture is either well-rotted manure or compost, or a combination of both. Homemade compost is ideal, and horse manure mixed with stable litter is also an excellent soil additive. If the soil is light and sandy, the organic matter should be incorporated several weeks prior to planting. If the soil is a heavy clay it will need more time to break down, so preparation should be done several months in advance.

Summary

• Roses prefer well-drained, fertile loam.
• Add organic matter to soils that are clay, sandy, chalk or gravel.

PLANT SELECTION

Roses are sold either potted up in a container, or bare-rooted wrapped in plastic or hessian. Container-grown roses can be planted at any time of the year, although late spring and summer are the preferred times.

Bare-rooted roses are sold and planted only from late autumn to early spring. Neither type should be planted when there is hard frost or snow on the ground. The soil is just too cold for the plants to survive the trauma of transplantation.

The advantage of buying container-grown roses is that the flower shape, colour and form can be properly appreciated, although bare-rooted roses often have a coloured label showing a photograph of the bloom.

Select roses to suit your particular climate. If special protection is not provided, certain tender roses will fail in cold climates. Look around and observe which roses grow well in your area by visiting public parks and gardens, nurseries and the gardens of friends. Keep in mind that roses susceptible to rust or black spot should not be grown in moist or humid climates. Always look for healthy, robust specimens, free from disease or pest infestation. Nursery

Perfect blooms, such as these of floribunda Escapade, are the result of good growing conditions and routine maintenance.

stock that has been neglected will be slow to recover.

Gardeners with little time for maintenance should avoid fussy, difficult-to-grow varieties. Give some thought to the colours of the blooms and how they will complement each other and other plants in the garden. Avoid beds of brightly coloured roses in clashing colours, instead try to co-ordinate flowers of a similar colour in various tones. Massed plantings of the one variety look spectacular, albeit contrived; consideration must also be given to the style of garden (formal, traditional, cottage) and the

space available, remembering that certain types of rose require plenty of growing space.

Summary

• Choose healthy plants that are suited to your climate.
• Avoid sensitive varieties if little time is available for maintenance.
• Select flower colours that complement each other.
• Avoid roses that will grow too large for your garden.

Dwarf (cluster-flowered) rose Sweet Dream

Hybrid tea (large-flowered) rose Alec's Red

Floribunda (cluster-flowered) rose City of Belfast

Miniature rose Baby Masquerade

Shrub rose Reine Victoria

ROSE TYPES

It helps when selecting plants to have an understanding of the various rose types, their size, shape and general appearance.

HYBRID TEA (LARGE-FLOWERED) ROSES

This very popular group can grow to 1.5 m (5 ft) in height, although they are generally about 1 m (3 ft), spreading to 80 cm (2½ ft) wide. They develop into an attractive bush shape, suitable for beds, borders and in some cases hedges, with large blooms on strong stems that make excellent cut flowers.

FLORIBUNDA (CLUSTER-FLOWERED) ROSES

Another popular group that can reach 2 m (7 ft) although more commonly 1 m (3 ft), spreading to 70 cm (2 ft) wide. Floribundas are prolific bloomers, although the flowers are slightly smaller than the hybrid tea roses. Useful for hedges, beds and borders.

MINIATURE ROSES

Small growers reaching 45 cm (1½ ft) at most, with some smaller varieties only growing to 25 cm (10 in). Flowers are on a small scale, and the shape of the plant depends on how it was propagated. Excellent pot or tub specimens, or for use as edging plants in the garden.

DWARF (CLUSTER-FLOWERED) ROSES

Scaled-down, floribunda-style roses, growing up to 70 cm (2 ft) with prolific flowers. Can be used to fill a small gap in the garden, as an edging plant or pot specimen.

SHRUB ROSES

This group takes in many varieties including wild roses, old garden roses, modern shrub and ground-covering roses. Their size, shape and habit vary according to the variety, however in general they are larger and leafier than hybrid tea roses and

Climber Dortmund

floribundas. In landscaping they can be used in beds, as part of a garden border or as an individual specimen.

CLIMBING AND RAMBLING ROSES

The size and habit of this group vary tremendously, from 2 m (7 ft) to 15 m (50 ft) in height. Some varieties are relatively slow-growing and easy to control, while others feature vigorous, rampant growth and require a large, open area in which to develop. Climbers and ramblers have a multitude of uses, from covering a fence or wall, to training over a classical archway or pergola. Most benefit from some support upon which to climb or ramble.

STANDARD ROSES

Noted for providing a background shape to the garden, standards have been propagated onto tall, slender stems, forming a bush shape at the top. There are weeping standards, which emerge from the top of the central stem with trailing shoots. The height of standards varies considerably according to the variety that has been propagated. Standards are generally used as specimen plants or as background plants in the garden.

PLANTING

Both bare-rooted and container-grown roses should be planted immediately after purchase. If this is not possible, they must be stored in a cool, sheltered place away from direct sunlight. The packing surrounding bare-rooted plants should

Weeping standard rose Minnehaha

Rambler rose Ghislaine de Féligonde

not be disturbed or the roots will dry out—if in doubt unwrap them, dip the roots in water and re-pack in moist peat or sphagnum moss, wrapping them again in plastic to retain moisture. Potted roses will need to be regularly watered when stored. In both cases, two to three weeks is the maximum storage time.

Never plant roses in soil that is either completely dry or water-logged. The ground should be lightly damp, so that the soil structure is not damaged by cultivation.

Do not overcrowd the garden with too many roses, or other species. Air circulation around plants is vital to avoid fungal-forming conditions.

To plant bare-rooted roses excavate a hole wide and deep enough to comfortably contain the roots, positioning a firm stake in the centre.

Make a mound in the middle of soil mixed with compost, and arrange the roots around it carefully, with the stem beside the stake.

Refill the hole with the soil and compost mixture, then press down firmly, but not hard enough to compact the ground. Water well.

Bare-rooted roses

These are planted from late autumn to early spring, during the dormant season. Dig a hole that is large enough to accommodate the spread of the roots, which generally run at right-angles to the stem. A mound of soil can be made in the centre of the hole to support the central stem, and the roots splayed out over the mound from the centre. Any long roots should be neatly shortened with clean, sharp secateurs. Use fine soil or a mixture of soil and bonemeal to fill in the hole, treading down firmly as the hole is filled. The planting depth is an important factor. The correct depth to plant is so that a shallow covering of soil covers the rootstock. If not planted deeply enough the rose may be unstable in strong winds; if planted too deeply

new roots will form above those already emerging from the rootstock. Water well after planting.

Container-grown roses

Summer is the usual time for planting container-grown roses, as they are most popular when sold in full flower. Dig a hole that is twice the size of the root mass and then carefully remove the plant from its pot, either by cutting the pot away with sharp scissors, or by loosening the root mass, then gently up-end the pot, cradling the roots and potting mixture in one hand. Ensure that the soil in the pot and the ground where the rose is to be planted are lightly damp to prevent any transplanting trauma.

Position the rose and fill around it with a mixture of soil and bonemeal,

pressing down firmly. Water well, and press down firmly again to make sure the rose is well positioned. If the weather is dry, water daily until the rose is established, and mulch to help prevent the surface from becoming dry.

Summary

• Plant roses as soon as possible after purchase.
• Ensure the soil is well prepared and lightly moist prior to planting.
• Take care not to damage root material during planting.
• Always plant at the correct depth, and allow sufficient distance between plants.
• Water well until plants are established.

To plant container-grown grafted roses first carefully remove the base of the pot, trying not to disturb the root ball of the plant.

Use a clean, sharp knife to cut the side of the pot and place it in a prepared hole that is at least twice the size of the roots.

Firmly place a mixture of soil and compost around the rose so that the union is 2.5 cm (1 in) beneath ground level.

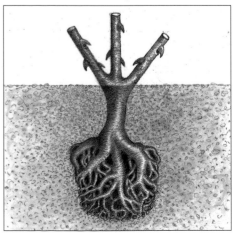

MAINTENANCE

Mulching around roses is the best way of preventing the soil surface drying out in hot weather, and also helps to suppress weeds. Organic mulches are the most satisfactory because they break down and help to maintain the texture and nutrient quality of the soil. Animal manures are excellent providing they are well rotted—avoid poultry manure which can release too much nitrogen into the soil causing rapid foliage growth and making the plants more vulnerable to disease.

Compost is also a good mulch, and can be mixed with well-rotted manure to make it spread further. The mulch layer can be quite thick, but avoid mounding it up around the base of the plants.

When feeding roses a specially formulated, all-purpose rose food will give the best results. This fertiliser has been developed to contain the right balance of nutrients required for healthy growth, and it is generally available in granulated form for mixing lightly into the mulch layer around the base of plants (and slightly beyond when plants have matured, as their roots will have spread out considerably). Roses are best fed in late winter or early spring to encourage the new season's growth, then again in mid to late summer to encourage a second flush of flowers. Those varieties that only flower once will still benefit from a late summer or autumn feeding.

In some climates roses will need regular watering, especially during long, hot summers. A deep watering every few days is more beneficial than a light sprinkling every day. Deep watering helps to encourage roots to travel downwards rather than to the soil surface in search of moisture. Avoid watering the foliage and flowers too heavily, in fact watering at ground level is preferred during daylight. Take care, however, not to overwater, as this can also cause fungal disease like black spot. Many gardeners find that a ground-level soaker hose is the most efficient method of watering roses, and the least wasteful of water.

A vigorous shrub rose like Bourbon Rose responds well to light winter pruning and the removal of dead or spindly wood.

Summary

• Mulch to suppress weeds and prevent the soil drying out.
• Feed to encourage strong growth and flower production.
• Water at ground level.

PRUNING

This is a controversial topic among rose enthusiasts, whose viewpoints vary considerably. Some rose-growers advocate a minimum of pruning, except to remove dead or diseased wood or spindly growth. However, most admit that the new varieties of hybrid tea roses and floribundas benefit greatly from a good pruning every year.

Pruning is undertaken to encourage new growth by removing old growth, and also to allow air and light circulation into the plant by discarding tangled or spindly growth. Pruning also improves flower production and helps to maintain the shape of the plant.

For the purpose of pruning, plants can be divided into four groups:

Floribundas, Hybrid Teas, Miniatures and Dwarf roses

These are pruned by cutting back the new growth by one-half to two-thirds to prevent them producing thin, straggly stems. The new growth is generally reddish green in colour, and smooth in appearance.

In the first year prune back all this new growth to about 12 cm (5 in), to form a solid basis for the bush. In subsequent years prune back new growth according to its vigour—weak varieties with thin shoots will need to be pruned back harder than those with strong growth. Moderate pruning is best.

To open out the bush and allow light and air to circulate, thin, weak stems should be pruned out completely. The dead or diseased wood should also be pruned out. Where two stems cross or overlap remove the weaker one.

Old and modern shrub roses

These are pruned according to the variety. Many of the old species (wild) and shrub roses are best left unpruned, apart from the removal of dead or spindly wood. Modern shrubs, however, can be pruned in similar fashion to hybrid teas, except not as hard. They all benefit from some reduction of new growth and the cutting back of side-shoots.

Standard roses

The same basic pruning regime applies to standards; however they resent hard pruning and therefore new growth should only be reduced by one-third.

Climbers and ramblers

These vigorous plants are generally pruned and trained to cover the structure (wall, fence, pergola or trellis) against which they are planted. Hard pruning will restrict their growth to a large bush. New climbers require no pruning, as the shoots emerge to create the foundation, or leading stems, of the plant. As new growth appears, often higher up from the old stems rather than from the base, it can be lightly pruned and trained while still young enough to be pliable. Remove dead and spindly wood each year, and also side shoots that are weak, but allow the new growths to develop.

PRUNING TECHNIQUES

Always use clean, sharp secateurs, and clear away pruned material from the base of the plants. When pruning new growth, the cut should be made just above an outward facing bud, at an angle that slopes back and away from the bud to allow moisture to run off. Cuts made too close to the bud can damage it, while those made more than ½ cm (¼ in) above the bud can cause dieback.

When pruning out an entire stem make the cut as close as possible to the parent stem—the cut may need to be tidied up with a sharp knife.

Old, hard wood may need to be removed with a narrow-bladed pruning saw, especially on an old, established plant. Again a sharp knife may be needed to tidy up the cut.

Dorothy Perkins grown as a pillar rose requires patient training and pruning techniques.

The three basic steps in pruning:
a) Use clean, sharp secateurs to remove dead wood from the centre of the plant.

b) Prune out all spindly growth and stems that overlap or grow into the centre of the plant.

c) New growth can now be pruned back by one-third to one-half according to the variety.

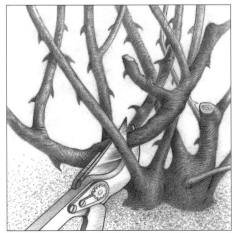

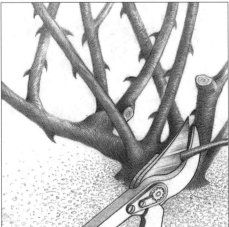

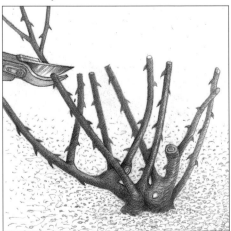

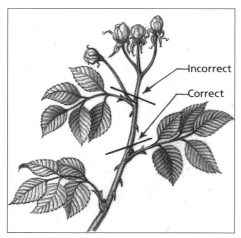

Dead-heading needs to be done routinely, cutting at the first growth bud using sharp secateurs.

Dead-heading

Many gardeners pick blooms for indoor display because it greatly benefits the plant. Indeed it does help to keep the plant tidy during summer, and if not done, the spent flowerheads will have to be routinely removed from the plant. Cutting the flowers also helps to encourage more blooms.

Dead-heading means that as soon as the blooms wither they should be cut back to a point just above an outward facing bud or a strong shoot. Floribundas especially appreciate having the entire truss removed by cutting back to the first bud below the truss.

Disbudding

This practice encourages larger blooms, and is popular with growers who exhibit their blooms. It simply involves pinching out several of the lower buds to ensure the remaining ones develop more vigorously. It is most commonly undertaken with hybrid tea roses.

When to prune

Most roses are pruned in winter or early spring. If pruning is undertaken during autumn or early winter in cool to cold climates, new growth can be stimulated which may be damaged by frosts. Therefore, the colder the area, the later the pruning should be undertaken. Some gardeners tidy up their plants at the end of the flowering period, then leave the pruning back of new growth until later.

Regular cutting of flowers for indoor display helps encourage growth, and decreases the need for dead-heading. Shrub rose Celsiana.

Summary

• Pruning rejuvenates plants and encourages flowering.
• Pruning varies according to the variety.
• Always use clean, sharp secateurs.
• Tidy up in late summer, and prune in winter.

PROPAGATION

Confident gardeners often propagate plants to produce their own stock, either to expand their gardens or to give as gifts to friends. Roses are not the easiest plants to propagate; however, even the inexperienced gardener can have success if the right methods are followed.

Cuttings

Even if cuttings strike, they may not grow into vigorous plants. However, wild roses, hybrid musks, rugosas, Scotch roses, gallicas, wild ramblers, and some floribundas can produce good results. It is certainly worth a try.

Hardwood cuttings are taken in autumn by using sharp secateurs to cut a pencil-thick section of stem about 15 cm (6 in) long, cutting just above the upper bud and below the lower one. Cut at an angle, as for

Hardwood cuttings should be taken in autumn and kept in a cool, sheltered position until spring, when they can be planted out.

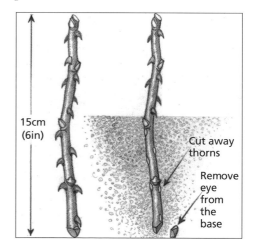

Growing from seed is unreliable, though an enjoyable experiment for many. The decorative seed-bearing hips of R. sweginzowii.

pruning, and remove the thorns from the lower portion that will be underground. The cutting should be planted to about half its length either in a container of rich potting mix or directly in the ground in a cool, sheltered part of the garden. These cuttings should have produced roots by spring.

Softwood cuttings are a little more tricky. They are taken in summer by removing a section about 15 cm (6 in) long of new growth. Remove all the foliage except for a few leaves at the top and also remove the lower bud. Place cuttings in a mixture of sand and peat in a pot, then cover with a plastic bag. Place in a warm but sheltered location. If successful, roots will form quickly and the cuttings will need to be repotted into a rich potting mixture and kept until the following spring.

Grafting

This is usually only done by professional nurserymen, and is a sophisticated means of propagation. It basically involves the joining together of two plants that are compatible, to produce a hybrid. The root stock of one variety is grown rapidly, then a scion (a section of one-year-old wood) from a second species or variety is grafted onto the rootstock. The join is held in place with tape, and sealed to make it watertight.

Budding

This method is more practical for the home gardener. It simply involves cutting a small section of ripe, flowering-shoot and removing a budding eye which is then grafted onto a one-year-old seedling. This process is done during the main growing period. Use a special sharp budding knife to make the cuts.

Layering

This is a useful method of propagating roses with long, pliable stems that can reach the ground. Simply take a one-year-old shoot and bend it to the ground so that part of the shoot can be covered with soil in a shallow trench. Before burying the section, first make a small nick in the wood on the underside to encourage rooting. A length of wire may be needed to hold the stem in place. Spring is a good time to attempt layering, as root growth will be rapid. When rooting has occurred the protruding tip will start to grow, and the section can be separated from the parent plant and potted, or planted where it is to grow.

Division

This can only be done to roses that naturally throw out suckers, which develop into plants in their own right. These young plants can be lifted and replanted elsewhere or potted up for gifts. Take care when lifting and dividing suckers from the parent plant, not to damage the root systems.

Seed

Rosehips are the seed-bearing fruit of the rose, and these can be collected when ripe and used to propagate. Only species are likely to breed true roses, although the seed of garden hybrids can be propagated with haphazard results. Start by gathering the hips in early winter and storing them in sand until spring, when they can be opened and the seeds removed. These seeds can then be removed and sown in a rich potting mix in seed trays and stored in a sheltered position not above 15°C (60°F) until successful germination— several weeks to months.

Summary

• In general, choose simple propagation methods, such as cuttings or layering.
• Results will vary according to the parent stock.

PESTS AND DISEASES

Prevention is the first requirement if pest and disease infestation is to be avoided. Healthy, well-grown plants will be far less vulnerable than those grown in less than ideal conditions.

Always plant roses that are suited to your climate, choose a sunny, open position and enrich the soil prior to planting. Keep weed growth down and avoid overcrowding with other roses or low-growing plants. All these factors will determine how robust and resilient the plants will become. Overfeeding plants with nitrogen-rich fertiliser will cause rapid stem and foliage growth, yet weaken plants and make them susceptible to infestation. Likewise, overwatering can cause fungal problems. Use care and commonsense in the maintenance of the rose garden, and many of the common problems can be avoided.

COMMON PROBLEMS

Aphids (greenfly or blackfly)

Aphids devour young shoots and are very prevalent in dry weather. They breed and spread quickly, causing stunting and distortion of new shoots. Check plants daily in the growing season, and remove aphids manually or spray with a specifically designed insecticide. All-purpose rose dust also helps reduce aphids.

Caterpillars

Caterpillars like to feed on tender young shoots and buds, causing plants to produce fewer flowers than expected. Constant checking will help to catch this problem before it develops. If there are just a few culprits remove them manually, or spray with a specific insecticide or rose dust.

Canker

This fungal problem is sometimes found on the prickles of bushes, causing yellow or reddish spots on the bark as the disease spreads. Prune off diseased canes using clean, sharp secateurs and as a preventive measure always prune away overlapping branches which rub together during wind, injuring the stem and leaving it open to infestation.

Red Spider Mite

Red spider mite causes yellowing of the foliage as the mites suck the juice from the leaves. They can be detected by looking for a fine web on the foliage undersides. This is usually more of a problem to roses grown under glass, and can multiply very rapidly unless checked. The spray Perimiphos-Methyl is reasonably effective, or jets of cold water directed at the undersides of the leaves will discourage the mites.

Scale

Affects the stems and branches, covering them with a flat white coating that stunts the development of the plant. Prune away badly affected stems and burn them, then spray with white oil to prevent a reinfestation.

Mildew

Mildew causes a fine covering of white powdery deposit on the surface of leaves and shoots. It occurs mostly during dry weather, when the ground around the roots of the rose is dry. Some plants are more susceptible than others. Spraying

with a systemic fungicide is the best solution. Downy mildew is another form which affects roses grown under glass, causing affected foliage to become limp and fall. Fungicides are available to treat mildew.

Black spot

Black spot is a disease of the foliage that can completely defoliate a bush. It is characterised by black or brown mottling of leaves, which spreads and can even affect stems. Affected foliage must be removed, including leaves that have fallen to the ground, to prevent the carry-over of spores to the next season. Chemical fungicide sprays are available to treat the disease.

Rust

Rust thrives in warm, moist conditions covering the undersides of foliage with an orange-brown coating that eventually turns black, destroying the leaf. Some roses are more susceptible, and should never be grown in warm, humid climates. All affected foliage should be quickly removed, and if a fungicide spray is used take care to spray the back of the leaves.

Summary

- Prevention is better than cure.
- Grow roses in good conditions to make them resistant.
- Check regularly to detect problems before they become serious.
- Use the appropriate spray or dust if required.

Rose canker: prune off diseased canes.

Rose scale covering stems: spray white oil.

Black spot: decrease ground-level humidity.

How Roses are Classified

Roses are grouped together in various classifications for both botanical and practical purposes. All roses are known by the term *Rosa*, which is Latin for 'rose', and within this sub-family are ten sections into which roses have been grouped according to their distinguishing characteristics.

It is interesting to note that wild roses are generally very pale in hue, either white, blush, pale yellow or medium pink, with only a very small percentage in the deeper shades of yellow, scarlet, crimson or purple. Deep yellow roses were only found growing wild in Asia, and deep red roses are native only to China. Roses that flower for long periods from summer through to autumn are all native to the eastern regions of Asia.

Modern hybridised roses are found in all shades, including orange, salmon, pink, yellow, red, lilac, purple and brownish-green, and can also be bicoloured and multicoloured.

R. foetida persiana (Pimpinellifoliae)

BOTANICAL GROUPINGS

PIMPINELLIFOLIAE

So called because of the foliage, said to resemble the plant *pimpinella* (salad burnet). There are only about twelve species roses in this group native to Europe and Asia, notably several bright yellow varieties (from Asia) as well as some in the cream, pink and purple colour range. The flowers are mostly produced singly on short stems. The hybridised garden groups classified are Austrian Briars, Burnet and Scotch roses.

GALLICANAE

Or 'French' roses, native to Europe, Turkey and Iraq. The foliage is large, usually made up of five leaflets, and the flowers are solitary in threes or fours on long stems. *R. gallica* is the major wild rose in this group, and the hybridised garden groups classified are gallicas, cabbage roses, damasks, mosses and Portlands.

CANINAE

Thought to be so named because the thorny stems resemble the teeth of canines. Native to Europe, western Asia and North Africa. Growth is upright and arching, with numerous hooked thorns and medium-sized leaves, often greyish-green in colour. The summer flowers are borne in small clusters, and the hips are generally oval to round in shape. Garden groups include albas, dog roses and sweet briars.

CAROLINAE

So named after Carolina, USA. There are six or seven species native only to North America, with shortish, upright growth and flowers mostly borne singly on short stalks. All the flowers are in shades of deep pink, and all flower in summer.

CASSIORHODON (CINNAMOMEAE)

A large group including fifty or more species, native to eastern Asia, Europe and North America. The European and North American species are pink, while the Asian species are also in shades of white, purple and red. Growth is mostly shrubby and upright and the thorns are often large and in pairs. Garden groups classified are boursaults and rugosas.

Charles de Mills (Gallicanae)

Honorine de Brabant (Chinensis)

Sparrieshoop (Synstylae)

Mme Legras de St. Germain (Caninae)

Paulii rosea (Cassiorhodon [Cinnamomae])

SYNSTYLAE

So named from the Greek 'fused pillars' which described the way the styles are formed at the centre of the flower. This group is mainly native to eastern Asia, although there are some species from Europe and the United Kingdom and one, *R. setigera* (Prairie Rose), from North America. Growth is vigorous, climbing and flexible. The wild roses in this group are in the white, cream or blush colour range. Garden groups are Ayrshires, hybrid musks, polyanthas, floribundas and modern climbing and rambling roses.

CHINENSIS

A group based on two wild roses from China, *R. chinensis* and *R. gigantea*, which changed the face of rose growing in the West, mainly due to their recurrent flowering. There are many garden groups under the sub-family Chinensis, including Chinas, teas, noisettes, bourbons, hybrid perpetuals, hybrid teas and climbing hybrid teas. Growth is very variable, usually upright, and the flowers are borne in small clusters.

R. laevigata (Laevigata)

BANKSIANAE

A distinctive group of four climbing roses, originally named after the wife of Sir Joseph Banks who was in charge of The Royal Botanic Gardens, Kew, *c.* 1807. The first form discovered was a beautiful white rose from China, and yellow forms were later discovered. They are all vigorous growers with virtually no thorns, smooth foliage, and generally have clusters of small blooms.

LAEVIGATA

A sub-family of one rose, *R. laevigata*, so named for its smooth, glossy foliage. Growth is sprawling or climbing, thorns irregular, and the foliage is virtually evergreen. There are various forms and hybrids including 'Cooper's Burmese', which is an excellent creamy-white single rose with a beautiful fragrance.

BRACTEATAE

So named after its leafy bracts which are borne close to the flower. There are only two wild roses in this group. They are native to South-East Asia, and are both creamy-white with recurrent flowers from late spring until autumn. There is a popular hybrid climber 'Mermaid' in this group, with single lemon yellow flowers and prominent golden brown stamens.

R. banksia alba plena (Banksianae)

Flower Forms

Roses vary considerably in their flower shapes and forms, from the simple five petals of the single wild rose, to the large full-petalled flowers seen on both modern hybrids and many old-fashioned varieties.

The basic shapes are illustrated here.

Flat or open: These blooms are usually either single, with just five petals, or semi-double with characteristic flat petals. Many wild roses feature this flower form.

Cupped: These flowers are also open, showing the central stamens, and can be single, semi-double, double or fully double. The petals are curved outwards from the centre.

Pointed: These roses have elegant pointed buds and can be semi-double or fully double with a high centre. They are the characteristic flowers of the hybrid tea rose.

Urn-shaped: This shape flower is also seen in hybrid tea roses, with a more curved shape and slightly flat top. They can be semi-double, double or fully double.

Rounded: This flower has a full bodied and rounded shape, either double or fully double, with overlapping petals of an even size.

Rosette: This fully-packed flower is either double or fully double, often with a flat shape and masses of overlapping petals of an uneven size. It is sometimes called 'muddled'.

Quartered: This flower is quite distinctive, with masses of uneven petals bunched in a quartered pattern. It is often flat, and is either double or fully double.

Pompon: These small, round flowers are either double or fully double with masses of even petals.

Wild Roses

Canary Bird

Wild roses are also known as species roses. This section is made up of the earliest recorded roses and a selection of their hybrids. These ancient roses were native to many regions of the northern hemisphere, including North America, Europe, North Africa, Asia Minor, Japan and Korea, where they can still be seen growing wild to this day.

   Many wild roses feature the single flower form of five petals; however, there are also more complex semi-double and double flower forms. The shape of the plants varies greatly too, from dwarf forms to the large banksiae roses, which can grow to 10 m (30 ft) or more.

ABBOTSWOOD

Botanical grouping: Caninae
Parentage: Unknown
Other names: Canina Abbotswood
Other varieties: None
Year: 1954
Origin: England
Description: Dense shrub grows to 2 m (7 ft) with arching, thorny branches and pale green leaves. The clear pink flowers are semi-double and very fragrant. The oval fruit is scarlet red.
Flowering: Summer only
Cultivation: A hardy shrub which tolerates poor soils and shady positions, including shady walls. Useful as an impenetrable hedging plant.

ARTHUR HILLIER

Botanical grouping: Cassiorhodon (Cinnamomeae)
Parentage: *R. macrophylla* x *R. moyesii*
Other names: None
Other varieties: None
Year: 1938
Origin: England
Description: The shrub grows to about 3 m (10 ft). The small clusters of flowers are a bright cerise and 7.5 cm (3 in) across. Attractive urn-shaped, orange-red fruit hang down in groups of three or four.
Flowering: Spring and summer
Cultivation: Will tolerate some shade and also poorer soils. Suited to a woodland setting. Little pruning necessary, except for the removal of dead wood.

Arthur Hillier

CANARY BIRD

Botanical grouping: Pimpinellifoliae
Parentage: Possibly *R. hugonis* x *R. xanthina*
Other names: Falsely called *R. xanthina spontanea*
Other varieties: None
Year: 1906
Origin: China, Mongolia, Turkestan
Description: Graceful shrub to 2 m (7 ft) with arching brown branches and smallish leaves. The bright yellow flowers are carried all along the stem and are moderately scented. The fruit is globular and blackish red.
Flowering: Late spring and occasionally again in autumn.
Cultivation: Needs full sun and moderately rich soil. Good as a hedging plant and will also do well as a standard rose if planted in rich soil. Inclined to die back but will recover if dead wood is removed.

Cantabrigiensis

CANTABRIGIENSIS

Botanical grouping: Pimpinellifoliae
Parentage: *R. hugonis* x *R. sericea*
Other names: *R. pteragonis cantabrigiensis*
Other varieties: None
Year: 1931
Origin: England
Description: Shrub to 2 m (7 ft) with arching, brown, thorny branches and fern-like foliage. The flowers are larger and paler than its parent *R. hugonis*, about 4 cm (1½ in) across, and medium yellow. The orange fruit is spherical.
Flowering: Spring only
Cultivation: Thrives in a sunny, sheltered position, although will tolerate poorer soils. Suitable for woodland planting. Prune out dead wood if necessary.

CARMENETTA

Botanical grouping: Caninae
Parentage: *R. glauca* x *R. rugosa*
Other names: *R. rubrifolia carmenetta*
Other varieties: None
Year: 1930
Origin: Canada
Description: A very similar shrub to *R. glauca* except for its thorns which it inherits from *R. rugosa*. Foliage colouring is the same, the flowers are larger and produced in larger bunches, and the fruit are similar.
Flowering: Summer only
Cultivation: A stronger growing shrub than its parent, it tolerates light, sandy soils but needs a sunny position. Useful as a hedging plant. Susceptible to rust, so care must be taken to avoid moist conditions.

CORYANA

Botanical grouping: Cassiorhodon (Cinnamomeae)
Parentage: *R. roxburghii* x *R. macrophylla*
Other names: None

Other varieties: None
Year: 1926
Origin: England
Description: Densely bushy shrub to 2.5 m (8 ft) with few prickles. Fern-like foliage similar to *R. roxburghii*. Produces large, single, dark pink flowers with abundant yellow stamens.
Flowering: Early summer
Cultivation: Will tolerate poorer soils and is ideal for woodland planting.

DUPLEX

Botanical grouping: Caninae
Parentage: Hybrid of *R. villosa* (*R. pomifera*)
Other names: Wolley-Dod's Rose, *R. villosa* Duplex, *R. pomifera* Duplex
Other varieties: None
Year: Unknown, garden form first noted *c*. 1900 in England
Origin: Europe
Description: A compact shrub to 2 m (7 ft) often with suckers. The foliage is greyish green and the large flowers are semi-double and clear pink with a slight fragrance. The shrub is best known for its very large, plum-red fruit but which it sets only occasionally.
Flowering: Summer only
Cultivation: May be grown in shade, including on shady walls, and is also tolerant of poorer soils. Suited to a woodland setting. Suckers can be invasive, so position where they will not affect other plants.

Eddie's Crimson

EDDIE'S CRIMSON

Botanical grouping: Cassiorhodon (Cinnamomeae)
Parentage: Donald Prior x *R. moyesii* hybrid
Other names: *R. moyesii* Eddie's Crimson
Other varieties: None
Year: 1956
Origin: Canada
Description: Shrub reaches 3 m (10 ft) with sparse, thorny stems and foliage similar to *R. moyesii*. The flowers are double and crimson-red, while the fruit is spherical and dark red.
Flowering: Summer only
Cultivation: Will tolerate some shade and poorer soils. Suited to woodland plantings.

Eddie's Crimson

EDDIE'S JEWEL

Botanical grouping: Cassiorhodon (Cinnamomeae)
Parentage: Donald Prior x *R. moyesii* hybrid
Other names: *R. moyesii* Eddie's Jewel
Other varieties: None
Year: 1962
Origin: Canada
Description: Shrub grows to 2.5 m (8 ft) with foliage and growth similar to other *R. moyesii* shrubs. New shoots are red-brown. The double flowers are vibrant red and in good seasons will repeat flower. The very large, round fruit is orangey red, although produced only occasionally.
Flowering: Repeating throughout summer and into autumn
Cultivation: Is shade tolerant and may be grown in poorer soils. Remove dead wood if necessary.

EOS

Botanical grouping: Cassiorhodon (Cinnamomeae)
Parentage: *R. moyesii* x Magnifica
Other names: *R. moyesii* Eos
Other varieties: None
Year: 1950
Origin: The Netherlands
Description: Vigorous shrub to 2.5 m (8 ft) with arching, stiff stems, *moyesii*-style foliage in dark green and red thorns. The abundant flowers are coral-red with white centres and yellow stamens produced singly all along the stem. It does not produce fruit.
Flowering: Summer only
Cultivation: Will tolerate poorer soils and some shade. It is best planted behind other shrubs to conceal its bare lower stems.

Eos

Geranium

FARGESII

Botanical grouping: Cassiorhodon (Cinnamomeae)
Parentage: Unknown
Other names: *R. moyesii* Fargesii
Other varieties: None
Year: 1913
Origin: Unknown
Description: This shrub is very similar to *R. moyesii* except for the colour of the flowers which is rose-red and the slightly smaller foliage. It is also somewhat less vigorous and produces fruit less abundantly than its parent.
Flowering: Summer only
Cultivation: Will tolerate some shade and poorer soils and may be used in a woodland planting. Not as hardy as some of the other *R. moyesii*.

GERANIUM

Botanical grouping: Cassiorhodon (Cinnamomeae)
Parentage: Seedling of *R. moyesii*
Other names: *R. moyesii* Geranium
Other varieties: None
Year: 1938
Origin: England
Description: More compact shrub than *R. moyesii*, grows to 2.5 m (8 ft) with lighter, more abundant foliage and few thorns. The flowers are crimson-red with cream stamens and the petals have a waxy feel. The large fruit is orange-red and very attractive.
Flowering: Summer only
Cultivation: Tolerant to poorer soil and some shade. It should be pruned only lightly after flowering.

HEADLEYENSIS

Botanical grouping: Pimpinellifoliae
Parentage: *R. hugonis* and possibly *R. pimpinellifolia altaica*
Other names: *R. headleyensis*
Other varieties: None
Year: 1920
Origin: England
Description: Graceful shrub to 3 m (10 ft) with attractive fern-like foliage on thorny, brownish green stems. The flowers are fragrant, single and primrose-yellow and are followed by reddish fruit.
Flowering: Spring only
Cultivation: Will tolerate poorer soils and some shade. Is suited to a woodland planting. Only requires pruning to remove dead or diseased wood.

Geranium with autumn fruit

Scarlet hips of Highdownensis

HIGHDOWNENSIS

Botanical grouping: Cassiorhodon
(Cinnamomeae)
Parentage: Seedling from *R. moyesii*
Other names: *R. moyesii highdownensis*
Other varieties: None
Year: 1928
Origin: England
Description: A more bushy shrub than
R. moyesii with dark green foliage and
coppery new growth reaching 3 m (10 ft).
The single, cerise-crimson flowers are
produced in clusters and are followed by
large flagon-shaped, plum-red fruit.
Flowering: Summer only
Cultivation: Tolerates poorer soils and
some shade. Light pruning recommended
after flowering.

HILLIERI

Botanical grouping: Cassiorhodon
(Cinnamomeae)
Parentage: Seedling of *R. moyesii* x *R.
multibracteata* or *R. willmottiae*
Other names: *R. pruhoniciana*
Other varieties: None
Year: 1924
Origin: England
Description: Strong growing, densely
branched shrub to 3 m (10 ft) with gracefully
arching stems and fern-like foliage. It is
considered the darkest of the single roses,
being a dusky, brownish red with golden
stamens. The orange-red fruit lasts long after
the leaves have fallen.
Flowering: Summer only
Cultivation: Thrives in an open, sunny
position, where the flowers also look their
best. Prune out dead wood or weak, spindly
growth.

MARGUERITE HILLING

Botanical grouping: Cassiorhodon
(Cinnamomeae)
Parentage: A sport from 'Nevada'

Other names: *R. moyesii* Marguerite Hilling
Other varieties: None
Year: 1959
Origin: England
Description: Vigorous, dense shrub
reaches at least 2.5 m (8 ft) with abundant,
pale green foliage carried on dark brown
stems with only a few thorns. The single
flowers are large and a soft rose-pink with
golden-yellow stamens and orange, pear-
shaped fruit following.
Flowering: First flush in early summer with
intermittent flowers through the rest of
summer and into autumn.
Cultivation: Requires plenty of sunshine
but can tolerate poor soil quality. Suitable as
a hedging plant or in a woodland setting. If
growing as a hedge, prune into shape during
winter.

R. ACICULARIS

Botanical grouping: Cassiorhodon
(Cinnamomeae)
Parentage: Unknown
Other names: Arctic Rose
Other varieties: Bourgeauiana (larger
flowers)

Year: 1805
Origin: North America, Asia, Europe
Description: Shrub reaches 1 m (3 ft) with
densely bristled stems and few thorns. Dull
green leaves. Solitary, pink, scented flowers,
occasionally in groups of two or three with
red, pear-shaped, smooth fruits.
Flowering: Early summer
Cultivation: Requires full sun but will
tolerate poorer soils. Suitable also as a
hedging plant.

R. acicularis

Marguerite Hilling

R. banksiae alba-plena

R. banksiae alba-plena

R. ACICULARIS NIPPONENSIS

Botanical grouping: Cassiorhodon
(Cinnamomeae)
Parentage: Unknown
Other names: None
Other varieties: None
Year: 1894
Origin: Japan
Description: Shrub grows to 1.5 m (5 ft)
with grey-green foliage on densely bristled
stems with few real thorns. Solitary flowers
of 4–5 cm (1¹/₂–2 in) in a deep pink, almost
red.
Flowering: Early summer
Cultivation: Can be grown in poor soil.
Does best in a sunny position. Suitable as a
hedging plant or as part of a woodland
setting. Little or no pruning required, except
for the removal of dead or spindly wood.

R. ANEMONEFLORA

Botanical grouping: Synstylae
Parentage: Hybrid of uncertain origin
Other names: *R. triphylla*, Three Leaf Rose
Other varieties: None
Year: 1844
Origin: China
Description: A vigorous, climbing rose
with sparsely prickled branches and very
narrow leaves. The flowers are dull white
and double in the garden form (single in the
wild). May be trained up into trees.
Flowering: Late summer
Cultivation: A difficult rose to grow,
requires attention. Does best in full sun.

R. BANKSIAE ALBA-PLENA

Botanical grouping: Banksianae
Parentage: Unknown
Other names: Lady Banks Rose, Banksian
Double White
Other varieties: None

Year: 1807
Origin: China
Description: Climbing shrub with arching,
thornless stems and pale green foliage
reaching to 6 m (20 ft). The small flowers are
double and pure white with a strong
fragrance and usually occur in clusters.

Flowering: Summer only
Cultivation: Requires a warm, sunny
position to thrive. Useful for covering
pergolas and garden arches and may be
grown into trees. Mulch the base to suppress
weed growth, and prune out dead or
straggly wood.

R. BANKSIAE LUTEA

Botanical grouping: Banksianae
Parentage: Unknown
Other names: Yellow Banksia
Other varieties: None
Year: 1824
Origin: China
Description: Climbing shrub to 6 m (20 ft)
with small, double, yellow, slightly fragrant
flowers produced in clusters on graceful,
arching stems covered in abundant foliage.
Flowering: Late spring or early summer
Cultivation: Needs a sheltered, sunny
position to thrive but it is usually hardier
than other banksia roses. Keep the area at
the base of the plant weed-free, and prune
out dead wood.

R. banksiae lutea

R. banksiae lutescens

R. banksiae lutescens

R. BANKSIAE LUTESCENS

Botanical grouping: Banksianae
Parentage: Unknown
Other names: None
Other varieties: None
Year: 1870
Origin: China
Description: Climbing shrub similar in form to the other banksia roses. The flowers are small, single, yellow and sweetly scented. Young leaves and shoots are occasionally copper toned.
Flowering: Summer only
Cultivation: Needs a sunny, sheltered position to do well. Train onto a trellis in a warm position, and mulch the surrounding soil to keep weeds down.

R. BANKSIAE NORMALIS

Botanical grouping: Banksianae
Parentage: Unknown
Other names: None
Other varieties: None
Year: 1877 or earlier
Origin: China
Description: This is the original wild species. Similar in form to the other banksia roses in foliage and shape. Stems are thornless. The flowers are small, white, single and sweetly scented.
Flowering: Summer only
Cultivation: Like all other banksia roses, requires a sunny, sheltered position to

R. banksiae normalis

thrive. Use as a climbing shrub to grow into trees or over fences and pergolas. Not considered especially hardy.

R. BEGGERIANA

Botanical grouping: Cassiorhodon (Cinnamomeae)
Parentage: Unknown
Other names: None
Other varieties: None
Year: 1881 or earlier
Origin: Central Asia
Description: Shrub grows to 2.5 m (8.ft) with abundant, prickled stems and long, greyish green leaves. The flowers are small and white and come in groups. The fruit is small, round and orange.
Flowering: A long season from mid-summer onwards
Cultivation: Will tolerate poorer soils and some shade and is suitable for a woodland setting. Prune out dead or straggly wood.

R. BELLA

Botanical grouping: Cassiorhodon (Cinnamomeae)
Parentage: Unknown, but possibly related to *R. moyesii*.
Other names: None
Other varieties: None
Year: 1910
Origin: China
Description: Upright shrub reaches 2.5 m (8.ft) with bristly stems. Flowers usually occur singly and are bright pink. The fruit is flask-shaped and may be orange or scarlet.
Flowering: Summer only
Cultivation: Can tolerate poor soils and some shade and is suitable for woodland planting.

R. BLANDA

Botanical grouping: Cassiorhodon (Cinnamomeae)
Parentage: Unknown, but related to *R. pendulina*
Other names: Hudson Bay Rose, Smooth Rose, Meadow Rose, Labrador Rose
Other varieties: None
Year: 1773
Origin: North America
Description: Shrub grows to 2 m (7 ft) with slim, brown, nearly thornless stems. The deep pink flowers occur singly or in groups of two or three. The attractive fruit is pear-shaped and red.
Flowering: Summer only
Cultivation: Grows in wet, stony areas and will tolerate poor soils and some shade. Little pruning required, except for the removal of dead wood.

R. bracteata

R. BRACTEATA

Botanical grouping: Bracteata
Parentage: Unknown
Other names: Macartney Rose, Chickasaw Rose
Other varieties: None
Year: 1793
Origin: China, Taiwan
Description: Evergreen shrub which grows to 3 m (10 ft). It may also be grown as a ground cover or climber. Hairy, prickled stems and dark green, glossy leaves. The flowers are large, white and lightly scented with prominent yellow stamens. The fruit is round and orange.
Flowering: Late summer
Cultivation: A rose which needs little attention, though not suited to colder climates. Prune out dead wood, and cut back weak or spindly stems.

R. BRUNONII

Botanical grouping: Synstylae
Parentage: Unknown
Other names: Himalayan Musk Rose
Other varieties: None
Year: 1822
Origin: Himalayas
Description: Vigorous climber to 5 m (16 ft) or more with strongly prickled stems. New

R. brunonii

R. canina

growth is purplish, older leaves are greyish green. The clusters of small, white flowers are fragrant. Fruit is very small and red.
Flowering: Summer only
Cultivation: Very vigorous but sensitive to cold winters. Does well in mild climates, especially in a sunny, sheltered position.

R. CALIFORNICA NANA

Botanical grouping: Cassiorhodon (Cinnamomeae)
Parentage: Unknown
Other names: None
Other varieties: None
Year: 1914
Origin: North America
Description: A dwarf shrub with multiple hooked prickles and dull green foliage. The flowers are pale pink and single with a strong scent. The fruits are small and globular with a distinct neck.
Flowering: Summer only
Cultivation: Very hardy, tolerating some shade and relatively poor soils. Suitable as a hedging or border plant. Little or no pruning necessary, except for the removal of dead or spindly wood.

R. CANINA

Botanical grouping: Caninae
Parentage: Unknown

R. canina

Other names: Dog Rose
Other varieties: At least 60 varieties
Year: Ancient
Origin: Europe, Asia
Description: The most common wild rose found in the northern hemisphere, this vigorous shrub reaches to 3 m (10 ft) with abundant, prickled growth. Solitary, scented flowers or groups of two or three are generally pale pink, although there is a white form. The abundant fruit is oval and scarlet red.
Flowering: Summer only
Cultivation: Tolerates poorer soils and shady positions and may be grown on south facing walls. Suitable for woodland plantings.

R. CAROLINA PLENA

Botanical grouping: Carolinae
Parentage: Unknown
Other names: Double Pennsylvanian Rose, *R. pennsylvanica*
Other varieties: None
Year: 1790
Origin: North America
Description: Small shrub reaching 50 cm (1 ¹/₂ ft) with densely bristled, slender stems and dark green foliage. Free suckering. The small, double flowers are a clear salmon pink, fading to almost white at the edges. The fruit is round and scarlet red.
Flowering: Summer only
Cultivation: Will tolerate poorer soils and can be grown in a pot. Avoid planting in a bed where suckering will be a problem.

R. DAVIDII

Botanical grouping: Cassiorhodon (Cinnamomeae)
Parentage: Unknown
Other names: None
Other varieties: var. *elongata*
Year: 1903

R. eglanteria

Origin: China
Description: Upright, vigorous shrub reaching 3 m (10 ft) with pale green, heavily veined foliage. It is late-flowering, with pale pink flowers carried in clusters or singly along the length of the stem. The fruit is flask-shaped and orange-red.
Flowering: Late summer
Cultivation: Will tolerate a shady position and poor soil quality and is useful as a woodland planting. Prune out dead or spindly wood.

R. EGLANTERIA

Botanical grouping: Caninae
Parentage: Unknown
Other names: Sweetbriar, *R. rubiginosa*, Eglantine Rose
Other varieties: None
Year: Unknown
Origin: Europe, South-west Asia
Description: Strong-growing shrub to 3 m (10 ft) with very prickly stems and dark green leaves with a strong apple smell. Small, pale pink flowers occur singly or in small groups with oval scarlet fruit following.

Flowering: Summer only
Cultivation: Will tolerate poor soils and a shady position. It is suitable as a hedging plant or pot-plant or for use in a woodland setting. Clipping each year will encourage new growth.

R. FEDTSCHENKOANA

Botanical grouping: Cassiorhodon (Cinnamomeae)
Parentage: Unknown
Other names: None
Other varieties: None
Year: *c.* 1875
Origin: Central Asia
Description: Upright shrub to about 2 m (7 ft) with very prickly stems. Foliage is pale greyish green. The solitary flowers are usually white with an unpleasant scent. Hairy, pear-shaped, red fruit follows. The shrub has attractively coloured foliage in autumn.
Flowering: Repeat flowering throughout summer
Cultivation: Tolerates poor soil. Suitable for hedging and in woodland settings.

R. FOETIDA

Botanical grouping: Pimpinellifoliae
Parentage: Unknown
Other names: Austrian Yellow, Austrian Briar, *R. lutea*
Other varieties: None
Year: 16th century or earlier
Origin: Asia
Description: Upright shrub to 1.5 m (5 ft) with brown stems, bright green foliage and few prickles. Flowers are usually solitary or in pairs and are deep yellow, 6 cm (2 ¹/₂ in) across. It has a somewhat disagreeable scent. The fruit is round, red and occasionally hairy. All modern orange and yellow roses ultimately derive from this variety.
Flowering: Early summer
Cultivation: Prone to black spot and dislikes being pruned. Will tolerate a poorer soil.

R. foetida

R. foetida bicolor

R. FOETIDA BICOLOR

Botanical grouping: Pimpinellifoliae
Parentage: Mutation from *R. foetida*
Other names: Austrian Copper, *R. lutea punicea*
Other varieties: None
Year: Before 1590
Origin: Asia
Description: Shrub grows to 2 m (7 ft) with long-leaved, bright green foliage. The flowers are a rich coppery-orange on the upper side and yellow underneath with prominent gold stamens. All modern orange and yellow roses derive from this variety. Occasionally, the plant will revert to the original yellow form and sometimes both colours appear on the plant at the same time.
Flowering: Summer only
Cultivation: Will tolerate poorer soils but has a tendency to black spot and dislikes being pruned. Keep the area at the base of plants free from weeds.

R. FOETIDA PERSIANA

Botanical grouping: Pimpinellifoliae
Parentage: Unknown
Other names: Persian Yellow
Other varieties: None
Year: 1837
Origin: South-west Asia
Description: The stems, foliage and thorns are similar to the other *R. foetida* varieties, although slightly less vigorous. The flowers are very double and golden yellow.

R. foetida persiana

Flowering: Summer only
Cultivation: Prone to black spot and dislikes being pruned. Tolerates poorer soils and does well in a warm, sunny position.

R. FORRESTIANA

Botanical grouping: Cassiorhodon (Cinnamomeae)
Parentage: Unknown
Other names: None
Other varieties: None
Year: 1918
Origin: Western China
Description: Very upright and vigorous shrub to 2 m (7 ft). The foliage is abundant and purplish green as are the branches. Solitary flowers are cerise-pink to crimson, about 5 cm (2 in) across and very fragrant. The fruit is red and bottle-shaped.
Flowering: Summer only
Cultivation: Tolerates poorer soils and is suitable for woodland planting.

R. GIGANTEA

Botanical grouping: Chinensis
Parentage: Unknown
Other names: None
Other varieties: Several different forms including *f. erubescens*
Year: 1888
Origin: Southern China and Burma
Description: Vigorous, climbing shrub to 10 m (30 ft) or more, with foliage changing from brownish green when young to pale green on maturity. The solitary, scented flowers are large, about 13 cm (5 in) across, and are white to creamy white. The fruit is orange to red and pear-shaped.
Flowering: Early to late spring
Cultivation: Reasonably hardy rose with good disease resistance. In cooler climates it requires a sunny, sheltered aspect.

R. gigantea

R. GLAUCA (R. RUBRIFOLIA)

Botanical grouping: Caninae
Parentage: Unknown
Other names: *R. ferruginea*
Other varieties: None
Year: Prior to 1830
Origin: Central Europe
Description: Upright shrub to 3 m (10 ft) grown mainly for its foliage which is violet when young, glaucous and purplish in mid-season and spectacularly varied in autumn. Foliage colours vary also depending on sun exposure. Shady spots produce greyish green leaves while a sunny position gives them a coppery mauve tint. The flowers are abundant, clear to dark pink with pale yellow stamens. The fruit is small and red, and is produced in bunches.
Flowering: Summer only
Cultivation: Will tolerate some shade. Susceptible to rust. Keep the area around the plant free from weeds, and avoid overhead watering in summer.

R. HELENAE

Botanical grouping: Synstylae
Parentage: Unknown
Other names: None
Other varieties: None
Year: 1907

R. helenae

R. glauca (R. rubrifolia)

R. glauca (R. rubrifolia)

R. hugonis

Origin: Central China
Description: Very tall and vigorous climbing shrub to 6 m (20 ft) with glossy green foliage and abundant thorns. Young growth is purplish red. Multiple small, creamy white, scented flowers are produced in large heads. The abundant fruit that follows is oval and red.
Flowering: Summer only
Cultivation: A hardy rose which does well in an open, sunny position. Prune, if necessary, to remove dead wood.

R. HUGONIS

Botanical grouping: Pimpinellifoliae
Parentage: Unknown
Other names: Golden Rose of China
Other varieties: None
Year: 1899
Origin: China
Description: Upright shrub to 2.5 m (8 ft) with dark brown, arching or straight branches and fern-like foliage, very thorny. Abundant, primrose-yellow flowers are carried on short branchlets. The foliage is also attractive in autumn when it turns an orange-bronze colour. The fruits are dark red and oval.
Flowering: Spring only
Cultivation: Will tolerate poorer soils, but needs an open, sunny position to thrive. Suitable for woodland plantings. Prune out dead or diseased wood.

R. LAEVIGATA

Botanical grouping: Laevigatae
Parentage: Unknown
Other names: Cherokee Rose, *R. sinica alba*
Other varieties: *Laevigata rosea,* a rare pink form
Year: 1759 or earlier
Origin: China
Description: Evergreen, vigorous climber

R. laevigata

growth which is virtually thornless. The flowers are small, double and lilac-pink, although varying in tone from pale to mid-pink. The fruit is round and of medium size.
Flowering: Usually late spring, but some-times later.
Cultivation: Requires an open sunny position and moderately rich soil.

R. MICRUGOSA ALBA

Botanical grouping: Cassiorhodon (Cinnamomeae)
Parentage: Second generation from original *R. micrugosa* cross
Other names: None
Other varieties: None
Year: Unknown
Origin: England
Description: More upright than *R. micrugosa*, but otherwise similar in growth. The beautiful flowers are white with golden yellow stamens and have a pleasant fragrance.
Flowering: Repeat flowering throughout season
Cultivation: Identical requirements and conditions to its parent *R. micrugosa*.

R. micrugosa alba

R. laevigata

to 5 m (16 ft) with bright green foliage and a few large thorns. The scented flowers are very large and white with yellow stamens. The fruits are pear-shaped and orange.
Flower: Spring only
Cultivation: Does well in warm, sunny positions. Flowers poorly in areas of heavy frost and is not especially hardy in cold climates.

R. LONGICUSPIS

Botanical grouping: Synstylae
Parentage: Unknown
Other names: None

Other varieties: None
Year: 1915
Origin: Western China, Himalayas
Description: Evergreen climber to 6 m (20 ft) with reddish brown, shiny branches, glossy, dark green foliage and long, hooked thorns. The flowers are white and about 4 cm (1 1/2 in) across with a strong banana scent. Fruits are small, ovoid and orangey scarlet.
Flowering: Late summer
Cultivation: Sensitive to frosts and extreme cold and not totally hardy. Does best in warm, sunny spots. Use as a climber or ground cover.

R. MAJALIS PLENA

Botanical grouping: Cassiorhodon (Cinnamomeae)
Parentage: Unknown
Other names: Whitsuntide Rose, *R. cinnamomea*, Rose du Saint Sacrement, Foecundissima
Other varieties: None
Year: Prior to 1600
Origin: Northern and Central Europe to Russia
Description: Upright, branching shrub grows to 2 m (7 ft) with purplish red, new

R. longicuspis

R. moschata grandiflora

R. MOSCHATA

Botanical grouping: Synstylae
Parentage: Unknown
Other names: Musk Rose
Other varieties: None
Year: 1540
Origin: Possibly India or southern China
Description: Shrubby, lax growth to 3 m
(10 ft). Branches are greyish with few
thorns. Flowers are produced in groups of
three, cream changing to white, with a
strong beeswax or musk scent.
Flowering: Repeated flowering to autumn
in warmer climates, otherwise summer only.
Cultivation: Has been widely used in
breeding. Best suited to open, sunny
positions but will tolerate some shade and
can even be grown on shady walls.

R. MOSCHATA GRANDIFLORA

Botanical grouping: Synstylae
Parentage: Unknown
Other names: *R. multiflora grandiflora*
Other varieties: None
Year: 1866
Origin: France
Description: A vigorous climbing shrub to
6 m (20 ft). The single white flowers are
large with yellow stamens and very fragrant.
The fruit is round and orange and is pro-
duced in autumn.
Flowering: Summer only
Cultivation: Will tolerate shade, poor soil
quality and even a south facing position.
Useful for training into trees.

R. MOYESII

Botanical grouping: Cassiorhodon
(Cinnamomeae)
Parentage: Unknown
Other names: None
Other varieties: *R. moyesii rosea* (*R.
holodonta*)—a pink form.
Year: 1893
Origin: Western China
Description: A tall, sparsely branched
shrub to 3 m (10 ft) with bluish green leaves
and thorny stems. Foliage is dense toward
the top of the shrub. The flower is consid-
ered one of the most beautiful of the red
roses with intense blood-red petals and dark
stamens. Grown mainly for its abundant
crop of orange-red, flagon-shaped fruit.
Flowering: Summer only
Cultivation: Will tolerate poorer soils.

R. moyesii

Plants grown from seeds or seedlings are
often sterile and will not produce fruit.
Flowers from mature wood, so should be
lightly pruned after flowering.

R. NITIDA

Botanical grouping: Carolinae
Parentage: Unknown
Other names: None
Other varieties: None
Year: 1807
Origin: North America
Description: A small shrub to around 1 m
(3 ft). Slender, erect, reddish stems are very
prickly and free suckering, with delicate,
fern-like foliage. The flowers are bright pink
with yellow stamens. The autumn foliage is
spectacular as are the long-lasting red fruits.
Flowering: Summer only
Cultivation: Tolerates some shade and
poorer soil quality. A good ground carpeting
rose, it will also do well in pots. Do not
position in beds where suckering or rapid
spreading is a problem.

R. NUTKANA

Botanical grouping: Cassiorhodon
(Cinnamomeae)
Parentage: Unknown but closely related to
R. blanda
Other names: None
Other varieties: var. *hispida*
Year: 1876
Origin: North America
Description: A small, upright shrub to
around 1.5 m (5 ft) with slender, dark brown
stems and dark green foliage. The flowers
are dark pink and single. The shrub is grown
mainly for the fruit which is red and lasts
long into winter.
Flowering: Summer only
Cultivation: A hardy and prolific flowerer,
it requires an open, sunny position but can
tolerate poor soils.

R. nitida

R. PENDULINA

Botanical grouping: Cassiorhodon (Cinnamomeae)
Parentage: Unknown
Other names: Alpine Rose
Other varieties: None
Year: 1683
Origin: Europe
Description: Vigorous, healthy shrub grows to 1–1.5 m (3–5 ft) with nearly thornless stems and dull, greyish green leaves. Flowers are single, purplish pink about 4 cm (1 1/2 in) across. The fruit is pendulous and urn-shaped. Attractive autumn foliage.
Flowering: Summer only
Cultivation: This is a hardy plant and does well under difficult conditions including poorer soils. Remove dead wood, otherwise only a light shaping required.

R. PERSICA

Botanical grouping: Hulthemia
Parentage: Unknown
Other names: Hulthemia persica, Barberry Rose
Other varieties: None
Year: c. 1788
Origin: Iran, southern Russia, Afghanistan

Description: A small, suckering shrub, growing to 70 cm (2 ft) with unique blue-green 'simple' leaves, and small vivid yellow flowers with a deep scarlet mark at the base of the five petals. The flower buds are covered with curious bristles.
Flowering: Early summer
Cultivation: Difficult to grow except in warm, dry climates with protection from cold, damp conditions. Must have full sun and well-drained soil. Can also be cultivated in a container.

R. PIMPINELLIFOLIA ALTAICA

Botanical grouping: Pimpinellifoliae
Parentage: Unknown
Other names: Altai Rose, *R. grandiflora*, *R. sibirica* , *R. spinosissima baltica*
Other varieties: None
Year: 1820
Origin: Siberia
Description: An upright, very vigorous shrub to 1.8 m (6 ft), freely suckering, with slender, dark brown branches, greyish green foliage and few thorns. The single, fragrant flowers are creamy ivory, with a primrose tinge on opening. The fruit is maroon-black.
Flowering: Spring only
Cultivation: Tolerates poor soils and some shade. Use as a hedging plant.

R. PISOCARPA

Botanical grouping: Cassiorhodon (Cinnamomeae)
Parentage: Unknown
Other names: Pea-Fruited Rose
Other varieties: None
Year: 1877
Origin: North America
Description: Arching shrub to 1 m (3 ft) with slender stems and small, sparse thorns. The small, single flowers are lilac-pink and are produced in clusters. The fruits from which the rose gets its name are small, round and abundant. The autumn foliage is attractive.
Flowering: Summer only
Cultivation: Needs a moderately rich soil but can tolerate some shade. May be grown as a ground cover or in a pot. Prune out dead wood or weak stem growth.

R. PRIMULA

Botanical grouping: Pimpinellifoliae
Parentage: Unknown
Other names: Incense Rose, Tien Shan Rose
Other varieties: None
Year: 1910
Origin: Turkestan, northern China
Description: An upright shrub to 2 m (7 ft)

R. persica

R. primula

R. pimpinellifolia altaica

R. primula

R. richardii

R. sericea pteracantha

with slender, arching branches and aromatic, reddish brown foliage when young. The flowers are solitary, pale translucent yellow like a primrose, fading to white as they age. Slightly scented. Small, inconspicuous red fruit follow the flowers

Flowering: Early spring
Cultivation: Plant in a warm, sunny position for best results. Tolerates poor soils.

R. PULVERULENTA

Botanical grouping: Caninae
Parentage: Unknown
Other names: *R. glutinosa*
Other varieties: var. *dalmatica*
Year: 1821
Origin: Mediterranean, Balkans, Asia Minor
Description: A small, dense shrub to 70 cm (2 ¼ ft), very prickly with small leaves. The foliage has a pine-like scent. The flowers are solitary on short branches, small and pink. The fruit is more attractive, being scarlet and rounded.
Flowering: Late spring
Cultivation: Will tolerate poorer soils and some shade and may be cultivated in a pot.

R. RICHARDII

Botanical grouping: Gallicanae
Parentage: Unknown, possibly *R. gallica* x *R. phoenicia*
Other names: *R. sancta*, Holy Rose, Rose of the Tombs, Abyssinian Rose
Other varieties: None
Year: 1897
Origin: Abyssinia
Description: A low, sprawling shrub to 1 m (3 ft) with dark green, dull leaves and many thorns. Flowers are single in clear pink. Its common names derive from its use as a courtyard planting in Ethiopian churches and tombs.
Flowering: Summer only
Cultivation: A hardy rose which can be planted in pots or near water and is tolerant

of some shade and poorer soils. May be used as a ground cover in a woodland setting.

R. ROXBURGHII PLENA

Botanical grouping: Platyrhodon
Parentage: Unknown
Other names: Chestnut Rose, Burr Rose
Other varieties: None
Year: 1824
Origin: China
Description: Spreading shrub grows to 1.5 m (5 ft) with stiff thorny branches, the bark of which is buff-coloured and flaky. The flowers are very double, with pale pink

outer petals and deeper pink inner petals. Slightly scented. The fruit is small and green. Worthwhile for its autumn foliage.
Flowering: Summer only
Cultivation: Tolerates shade and poor soil quality, making it useful for difficult situations. Little or no pruning necessary, except to remove dead wood.

R. SERICEA PTERACANTHA

Botanical grouping: Pimpinellifoliae
Parentage: Unknown
Other names: *R. omeiensis pteracantha*, Wing Thorn Rose
Other varieties: None

R. roxburghii plena

Stems and thorns of R. sericea pteracantha

Leaves of sericea pteracantha

R. sweginzowii

Year: 1890
Origin: China
Description: A shrub growing to 2.5 m (8 ft) with fern-like foliage on abundant, very upright, red stems. The rose is well known for its very large, translucent red thorns when young. The flowers are unusual in that they often have only four petals and are white with raised gold stamens.
Flowering: Summer only
Cultivation: Should be planted in the sun to show off the thorns. Older thorns turn grey so needs pruning to encourage new growth.

R. SETIGERA

Botanical grouping: Synstylae
Parentage: Unknown
Other names: Prairie Rose
Other varieties: None
Year: 1810
Origin: North America
Description: A sprawling shrub 1–3.5 m (3–12 ft) with arching bald stems and bright green foliage. The flowers are sparse, cerise-pink and single with a rich scent. The fruits are small, round and brownish green.
Flowering: Late summer
Cultivation: Thrives in sandy soils. May be grown as a ground cover or a climber. Flowers later than most other roses.

R. SOULIEANA

Botanical grouping: Synstylae
Parentage: Unknown
Other names: None
Other varieties: None
Year: 1896
Origin: Western China
Description: A large shrub to 4 m (13 ft) with arching, very thorny branches and attractive grey foliage. The flowers in bud are ivory yellow, fading to white as they open. Fruity fragrance. The fruit is tiny and orange.
Flowering: Summer only
Cultivation: Susceptible to autumn frosts. Is somewhat shade tolerant and may be planted close to water. May be used as a climber through trees or other shrubs, or as a ground cover.

R. SWEGINZOWII

Botanical grouping: Cassiorhodon (Cinnamomeae)
Parentage: Unknown
Other names: None
Other varieties: var. *macrocarpa*
Year: 1909
Origin: Northern China
Description: Graceful shrub to around 3 m (10 ft) with fern-like, bright green foliage and very prickly pale brown stems. The abundant, very attractive flowers are bright pink in groups of two or three and followed by orange-red, bristly, flagon-shaped fruit.
Flowering: Early summer
Cultivation: Tolerant of some shade and poorer soil quality. Cut out old or spindly wood to encourage new growth and better flowering.

R. VIRGINIANA PLENA

Botanical grouping: Carolinae
Parentage: Unknown
Other names: St Mark's Rose, Rose d'Amour
Other varieties: None
Year: Prior to 1870
Origin: Unknown
Description: Upright shrub to 2 m (7 ft) with reddish brown stems and glossy green leaves. Buds very attractive, double flowers open to clear pink, scrolled at the edges and deepening in colour toward the centre. Lightly scented. Useful where autumn colour is required.
Flowering: Repeats throughout summer.
Cultivation: Tolerates poorer soils and some shade. Prune out dead wood if necessary.

R. virginiana (the wild form of R. virginiana plena)

fragrant with yellow stamens. The fruit is oval and dark red and is bird-attracting.
Flowering: Summer only
Cultivation: If used as a climber, the weak stems need to be supported and tied up. Will tolerate poorer soils and may be grown close to water. Ideal as a ground cover plant.

R. WILLMOTTIAE

Botanical grouping: Cassiorhodon (Cinnamomeae)
Parentage: Unknown
Other names: None
Other varieties: None
Year: 1904
Origin: Western China
Description: Dense shrub to 1.8 m (6 ft) with arching stems, pinkish when young and dainty, greyish leaves that release a perfume when crushed. Very thorny. The single, cerise-pink flowers are scented with creamy stamens. The fruit is pear-shaped and orange-red.
Flowering: Early summer
Cultivation: Will tolerate poorer soils and some shade but prefers a sunny, open position. A good rose for potting.

R. WOODSII FENDLERI

Botanical grouping: Cassiorhodon (Cinnamomeae)
Parentage: Unknown
Other names: None
Other varieties: None
Year: 1888
Origin: North America
Description: Attractive, rounded shrub to 2 m (7 ft) with graceful, greyish green, fern-like foliage. Very thorny. The plentiful flowers are single, lilac-pink with cream stamens and a light scent. The abundant fruit is bright red, round and lasts well into winter.
Flowering: Summer only
Cultivation: Tolerant of poor soil and shade but does better in a sunny position. Use in woodland settings or as a hedging plant.

R. webbiana

R. WEBBIANA

Botanical grouping: Cassiorhodon (Cinnamomeae)
Parentage: Unknown
Other names: None
Other varieties: None
Year: 1879
Origin: Himalayas, India
Description: Dense shrub to 1.8 m (6 ft) with arching stems of plum-brown, purplish when young. Yellowish thorns at the base.The flowers are single and lilac-pink with yellow stamens. Slightly scented. The fruits are bottle-shaped and scarlet.
Flowering: Early summer only
Cultivation: Needs a sheltered position in cold climates. Will tolerate poorer soils and some shade. Makes an attractive potted shrub.

R. wichuraiana

R. WICHURAIANA

Botanical grouping: Synstylae
Parentage: Unknown
Other names: Memorial Rose
Other varieties: None
Year: 1891
Origin: Japan, eastern China
Description: Climbing, semi-evergreen shrub to 6 m (20 ft) with dark green, fern-like foliage. The single flowers are white and

R. woodsii fendleri

R. x Dupontii

R. X DUPONTII

Botanical grouping: Synstylae
Parentage: Unknown
Other names: Dupont Rose, Snow-Bush Rose
Other varieties: None
Year: Before 1817
Origin: France
Description: Shrub grows to 2.5 m (8 ft) with stems at first upright then with a tendency to spread. Foliage is greyish green. The flowers are very fragrant, creamy white on opening and then changing to pinkish white.The fruit is orange and ripens very late.
Flowering: Early summer with the occasional later flower.
Cultivation: Tolerant of poorer soils but needs a sunny position to thrive. Suitable as a hedging plant or in a woodland setting.

R. X HARDII

Botanical grouping: Hulthemia
Parentage: Seedling of *R. persica*
Other names: x *Hulthemosa hardii*
Other varieties: None
Year: 1836
Origin: France
Description: Spreading, usually grows up to 1 m (3 ft) but may reach 2 m (7 ft) on a wall, with dense, twiggy growth and abundant thorns. Unusual small, golden-yellow flowers with a crimson mark at the base of each petal.
Flowering: Spring flowering
Cultivation: A short-lived, not especially hardy rose which requires an open, sunny position to thrive. It is very difficult to propagate. Can be grown in a pot.

R. X HARISONII

Botanical grouping: Pimpinellifoliae
Parentage: Unknown, probably *R. pimpinellifolia* x *R. foetida*

R. x Dupontii

Other names: Harison's Double Yellow, Yellow Rose of Texas
Other varieties: None
Year: 1830
Origin: North America
Description: Shrub grows to over 1 m (3 ft) with rich green foliage but a rather sparse, upright habit. Flowers are semi-double and very deep, sulphur yellow with a delicate scent. The fruit is nearly black.
Flowering: Early spring
Cultivation: A very hardy rose which will tolerate some shade and poor soil. May be used as a hedging plant. Prune out dead wood if necessary.

R. X HIBERNICA

Botanical grouping: Pimpinellifoliae
Parentage: Possibly *R. canina* x *R. pimpinellifolia*
Other names: Irish Rose
Other varieties: None
Year: 1802

R. x hardii

R. x harisonii

Origin: Northern Ireland
Description: Shrub grows to 1–2 m (3–7ft) with dark red, upright or arching shoots. Flowers are single, bright pink and faintly scented. The fruit is red and egg-shaped and is considered the best feature of this rose.
Flowering: Summer only
Cultivation: Requires an open, sunny position to thrive but can make do with poorer soils. Use in a woodland-style planting.

R. X MACRANTHA

Botanical grouping: Gallicanae
Parentage: *R. gallica* x unknown
Other names: None
Other varieties: None
Year: 1880
Origin: France

R. x harisonii

Description: A vigorous shrub with arching, green stems to 2 m (7 ft). Multiple light pink flowers, later fading to white with a strong scent and prominent stamens. Fruit is globular and dull red in autumn.
Flowering: Summer only
Cultivation: Will tolerate poorer soils. May be grown as a ground cover and is suited to woodland plantings.

R. X MICRUGOSA

Botanical grouping: Cassiorhodon (Cinnamomeae)
Parentage: *R. rugosa* x *R. roxburghii*
Other names: None
Other varieties: None
Year: Before 1905
Origin: Strasbourg Botanical Institute
Description: A very dense shrub to 1.5 m

R. x hibernica

R. x macrantha

(5 ft) with foliage similar to *R. rugosa*. The flowers are large, single and pale pink with orangey green fruit following.
Flowering: Repeat flowering throughout the season
Cultivation: Tolerates poorer soils and some shade and is considered very hardy. Will make an impenetrable hedging plant; also useful as a potted specimen and suitable for a woodland setting. Prune to remove weak or straggly stems and dead wood.

SEALING WAX

Botanical grouping: Cassiorhodon (Cinnamomeae)
Parentage: A form of *R. moyesii rosea*. Possibly a hybrid with *R. sweginzowii*.
Other names: *R. moyesii* Sealing Wax
Other varieties: None
Year: 1938
Origin: England
Description: Shrub grows to 2.5 m (8 ft) with foliage and habit similar to *R. moyesii* Geranium. The flowers are vivid cerise-pink. The scarlet fruit is large and flagon-shaped.
Flowering: Summer only
Cultivation: Will tolerate poorer soils and some shade. Prune lightly after flowering.

Gallica Roses

This ancient group of roses is characterised by a compact and rounded shape, well covered with foliage right to the base of the bush. Gallica stems are covered with bristles, especially the young stems, and needle-like thorns. Foliage is generally a rather dull, deep green with pale undersides. Flowers are commonly small to medium in size, and many are in the deep maroon-purple colour range. There are also paler pink forms, including some pale pink striped with deep maroon or deep pink.

Gallicas are quite vigorous growers, and some will quickly spread suckers that can be invasive.

Agathe Incarnata

AGATHE INCARNATA

Botanical grouping: Gallicanae
Parentage: Unknown
Other names: None
Other varieties: None
Year: Before 1815
Origin: Europe
Description: Light green, soft foliage on a thorny bush to 1.5 m (5 ft) high and 1.5 m (5 ft) wide. Arching branches carry the pale pink, very fragrant flowers, which are double, quartered and have a button centre.
Flowering: Summer only
Cultivation: Tolerates poorer soils, but requires full sun. Best grown as a specimen. After flowering, remove some of the old wood, and shorten long new stems by one-third.

ALAIN BLANCHARD

Botanical grouping: Gallicanae
Parentage: probably *R.* x *centifolia* and *R. gallica*
Other names: None
Other varieties: None
Year: 1839
Origin: France
Description: Thin, wiry branches, dense dark green foliage on a shrub 1.5 m (5 ft) high and 1.5 m (5 ft) wide. The almost single crimson flowers become spotted purple with age, have prominent golden stamens and a good scent.
Flowering: Summer only
Cultivation: Can be grown in poorer soils and partial shade. After flowering, remove some of the old wood, and shorten long new stems considerably.

ANAÏS SÉGALAS

Botanical grouping: Gallicanae
Parentage: Unknown, possibly a Gallica and centifolia hybrid
Other names: None
Other varieties: None

Year: 1837
Origin: France
Description: A small shrub with arching and thorny stems to 1 m (3 ft) high and 1 m (3 ft) wide with small, dark foliage. Highly scented, mauve-lilac flowers fade to paler at the edges and are very prolific.
Flowering: Summer only
Cultivation: Tolerates poorer soils but needs full sun. Makes a good tub specimen.

ANTONIA D'ORMOIS

Botanical grouping: Gallicanae
Parentage: Unknown
Other names: None
Other varieties: None
Year: Unknown
Origin: France
Description: An upright shrub with clear green foliage, growing to 1.5 m (5 ft) high and 1 m (3 ft) across. The loose pink flowers fade to almost white, and are about 10 cm (4 in) wide and full double.
Flowering: Summer only, but generally later than other Gallicas.
Cultivation: Tolerates poorer soils, but requires full sun. Remove some of the old wood after flowering and shorten long new stems by one-third for good results the following season.

ASSEMBLAGE DES BEAUTÉS

Botanical grouping: Gallicanae
Parentage: Unknown
Other names: Rouge eblouissante
Other varieties: None
Year: 1823
Origin: France
Description: A dense, compact shrub to 1.5 m (5 ft) and 1 m (3 ft) across, with few thorns and rich green foliage. The scented flowers are bright crimson, very double and darken to purple with age. They have a green eye, are very abundant, and contrast effectively with the foliage.

Alain Blanchard

Anaïs Ségalas

Assemblage des Beautés

Flowering: Summer only
Cultivation: Hardy shrub which tolerates poorer soils and light shade. Considered one of the best of the Gallicas and an excellent tub specimen. After flowering, remove some of the old wood, and shorten long new stems by one-third.

BELLE DE CRECY

Botanical grouping: Gallicanae
parentage: Unknown
Other names: None
Other varieties: None
Year: Mid-19th century
Origin: Unknown
Description: An upright shrub, reaching 1.2 m (4 ft) in height, with attractive grey-green foliage and a wonderful mixture of pink, greyish and mauve flowers that are flat and quartered, often with a distinctive green centre. Flowers are very fragrant.
Flowering: Summer
Cultivation: Rather unreliable in its flowering, this rose needs very good growing conditions to be a success. Protect from strong winds, and provide warmth and full sun.

BELLE ISIS

Botanical grouping: Gallicanae
Parentage: Unknown, possibly some centifolia
Other names: None
Other varieties: None
Year: 1845
Origin: Belgium
Description: A small, compact and upright shrub, growing to 1.5 m (5 ft) high and 1 m (3 ft) across with thorny stems. The fully double flowers, which open flesh-pink and fade to white on the edges, have a strong fragrance. This rose is well known as one of the parents of 'Constance Spry'.
Flowering: Summer only
Cultivation: Tolerates poorer soils, but needs full sun to produce good results. After flowering, remove some of the old wood, and shorten long new stems by one-third.

BOULE DE NANTEUIL

Botanical grouping: Gallicanae
Parentage: Unknown
Other names: None
Other varieties: None
Year: Before 1848
Origin: Unknown
Description: A strong, upright and twiggy shrub growing to 1.5 m (5 ft) and 1 m (3 ft) across, with dark green foliage. The fragrant, fully double flowers are flat and quartered, deep pink.

Camaieux

Belle de Crecy

Belle Isis

Flowering: Summer only
Cultivation: Although it tolerates poorer soils, this rose is prone to mildew and needs full sun. Can be grown as a hedge plant. After flowering, remove some of the old wood, and shorten long new stems by one-third.

CAMAIEUX

Botanical grouping: Gallicanae
Parentage: Unknown
Other names: None
Other varieties: None
Year: 1830

Origin: France
Description: A short, dense bush, with arching branches and grey-green foliage. It grows to 1 m (3 ft) high and 1 m (3 ft) wide. The striking white flowers are striped with crimson, pink, lilac and grey as the flower ages. The loose-petalled flowers sometimes have a green centre.
Flowering: Summer only
Cultivation: Sometimes not a strong plant, it will nevertheless tolerate poorer soils, and tub planting. Can be grown as a hedge. After flowering, remove some of the old wood, and shorten long new stems by one-third.

Cardinal de Richelieu

CARDINAL DE RICHELIEU

Botanical grouping: Gallicanae
Parentage: Unknown
Other names: None
Other varieties: None
Year: 1840
Origin: France
Description: Dense and smooth dark green foliage on an almost thorn-free bush 1.5 m (5 ft) high and 1 m (3 ft) across. The royal-purple flowers are rich and velvety, spherical, and clustered on the stems. Flowers often have a green eye.
Flowering: Summer only
Cultivation: Tolerates poorer soils, but benefits from generous fertilising. Suitable as a hedge or as a tub specimen. After flowering, remove some of the old wood, and shorten long new stems by one-third.

CHARLES DE MILLS

Botanical grouping: Gallicanae
Parentage: Unknown

Charles de Mills

Other names: Bizarre Triomphant
Other varieties: None
Year: Unknown
Origin: Unknown
Description: Lush, dark green foliage on an almost thornless shrub to 1.5 m (5 ft) high and across. The large flat and circular flowers grow up to 13 cm (5 in) wide and are mixed purples and reds, fading to lilac and grey. Scented.
Flowering: Summer only
Cultivation: Tolerates poorer soils, but is at its best in good soils. Requires full sun and can be used as a hedging plant. After flowering, remove some of the old wood, and shorten long new stems by one-third.

COMPLICATA

Botanical grouping: Gallicanae
Parentage: Unknown, possibly some *R. canina*, or *R. macrantha*
Other names: None
Other varieties: None
Year: Unknown
Origin: Unknown
Description: A tall shrub with lax, arching branches which can reach 3 m (10 ft) high if supported, and 2 m (7 ft) wide. Has a vigorous habit and grey-green foliage. The large single flowers can be 13 cm (5 in) across and are a clear, bright pink with pale centres. Globular orange fruits follow.
Flowering: Summer
Cultivation: Particularly tolerant of poorer soils, but needs full sun. Remove some of the old wood, and shorten long new stems by one-third. Can be used as a pillar rose, a scrambler on old trees, or as an informal hedge.

CONDITORUM

Botanical grouping: Gallicanae
Parentage: Unknown
Other names: Hungarian Rose
Other varieties: None
Year: Ancient
Origin: Possibly Hungary
Description: A neat, upright and dense shrub growing to 1.5 m (5 ft) high and 1 m (3 ft) across with dark foliage. The fragrant double flowers have thick ruby-red petals and are very prolific.
Flowering: Summer only
Cultivation: Tolerates poorer soils and

Complicata

requires full sun. Can be used as a low informal hedge, as a tub plant, and the flowers are excellent for potpourri. After flowering, remove some of the old wood, and shorten long new stems by one-third.

COSIMO RIDOLFI

Botanical grouping: Gallicanae
Parentage: Unknown
Other names: Cosimo Ridolphi
Other varieties: None
Year: 1842
Origin: France
Description: A small compact shrub growing to 1 m (3 ft) high and 1 m (3 ft) wide with grey-green foliage. The fragrant lilac flowers are cupped at first and later become open and flat.
Flowering: Summer only
Cultivation: Tolerates poorer soils, but needs full sun. Can be grown as a low hedge, and its habit makes it an excellent tub specimen. After flowering, remove some of the old wood, and shorten long new stems by one-third.

CRAMOISI PICOTÉ

Botanical grouping: Gallicanae
Parentage: Unknown
Other names: None
Other varieties: None
Year: 1834
Origin: France
Description: An upright, densely foliated shrub with thin, thornless branches to 1 m (3 ft) high and up to 70 cm (2 ft) across. The almost scentless flowers are crimson changing to deep pink with an edge of crimson-red. This rose has an unusual flower form with deeply reflexed outer petals forming a chrysanthemum-like pompon.
Flowering: Summer
Cultivation: Tolerates poor soils, but needs full sun. An excellent tub specimen. After flowering, remove some of the old wood, and shorten long new stems by one-third.

D'AGUESSEAU

Botanical grouping: Gallicanae
Parentage: Unknown
Other names: None
Other varieties: None
Year: 1823
Origin: France
Description: Strong upright shrub to 1.5 m (5 ft) high and 1 m (3 ft) across with dark foliage. Fragrant flowers deep crimson at first, fading to deep pink, doubled and quartered with a green eye.
Flowering: Summer only

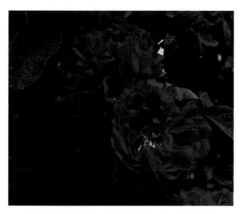

Conditorum

Cultivation: Needs full sun, but tolerates poorer soils. After flowering, remove the old wood, and prune new stems by about one-third.

DU MAÎTRE D'ECOLE

Botanical grouping: Gallicanae
Parentage: Unknown
Other names: Rose du Maître d'Ecole
Other varieties: None
Year: 1840
Origin: France
Description: An upright, nearly thornless shrub growing to 1 m (3 ft), with dense foliage. Red buds open to large, 13 cm (5 in) fragrant rose, lilac and pink flowers which fade in the sun. They are clustered on the canes.
Flowering: Summer only
Cultivation: Tolerates poorer soils but needs full sun. An excellent hedge plant, and tub specimen. Encourage next year's flowers and foliage by reducing long canes by one-third, and pruning out old wood.

Du Maître d'Ecole

D'Aguesseau

Duc de Fitzjames

DUC DE FITZJAMES

Botanical grouping: Gallicanae
Parentage: Unknown
Other names: None
Other varieties: None
Year: About 1885
Origin: Unknown
Description: A strong growing shrub to 1.5 m (5 ft) high and about 1 m (3 ft) wide.

Flowers are a rich, clear pink.
Flowering: Summer only
Cultivation: Tolerates poorer soils, but requires full sun. After flowering, remove some of the old wood, and shorten long new stems by one-third.

DUC DE GUICHE

Botanical grouping: Gallicanae
Parentage: Unknown
Other names: Sénateur Romain, Senat Romain
Other varieties: None
Year: 1835
Origin: France
Description: Spreading, arching branches on a shrub to 1.5 m (5 ft) high and wide, with dark foliage. Flowers double, globe-shaped, and crimson with purple veins or stripes.
Flowering: Summer only
Cultivation: Can be grown in a wide range of soils and conditions, providing there is adequate sun. Prune out dead wood and shorten new stems considerably after flowering.

Duc de Guiche

Duchesse d'Angoulême

DUCHESSE D'ANGOULÊME

Botanical grouping: Gallicanae
Parentage: Unknown
Other names: Duc d'Angoulême, Wax Rose
Other varieties: None
Year: 1827
Origin: France
Description: A low-growing, compact

Duchesse de Buccleugh

shrub to 1.5 m (5 ft) high and 1 m (3 ft) wide, with arching, light green, almost thornless branches which are weighed down with the flowers. Deep pink buds which open to fragrant, light, almost transparent pink blooms, sometimes have a darker margin.
Flowering: Summer only
Cultivation: Tolerates poorer soils, but needs full sun. Can be grown as a hedge, and is a good tub specimen. After flowering, remove some of the old wood, and shorten long new stems by one-third.

DUCHESSE DE BUCCLEUGH

Botanical grouping: Gallicanae
Parentage: Unknown
Other names: None
Other varieties: None
Year: 1846
Origin: France
Description: A large and vigorous shrub, reaching 2 m (7 ft) high and 1.5 m (5 ft) wide, with twiggy, almost thornless stems and grey-green foliage. The mildly scented flowers open large and flat, and are cerise, paling to lavender edges.
Flowering: Summer only, but later than some others in the group.
Cultivation: Hardy, and tolerant of poorer soils, but needs full sun for success. After flowering, remove some of the old wood, and trim back long new stems by one-third.

DUCHESSE DE MONTEBELLO

Botanical grouping: Gallicanae
Parentage: Unknown
Other names: None
Other varieties: None
Year: 1829
Origin: France
Description: A vigorous upright shrub to 1.5 m (5 ft) high and 1 m (3 ft) across with

Duchesse de Montebello

dark grey-green foliage. The fragrant flowers reach 7.5 cm (3 in) across, are fragrant, fully double and pale pink.

Flowering: Summer only, earlier than most

Cultivation: Can be cultivated in poorer soils and light shade. Suitable as an informal hedge, and is a good tub specimen. After flowering, remove some of the old wood and shorten long new stems.

EMPRESS JOSEPHINE

Botanical grouping: Gallicanae

Parentage: Unclear, but may be *R. gallica* and *R. pendulina*

Other names: *R. x francofurtana*

Other varieties: None

Year: *c.* 1820

Origin: Unknown

Description: A sprawling yet dense shrub growing to 1.5 m (5 ft) high and 1.5 m (5 ft) wide with grey-green foliage and almost thornless stems. Loose, wavy petals on double flowers, deep pink with paler highlights, and slightly scented.

Flowering: Summer only

Cultivation: Tolerates poorer soils, and light shade. Can be cultivated as a hedge or as a tub specimen. Prune back the old wood and shorten long, new stems by one-third after flowering.

GEORGES VIBERT

Botanical grouping: Gallicanae

Parentage: Unknown

Other names: La Pintade, Gallica Meleagris

Other varieties: None

Year: 1853

Origin: France

Description: Coarse, dark foliage on an upright shrub to 1 m (3 ft) high and wide. The flowers are purple or carmine, depending on climate, with darker stripes, and very double. The flowers fade with age.

Empress Josephine

Georges Vibert

Flowering: Summer only

Cultivation: Requires full sun but can be cultivated in poorer soils. Suitable as a hedging plant or a tub specimen. After flowering, remove some of the old wood, and shorten long new stems by one-third.

GLOIRE DE FRANCE

Botanical grouping: Gallicanae

Parentage: Unknown

Other names: Fanny Bias

Other varieties: None

Gloire de France

Year: Before 1819

Origin: Unknown

Description: A spreading and low-growing shrub to 1 m (3 ft) high and up to 1.5 m (5 ft) wide with dark foliage. The fully double flowers are medium-sized, very prolific, and fading from lilac-rose to pale pink.

Flowering: Summer only

Cultivation: Tolerates poorer soils and light shade. The spreading habit makes it an interesting tub specimen. After flowering prune out the old wood, and shorten long new stems by one-third.

Hippolyte

James Mason

Ipsilanté

Jenny Duval

JAMES MASON

Botanical grouping: Gallicanae
Parentage: Scharlachglut x Tuscany Superb
Other names: None
Other varieties: None
Year: 1982
Origin: England
Description: A medium-sized shrub with lush, dark green foliage, growing to 1.5 m (5 ft) high and 1.5 m (5 ft) across. The large, almost single flowers are 10 cm (4 in) across, fragrant and prolific.
Flowering: Summer only
Cultivation: Tolerates poorer soils, but needs full sun. Makes an excellent tub specimen. As with other Gallicas, prune by removing some of the old wood, and reduce long new stems by one-third, each year.

JENNY DUVAL

Botanical grouping: Gallicanae
Parentage: Unknown
Other names: None
Other varieties: None
Year: Mid-18th century
Origin: Unknown
Description: A neat, upright shrub to 1.5 m (5 ft) high and about 1 m (3 ft) wide, with green-grey foliage. The fragrant flowers are crimson-mauve and lilac, fading to pale lilac at the edges, depending on weather and climate.
Flowering: Summer only
Cultivation: Tolerates poorer soils, but needs full sun. Can be grown as a hedge, or as a tub specimen. Promote following year's foliage and flowers by reducing long stems by one-third, and removing some old canes altogether.

LA BELLE SULTANE

Botanical grouping: Gallicanae
Parentage: Unknown, possibly some centifolia
Other names: *R. gallica* Violacea,

La Belle Sultane

HENRI FOUCQUIER

Botanical grouping: Gallicanae
Parentage: Unknown
Other names: None
Other varieties: None
Year: Unknown
Origin: Unknown
Description: A sprawling shrub with lax, almost thornless stems, 1.5 m (5 ft) high and 1.5 m (5 ft) wide with dark green foliage. The scented flowers open clear pink, with reflexed petals and a small eye.
Flowering: Summer only
Cultivation: Needs full sun to grow well, but is tolerant of poorer soil conditions. Makes a good hedge, or tub specimen. Remove some of the old wood, and shorten long new stems by one-third when flowering has finished.

HIPPOLYTE

Botanical grouping: Gallicanae
Parentage: Unknown
Other names: Souvenir de Kean
Other varieties: None
Year: Early nineteenth century
Origin: Unknown
Description: Dark green, smooth foliage on thin arching stems. A shrub growing to 1.5 m

(5 ft) high and wide, with almost no thorns. The clusters of magenta flowers with soft highlights are flat with a button eye.
Flowering: Summer only
Cultivation: Suitable for cultivation in poorer soils, but needs full sun. Best as a specimen, or as a tub plant. Encourage new foliage and blooms for the following season by reducing longer stems by one-third, and removing some of the old wood.

IPSILANTÉ

Botanical grouping: Gallicanae
Parentage: Unknown
Other names: None
Other varieties: None
Year: 1821
Origin: Unknown
Description: A prickly shrub with coarse but dense foliage, growing to 1.5 m (5 ft) high and about 1 m (3 ft) wide. The sweetly scented flowers are full double, large and lilac-pink.
Flowering: Summer only, later than most Gallicas.
Cultivation: Will tolerate poorer soils, but requires sunny conditions. Can be grown as an informal hedge, and as a tub specimen. After flowering, reduce long stems by one-third, and remove some of the old wood.

Cumberland, Maheka
Other varieties: None
Year: Possibly 18th century
Origin: Unknown
Description: A tall, almost thornless shrub growing to 2 m (7 ft) tall and about 1.5 m (5 ft) wide, with sparse foliage. The almost single, fragrant flowers are violet-purple, 10 cm (4 in) wide, with fine golden stamens, and fade to violet.
Flowering: Summer only
Cultivation: Can be used as a hedging plant. Plant in full sun and encourage next year's flowers and foliage by reducing long canes by one-third, and removing some old wood.

MARCEL BOURGOUIN

Botanical grouping: Gallicanae
Parentage: Unknown
Other names: Le Jacobin
Other varieties: None
Year: 1899
Origin: France
Description: An upright shrub growing to 1.5 m (5 ft) high and about 1 m (3 ft) wide, with dark foliage. The magenta or purple flowers are paler beneath, semi-double, sometimes with prominent yellow stamens.
Flowering: Summer only
Cultivation: Tolerant of light shade. Can be grown as a hedge plant.

ORPHELINE DE JUILLET

Botanical grouping: Gallicanae
Parentage: Unknown, possibly some damask
Other names: None
Other varieties: None
Year: 1848
Origin: England
Description: An open, upright and thorny shrub growing to 1.5 m (5 ft) high and 1 m (3 ft) wide, with grey-green foliage. The abundant medium-sized, purple-crimson flowers turn fiery red in the centre, and are fully double.
Flowering: Summer only
Cultivation: Tolerates poorer soils, but needs full sun. Can be used as a tub specimen, and as a hedging plant. Encourage next year's flowers and foliage by reducing long canes by one-third, and removing some old wood.

PRÉSIDENT DE SÈZE

Botanical grouping: Gallicanae
Parentage: Unknown
Other names: Mme Hébert
Other varieties: None

Président de Sèze

Year: Before 1836
Origin: Unknown
Description: A thorny, loose shrub to 1.5 m (5 ft) high and 1 m (3 ft) across with grey-green foliage. The soft pink buds open to full-petalled flowers with magenta-crimson hearts, paling to lilac-pink at the edges, with a neat cushion of inward folding petals in the centre.

Marcel Bourgouin

Flowering: Summer only
Cultivation: Tolerates poorer soils, but needs full sun. Makes a good potted plant.

R. GALLICA OFFICINALIS

Botanical grouping: Gallicanae
Parentage: Oldest known form of *R. gallica*
Other names: *R. gallica* maxima, Apothecary's Rose, Red Rose of Lancaster
Other varieties: *R. gallica* variegata (Rosa Mundi)
Year: Ancient, known since the 13th century
Origin: Thought to be Damascus
Description: A spreading and suckering shrub growing to 1.5 m (5 ft) high, with dense foliage and few thorns. The semi-double, light red flowers have prominent yellow stamens and are fragrant. Small, round, red hips appear in autumn.
Flowering: Summer only, later than most
Cultivation: Oldest known Gallica in cultivation. Tolerates poorer soils. Encourage next year's flowers and foliage by reducing long canes by one-third and removing some old wood.

Orpheline de Juillet

R. gallica officinalis

Rosa Mundi

Sissingburst Castle

Tricolore de Flandre

ROSA MUNDI

Botanical grouping: Gallicanae
Parentage: Variegated sport of *R. gallica* officinalis
Other names: *R. gallica* versicolor, *R. gallica* variegata
Other varieties: None
Year: Known since the 16th century
Origin: Unknown
Description: A hardy shrub growing to 1.2 m (4 ft) high with few thorns and matt, green foliage. The striking flowers are all different, with combinations of light red, pink and white, with prominent yellow stamens.
Flowering: Summer only
Cultivation: A hardy shrub tolerant of poorer soils. To promote new foliage and flowers each year, reduce new branches by one-third and remove some of the old wood.

SISSINGHURST CASTLE

Botanical grouping: Gallicanae
Parentage: Unknown
Other names: Rose des Maures
Other varieties: None
Year: Unknown
Origin: Found at Sissinghurst Castle by Vita Sackville-West. Otherwise, origin unknown.
Description: A many-stemmed shrub growing to 1 m (3 ft) high and wide, with small but dense foliage and thin stems with few thorns. The fragrant flowers are maroon-crimson with paler edges, rather muddled, to 7.5 cm (3 in) across, and have prominent golden anthers.
Flowering: Summer only
Cultivation: Tolerates light shade and poorer soils, suckering freely. Can be cultivated as a tub specimen. Promote foliage and flowers by removing some of the old wood, and reducing new canes by one-third each year.

Surpasse Tout

SURPASSE TOUT

Botanical grouping: Gallicanae
Parentage: Unknown
Other names: None
Other varieties: None
Year: Before 1832
Origin: Unknown
Description: A leggy shrub growing to 1.5 m (5 ft) high and 1 m (3 ft) across, with less foliage than most others. The highly fragrant flowers open rose-crimson and fade to pink-cerise, petals are reflexed and there is a button eye.
Flowering: Summer only
Cultivation: Tolerates poorer soils, but is temperamental for some. Needs full sun. Remove some of the old wood and reduce new stems by one-third length, to promote flowers and foliage the following year.

TRICOLORE DE FLANDRE

Botanical grouping: Gallicanae
Parentage: Unknown
Other names: None
Other varieties: None
Year: 1846
Origin: Belgium
Description: A fine upright shrub to 1 m (3 ft) by 70 cm (2 ft) across, with abundant smooth dark foliage. The fully double flowers are pale pink with purple and magenta striping, and are scented.
Flowering: Summer only
Cultivation: Requires full sun, but will withstand quite poor soils. Can be grown as a hedge, but is a particularly fine tub specimen. Remove some of the old wood and reduce new stems by one-third length, to encourage flowers and foliage the following year.

TUSCANY

Botanical grouping: Gallicanae
Parentage: Unknown
Other names: Old Velvet Rose
Other varieties: Tuscany Superb
Year: Before 1596
Origin: Unknown
Description: A small, upright shrub growing to 1 m (3 ft) high and 1 m (3 ft) wide. Has been superseded by Tuscany Superb. The deep dark red flowers with golden stamens contrast with the rich green foliage.
Flowering: Summer only
Cultivation: Requires full sun. A good plant for a tub. To promote flowers and foliage the following year, remove dead wood and reduce new stems by one-third after flowering.

TUSCANY SUPERB

Botanical grouping: Gallicanae
Parentage: Sport from Tuscany
Other names: None
Other varieties: None
Year: 1848
Origin: England
Description: An upright shrub to 1.5 m (5 ft) high and 1 m (3 ft) wide, with strong stems and few thorns. The dark crimson flowers are strongly scented, semi-double and display a prominent circle of golden stamens.
Flowering: Summer only
Cultivation: Tolerates poorer soils, but needs full sun. A good hedge plant, or tub specimen. Remove some of the old wood and reduce new stems by one-third length, to promote flowers and foliage the following year.

Tuscany

Tuscany Superb

VELUTINAEFLORA

Botanical grouping: Gallicanae
Parentage: Unknown
Other names: None
Other varieties: None
Year: Unknown
Origin: France
Description: A low-growing shrub to 1.2 m (4 ft) high and wide, with dense grey-green foliage and thorny stems. The single flowers are 7.5 cm (3 in) across and pinkish purple with prominent stamens. Buds are pointed, and sepals are downy.
Flowering: Summer only
Cultivation: Tolerates light shade and poor soils. Makes an excellent tub specimen. Remove some of the old wood and reduce new stems by one-third of their length after flowering.

Damask Roses

A fascinating group of roses that includes *R. damascena* which is distilled to produce attar, the basis of many expensive perfumes and cosmetics. Damasks are generally rather untidy bushes, with an open or lax habit. The foliage is grey-green and downy and the flowers develop slowly and therefore extend the flowering season. The flowers are in a wide range of colours from pure white to clear pink and the older varieties are muddled and semi-double in form, while the newer hybrids tend to be cupped and quartered.

As damasks mostly flower only once a year, they should be pruned only after this flowering period. Removal of some old wood will help stimulate the growth of new wood.

Blush Damask

BLUSH DAMASK

Botanical grouping: Gallicanae
Parentage: Unknown
Other names: Blush Gallica
Other varieties: None
Year: Unknown, before 1759 and probably ancient
Origin: Unknown
Description: A vigorous, spreading shrub growing to 1.5 m (5 ft) high by 1 m (3 ft) wide with dense foliage. The many short-lived flowers are medium sized and double, rich pink, faded at the edges.
Flowering: Summer only
Cultivation: Tolerates poorer soils, and needs full sun. Can be grown as a hedge or as a woodland planting. Remove dead flower heads and some of the old wood and shape the shrub after flowering in summer.

BOTZARIS

Botanical grouping: Gallicanae
Parentage: Unknown, but may include *R. alba*
Other names: None
Other varieties: None
Year: 1856
Origin: Unknown

Botzaris

Description: A medium, thorny shrub growing to 1.5 m (5 ft) high by 1 m (3 ft) wide, with light green foliage. The flat flowers are at least 7.5 cm (3 in) across, fragrant, creamy white with a button centre.
Flowering: Summer only
Cultivation: Requires full sun but can tolerate poorer soil. Can be planted as a hedge, or in a woodland situation. After flowering remove some of the old wood and shape the plant as desired.

CELSIANA

Botanical grouping: Gallicanae
Parentage: Unknown

Other names: None
Other varieties: None
Year: 1732
Origin: Unknown, possibly The Netherlands
Description: A medium shrub growing to 1.5 m (5 ft) high by 1.5 m (5 ft) wide, fairly neat with grey-green foliage. Clusters of semi-double flowers are soft pink, with open centres displaying the yellow stamens. Flowers are fragrant and may fade in hot sun.
Flowering: Summer only
Cultivation: Tolerates poorer soils and requires full sun. May be used as a hedging plant or in woodland. Remove some of the old wood and shape the shrub after flowering in late summer.

Celsiana

DAMASCENA BIFERA

Botanical grouping: Gallicanae
Parentage: Thought to be a hybrid of *R. gallica* and *R. moschata*
Other names: Quatre Saisons, Autumn Damask, Rose of Paestum, Pompeii Rose
Other varieties: *R. x damascena* Bifera Alba Muscosa
Year: Very ancient
Origin: Middle East
Description: A loose, upright, medium-sized shrub 1.5 m (5 ft) high by 1 m (3 ft) wide, with downy, grey-green leaves. the loose-petalled pink flowers are fragrant and double, with characteristic long, thin sepals.
Flowering: Summer through to winter
Cultivation: Tolerates poorer soils, but requires full sun. Can be planted in a woodland setting. Particularly responsive to pruning as bushes should be shaped, and old growth reduced after flowering. Petals are used for potpourri

DUC DE CAMBRIDGE

Botanical grouping: Gallicanae
Parentage: Unknown
Other names: None
Other varieties: None
Year: Before 1848
Origin: Unknown
Description: A medium shrub to 1 m (3 ft) in height, with young brownish foliage contrasting with the bright green older leaves. Flowers are deep purple, very full, and delightfully fragrant.
Flowering: Summer only
Cultivation: Bushes should be shaped, and old growth reduced as soon as flowering is finished.

GLOIRE DE GUILAN

Botanical grouping: Gallicanae
Parentage: Unknown
Other names: None
Other varieties: None
Year: Possibly ancient in the Middle East, but introduced in 1949
Origin: Middle East
Description: A sprawling shrub, growing to 1.5 m (5 ft) high and 1.5 m (5 ft) across, with light green foliage and many small thorns. The highly fragrant flowers are medium pink, flat, double and quartered. This is one species used to produce attar of roses.
Flowering: Summer only
Cultivation: Tolerates poorer soils. Will grow in woodland providing there is good sunlight. Bushes should be shaped, and old growth reduced, as soon as flowering is finished. This rose may need support to increase height.

HEBE'S LIP

Botanical grouping: Caninae
Parentage: Unknown, but perhaps a damask hybrid
Other names: Rubrotincta, Margined Hip, Reine Blanche
Other varieties: None
Year: Before 1846, reintroduced 1912
Origin: England
Description: Medium-sized shrub to 1.5 m (5 ft) high with distinctive long, down-curving thorns on stems. Attractive buds open to creamy white, rosy-edged, flat flowers which look single but are technically double. Prominent yellow stamens.
Flowering: Prominent and ornamental hips
Cultivation: Plant in full sun. Can be used as a hedge if desired. In late summer, prune out dead or diseased wood , and then shape if necessary.

ISPAHAN

Botanical grouping: Gallicanae
Parentage: Unknown
Other names: Pompon des Princes, Rose d'Isfahan
Other varieties: None

Ispahan

Year: Before 1832
Origin: Middle East
Description: Upright shrub to 1.8 m (6 ft) high by about 1 m (3 ft) wide with good foliage. Fragrant flowers are medium pink and semi-double, and maintain good shape and colour.
Flowering: Longer flowering than most, in summer.
Cultivation: Tolerates poorer soil conditions, but needs full sun to flower successfully. Does well as a hedge plant, and can also be used as a tub specimen. After summer flowering, shape the shrub, and remove some of the old wood.

Hebe's Lip

Kazanlik

La Ville de Bruxelles

Léda

Léda

KAZANLIK

Botanical grouping: Gallicanae
Parentage: Unknown
Other names: Kazanluk, *R. damascena trigintipetala*
Other varieties: None
Year: Ancient
Origin: Middle East
Description: Tall, lax shrub to 2 m (7 ft) with support, 1.5 m (5 ft) wide with dark green foliage. Very fragrant flowers are soft pink, double, and tend to be shaggy. Used for the production of attar of roses, and as an ingredient of potpourri.
Flowering: Summer only
Cultivation: Will tolerate poorer soils, and light shade. Can be planted in a woodland setting. After flowering, remove some old wood, and shape the bush.

LA VILLE DE BRUXELLES

Botanical grouping: Gallicanae
Parentage: Unknown
Other names: None
Other varieties: None
Year: 1849
Origin: France
Description: A rounded, upright, strong shrub growing to 1.5 m (5 ft) high by 1 m (3 ft) wide, with prolific foliage and many thorns. The large, rich pink flowers are full and double, fairly flat and very fragrant.
Flowering: Summer only
Cultivation: Capable of cultivation in poorer soils, although it requires full sun. Can be used as a woodland planting. At the end of summer reduce old wood and shape the shrub as required.

LÉDA

Botanical grouping: Gallicanae
Parentage: Unknown
Other names: Painted Damask
Other varieties: Pink Leda

Year: Before 1827
Origin: Unknown, probably England
Description: A compact and tidy shrub growing to 1 m (3 ft) high and 1 m (3 ft) wide with lush, dark, grey-green foliage. The red-brown buds open to strongly scented white, full, double flowers with carmine edges.
Flowering: Summer only, sometimes repeating
Cultivation: Tolerant of poorer soils, but requires full sun to produce results. May be used as a hedge or for tub planting. Old wood needs to be reduced, and the bush shaped, after flowering in summer.

MARIE LOUISE

Botanical grouping: Gallicanae
Parentage: Unknown, probably a Gallica hybrid
Other names: None
Other varieties: None
Year: 1813
Origin: France

Description: A procumbent shrub to 1.5 m (5 ft) high, with arching branches weighed down by the many flowers. The flowers are very large, double, flat and a rich pink with a strong fragrance.
Flowering: Summer only
Cultivation: Will tolerate poorer soils, and requires full sun. Can be grown as a hedge plant and tub specimen. Reduce older wood and shape the shrub after flowering in summer.

MME HARDY

Botanical grouping: Gallicanae
Parentage: Unknown, possibly some alba
Other names: None
Other varieties: None
Year: 1832
Origin: France
Description: A graceful, strong shrub growing to 1.5 m (5 ft) high and 1.5 m (5 ft) wide. The foliage is lush and light, rich green, especially when young. Fragrant flowers are open, rounded and flat, pale

Mme Hardy

Mme Zöetmans

Omar Khayyam

Marie Louise

OMAR KHAYYAM

Botanical grouping: Gallicanae
Parentage: Unknown
Other names: None
Other varieties: None
Year: 1893. Raised from seeds collected from a rose growing over the grave of Omar Khayyam in Iran.
Origin: Unknown
Description: An erect and prickly shrub, varying in height, with foliage of grey-green. The flat, quartered flowers are about 7.5 cm (3 in) across and light pink, with a sweet fragrance.
Flowering: Summer only
Cultivation: Requires full sun and good soils. May be used as a tub specimen. Reduce the old wood, and shape the shrub after flowering.

PETITE LISETTE

Botanical grouping: Gallicanae
Parentage: Unknown
Other names: None
Other varieties: None
Year: 1817
Origin: France
Description: A low, neat shrub 1 m (3 ft) high and wide with grey-green, fine foliage featuring deeply serrated margins. The flowers are small pompons 2.5 cm (1 in) wide, appearing prolifically in clusters evenly over the shrub.
Flowering: Summer only
Cultivation: Prefers a richer soil. Can be grown as a hedge, and is an excellent tub specimen as well as being useful in front of borders. Reduction of long new growths by half after flowering will encourage next season's growth and flowers. Prune dead and spindly wood, and in late winter cut lateral flowering branches back to two or three buds.

pink at first, later pure white with a green centre.
Flowering: Summer only
Cultivation: Tolerates poorer soils and light shade. Reduce old wood and shape the shrub when flowering finishes in summer.

MME ZÖETMANS

Botanical grouping: Gallicanae
Parentage: Unknown
Other names: None

Other varieties: None
Year: 1830
Origin: France
Description: A spreading shrub to 1.2 m (4 ft) high, with dark green foliage. The flowers are fragrant, double, quartered, creamy pink fading to blush-white, with a green eye.
Flowering: Summer only, earlier than most
Cultivation: Can be grown as a hedge, and as a container specimen. Plant in full sun and reduce old wood by half to promote new foliage and flowers. Shape shrub and prune in summer after flowering.

QUATRE SAISONS BLANC MOUSSEUX

Botanical group: Gallicanae
Parentage: Sport of Quatre Saisons
Other names: *R. x damascena,* Bifera Alba Muscosa, Perpetual White Moss, Rosier de Thionville, Four Seasons White Moss
Other varieties: None
Year: First known 1835
Origin: France
Description: This rose is a double sport of Quatre Saisons, with white rather than pink flowers and dense, stiff, brownish green mossing on both buds and stems. The flowers are borne in quite tight, large clusters, opening from the centre of the cluster outward. The buds are elegant with long, ferny sepals and open to semi-double, rather floppy and muddled, thin-petalled, white flowers with a very sweet scent. The shrub is fairly stiff and can reach 1.5 m (5 ft) high and 1 m (3 ft) wide.
Flowering: Repeat flowers in autumn
Cultivation: Extremely tough, but with a little pampering yields quantities of blooms that have charm at all stages. Annual mulching, application of compost and an organic fertiliser are well rewarded. Prune immediately after flowering if required.

ROSE DE RESCHT

Botanical grouping: Gallicanae
Parentage: Unknown
Other names: Gul e Rescht
Other varieties: None
Year: Unknown
Origin: Uncertain, probably Iran
Description: An unusual small rose, growing to 1 m (3 ft) with gallica-like foliage and rich fuchsia-red flowers borne on small, slender stems. The flowers have strong purple tints, and lighten to a magenta-pink with age. They are strongly fragrant.
Flowering: Summer
Cultivation: Easy to cultivate in a wide range of soils and conditions, this rose needs hard pruning to produce flowers over a long period.

ROSE D'HIVERS

Botanical grouping: Gallicanae
Parentage: Unknown
Other names: None
Other varieties: None
Year: Unknown
Origin: Unknown
Description: Atypical of the damasks, this rose has a small and compact habit, 1 m (3 ft) high and wide, with pale green and twiggy new growth and greyish older foliage. The small but shapely flowers pink

at the centre paling to white at the margins.
Flowering: Repeating
Cultivation: Tolerates poorer soils and light shade. An interesting tub plant, it can also be planted as a woodland understorey. Reduce old wood to encourage new growth and flowers, and shape the bush, after flowering.

ST NICHOLAS

Botanical grouping: Gallicanae
Parentage: Unknown, possibly *R. gallica* and a damask
Other names: None
Other varieties: None
Year: 1950
Origin: England
Description: A thorny shrub growing to at least 1 m (3 ft) high and the same width, with dark, downy foliage. The semi-double, mildly fragrant flowers open flat to display pink petals and prominent golden anthers. Produces ornamental orange hips.
Flowering: Recurrent through summer

Cultivation: Requires good soil and full sun. An interesting tub plant. Encourage new foliage and flowers by removing some dead wood, and shape the shrub in winter.

YORK AND LANCASTER

Botanical grouping: Gallicanae
Parentage: Unknown
Other names: *R. x damascena* versicolor
Other varieties: None
Year: Before 1551
Origin: Unknown
Description: A tall, untidy shrub to 2 m (7 ft) high and about 1.5 m (5 ft) wide with downy grey foliage and prominent thorns. The loose, double flowers are distinguished by their unstable colour, ranging from pink to white, in all combinations.
Flowering: Summer only
Cultivation: Tolerates poorer soils and light shade, but responds well to good conditions. Can be used as understorey to woodland. Remove some of the old wood, and shape the bush after flowering.

St Nicholas

York and Lancaster

Rose de Rescht

Alba Roses

A beautiful group of hardy old roses noted for their glorious fragrance. Albas are quite large plants, most growing to 2 m (7 ft) or more, with large leaves and slender stems. The distinctive flowers are in the white, creamy white, blush and pale pink colour range—there are no stripes or dark colours.

Albas are prized for their hardiness and ease of cultivation. As vigorous growers they appreciate being well pruned back each season after flowering, with old wood removed to encourage fresh young growth.

Amélia

Belle Amour

AMÉLIA

Botanical grouping: Caninae
Parentage: Unknown, possibly some damask
Other names: None
Other varieties: None
Year: 1823
Origin: France
Description: Upright shrub to 1.5 m (5 ft) high and 1 m (3 ft) wide. Less vigorous than other albas. Grey-green foliage with prickly stems. Flowers are medium pink fading to pale pink, large, semi-double to 7.5 cm (3 in) with prominent golden anthers. Superb sweet fragrance.
Flowering: Summer only
Cultivation: Hardy, tolerates poor soils. Can be grown as a hedge. Remove some of the old wood after flowering. Long stems may be shortened by one-third.

BELLE AMOUR

Botanical grouping: Caninae
Parentage: Unknown
Other names: None
Other varieties: None
Year: Unknown
Origin: Unknown, possibly France

Belle Amour

Description: Large, vigorous shrub to 2 m (7 ft) with distinctive thorns. Flowers are a clear, soft pink, semi-double with prominent yellow stamens. Fragrant scent with a dash of aniseed.
Flowering: Summer only
Cultivation: Remove some of the old wood after flowering. Long stems may be shortened by about one-third to encourage flowering.

BLANCHE DE BELGIQUE

Botanical grouping: Caninae
Parentage: Unknown

Other names: Blanche Superbe
Other varieties: None
Year: 1817
Origin: France
Description: Vigorous, bushy upright shrub to 2 m (7 ft) high, 1.5 m (5 ft) wide. Grey-green foliage. Flowers are well sized and shaped, white, and superbly perfumed.
Flowering: Summer only
Cultivation: Tolerates poorer soils, prefers sun but will tolerate shade. Can be grown as a hedge. Remove some of the old wood after flowering and trim back long stems to aid flowering.

Celestial

Celestial

Félicité Parmentier

CELESTIAL

Botanical grouping: Caninae
Parentage: Unknown
Other names: Celeste
Other varieties: None
Year: Unknown, possibly ancient
Origin: Unknown, possibly The Netherlands
Description: Large round shrub to 2 m (7 ft) high and 1.5 m (5 ft) wide. Reddish stems, grey foliage. Flowers are a soft, even pink, open-cupped in shape, 10 cm (4 in) across, with a sweet perfume. Elongated red fruit.
Flowering: Summer only
Cultivation: Prefers sun but will tolerate shade. Tolerant of poorer soils. Suitable for hedging. Remove some of the old wood and shorten stems after flowering.

CHLORIS

Botanical grouping: Caninae
Parentage: Unknown
Other names: Rosée du Matin
Other varieties: None
Year: Unknown, very ancient
Origin: Unknown
Description: Relatively uncommon 1.5 m

(5 ft) high by 1.5 m (5 ft) wide shrub with dark green leaves and few thorns. Soft pink double flowers, with a satin texture and petals curving into a tight button. Scented.
Flowering: Summer only
Cultivation: Prefers sun but will tolerate shade. Tolerates poorer soils. Suitable as hedging. Remove some of the old wood after flowering. Encourage flowering by shortening long stems by one-third.

FÉLICITÉ PARMENTIER

Botanical grouping: Caninae
Parentage: Unknown. Some damask characteristics
Other names: None
Other varieties: None
Year: 1834
Origin: Unknown
Description: Upright bushy shrub to 1.5 m (5 ft) by 1 m (3 ft) wide with healthy grey-green foliage. Prolific flowers open salmon pink and fade to pale creamy pink, contrasting with the foliage. Petals reflex to form a sphere. Sweet scent.
Flowering: Summer only
Cultivation: Prefers sun, but tolerates shade

and poorer soils. Suitable for cultivation as a hedge. Prune by removing some of the old wood after flowering, and shortening long stems by about one-third.

JEANNE D'ARC

Botanical grouping: Caninae
Parentage: Unknown
Other names: None
Other varieties: None
Year: 1818
Origin: France
Description: Attractive shrub growing to 1.5 m (5 ft) in height. Sprawling, twiggy, dark foliage which contrasts with the creamy flowers, fading to white in bright sun. Flowers 7.5 cm (3 in) wide with muddled centres.
Flowering: Summer only
Cultivation: Prefers sun, but will tolerate shade and poorer soils. Also useful as a hedging plant. Remove some of the old wood after flowering. Long stems may be shortened by about one-third to encourage flowering.

KÖNIGIN VON DÄNEMARK

Botanical grouping: Caninae
Parentage: Unknown, possibly an alba crossed with a damask
Other names: Queen of Denmark, Belle Courtisanne
Other varieties: None
Year: 1826
Origin: Hamburg
Description: A beautiful open shrub 1.5 m (5 ft) high and 1.5 m (5 ft) wide, with lax branches usually weighed down with flowers. Stems more thorny than usual for albas, foliage coarse and blue-green. Flowers are bright pink fading with age, with a yellow button eye. Superb scent.
Flowering: Summer only
Cultivation: Tolerates shade and poorer soils, though it prefers an open, sunny position. Suitable as a hedging plant. Long stems may be shortened by about one-third to encourage flowering, and dead wood should be cut out after flowering.

LA VIRGINALE

Botanical grouping: Caninae
Parentage: Unknown
Other names: None
Other varieties: None
Year: Unknown
Origin: Unknown
Description: This rose grows to 1.5 m (5 ft) high, and has a shrubby shape with bright green foliage. Abundant flowers to 5 cm (2 in) across are pure white and fragrant.
Flowering: Summer only
Cultivation: Remove some of the old wood after flowering. Long stems may be shortened by about one-third. Prefers an open, sunny aspect.

MAIDEN'S BLUSH

Botanical grouping: Caninae
Parentage: Unknown
Other names: La Royale, La Séduisante, Cuisse de Nymphe, La Virginale, Incarnata, Maiden's Blush (Great), *R. alba regalis* of Redouté
Other varieties: Maiden's Blush (Small), Cuisse de Nymphe Emue
Year: Known by 15th century
Origin: Unknown
Description: This is a large shrub, growing to 2 m (7 ft) high by 1.5 m (5 ft) across. Light blue-grey foliage and arching branches which can be heavy with flower. The abundant blush-pink flowers are sweetly scented and up to 7.5 cm (3 in) across.
Flowering: Free-flowering in summer only
Cultivation: Tolerant of poorer soils. Suitable for cultivation as a hedge. Remove some of the old wood after flowering, and shorten stems to encourage next season's flowering.

MAXIMA

Botanical grouping: Caninae
Parentage: Possibly *R. canina* x *R. gallica*, or *R. alba semiplena* sport
Other names: Jacobite Rose, Great White Rose, Great Double White, White Rose of York, Cheshire Rose
Other varieties: None
Year: 15th century or earlier
Origin: Unknown
Description: One of the largest shrub roses, 2 m (7 ft) high or more, and 1.5 m (5 ft) wide. New stems arch from the base. The foliage is coarse and grey-green and the flowers are creamy white and fragrant doubles with muddled centres. Orange-red fruit is sometimes oval shaped.
Flowering: Upright clusters in summer only
Cultivation: Will tolerate poorer soils, although it needs full sun to thrive. Suitable as a hedging plant. Remove some of the old wood after flowering and shorten long stems by one-third to encourage flowering.

MME LEGRAS DE ST GERMAIN

Botanical grouping: Caninae
Parentage: Unknown, possibly alba-damask hybrid
Other names: None
Other varieties: None
Year: Before 1848
Origin: Unknown
Description: Medium-sized shrub 2 m (7 ft) high and 2 m (7 ft) wide, capable of reaching twice the height if supported. Relatively few thorns, pale grey-green foliage. Superb, white-cupped flowers with yellow centres and good scent.
Flowering: Summer only
Cultivation: Prefers sun, although it will tolerate shade, poorer soils and a cold aspect. Prune long stems by about one-third to encourage flowering, and cut out dead or diseased wood if necessary when flowering has finished.

Maiden's Blush

Maxima

Königin von Dänemark

Mme Legras de St Germain

Mme Plantier

Semi-plena

MME PLANTIER

Botanical grouping: Caninae
Parentage: Unknown, may include
R. moschata
Other names: None
Other varieties: None
Year: 1835
Origin: Unknown
Description: Very hardy shrub with lax branches which can be used to climb trees or trained as a pillar rose. Height to 3.5 m (12 ft) and width 2.5 m (8 ft). Fewer thorns and light grey-green leaves and stems. Large clusters of scented, small double and creamy flowers ageing to white.
Flowering: Summer only
Cultivation: Vigorous and tall climbing if given support. Will tolerate a cold aspect, poorer soils and some shade, although sunny conditions are ideal. Remove some of the old wood after flowering, and prune back long stems.

POMPON BLANC PARFAIT

Botanical grouping: Caninae
Parentage: Unknown
Other names: None
Other varieties: None
Year: 1876
Origin: Unknown, probably France
Description: An erect, neat shrub, reaching 1.5 m (5 ft) by 1 m (3 ft). Tight groups of small, fat pink buds opening to white flowers with button centres. The flowers are long-lasting and foliage is small and grey-green in color.
Flowering: Summer
Cultivation: Prefers full sun but will tolerate shade, poorer soils and even a cold aspect. Can be grown as a hedge. Prune out some of the old wood after flowering, and trim back long stems to encourage flowering.

PRINCESSE DE LAMBALLE

Botanical grouping: Caninae
Parentage: Unknown, possibly alba and *R. moschata*
Other names: None
Other varieties: None
Year: Unknown
Origin: Unknown
Description: This is an obscure old rose.

Attractive shrub shape with pure white, cupped double flowers to 5 cm (2 in) across. Blooms are abundant and fragrant.
Flowering: Summer only
Cultivation: Remove old wood after flowering and trim long stems by one-third.

SEMI-PLENA

Botanical grouping: Caninae
Parentage: Unknown
Other names: *R. x alba suaveolens,*
R. x alba nivea, White Rose of York
Other varieties: None
Year: 16th century or earlier
Origin: Europe
Description: A large, upright shrub with lax branches, 2.5 m (8 ft) high by 1.5 m (5 ft) wide and grey-green foliage. Flowers are pure white and semi-double with golden stamens, up to 7.5 cm (3 in) across. Elongated, orange-red autumn fruit.
Flowering: Summer only
Cultivation: Tolerant of poorer soils, suitable as an informal hedge. Remove some of the old wood after flowering. Long stems can be pruned by one-third to encourage next season's flowering.

Pompon Blanc Parfait

Centifolia Roses

Also known as cabbage roses, the centifolia's distinctive flowers have abundant petals (hence the name centifolia, the hundred-leaved-rose). Centifolia bushes are medium in size, neither lax or erect but featuring graceful arched stems and soft, mid-green foliage which is often reflexed. Thorns are variable in size, and the showy flowers appear in clusters of three to five. The tightly packed petals are in a range of colours from creamy white and palest pink, through mauve and lavender to a spicy warm shade of mid-pink. There are also dwarf forms.

After flowering new growths can be cut back by one half, and all dead, twiggy or spindly wood should be removed.

Bullata

BLANCHEFLEUR

Botanical grouping: Gallicanae
Parentage: Unknown
Other names: None
Other varieties: None
Year: 1835
Origin: France
Description: Relatively neat, medium-sized shrub 1.5 m (5 ft) by 1.5 m (5 ft) with pale grey-green foliage. The white, flat double flowers have an occasional pale pink blush and are scented. Heavy bunches weigh down the branches and open the centre of the shrub.
Flowering: Summer only
Cultivation: Prefers sun, will tolerate some shade and poorer soils. Reduce long new growths by half after flowering, remove all dead and spindly wood, and cut lateral flowering branches back to two or three buds in late winter.

BULLATA

Botanical grouping: Gallicanae
Parentage: Unknown, may be a mutant centifolia
Other names: Lettuce-leaf Rose, Rose à Feuilles de Laitue
Other varieties: None
Year: Before 1801, possibly 16th century
Origin: Unknown
Description: A medium-sized shrub, 1.5 m (5 ft) high by 1.5 m (5 ft) wide, with a lax growing habit. Atypical brown and veined young foliage which appears to be crinkled. Double flowers are medium pink and cupped or cabbage-like, with a strong fragrance.
Flowering: Summer only
Cultivation: Tolerant of poorer soils. Suitable for woodland planting. Reduce long new growths by half after flowering, prune all dead and spindly wood, and cut lateral flowering branches back to two or three buds in late winter.

CHAPEAU DE NAPOLÉON

Botanical grouping: Gallicanae
Parentage: Unknown
Other names: Crested Moss, Cristata
Other varieties: None
Year: 1826
Origin: Switzerland
Description: One of the most charming of the old roses with flowers of exquisite beauty. The buds open to very sweetly scented, fully double, deeply cupped, clear pink blooms. It will grow to 1.5 m (5 ft) and is somewhat lax although sturdy in form, reaching 1.2 m (4 ft) wide. The foliage consists of large, drooping leaves which clothe the shrub well.
Flowering: Summer
Cultivation: A sturdy, easy variety in most areas but will benefit from regular watering and mulching, and an annual application of compost or rotted manure. Prune immediately after flowering, but only if necessary. Some support is helpful, for example a tripod of appropriate height.

Chapeau de Napoléon

De Meaux

DE MEAUX

Botanical grouping: Gallicanae
Parentage: Unknown
Other names: Rose de Meaux, *R.* x *centifolia pomponia*
Other varieties: Rose de Meaux White
Year: Before 1789
Origin: France
Description: Short, neat, upright shrub to 7 cm (2 ft) high and the same in width. Abundant small leaves and flowers, which are pink and double, up to 2.5 cm (1 in) across, almost pompon shaped. Very fragrant.
Flowering: Very abundant in summer
Cultivation: May be difficult to grow in poor soils. Excellent tub specimen, and as low hedge. Remove all dead and spindly wood, and cut lateral flowering branches back to two or three buds in late winter. Shorten longer stems.

DUCHESSE DE ROHAN

Botanical grouping: Gallicanae
Parentage: Unknown
Other names: Duc de Rohan
Other varieties: None
Year: *c.* 1860
Origin: Unknown
Description: Medium-sized shrub 1.5 m (5 ft) high by 1.5 m (5 ft) wide. The flowers are rich pink fading to lavender with many petals and occasional repeat flowering. Strong fragrance.
Flowering: Unusual recurrent or repeat flowering.
Cultivation: Requires full sun and good soils. Reduce long new growths by half after flowering, remove all dead and spindly wood, and in late winter cut lateral flowering branches back to two or three buds.

FANTIN-LATOUR

Botanical grouping: Gallicanae
Parentage: Unknown
Other names: None
Other varieties: None
Year: *c.* 1900
Origin: Unknown
Description: Large, spreading shrub at least 1.5 m (5 ft) high and 1.5 m (5 ft) across. Leaves are atypically darker and smoother with stems less thorny. Flowers are pale pink, to 10 cm (4 in) across in large clusters, cup-shaped at first, outer petals reflexing

Fantin-Latour

later, good fragrance.
Flowering: Mid-summer
Cultivation: Will tolerate poorer soils, but requires full sun. Reduce long new growths by half after flowering, remove all dead and spindly wood, and cut lateral flowering branches back to two or three buds in late winter.

JUNO

Botanical grouping: Gallicanae
Parentage: Unknown, possibly gallica-China hybrid
Other names: None
Other varieties: None
Year: 1832

Juno

Origin: Unknown
Description: Medium spreading shrub with arching canes to 1.5 m (5 ft) high and 1.5 m (5 ft) wide. Very pale, double, pink flowers are globular, have a yellow centre when fully open, and are highly fragrant.
Flowering: Summer only
Cultivation: Will tolerate poorer soils, but requires full sun. Can be grown as a tub specimen. Reduction of long new growths by half after flowering will encourage new growth and flowers. Remove all dead and spindly wood, and toward the end of winter cut the lateral flowering branches back to two or three buds.

LA NOBLESSE

Botanical grouping: Gallicanae
Parentage: Unknown
Other names: None
Other varieties: None
Year: 1856
Origin: Unknown
Description: A relatively neat shrub 1.5 m (5 ft) high by 1.5 m (5 ft) wide. The very fragrant blooms are a rich pink and double in form, although quite flat in shape when they open.
Flowering: Late summer, possibly the latest to flower
Cultivation: Will tolerate poorer soils, although it requires full sun. May be grown as a hedging plant. Reduction of long new growths by half after flowering will encourage new growth and flowers. Cut lateral flowering branches back to two or three buds in late winter and remove all dead or spindly wood.

LA RUBANÉE

Botanical grouping: Gallicanae
Parentage: Unknown
Other names: Village Maid, Cottage Maid, Belle des Jardins, *R.* x *centifolia variegata*
Other varieties: None
Year: 1845
Origin: France
Description: A vigorous shrub growing to 1.5 m (5 ft) high and to 1.5 m (5 ft) across, it has strong branches and many thorns. Flowers are abundant, off-white with purple and crimson stripes to 10 cm (4 in) across, cupped and very fragrant.
Flowering: Mid-summer, with occasional repeats
Cultivation: Prefers full sun, although will tolerate poorer soil conditions. Reduce long new growths by half after flowering to encourage new growth and flowers. Remove all dead and spindly wood, and cut lateral flowering branches back to two or three buds in late winter.

Ombrée Parfaite

Petite de Hollande

Petite Orléanaise

OMBRÉE PARFAITE

Botanical grouping: Gallicanae
Parentage: Unknown, possibly a Gallica-China hybrid
Other names: None
Other varieties: None
Year: 1823
Origin: France
Description: A spreading, ornamental shrub growing to 1 m (3 ft) and 1 m (3 ft) wide, with small, rich green leaves. The flowers have many coloured petals ranging from crimson-purple through to the lightest pink. Flowers are delightfully fragrant.
Flowering: Summer only
Cultivation: Excellent tub specimen that tolerates poorer soils but requires full sun to produce good results. Reduction of long new growths by half after flowering will encourage next season's growth and flowering. After flowering remove all dead and spindly wood, and in winter cut lateral flowering branches back to two or three buds.

PETITE DE HOLLANDE

Botanical grouping: Gallicanae
Parentage: Unknown
Other names: Pompon des Dames, Petite Junon de Hollande

Other varieties: None
Year: 1800
Origin: The Netherlands
Description: This compact, small shrub to 1.5 m (5 ft) high by 1 m (3 ft) wide has prolific small flowers 4 cm (1 ½ in) wide appearing in clusters. The flowers are pink with darker centres and a rich fragrance.
Flowering: Summer only
Cultivation: Requires full sun, but tolerates poorer soils. Ideal in small gardens, and makes an excellent tub specimen. Reduction of long new growths by half after flowering will encourage next season's growth and flowers. Remove all dead and spindly wood, and cut lateral flowering branches back to two or three buds in late winter.

PETITE ORLÉANAISE

Botanical grouping: Gallicanae
Parentage: Unknown
Other names: None
Other varieties: None
Year: *c.* 1900
Origin: Unknown
Description: An attractive shrub with a neat, leafy habit. Similar to other pompon-type flowers, but the shrub is taller, 1.5 m (5 ft) and 1 m (3 ft) wide.
Flowering: Summer only

Cultivation: Can be grown in a wide range of soils and conditions. Suitable as a hedge and for larger containers. Pruning of long, new growths by half after flowering will stimulate next season's growth and flowers. Cut lateral flowering branches back to two or three buds at the end of winter, and remove all dead and spindly wood.

POMPON DE BOURGOGNE

Botanical grouping: Gallicanae
Parentage: Unknown
Other names: Parvifolia, *R. burgundica*
Other varieties: None
Year: Prior to 1664
Origin: Unknown
Description: A small and upright shrub, 70 cm (2 ft) high and wide. The foliage is packed densely along stiff stems, while the small, pompon flowers are claret or purple, with pink flecks.
Flowering: Summer only
Cultivation: Prefers good soil and needs full sun to flower freely. Can be planted as a hedge and is an excellent miniature tub specimen. Reduction of longer new growths by half after flowering will encourage next season's growth and flowers. Remove all dead and diseased wood.

R. CENTIFOLIA

Botanical grouping: Gallicanae
Parentage: Not known. Thought to be a complex hybrid.
Other names: Cabbage Rose, Provence Rose, Rose des Peintres
Other varieties: *R.* x *centifolia alba* (White Provence), *R.* x *centifolia muscosa*
Year: Early 17th century, but may be much older.
Origin: Europe
Description: Medium, lax shrub, 2 m (7 ft) high by 1.5 m (5 ft) wide with lush, grey-green, coarse-toothed leaves and varied thorns. The double flowers are cabbage-shaped, rich pink and strongly scented, carried as a single bloom or clustered on the stem. No rose hips, as double flowers prevent seed production.
Flowering: Summer only
Cultivation: Requires full sun, but will tolerate poorer soil. May be planted in woodland. Reduce long new growths by half after flowering and remove all dead and spindly wood.

REINES DES CENTFEUILLES

Botanical grouping: Gallicanae
Parentage: Unknown
Other names: None
Other varieties: None
Year: 1824
Origin: Belgium
Description: An untidy, open shrub of medium height, 1.5 m (5 ft) by 1 m (3 ft) wide. The prolific flowers are double, deep pink and quartered with button centre. Petals are reflexed, and the flower appears flat on top.

Robert le Diable

R. centifolia

Flowering: Summer only
Cultivation: Will tolerate poorer soils and requires full sun to produce good results. Reduce longer new growths by half after flowering to encourage next season's growth and flowers. If required, lateral flowering stems can be reduced to two or three buds' length in winter.

ROBERT LE DIABLE

Botanical grouping: Gallicanae
Parentage: Unknown
Other names: None
Other varieties: None
Year: Unknown
Origin: France
Description: A small procumbent shrub growing to 1 m (3 ft) high and wide with abundant foliage. Tends to be late flowering. The unusual flowers change colours from crimson to lilac with pink and grey, and have a green centre.
Flowering: Summer only, but later than most
Cultivation: Requires full sun, and will tolerate poorer soils. Can be an interesting tub specimen. Sometimes prone to black spot and rain damage. Reduction of longer new growths by half after flowering will encourage next season's growth and flowers. Remove all dead and spindly wood.

ROSE DES PEINTRES

Botanical grouping: Gallicanae
Parentage: Unknown
Other names: *R.* x *centifolia*, Major, Centfeuille des Peintres
Other varieties: None
Year: Before 1800
Origin: Unknown
Description: Similiar to *R.* x *centifolia*. A spreading, medium sized shrub growing to 2 m (7 ft) high and 1.5 m (5 ft) wide with dark foliage. Flowers are large, double, and deep pink, with good petal texture. There is a well-defined centre to the flowers.
Flowering: Summer only
Cultivation: Will tolerate poorer soils. Suitable for planting near large trees, as long as there is direct sun. Reduction of longer new growths by half after flowering will encourage next season's growth and flowers. Remove all dead and spindly wood. Lateral branches may be cut back in winter to two or three buds.

SPONG

Botanical grouping: Gallicanae
Parentage: Unknown
Other names: None
Other varieties: None
Year: 1805

Origin: Uncertain, possibly England
Description: A small to medium size, compact and upright shrub to 1.2 m (4 ft) high by 1 m (3 ft) wide. It has abundant grey-green rounded leaflets and showy, scented flowers which are a rich, deep pink, slightly larger than De Meaux.
Flowering: Long season in summer only
Cultivation: Will tolerate poorer soils and some shade, although prefers full sun. An excellent tub specimen and hedge plant. Dead-heads should be removed after flowering, and reduction of longer new growths by half after flowering will encourage next season's growth and flowers. Prune back dead and spindly wood.

Spong

Tour de Malakoff

THE BISHOP

Botanical grouping: Gallicanae
Parentage: Unknown, but may include Gallica
Other names: L'Evêque
Other varieties: None
Year: By 1821
Origin: Unknown
Description: An upright, medium-sized shrub to 1.5 m (5 ft) high. The double flowers are flat rosettes, magenta-cerise fading to grey-blue, and are wonderfully scented.
Flowering: Summer only, but earlier than most other centifolias
Cultivation: Requires full sun, although it can be grown in relatively poor soil. A good tub specimen. Prune new growths by half after flowering in order to encourage next season's growth and flowers, and remove all dead and spindly wood.

TOUR DE MALAKOFF

Botanical grouping: Gallicanae
Parentage: Unknown, possibly a gallica–China hybrid
Other names: Black Jack
Other varieties: None
Year: 1856
Origin: Luxembourg
Description: Probably the tallest centifolia, growing to 2.5 m (8 ft) and 1.5 m (5 ft) wide with lax branches which may require support. Large flowers grow to 10 cm (4 in) across, loosely double, magenta with a purple flush which fades with age to blue-violet. Flowers are abundant and scented.
Flowering: Summer only
Cultivation: Needs full sun, but will tolerate poorer soils. Pruning back longer new growths by half after flowering will encourage next season's growth and flowers. Lateral branches may be reduced to two or three buds' length in winter.

WHITE PROVENCE

Botanical grouping: Gallicanae
Parentage: Unknown. Thought to be a centifolia sport.
Other names: Unique Blanche, Vierge dé Cléry, R. x *centifolia alba*
Other varieties: None
Year: 1775
Origin: Suffolk, England
Description: A medium-sized shrub growing to 1.5 m (5 ft) high and up to 1.5 m (5 ft) wide. It has white flowers with a superb, silky texture.
Flowering: Summer, and into autumn
Cultivation: Wet weather may spoil the flowers of this rose. Can be grown in poorer soils, but requires full sun to bring results. Reduction of longer new growths by half after flowering will encourage next season's growth and flowers. Prune out dead and spindly wood every year.

The Bishop

Moss Roses

This group of roses is relatively easy to recognise because of the moss-like growth which covers the stems and buds, and sometimes the back of the stems which support the leaves. The extent and form of this mossy growth varies in colour from green to brown and can be very thick and feathery, or sparse and stiff in appearance. Moss roses are noted for their beautiful fragrance.

In appearance the bushes are smaller and more compact than those of the centifolia, and often the flowers and foliage are smaller too. The flower colours range from deep purple-black through pink to pure white and there is also a striped form.

Pruning involves cutting back about a third to a half of the long, new growths and removing dead wood.

Alfred de Dalmas

A LONGUES PÉDONCULES

Botanical grouping: Gallicanae
Parentage: Unknown
Other names: None
Other varieties: None
Year: 1854
Origin: France
Description: A graceful, vigorous, arching shrub to 1.8 m (6 ft) high and 1.2 m (4 ft) high with neat, plentiful, soft grey-green foliage. Produces a profusion of small, double, soft pink flowers infused with lilac which are sweetly fragrant. The flowers open from buds with plentiful green moss, borne on long peduncles (flower stalks).
Flowering: Summer
Cultivation: Reliable soil moisture levels ensure abundant flowering. Mulch and water well during the growing season. It responds to an annual application of rotted manure or compost. Prune immediately after flowering, or leave unpruned other than removal of twiggy or dead growth and branches rubbing against each other.

ALFRED DE DALMAS

Botanical grouping: Gallicanae
Parentage: Unknown, but shows damask or Portland influence
Other names: Mousseline, though some say this is a different rose, dating from 1881
Other varieties: None
Year: 1855
Origin: France
Description: A medium, compact shrub with few thorns growing to 1.2 m (4 ft) and spreading to 1.2 m (4 ft), with lush, fresh green, spoon-shaped foliage. The elegant buds are lightly mossed, the moss colouring from fresh green to rose pink to russet shades. The buds open to creamy, blush pink, cupped, double blooms which are sweetly scented.
Flowering: Repeat flowering for up to six months of each year.
Cultivation: A hardy variety which is suitable for pot culture and can be used effectively as a bedding rose. Cut back by up to one-third when dormant and dead-head in summer when necessary.

BARON DE WASSENAER

Botanical grouping: Gallicanae
Parentage: Unknown
Other names: None
Other varieties: None
Year: 1854
Origin: France
Description: A vigorous upright-growing shrub to 1.8 m (6 ft) well clothed in dark green foliage. The buds are lightly mossed opening to cupped fragrant very double rich bright crimson blooms borne in very large trusses. A damask moss by breeding.
Flowering: Summer flowering over a long period
Cultivation: Mulch and water well during the growing season. Responds to an annual application of manure or compost. Prune immediately after flowering if pruning is required for shaping.

BLANCHE MOREAU

Botanical grouping: Gallicanae
Parentage: Comtesse de Murinais x Quatre Saisons Blanc
Other names: None
Other varieties: None
Year: 1880
Origin: France
Description: A slender, lax shrub to 1.5 m (5 ft) high and 1 m (3 ft) wide. A beautiful damask moss rose with purest white, double

A Longues Pédoncules

Baron de Wassenaer

blooms of near-perfect, camellia-like conformation and with a button eye. The flowers are sweetly fragrant with dark mossing on the buds and are borne in small clusters.
Flowering: Summer flowering; one of the later flowering mosses, but often with a light second flush of flowers in autumn.
Cultivation: Mulch and water well to achieve perfection of flower and control mildew where perfect mossed buds are required.

CAPITAINE JOHN INGRAM

Botanical grouping: Gallicanae
Parentage: Unknown
Other names: None
Other varieties: None
Year: 1856
Origin: France
Description: The flowers have a rich sweet scent and are fully double, pompon shaped, richly coloured in velvety purple infused with dark crimson shaded to maroon. The reverse of the petals is a soft lilac-pink. Stems and buds are well mossed, the mossing being russet coloured, and the foliage is infused with purple when young. Grows to 1.2 m (4 ft) high and 1 m (3 ft) wide. In rich soil and warm climates it will reach 1.5 m (5 ft).
Flowering: Summer
Cultivation: Responds to mulching and regular watering to maintain even summer moisture, and to an annual top dressing of well-rotted manure or compost. Prune immediately after flowering, if required.

CÉLINA

Botanical grouping: Gallicanae
Parentage: Unknown
Other names: None
Other varieties: None
Year: 1855
Origin: France
Description: A smaller moss of tidy habit to 1.2 m (4 ft) with charming semi-double, fragrant flowers of deep crimson infused with cerise and lavender, and with a central boss of golden stamens. The mossing on this variety is slight.
Flowering: Summer
Cultivation: In areas where rose mildew is common, control measures are advised as this variety is prone to mildew. Prune soon after flowering is finished. Mulch and maintain the soil moisture with regular watering during the growing season. Top dress the soil annually with compost or well-rotted manure.

COMMON MOSS

Botanical grouping: Gallicanae
Parentage: Unknown
Other names: Old Pink Moss, Communis; *R. centifolia muscosa*
Other varieties: Several forms are sold under the name Common Moss.
Year: Before 1700
Origin: Unknown
Description: This is the original moss rose. Considered by many to be unexcelled in beauty by any varieties which followed. An open shrub, 1.5 m (5 ft) tall and 1.5 m (5 ft) wide, very well clothed with large coarsely toothed, handsome foliage. The buds are exquisite, covered in soft, fresh green, abundant mossing, opening to clear pink, very double globular blooms which finish flat with a button eye. The flowers are exceptionally fragrant.
Flowering: Summer flowering for up to two months
Cultivation: A tough variety but prolonged flowering and optimum flower quality are ensured by regular summer mulching and watering, and by an annual top dressing of compost or well-rotted manure. Pruning, if required, should be carried out immediately after flowering.

COMTESSE DE MURINAIS

Botanical grouping: Gallicanae
Parentage: Unknown
Other names: None
Other varieties: None
Year: 1843

Common Moss

Comtesse de Murinais

Origin: France
Description: A tall, graceful damask moss with arching stems, growing to 2 m (7 ft) high and 1.2 m (4 ft) wide, with handsome light green leaves. The buds are well mossed, the moss being quite stiff to the touch, fresh green in colour and with a strong pink-like resinous fragrance. The buds open to flowers of an exquisite blush, for example, cream paling to creamy white when fully open. The flowers are very double opening flat and quartered, of classic formation, borne in graceful sprays.
Flowering: Summer
Cultivation: Provide support for this tall rose. Prune immediately after flowering, if required. This is a vigorous variety but in areas with hot dry summers it responds to mulching and regular watering. A top dressing of compost or well rotted manure should be given annually for quality blooms.

Capitaine John Ingram

Crested Jewel

Deuil de Paul Fontaine

Général Kléber

CRESTED JEWEL

Botanical grouping: Gallicanae
Parentage: Unknown
Other names: None
Other varieties: None
Year: 1971
Origin: United States
Description: A fairly modern-looking rose on a medium bush to 1.2 m (4 ft) high and 1.2 m (4 ft) wide. The flowers are semi-double in a bright, rich rose pink, fragrant, and usually borne in small clusters. They open from lightly mossed buds. The foliage is green.
Flowering: Recurrent flowering although the major display for most places is at the beginning of the season.
Cultivation: Prune lightly after the initial flowering. If further pruning is required for shaping it may be done in winter.

CRIMSON MOSS

Botanical grouping: Gallicanae
Parentage: Unknown
Other names: None
Other varieties: None
Year: Before 1846
Origin: England
Description: The bush is of typical centifolia conformation, to 1.5 m (5 ft) high and 1.2 m (4 ft) wide. The flowers are very richly coloured in crimson and purple and are cupped and very double.
Flowering: Summer
Cultivation: Probably not worthy of planting other than in areas with a reliably warm dry flowering season. The guard petals are very prone to failing to separate causing the flowers to be malformed or to fail to open properly whenever it rains. Regular mulching in summer is necessary and watering should be confined to the soil surface during flowering. It responds well to an annual application of compost or well-rotted manure.

DEUIL DE PAUL FONTAINE

Botanical grouping: Gallicanae
Parentage: Unknown
Other names: None
Other varieties: None
Year: 1873
Origin: France
Description: A damask moss rose for smaller gardens, being a slender shrub rarely exceeding 1.2 m (4 ft), repeat flowering in most years. The blooms are a rich deep crimson to maroon and purple-black mixture, cupped, revealing golden stamens. There is a hard, crimson-coloured mossing on the sepals and pedicels, and sparse dark foliage.
Flowering: Repeats in most seasons.
Cultivation: This is a rose that repays some kindness, yielding good quality flowers and more reliable repeat flowering.

FÉLICITÉ BOHAIN

Botanical grouping: Gallicanae
Parentage: Unknown
Other names: None
Other varieties: None
Year: c.1865
Origin: Unknown
Description: A moderate growing moss rose that is surprisingly little known. The smallish sweetly scented flowers are very double, quartered with a button eye in rich bright pink. The bush is neat, reaching 1.2 m (4 ft) high and 1 m (3 ft) wide.
Flowering: Summer
Cultivation: A hardy variety. Prune immediately after flowering, if required. Mulching and an annual application of compost or well-rotted manure is recommended.

GÉNÉRAL KLÉBER

Botanical grouping: Gallicanae
Parentage: Unknown

Other names: None
Other varieties: None
Year: 1856
Origin: France
Description: An excellent garden variety of moss rose growing to approximately 1.5 m (5 ft) high and 1.2 m (4 ft) wide, forming a very well-clothed shrub. The foliage is a bright green, large and healthy. The buds are well mossed with soft, bright green moss and open to large, informal, double, shining fragrant flowers of soft to bright pink. A floriferous and very reliable garden variety.
Flowering: Summer
Cultivation: Prune after flowering if required. One of the toughest of the moss roses growing well under a variety of conditions. Mulching and the annual addition of compost or well rotted manure is recommended.

GLOIRE DES MOUSSEUX

Botanical grouping: Gallicanae
Parentage: Unknown
Other names: Mme Alboni

Gloire des Mousseux

Other varieties: None
Year: 1852
Origin: France
Description: An excellent garden variety. A damask moss which makes a substantial upright bush to 1.2 m (4 ft) or a little more. The fully double flowers, opening from lightly mossed buds of bright green, are very lovely and borne in small clusters. These are perhaps the largest of all moss rose flowers and are a clear soft pink with a very sweet strong scent. The foliage is large, plentiful and bright green. A thoroughly romantic rose!
Flowering: Slightly recurrent
Cultivation: A strong healthy variety over a wide climatic range. A light pruning immediately after summer flowering can be carried out if required. Annual mulching and an application of compost or well-rotted manure are recommended.

GOETHE

Botanical grouping: Gallicanae
Parentage: Unknown
Other names: None
Other varieties: None
Year: 1911
Origin: Germany
Description: The only single moss rose available today although several were known in the 19th century. It bears large, open, rather angular clusters of single flowers in a deep carmine-pink with a white eye and central boss of prominent golden stamens. The buds and pedicels are well mossed with a rather stiff, bristled, reddish-brown mossing. Younger shoots have a distinct crimson colouration. The shrub is very thorny with dark green foliage, and is very vigorous, easily gaining a height of 2 m (7 ft) and a width of 1.5 m (5 ft).
Cultivation: It grows rapidly and is tolerant of a wide variety of climatic conditions. Requires no pruning other than to control inconvenient growth or broken branches. If pruning is carried out take care to prune evenly to maintain the balanced shape of this shrub. Like all moss roses it responds to annual mulching and the application of well-rotted manure or compost.

GOLDEN MOSS

Botanical grouping: Gallicanae
Parentage: Frau Karl Druschki x (Souvenir de Claudius Pernet x Blanche Moreau)
Other names: None
Other varieties: None
Year: 1932
Origin: Spain
Description: From Frau Karl Druschki comes the enormous vigour of this rose

Henri Martin

which in warmer climates is perfectly capable of sending up canes to 3 m (10 ft) although its width is more modest at around 1 m (3 ft). In cooler climates it behaves in a more restrained fashion reaching around 1.5 m (5 ft). It is a shy flowerer under all climatic conditions but in areas with a dry summer the blooms can be quite lovely, cupped, pale gold and sweetly fragrant. Areas with predictably wet weather in the old rose flowering season experience discolouration and balling of the flowers.
Flowering: Summer
Cultivation: Firm pruning soon after flowering will help to develop a better shape to the bush and hold ambitious canes in check. It also seems to assist in promoting flowering. This is a tough variety but like all moss roses annual mulching and the application of compost or well-rotted manure is advised.

HENRI MARTIN

Botanical grouping: Gallicanae
Parentage: Unknown
Other names: Red Moss
Other varieties: None
Year: 1863
Origin: France
Description: This is a damask moss which makes a tall, graceful shrub, growing to 1.8 m (6 ft) high and 1.2 m (4 ft) wide. It is once-flowering but very floriferous bowing

Golden Moss

down under the weight of clusters of sweetly scented, double, intensely bright, crimson flowers which reveal golden stamens in the centre. The clear green mossing, although present, is not prolific.
Flowering: Summer
Cultivation: This rose looks best supported by a substantial tripod or other structure which will allow the long graceful canes to be displayed to advantage and form a cascade of flowers in summer. A very cold tolerant rose, yet will survive very hot, dry summers well too. It is also a rose for difficult north-facing aspects in the northern hemisphere. Prune immediately after flowering if required.

Hunslett Moss

James Veitch

James Mitchell

James Veitch

HUNSLETT MOSS

Botanical grouping: Gallicanae
Parentage: Unknown
Other names: Original name unknown
Other varieties: None
Year: 1984 (reintroduction)
Origin: Unknown, grown in England for generations
Description: A moderate, sturdy bush to 1.2 m (4 ft) high and 1 m (3 ft) wide, with dark green foliage. The flowers have a delightful, strong fragrance and are a rich, deep pink, large and very double. They have excellent mossing which sets the flowers off very well.
Flowering: Summer
Cultivation: This rose has limited distribution as yet and its performance in a wide variety of climates has not been evaluated. However, its performance in England has indicated that normal mulching, an annual application of rotted manure or compost, and pruning immediately after flowering will yield very good results.

JAMES MITCHELL

Botanical grouping: Gallicanae
Parentage: Unknown
Other names: None
Other varieties: None
Year: 1861
Origin: France
Description: A substantial, graceful bush to 1.5 m (5 ft) high and 1.2 m (4 ft) wide. It is an early flowering variety and a prolific flowerer. The individual sweetly scented flowers are quite small, flat, very double with a button eye and quilled petals, of a bright clear cerise-pink which fades with age to lilac-pink. The dainty buds are covered in brownish green moss.
Flowering: Summer
Cultivation: Tends to spray outward, particularly under the weight of blossom, so support with stakes. Otherwise a very tough variety performing well over a wide climatic range provided soil moisture is maintained during the summer. Prune immediately after flowering.

JAMES VEITCH

Botanical grouping: Gallicanae
Parentage: Unknown
Other names: None
Other varieties: None
Year: 1865
Origin: France
Description: With a relationship to the Portland roses, this moss rose is a good, reliably repeat flowering variety forming a smallish, neat bush to 1 m (3 ft) high and 1 m (3 ft) wide. The buds are only lightly mossed but the very double, fragrant flowers are medium-sized with a button eye and are a rich, subtle plum purple with a slate grey cast.
Flowering: Repeat flowering over an extended period.
Cultivation: In some areas this rose has shown a tendency to be susceptible to mildew. Prune lightly after the final flowering for the season, if required.

JEANNE DE MONTFORT

Botanical grouping: Gallicanae
Parentage: Unknown
Other names: None
Other varieties: None
Year: 1851
Origin: France
Description: A very tall variety to a height of 2.5 m (8 ft) and a width of 1.5 m (5 ft) with shiny, dark green foliage. It bears abundant clusters of very heavily and prettily mossed buds which open to clear, rose pink, semi-double flowers which are very fragrant and show golden stamens.
Flowering: Summer
Cultivation: Best grown as a pillar rose or shorter climber as it requires support. Alternatively, it can be allowed to make a large shrub. Prune lightly when flowering is complete. Mulch to maintain soil moisture levels in summer and provide an application of well-rotted manure or compost annually.

LANEII

Botanical grouping: Gallicanae
Parentage: Unknown
Other names: Lane's Moss
Other varieties: None
Year: 1846
Origin: France
Description: An unusual Gallica–hybrid moss forming a leggy, prickly, vigorous bush growing to 1.5 m (5 ft) high and 1 m (3 ft) wide. It is a prolific bloomer producing mossed, large round buds which open to scented, very double, purplish mauve flowers.
Flowering: Summer
Cultivation: This variety is best grown with support. Prune immediately after flowering. Mulch well and supply an annual application of compost or well-rotted manure.

LITTLE GEM

Botanical grouping: Gallicanae
Parentage: Unknown
Other names: Validé
Other varieties: None
Year: 1880
Origin: England
Description: A miniature damask moss reaching a height of only 1 m (3 ft) even under sub-tropical conditions and a width of 70 cm (2 ft). The foliage is dense, small, and deep green. The clusters of plump, lightly mossed buds open to small, very double, pompon-like flowers in rosy carmine.
Flowering: Summer
Cultivation: A tough little rose requiring no pruning. It responds to mulching to preserve soil moisture in summer and the annual application of well-rotted manure or compost. It can be grown in a pot.

LOUIS GIMARD

Botanical grouping: Gallicanae
Parentage: Unknown
Other names: None
Other varieties: None
Year: 1877
Origin: France
Description: This is a damask–China moss which grows to a maximum of 1.5 m (5 ft) high and 1 m (3 ft) wide. The dark green foliage is a foil for the abundant, fragrant, very double, quartered flat blooms of rich deep pink frosting to paler pink toward the edges. The mossing is hard and crimson in colour.
Flowering: Summer
Cultivation: An easily grown variety over a wide climatic range. It should be pruned, if required, immediately after flowering. Apply well-rotted manure or compost annually. Mulch to maintain soil moisture during the summer.

MARÉCHAL DAVOUST

Botanical grouping: Gallicanae
Parentage: Unknown
Other names: None
Other varieties: None
Year: 1853
Origin: France

Louis Gimard

Description: This variety is worthy of growing for the colour of the very double flowers which is a subtle rich mixture of purple, dove grey and rich pink. A small green eye is sometimes revealed and the light mossing is dark coloured. The bush is very free flowering and reaches a neatly shaped 1.2 m (4 ft) and a width of 1 m (3 ft). The foliage is dark green and narrow.
Flowering: Summer
Cultivation: Prune immediately after flowering. An annual application of compost or well-rotted manure and a summer mulch to maintain even soil moisture is beneficial.

Maréchal Davoust

Mme Louis Lévêque

The mossing is thick and a dark crimson-purple in colour. The healthy foliage is also dark. The medium-sized, nicely shaped shrub reaches 1.2 m (4 ft) high and 1 m (3 ft) wide.
Flowering: Repeat flowers in autumn in most years.
Cultivation: This makes a good contrasting planting and is often used for that purpose. Prune lightly after the first flowering if required. A tough variety that performs well over a wide climatic range. An annual application of well-rotted manure or compost, and summer mulching is beneficial.

MME LOUIS LÉVÊQUE

Botanical grouping: Gallicanae
Parentage: Unknown
Other names: None
Other varieties: None
Year: 1898 or earlier
Origin: France
Description: Without doubt one of the loveliest of the moss roses with very fragrant, large ,double, clear pink, cupped blooms. The silken texture of the petals contrasts exquisitely with the moss. The bush grows to approximately 1.5 m (5 ft) high and 1 m (3 ft) wide, and is well clothed with large dark green foliage.
Flowering: Repeat flowering in late summer or autumn.
Cultivation: An easily grown variety performing well over a wide range of climates. Prune lightly immediately after the first flowering if required.

Mme de la Roche-Lambert

MARIE DE BLOIS

Botanical grouping: Gallicanae
Parentage: Unknown
Other names: None
Other varieties: None
Year: 1852
Origin: France
Description: A cheerful rose with large, informal, double frilled, very fragrant blooms in a bright rich pink, borne in profusion. The bush grows to 1.5 m (5 ft) high and 1 m (3 ft) wide. The foliage is a bright clean green and the mossing tinged is with crimson.
Flowering: Repeat flowering
Cultivation: Prune lightly immediately after the first flowering, if required. An annual application of compost or well-rotted manure and a mulch to maintain even soil moisture is beneficial.

MME DE LA ROCHE-LAMBERT

Botanical grouping: Gallicanae
Parentage: Unknown
Other names: None
Other varieties: None
Year: 1851
Origin: France
Description: An autumn damask moss which creates an overall dark effect providing an excellent contrast with the pink varieties. The flowers are globular at first, then flat with a muddled centre, fragrant, very double, and of rich purple. The colour holds well even in areas with hot summers.

MOUSSEUX DU JAPON

Botanical grouping: Gallicanae
Parentage: Unknown
Other names: Japonica, Moussu du Japon
Other varieties: None
Year: Unknown
Origin: Unknown
Description: This is the mossiest of all the moss roses with plump buds entirely covered in very dense, soft, clear green, fragrant moss which extends far down the stem. Even the compound leaves have mossed petioles. The bush is of moderate size, reaching 1.2 m (4 ft) high and 1 m (3 ft) wide, and of lax habit. The blooms are semi-double, fragrant, of a soft, lilac-pink with golden stamens, and rather fleeting. This variety makes a wonderful talking point in the garden.
Flowering: Summer
Cultivation: Quite an easily grown and tough moss rose, but it often takes a while to settle down and begin to grow. In drought-prone areas it is essential that mulch be used to maintain even soil moisture, particularly in the first few years.

MOUSSU ANCIEN

Botanical grouping: Gallicanae
Parentage: Unknown
Other names: None
Other varieties: None
Year: Unknown (19th century)
Origin: France
Description: A relatively little known variety which forms a compact well-clothed bush to just over 1 m (3 ft) high and 1 m (3 ft) wide. The blooms are plentiful, medium-sized, fragrant, of pure pink blushed deeper pink in the centre, opening from nicely mossed buds.
Flowering: Summer
Cultivation: This is a useful variety for the smaller garden and can also be grown in a pot. As with most moss roses pruning is normally unnecessary but if required for any reason should be carried out immediately after flowering.

NUITS DE YOUNG

Botanical grouping: Gallicanae
Parentage: Unknown
Other names: Old Black
Other varieties: None
Year: 1845
Origin: France
Description: A rather wiry shrub, compact, erect, with small dark green foliage. It reaches approximately 1.2 m (4 ft) high and up to 1 m (3 ft) wide. The small flowers are not fully double but they are of the darkest maroon, velvety textured, with a contrasting golden boss of stamens. The mossing, although not heavy, is also dark.
Flowering: Summer
Cultivation: This variety makes an excellent dark colour contrast to other lighter coloured varieties. Prune immediately after flowering if required. Mulch to maintain even soil moisture in summer. An annual application of compost or well-rotted manure is beneficial, as is an annual application of organic fertiliser. It is tolerant of a wide variety of climatic conditions.

PÉLISSON

Botanical grouping: Gallicanae
Parentage: Unknown
Other names: Monsieur Pélisson
Other varieties: None
Year: 1848
Origin: France
Description: This variety forms a vigorous, upright, small shrub to approximately 1.2 m (4 ft) high and 1 m (3 ft) wide. The flowers are sweetly fragrant, fully double, and in red gradually infusing with purple as they age. The mossing is dark green as is the rather coarse foliage.

Flowering: Summer
Cultivation: This is a tough little rose growing well over a wide climatic range. Prune immediately after flowering if required. Mulch in summer. An annual application of compost or well-rotted manure is very beneficial.

RÉNÉ D'ANJOU

Botanical grouping: Gallicanae
Parentage: Unknown
Other names: None
Other varieties: None
Year: 1853
Origin: France

Description: A relatively little known damask moss variety, reaching a 1.5 m (5 ft) high and 1 m (3 ft) wide The flowers are exquisitely fragrant, opening from buds covered in brownish green moss, and are a pretty, medium pink fading to lilac-pink, double with muddled centres. The foliage is bronze coloured and the mossing is also bronzed.
Flowering: Summer
Cultivation: A sturdy, compact growing variety that tolerates a wide climatic range. Prune immediately after flowering if required. Mulch to retain soil moisture in summer. A yearly application of compost or rotted manure is very beneficial.

Pélisson

Réné D'Anjou

Nuits de Young

SALET

Botanical grouping: Gallicanae
Parentage: Unknown
Other names: None
Other varieties: None
Year: 1854
Origin: France
Description: A damask moss with endearing qualities. The blooms, opening from lightly mossed buds, are very double and charmingly muddled, of clear rose pink

which deepens in cooler weather, and sweetly fragrant. The bush grows to approximately 1.2 m (4 ft) high and 1 m (3 ft) wide. The foliage is a bright green.
Flowering: Repeat flowering in autumn.
Cultivation: A sturdy variety but it requires regular watering and mulching to achieve its optimum flowering capacity in hot dry summers. An annual application of compost or well rotted manure is also beneficial. Prune lightly immediately after the first flowering each summer if required.

Salet

Shailer's White Moss

Soupert et Notting

SHAILER'S WHITE MOSS

Botanical grouping: Gallicanae
Parentage: Sport of Common Moss
Other names: *R. centifolia muscosa alba*
Other varieties: None
Year: 1788
Origin: England
Description: The flowers are large, fully double, pure white but occasionally faintly blushed, and very fragrant. The buds are exquisitely densely and fragrantly mossed in a fresh soft green. The shrub is slightly lax in form and grows to 1.5 m (5 ft) high and 1.2 m (4 ft) wide. (See White Bath.)
Flowering: Summer
Cultivation: Prune immediately after flowering if required. Hot dry summers can spoil the abundance and delicate beauty of the flowers. Well-composted soils, a summer mulch and regular watering are very beneficial in such climates.

SOUPERT ET NOTTING

Botanical grouping: Gallicanae
Parentage: Unknown
Other names: None
Other varieties: None
Year: 1874
Origin: France
Description: A useful repeat flowering autumn damask moss which forms a dense lower growing bush to 1 m (3 ft) high and 70 cm (2 ft) wide. It is quite well mossed and the quite large flowers, borne in small clusters, are double and quartered, of a deep soft pink and delightfully fragrant. The name derives from the name of the nursery firm from Luxembourg.
Flowering: Repeat flowering in autumn, often with a sprinkle of blooms between the first and second blooming.
Cultivation: This is a reliable variety very suited to pot culture provided soil moisture is maintained. In some areas mildew can be a problem in autumn and should be controlled.

STRIPED MOSS

Botanical Grouping: Gallicanae
Parentage: Unknown
Other names: Oeillet Panachée
Other varieties: None
Year: 1888
Origin: France
Description: A quaint little pale pink rose, striped and parti-coloured in a rich crimson which softens as it fades. Fragrant. Small bush to 1 m (3 ft) or more and 70 cm (2 ft) wide.
Flowering: Summer
Cultivation: A good variety for small gardens and for pot culture provided soil moisture is maintained. Prune lightly immediately after flowering if required.

WHITE BATH

Botanical grouping: Gallicanae
Parentage: Sport of Common Moss
Other names: Clifton Moss, White Moss
Other varieties: None
Year: Discovered 1810
Origin: England
Description: The rose now sold under this name has large, fully double, pure white, very fragrant flowers with buds, pedicels, stems and foliage all well mossed. It is of medium vigour and attains a height of 1.2 m (4 ft) and width of 1 m (3 ft), which is lower than Shailer's White Moss. It is fairly lax in growth habit and has lighter green foliage than Shailer's White Moss.
Flowering: Summer
Cultivation: The full beauty of this rose will not be revealed in areas with hot dry summers without regular watering, mulching and composting. Prune if required immediately after flowering. (See also Shailer's White Moss.)

WICHMOSS

Botanical grouping: Gallicanae
Parentage: *R. wichuraiana* x Salet
Other names: None
Other varieties: None
Year: 1911
Origin: France
Description: This is the only climbing moss rose now reasonably widely available, and is a plant of considerable charm. The individual flowers are small, semi-double, sweetly fragrant and well mossed in fresh green. They are a delicate pale pink to milky white with a centre of golden stamens and are borne in clusters. It will grow to approximately 3.5 m (10 ft) and has shiny, fresh, healthy foliage.
Flowering: Summer
Cultivation: This is a tough variety. It can be disfigured by mildew in some areas where mildew is a frequent problem and appropriate measures should be taken if necessary. Use on arches or pergolas.

WILLIAM LOBB

Botanical grouping: Gallicanae
Parentage: Unknown
Other names: Duchesse d'Istrie, Old Velvet Moss
Other varieties: None
Year: 1855
Origin: France
Description: A very tall, vigorous damask moss which may reach 2.5 m (8 ft) high and 1.5 m (5 ft) wide. This can be a stunningly beautiful rose smothering in sprays of heavily mossed buds opening to rich, crimson-purple, large, sweetly scented

White Bath

William Lobb

Wichmoss

flowers that ring the changes through dove grey, mauve and cerise. The foliage is large and ample.
Flowering: Summer
Cultivation: This rose needs support to display itself to advantage and can be treated as a pillar rose, trained up a pergola, supported by a tripod or allowed to grow in a shrubbery supported by other bushes. It is a very tough variety growing well over a wide climatic range.

ZENOBIA

Botanical grouping: Gallicanae
Parentage: Unknown
Other names: None
Other varieties: None

Year: 1892
Origin: England
Description: A tall, lanky shrub which reaches approximately 1.8 m (6 ft) high and 1.2 m (4 ft) wide. The flowers have much of the character of the old hybrid perpetuals being large, globular, very fragrant, of a striking cerise to satin pink. The buds are well mossed in clear green, and the foliage is dense, healthy and rather coarse.
Flowering: Summer
Cultivation: A short tripod or stakes help to support and show this rose to advantage. If pruning is necessary, carry it out immediately after flowering. This is a rose that rewards attention to mulching and the maintenance of high levels of organic matter in the soil.

Scotch Roses

These roses enjoyed a brief heyday from the 1790s to the 1830s. There were several hundred cultivated forms, but only a handful survive. They take their name from the wild Scotch or Burnett Rose, known to botanists as *R. pimpinellifolia*. It is a very hardy species and can tolerate sandy or rocky soils near the sea, where the 'hedgehog' type growth, fierce prickles and small, dark ferny leaves make it easy to recognise. The flowers open like saucers, have a sweet musky scent and vary in colour from white to cream, pink to purple.

They enjoy an open site in well drained soil, and will sucker freely so care must be taken in siting in relation to other plants. The flowering period is brief, just two or three weeks in early summer. Pruning is a matter of shaping rather than cutting back; a clip after flowering will do, unless you want to enjoy a crop of round black hips.

Bicolor

BICOLOR

Botanical grouping: Pimpinellifoliae
Parentage: Unknown
Other names: None
Other varieties: None
Year: Unknown, probably before 1822
Origin: Unknown
Description: Dense, vigorous shrub to around 1 m (3 ft) with small, greyish foliage and many prickles. The flowers are double and rosy-pink, fading to lilac-white with age. Stamens are yellow and the fruit is black.
Flowering: Spring only
Cultivation: Tolerates poor soils but does best in a sunny position. Suitable as a hedging plant.

DOUBLE BLUSH

Botanical grouping: Pimpinellifoliae
Parentage: Unknown
Other names: None
Other varieties: None
Year: Unknown
Origin: Unknown
Description: A vigorous, bushy shrub to around 1 m (3 ft). The double flowers are pale pink, darker in the centre and very fragrant. Blackish fruit.
Flowering: Summer only
Cultivation: Tolerates some shade and poorer soil quality. Suitable as a hedging plant. Trim into a hedge shape, if required, during winter.

DOUBLE YELLOW

Botanical grouping: Pimpinellifoliae
Parentage: Possibly *R. foetida* x *R. pimpinellifolia*
Other names: *R. spinosissima lutea* plena, William's Double Yellow, Old Double Yellow Scots Rose, Prince Charlie's Rose
Other varieties: None
Year: 1828
Origin: England
Description: Another vigorous and dense shrub to about 1 m (3 ft). The double flowers are bright yellow with greenish stamens. Very fragrant.
Flowering: Spring only
Cultivation: A good hedging plant, however, the spent petals stay on the plant too long after the flower is dead. Dead-heading will encourage healthy growth.

FALKLAND

Botanical grouping: Pimpinellifoliae
Parentage: Unknown
Other names: None
Other varieties: None
Year: Unknown
Origin: England
Description: Similar in habit and foliage to

Double Yellow

other *R. pimpinellifolia*, this compact shrub grows to 1 m (3 ft). The rose is semi-double in pinky-lilac, fading to white in the sun. The fruit is wine-red.
Flowering: Spring only
Cultivation: Will tolerate some shade and poorer soils. Suitable as a hedging plant.

IRISH RICH MARBLED

Botanical grouping: Pimpinellifoliae
Parentage: Unknown
Other names: None
Other varieties: None
Year: Unknown
Origin: Unknown
Description: The flowers in bud are soft pink and rounded, on opening are deep pink with lilac-pink reverse, fading toward the edges. A very attractive rose. Follows the form of *R.spinosissima* in foliage. Grows to 1 m (3 ft).
Flowering: Spring only
Cultivation: Has the same requirements as the other *R. pimpinellifolias*.

Falkland's colourful rosehips

MARY QUEEN OF SCOTS

Botanical grouping: Pimpinellifoliae
Parentage: Unknown
Other names: None
Other varieties: None
Year: Unknown
Origin: Unknown
Description: Well-known, compact shrub to 1 m (3 ft) with foliage in the *R. pimpinellifolia* style. The flowers in bud are plump and lilac-grey, opening to doubles of plum-purple with a paler reverse. The fruit is globular and maroon to black.
Flowering: Spring only
Cultivation: Thrives in poor soil but prefers a sunny, open spot. Useful as a pot-plant. Little or no pruning required, apart from cutting out dead wood.

Irish Rich Marbled

William III

SINGLE CHERRY

Botanical grouping: Pimpinellifoliae
Parentage: Unknown
Other names: None
Other varieties: None
Year: Unknown
Origin: Unknown
Description: Shrub reaches around 1 m (3 ft) with bluish green foliage. Buds are rose-pink, opening to single flowers of bright cherry-red with a lighter pink reverse. Stamens are very prominent and the fruit is small and black.
Flowering: Spring only
Cultivation: Tolerates poorer soil but prefers a sunny position. Suitable as a hedging plant or potted specimen. Mulch well around base of plant, to keep weeds down.

Stanwell Perpetual

Single Cherry

STANWELL PERPETUAL

Botanical grouping: Pimpinellifoliae
Parentage: Possibly *R. pimpinellifolia* x *R. damascena semperflorens* (bifera)
Other names: None
Other varieties: None
Year: 1838
Origin: England
Description: Dense shrub grows to around 1.5 m (5 ft) with many suckers. Foliage is small and greyish although occasionally becomes a mottled purple colour. Very prickly. Considered one of the prettiest of the *R. pimpinellifolia* group, the flowers are pale pink, fading to white with the heat. Fragrant.
Flowering: Continuous, but at their best in mid-summer.
Cultivation: Tolerates poor soils. Suitable as a hedging plant. If growing as a hedge, trim into shape during winter.

WILLIAM III

Botanical grouping: Pimpinellifoliae
Parentage: Unknown
Other names: None
Other varieties: None
Year: Unknown
Origin: Unknown
Description: Very dwarf shrub to 70 cm (2 ft), vigorous, with grey-green leaves densely covering the very twiggy bush. The flowers are semi-double, crimson-cerise darkening to plum with a paler reverse. The fruit is dark brown to black.
Flowering: Spring only
Cultivation: Tolerates poorer soils and some shade although does better in a sunny position. Useful as a hedging plant and may be planted in a pot.

Portland Roses

This small group of roses became popular after 1800, the varieties being remarkable for their recurrent flowering, a rare quality at that time. They share many of the characteristics of old-fashioned roses, although they were superseded in cultivation and popularity by the hybrid perpetuals. The Portland rose is characterised by short stems and fragrant very-double flowers in the deep red to deep pink colour range.

To produce good results, provide rich, well-drained soil and prune out all dead and twiggy wood in late winter, cutting back strong growths by one-third to one-half at the same time.

Arthur de Sansal

ARTHUR DE SANSAL

Botanical grouping: Gallicanae
Parentage: Said to be a seedling of Géant des Batailles
Other names: None
Other varieties: None
Year: 1855
Origin: France
Description: A very fragrant variety with very double, rich crimson-purple flowers with paler reverse. They are flat, quartered with a button eye, and borne in generous quantities. The bush is neat and upright growing to approximately 1 m (3 ft) and 70 cm (2 ft) wide, and is well clothed in light green foliage.
Flowering: Particularly in warmer climates this variety repeat flowers
Cultivation: Prune in winter, removing all dead and weak twiggy growth and cutting back the remaining framework stems by one-third or a little more. This otherwise excellent variety is marred by a tendency to mildew.

COMTE DE CHAMBORD

Botanical grouping: Gallicanae
Parentage: Baronne Prévost x Portland Rose
Other names: None
Other varieties: None
Year: 1860
Origin: France
Description: Surely one of the loveliest of the old roses with large flowers filled with clear rose pink petals and breathing the most delicious rich fragrance. This small shrub reaching only 1 m (3 ft) with a width of 70 cm (2 ft) is very showy and the abundant large-leafed grey-green foliage is a perfect foil for the continuous display of blooms.
Flowering: Recurrent flowering
Cultivation: This is a very reliable variety performing well over a wide climatic range. Its small stature and very repeat flowering

Comte de Chambord

nature makes it the perfect choice for a small garden. Prune in winter removing all dead and twiggy wood and cutting the remaining strong framework back by approximately one-third or a little more.

DELAMBRE

Botanical grouping: Gallicanae
Parentage: Unknown
Other names: None
Other varieties: None
Year: 1863
Origin: France
Description: A compact, upright, small

bush well clothed with dark green, healthy foliage, reaching 1 m (3 ft) high and 70 cm (2 ft) wide. It has fully double, medium-sized flowers which are a deep pink verging on crimson-red and sweetly fragrant. Like all the Portlands it flowers prolifically.
Flowering: Recurrent flowering
Cultivation: A tough variety accommodating to a wide range of climates and soils. Excellent for the smaller garden and pot culture. Prune in winter. Regular mulching and maintenance of adequate organic material in the soil are very beneficial to quality of bloom and repeat flowering performance.

Jacques Cartier

JACQUES CARTIER

Botanical grouping: Gallicanae
Parentage: Unknown
Other names: None
Other varieties: None
Year: 1868
Origin: France
Description: One of the most popular of the Portland roses, this is a rose of singular perfection of form and great charm. The blooms are large, very double, of exquisite old rose formation being quartered with a button eye. It is very sweetly fragrant, in a clear pink fading to paler pink at the edges. It flowers reliably and abundantly and is healthy and resilient. The bush is compact and upright growing reaching approximately 1.2 m (4 ft) high and 1 m (3 ft) wide. The foliage is light green.
Flowering: Repeat flowering
Cultivation: A variety that grows well over a wide range of climatic conditions and soils. However, to obtain the finest displays, ensure that regular mulching is maintained, as well as an adequate level of organic matter in the soil with the use of compost or well-rotted manure. Prune in winter.

MARIE DE SAINT JEAN

Botanical grouping: Gallicanae
Parentage: Unknown
Other names: None
Other varieties: None
Year: 1869
Origin: France
Description: One of the loveliest Portland roses, with the typical high-shouldered flowers of the Portlands. It has very double, very fragrant, pure white blooms of beautiful old rose formation just touched here and there at the edge with carmine. The bush is strong, compact, and healthy, growing to approximately 1 m (3 ft) high and 1 m (3 ft) wide. The foliage is mid-green. A slight tendency to mildew is a minor fault in an otherwise outstanding variety.

Panachée de Lyon

Flowering: Recurrent flowering
Cultivation: Prune in mid-winter removing any unproductive wood and pruning back by approximately one-third. Maintain even soil moisture to promote maximum flowering and quality of flower by the use of mulch and incorporation of organic material in the soil. In 'mildew seasons' control any tendency to develop mildew.

MME KNORR

Botanical grouping: Gallicanae
Parentage: Unknown
Other names: None
Other varieties: None
Year: 1855
Origin: France
Description: A delightfully fragrant variety with large, bright rose pink, semi-double flowers with paler reverse which are borne in abundance. It forms a rather taller bush than many of the other Portlands, growing to a height of approximately 1.2 m (4 ft) and width of 1 m (3 ft). The foliage is healthy and abundant.
Flowering: Recurrent flowering
Cultivation: This is a good, tough, easily grown variety. Nevertheless, it is encouraged to give of its best, particularly when it repeat flowers, by the regular application of mulch and maintenance of good levels of organic matter in the soil by the addition of compost or well-rotted manure. Prune in winter, removing all weak or dead growth and cutting back the remaining by one-third or a little more.

PANACHÉE DE LYON

Botanical grouping: Gallicanae
Parentage: Reputedly a sport of Rose du Roi
Other names: None
Other varieties: None
Year: 1895
Origin: France

Description: The flowers of this variety are medium-sized, double, flat, sweetly fragrant, and rose pink, flaked and parti-coloured with crimson and purple. It forms an erect, rather slender shrub, to approximately 1 m (3 ft) high and 70 cm (2 ft) wide. Flowering is less abundant than with some Portland roses. The foliage is mid-green.
Flowering: Recurrent flowering
Cultivation: Prune in winter removing any dead or non-bearing twiggy growth. Cut back the remaining stems by approximately one-third or a little more. Mulch well and maintain the organic matter in the soil with regular applications of compost or well-rotted manure.

PERGOLÈSE

Botanical grouping: Gallicanae
Parentage: Unknown
Other names: None
Other varieties: None
Year: 1860
Origin: France
Description: An excellent, abundant-flowering variety forming a smallish compact, upright plant with beautiful medium-sized, fully double, fragrant blooms of rich bright plum-purple infused with cherry-crimson, resembling an old-fashioned tulle rose. The bush reaches approximately 1.2 m (4 ft) high and 1 m (3 ft) wide. This rose has Gallica-like foliage and is often classified with the Gallica roses.
Flowering: Recurrent flowering
Cultivation: Prune in winter removing any weak unproductive growth and cut back the remaining stems by approximately one-third. This variety is tough and grows well over a wide climatic range and succeeds in many soil types. Regular mulching and maintenance of good levels of organic matter in the soil are beneficial. This is a good pot variety.

PORTLAND ROSE

Botanical grouping: Gallicanae
Parentage: Unknown, but reputedly Quatre Saisons x Slater's Crimson China, with possible *R.centifolia* involvement. It is also suggested that Quatre Saisons and a Gallica rose were responsible.
Other names: Duchess of Portland, *R. portlandica*, *R. paestana*, Le Rosier de Portland, Scarlet Four Seasons
Other varieties: None
Year: Prior to 1809
Origin: Released by Dupont in Paris in 1809, possibly originating from Italy as a natural hybrid and reaching Dupont via England.
Description: This variety was the progenitor of the Portland group. Reputed to have

Portland Rose

Portland Rose

Rose du Roi

been brought to England from Paestum in Italy by the Duchess of Portland early in the 19th century and that it was for her that Dupont later named it. Also reputedly named after the second Duchess of Portland who died in 1785 and who never travelled out of England; the rose was apparently listed in a nursery catalogue in 1782. It caused a sensation at the time with its bright red colouring and ability to reflower in the autumn. This reflowering ability appears to be far more reliable in warm climates which certainly suit roses with China rose ancestry. The sweetly scented blooms are usually semi-double (some are single) and are borne with considerable freedom on a low, compact, well-clothed shrub.

Flowering: Recurrent flowering
Cultivation: Prune in winter removing all non-productive wood and cutting back the remaining stems by one-third. Dead-heading improves the summer display.

ROSE DU ROI

Botanical grouping: Gallicanae
Parentage: Reputedly Portland Rose x *R. gallica officinalis* although the Gallica involvement has been questioned.
Other names: Rose Lelieur, Lee's Crimson Perpetual, Crimson Perpetual
Other varieties: None
Year: 1815 (Under its former name of Rose

Lelieur it was released in 1812, and in England it was released as Lee's Crimson Perpetual in 1819)
Origin: France
Description: On seeing this rose King Louis XVIII asked for its name to be changed from Rose Lelieur to Rose du Roi. The flowers have a delightful, strong fragrance and are large, semi-double, and of a rich bright red. They are borne over a long flowering period. The bush is fairly compact and quite short, to 1 m (3 ft) high and 1 m (3 ft) wide. The foliage is small and dark. This rose was important as a forerunner for the magnificent 19th century rose group Hybrid Perpetuals.
Flowering: Flowers over a long season and may repeat in autumn.
Cultivation: Prune in winter, removing non-productive twiggy growth to leave a strong framework; prune the remaining stems back by one-third.

ROSE DU ROI À FLEURS POURPRES

Botanical grouping: Gallicanae
Parentage: Sport of Rose du Roi
Other names: Roi des Pourpres, Mogador
Other varieties: None
Year: 1819
Origin: France
Description: This variety closely resembles Rose du Roi but the flowers are slightly more

double and of a deeper colour. It forms a short, fairly compact bush to 1 m (3 ft) high and 1 m (3 ft) wide.
Flowering: Repeat flowering
Cultivation: Prune in winter if required, removing any weak or unproductive wood and cutting back the remaining framework by approximately one-third. The regular application of mulch and incorporation of organic material in the soil is very beneficial.

Rose du Roi à Fleurs Pourpres

Bourbon Roses

The first bourbon rose is believed to have been a natural cross between *R. chinensis* and *R. damascena,* arriving on the French mainland in the early 1800s from Ile de Bourbon. These delightful plants can be shrubby or have long canes like a climber. They have glossy foliage that almost always features the characteristic reddish tints associated with China roses. The flowers are quite small, borne in clusters of three to seven and sometimes more, in the pale to deep pink colour range with many outstanding striped forms.

Little pruning is required except to cut back new recent growth to encourage new the season's flowering, and to cut out dead or spindly wood after flowering has finished.

Bourbon Queen

Boule de Neige

Commandant Beaurepaire

ADAM MESSERICH

Botanical grouping: Chinensis
Parentage: Frau Oberhofgärtner Singer x (Louise Odier seedling x Louis Phillipe)
Other names: None
Other varieties: None
Year: 1920
Origin: Germany
Description: Makes a substantial upright bush well clothed to 1.5 m (5 ft) high and wide. It bears abundant quantities of large, semi-double, bright rose pink flowers in clusters. Their fragrance is sweet and fresh, reminiscent of raspberries particularly in the morning. The flowers do fade somewhat, but becomingly. This variety has the advantage of not being too heavily thorned.
Flowering: Repeat flowering
Cultivation: Prune in winter if required, removing non-productive wood and pruning back the remaining wood by one-third to one-half.

BOULE DE NEIGE

Botanical grouping: Chinensis
Parentage: Blanche Lafitte x Sappho
Other names: None
Other varieties: None
Year: 1867
Origin: France
Description: A superb variety, truly a 'snowball' rose with quantities of very double, medium-sized flowers in clusters of purest white, of the perfect symmetry of camellias, each rose reflexing with maturity to an almost spherical snowball. It forms a fairly slender, compact, upright shrub reaching 1.5 m (5 ft) high and 1 m (3 ft) wide, with smooth mid-green foliage. The plump buds are tinted with rich crimson, and are deliciously fragrant.
Flowering: Repeat flowering, almost continuously in bloom.

Cultivation: This variety can produce twiggy growth particularly when under water stress or poorly fed. Regular mulching and applications of organic matter are beneficial. Prune in winter, if required.

BOURBON QUEEN

Botanical grouping: Chinensis
Parentage: Unknown
Other names: Queen of Bourbons, Reine de l'Ile Bourbon, Souvenir de la Princesse de Lamballe
Other varieties: None
Year: 1834
Origin: France
Description: A very lovely variety which will reach 3 m (10 ft) with long graceful canes. Less recurrent than most bourbon roses but compensates with an abundance of bloom in summer. The flowers are borne in clusters and are almost double, cupped, of rich rose pink paling toward the edges, and have a strong, sweet fragrance. The flowers are borne on last year's growth. While an autumn flowering is common but rarely generous, the autumn display of large hips is a bonus.
Flowering: Recurrent flowering but the autumn display is not fully reliable.
Cultivation: As this rose flowers on the previous summer's wood it is important that any necessary pruning is carried out immediately after the initial flowering. It makes a spectacular hedge, and can be used as a specimen shrub or trained against a wall.

COMMANDANT BEAUREPAIRE

Botanical grouping: Chinensis
Parentage: Unknown
Other names: Panachée d'Angers
Other varieties: None
Year: 1874
Origin: France
Description: A very desirable variety forming a tallish, strong, dense shrub to 1.5 m (5 ft) high and wide. It flowers generously from every shoot in summer but rarely flowers in autumn. The individual flowers are fully double, globular, beautifully fragrant, of a rich, soft rose pink striped and flaked with deep, bright carmine and fuchsia purple. An outstanding striped rose, healthy, vigorous and beautiful. The foliage is light green.
Flowering: Occasionally repeat flowers, but lightly
Cultivation: An easy rose to grow in a wide variety of climates. Some support is advisable in windy and exposed positions and annual mulching and application of compost is beneficial.

COUPE D'HÉBÉ

Botanical grouping: Chinensis
Parentage: Bourbon x China
Other names: None
Other varieties: None
Year: 1840
Origin: France
Description: A tall shrub, vigorous and lax, reaching approximately 2.5 m (8 ft) and a width of 1.5 m (5 ft). It is very free-flowering in summer, bearing quantities of globular, soft pink double roses that are not infrequently quartered when fully open. They are very sweetly fragrant. The autumn display is far from reliable, and may be little more than a light scatter of blooms or none whatsoever. The foliage is light green and rather prone to mildew as the season lengthens.
Flowering: Occasionally repeat flowers
Cultivation: Any tendency to mildew in late summer or autumn can be checked at that time. Prune immediately after flowering if required as it flowers on the previous season's wood. In most positions it will welcome support.

FULGENS

Botanical grouping: Chinensis
Parentage: Unknown
Other names: Malton
Other varieties: None
Year: 1830
Origin: France
Description: The chief importance of this rose lies in the fact that it was one of the most fertile bourbon roses. It is thought to have been involved in the development of the hybrid perpetual class. The blooms are almost double, of a bright crimson colour verging on cerise pink, with some fragrance. It forms a rather lax, tallish shrub to 1.5 m (5 ft) high and 1.2 m (4 ft) wide.
Flowering: Recurrent
Cultivation: Some support is recommended for this rose, particularly in more exposed positions. Regular mulching and adequate levels of organic matter to maintain even soil moisture and minimise soil temperature fluctuations are beneficial.

GREAT WESTERN

Botanical grouping: Chinensis
Parentage: Unknown
Other names: None
Other varieties: None
Year: 1840
Origin: France
Description: A singularly beautiful variety producing an abundance of sumptuous, large, double, quartered blooms of crimson-purple infused with maroon which are sweetly scented. The foliage is dark and trouble free. The bush reaches 1.5 m (5 ft) high and 1.2 m (4 ft) wide, forming a nicely shaped, quite dense bush.
Flowering: Summer flowering, crimson hips in autumn
Cultivation: An easily grown variety over a wide climatic range. Prune immediately after flowering, if required. Regular mulching and maintenance of good levels of organic matter in the soil are beneficial.

GROS CHOUX D'HOLLANDE

Botanical grouping: Chinensis
Parentage: Unknown
Other names: None
Other varieties: None
Year: Unknown
Origin: Unknown
Description: A bushy, vigorous old rose, reaching 2 m (7 ft) in height, with a good covering of matt, mid-green foliage. The flowers of this bourbon are outstanding: large and cup-shaped, fully double and very fragrant, in shades of soft pink.
Flowering: Recurrrent through summer and autumn
Cultivation: A hardy and easy-to-grow rose, tolerant of most soils and climate conditions. Prefers full sun. Prune back in winter to maintain a bushy shape.

HONORINE DE BRABANT

Botanical grouping: Chinensis
Parentage: Unknown
Other names: None
Other varieties: None
Year: Unknown
Origin: Unknown
Description: A lovely rose making a densely foliaged rather lax shrub to approximately 1.5 m (5 ft) high and 1.5 m (5 ft) wide. It produces an abundance of large double blooms of pale pink delicately striped with lilac-pink and purple. The long smooth canes have few thorns and the foliage is lush, large and light green. It creates that romantic soft spillover effect that has maintained the popularity of the bourbon class.
Flowering: Repeat flowering usually giving an excellent autumn display
Cultivation: An excellent rose over a wide climatic range. Can be trained as a short climber or allowed to form an arching shrub. Prune in winter removing any weak twiggy growth to leave a framework of strong canes which should be reduced by approximately one-third of their length.

Coupe D'Hébé

Great Western

Honorine de Brabant

Kathleen Harrop

KATHLEEN HARROP

Botanical grouping: Chinensis
Parentage: A sport of Zéphirine Drouhin
Other names: None
Other varieties: None
Year: 1919
Origin: Northern Ireland
Description: This is a very lovely and very long flowering and generous variety with sweetly fragrant semi-double shell pink flowers in clusters. The flowers are of refined form and never fail to charm. It is equally as thornless as Zéphirine Drouhin, and grows to approximately 3 m (10 ft) high and 1.8 m (6 ft) wide.
Flowering: Very repeat flowering
Cultivation: Prune, if required, in winter. Attention to regular mulching and incorporation of compost into the soil is amply rewarded. Use as a pillar rose, over arches and pergolas, or pruned back to a very attractive hedge.

KRONPRINZESSIN VIKTORIA

Botanical grouping: Chinensis
Parentage: Sport of Souvenir de la Malmaison
Other names: White Malmaison; Souvenir de la Malmaison Jaune
Other varieties: None
Year: 1888
Origin: Germany
Description: A rose of exquisite beauty with large, slightly cupped, double quartered blooms of pure white shading to creamy white and palest lemon in its heart. It has exquisite fragrance. The bush is short and compact, growing to 1.2 m (4 ft) high

and 1 m (3 ft) wide. The flowers are gracefully disposed over the bush which flowers abundantly for up to six months of the year.
Flowering: Continuously from early summer to late autumn
Cultivation: An excellent rose for the small garden. Prune in winter removing any unproductive, old and twiggy growth and cut the remaining strong stems back by approximately one-third. This is a strong, healthy variety, but regular mulching and additions of compost are beneficial.

LOUISE ODIER

Botanical grouping: Chinensis
Parentage: Unkown
Other names: Madame de Stella
Other varieties: None
Year: 1851
Origin: France
Description: Noted for the perfection of its large blooms which are very double, saucer-shaped, and of camellia-like precision in the arrangement of their petals. The flowers are produced in clusters, have an exquisite fragrance, and are a lovely, clear, rich rose pink with a hint of lilac. The bush is quite tall and vigorous, up to 1.8 m (6 ft) high and 1.2 (4 ft) wide, with long slender canes bearing few thorns and bowing down with the weight of their blossom.
Flowering: Repeats generously well into autumn
Cultivation: While this is quite a tough variety it greatly repays kindness and is certainly not a variety to abandon in a forgotten corner. Prune each winter removing all weak and unproductive wood and pruning back the remaining canes by approximately one-third. Regular mulching and incorporation of compost or well-rotted manure in the soil is very beneficial.

MME ERNST CALVAT

Botanical grouping: Chinensis
Parentage: Sport of Mme Isaac Pereire
Other names: None
Other varieties: None
Year: 1888
Origin: France
Description: This is a rewarding variety in the right climate, which is not in places which greatly encourage mildew. It forms a large, strong, rather coarse shrub to 2.5 m (8 ft) high and 1.2 m (4 ft) wide, and bears quantities of large very double, globular, light pink blooms which are very fragrant. Early growth is a bronze-purple.
Flowering: Recurrent flowering, the autumn flowers often being much finer.
Cultivation: Early blooms may be subject to malformation but this is a characteristic of

Kronprinzessin Viktoria

Louise Odier

Mme Ernst Calvat

the variety. Mildew may be a problem, particularly if planted in an area of poor air circulation. Not a rose for the small garden, but in more spacious surroundings or country gardens it grows well, either as a shrub or used against a pillar (provided there is good air circulation).

Mme Isaac Pereire

Mme Lauriol de Barny

Mme Pierre Oger

Mrs Paul

MME ISAAC PEREIRE

Botanical grouping: Chinensis
Parentage: Unknown
Other names: None
Other varieties: None
Year: 1881
Origin: France
Description: Widely held to be the most fragrant of all roses, not entirely without reason. The perfume is very rich and heady, reminiscent of ripe raspberries. A very strong grower to 2 m (7 ft) high and 1.5 m (5 ft) wide. Early blooms are huge, informal and showy, of a rich deep purplish-cerise, often finer in autumn than in summer when they sometimes suffer from malformation.
Flowering: Repeat flowering
Cultivation: Has some tendency to mildew which should be dealt with early. Pruning should be carried out in winter, pruning out all poorly flowering wood and cutting back each remaining cane by approximately one-third. It makes a good climber but only where there is good air circulation.

MME LAURIOL DE BARNY

Botanical grouping: Chinensis
Parentage: Unknown
Other names: None
Other varieties: None
Year: 1868
Origin: France
Description: A variety of great charm with long canes flowering along almost their entire length, bowing outward with the weight of blossom. It grows to 1.5 m (5 ft) high and 1.2 m (4 ft) wide. The flowers are quite lovely being large, very double, flat. quartered, in silver-pink with a fresh, fruity fragrance. The weeping tendency causes flowers to break all along the canes but this can be encouraged by pegging the canes down at the tips in the Victorian manner.
Flowering: Repeat flowering
Cultivation: A vigorous, healthy variety which performs well in a wide range of climates. Prune in winter if required. Although usually grown as a shrub, it makes an excellent pillar rose.

MME PIERRE OGER

Botanical grouping: Chinensis
Parentage: Sport of Reine Victoria
Other names: None
Other varieties: None
Year: 1878
Origin: France
Description: At its best, which is not infrequently, one of the most beautiful of the old roses. It has exactly the same exquisite, cupped form of flower as Reine Victoria but is milky white to pale silvery pink (depend-

ing on the temperature), touched at the tips of the petals with crimson. The fragrance is delicious, and the buds small and rosy. It forms a rather lax, slender shrub with relatively few thorns on its long clean canes, reaching a height of 1.8 m (6 ft) if unpruned and a width of 1.2 m (4 ft) with mid-green foliage. The flowers are borne along the entire length of the cane.
Flowering: Repeat flowering with magnificent opening and closing displays each season. The autumn display is often the finest.
Cultivation: Cut back hard in the winter to produce a much denser shrub flowering in clusters, or allow the natural willowy effect of this rose to develop. It can be pegged down or trained up an archway or pillar if desired. A slight tendency to black spot should be controlled.

MRS PAUL

Botanical grouping: Chinensis
Parentage: Seedling of Mme Isaac Pereire
Other names: None
Other varieties: None
Year: 1891
Origin: England
Description: An excellent variety being restored to lists around the world for its excellent garden qualities. It forms a good, vigorous, rather floppy shrub to approximately 1.5 m (5 ft) high and 1 m (3 ft) wide, very well clothed in somewhat coarse foliage with quantities of large, fully double, richly perfumed blush-white flowers. It creates an excellent garden effect.
Flowering: Repeat flowering
Cultivation: A vigorous variety easily grown in a wide range of conditions. Prune in winter if required.

PAUL VERDIER

Botanical grouping: Chinensis
Parentage: Unknown
Other names: None
Other varieties: None
Year: 1866
Origin: France
Description: Forms an arching bush bearing along the length of its canes globular, double flowers of a rich pink to crimson-red, finally opening flat and slightly frilled. It has a sweet fragrance and good foliage, and forms a medium-sized shrub to 1.5 m (5 ft) in reasonable conditions with a width of approximately 1.2 m (4 ft).
Flowering: Repeat flowering
Cultivation: Prune in winter removing all poorly producing wood and cutting back the remaining strong canes by one-third. Mulch and add compost regularly to the soil.

PRINCE CHARLES

Botanical grouping: Chinensis
Parentage: Unknown
Other names: None
Other varieties: None
Year: Known since 1842
Origin: Unknown
Description: A lovely variety with large double blooms of rich deep crimson to maroon with a delightful sweet fragrance and golden stamens. The blooms fade to lilac and rose madder mixture with crimson veining. The shrub is rather lax reaching 1.5 m (5 ft) high and 1.2 m (4 ft) wide. The foliage is dark green and large and tough, giving it good disease resistance.
Flowering: Summer flowering only
Cultivation: Prune immediately after flowering is completed. Regular mulch application and incorporation of compost or well-rotted manure into the garden is advisable.

QUEEN OF BEDDERS

Botanical grouping: Chinensis
Parentage: Seedling of Sir Joseph Paxton
Other names: None
Other varieties: None
Year: 1871
Origin: England
Description: A short growing, compact variety reaching a height of approximately 1 m (3 ft) and the same width. It produces quantities of fragrant, shapely, double, rich carmine-red flowers which fade with age to a deep, soft rose.
Flowering: Repeat flowering
Cultivation: This is a healthy, tough, sturdy variety growing well over a range of climates. A good choice for the small garden or for a large pot. The colour can be difficult to place but it comes into its own in the bright cheerful colour schemes of the true cottage garden. Prune in winter if necessary.

REINE VICTORIA

Botanical grouping: Chinensis
Parentage: Unknown
Other names: The Shell Rose
Other varieties: None
Year: 1872
Origin: France
Description: One of the best known of the old-fashioned roses, this variety forms a tall, slender shrub with long willowlike, relatively slender canes which flower along their entire length. The individual blooms are medium-sized, perfectly cupped, rose pink and exquisitely fragrant. Cared for, it is rarely out of bloom for many months of the year. Grows to 1.8 m (6 ft) high if unpruned,

and 1 m (3 ft) wide.
Flowering: Very repeat flowering
Cultivation: This is not a rose to be stuck in an abandoned corner of the garden and left to fend for itself. It may struggle on but only pampering will produce the Valentine card picture most people have in mind when purchasing this rose. Incorporate plenty of compost or well-rotted manure in the soil and maintain a substantial organic mulch. It is prone to black spot.

REVEREND H. D'OMBRAIN

Botanical grouping: Chinensis
Parentage: Unknown
Other names: None
Other varieties: None
Year: 1863

Reine Victoria

Prince Charles

Souvenir de la Malmaison

Souvenir de St Annes

Variegata di Bologna

Origin: France
Description: Despite the name, a lady-like rose with double, flat blooms of clear pink blushed deeper in the centre, with a sweet, refined fragrance. The bush is of medium height, compact, reaching 1.5 m (5 ft) high and 1.2 m (4 ft) wide. The foliage is plentiful although it can show some mildew.
Flowering: Repeat flowering
Cultivation: Prune in winter. Mildew should be controlled if it appears. Regularly mulch and incorporate compost into the soil.

ROSE EDOUARD

Botanical grouping: Chinensis
Parentage: China x Damask, suggested as Old Blush x Quatre Saisons.
Other names: Rose Edward, Temple Rose
Other varieties: None
Year: Known from *c*.1818
Origin: India
Description: Very fragrant, forming a lax growing shrub to 1.8 m (6 ft), with bright crimson blooms.
Flowering: Repeat flowering
Cultivation: Prune in winter. This, like so many bourbons, is a variety that comes into its own in the warmer parts of the world. Mulch and incorporate compost into the soil regularly.

SOUVENIR DE LA MALMAISON

Botanical grouping: Chinensis
Parentage: Mme Desprez x Tea rose
Other names: Queen of Beauty and Fragrance
Other varieties: Climbing Souvenir de la Malmaison
Year: 1843
Origin: France
Description: Perhaps the best known of all the old roses, this is a superb variety with an abundance of large, very double, quartered blooms of exquisite pale pink. The fragrance is always beautiful but there are times when it is the most extraordinary mixture of

cinnamon and ripe bananas. At any time there is a distinct hint of spice. After it has rained for some time the guard petals brown and shrink so that the flower is trapped inside, unable to expand, a phenomenon called balling. But in places with Mediterranean summers such as California, South Africa, and southern Australia, as well as the Mediterranean countries, it is a singularly glorious creature. It grows to approximately 1.2 m (4 ft) high and 1.2 m (4 ft) wide.
Flowering: Highly recurrent flowering
Cultivation: A healthy, high yielding variety over a wide climatic range. Prune in winter. Attention to regular mulch application and addition of compost to the soil is well rewarded.

SOUVENIR DE LA MALMAISON ROSÉ

Botanical grouping: Chinensis
Parentage: Sport of Souvenir de la Malmaison
Other names: Rose Malmaison, Leveson Gower
Other varieties: None
Year: 1846
Origin: France
Description: A very fine variety in its own right, still very widely grown, this rose is fully double, flat and quartered, of perfect form, in a soft, warm, deep pink. The blooms are borne in abundance on a slightly less upright shrub than the parent and have an exquisitely sweet fragrance. This variety forms a medium-sized bush to around 1.2 m (4 ft) high and 1 m (3 ft) wide.
Flowering: Very repeat flowering with good flushes well into autumn.
Cultivation: This variety is very little trouble to grow, but it really comes into its own in Mediterranean climates with their long, dry summers as, like the parent, it has a tendency to balling in wet weather. With a long flowering season, however, perfect blooms will be found anywhere it is grown. Prune in winter.

SOUVENIR DE ST ANNES

Botanical grouping: Chinensis
Parentage: Sport of Souvenir de la Malmaison
Other names: None
Other varieties: None
Year: 1950
Origin: Ireland
Description: Jack Harkness declared that this rose 'could well be taken as the emblem of purity'. Only Shropshire Lass can rival it for the title. Almost single, this quite large rose of delicate pearly pink has perfect formation, an airy loveliness and delightful, fresh sweet fragrance. It forms an excellent, well-clothed shrub to approximately 1.5 m (5 ft) and a little less in width. It takes its name from a famous garden near Dublin.
Flowering: Very recurrent
Cultivation: An easily grown variety and, of course, with none of the 'balling' problem of the parent. It rewards regular mulching and digging in of compost with a great bounty of exquisite flowers.

VARIEGATA DI BOLOGNA

Botanical grouping: Chinensis
Parentage: Unknown
Other names: None
Other varieties: None
Year: 1909
Origin: Italy
Description: One of the most spectacular of all roses bearing masses of large, full-cupped blooms in long sprays of pure, pearly white, crisply striped and finely splashed with deep purple-crimson. The fragrance is ravishing and the effect is that of an old Dutch painting come to life. It forms a strong, arching shrub to 1.8 m (6 ft) high and 1.5 m (5 ft) wide.
Flowering: Magnificent display in summer; only slightly recurrent in autumn
Cultivation: A tough, easy variety in a wide range of climates but particularly good in warmer areas. Regular attention to mulching and the addition of compost is infinitely rewarded. Prune in winter.

VIVID

Botanical grouping: Chinensis
Parentage: Unknown
Other names: None
Other varieties: None
Year: 1853
Origin: England
Description: A variety that earns its name with sweetly scented, vividly coloured, double blooms of rich magenta-pink on a tallish growing bush to 1.5 m (5 ft) with a width of 1.2 m (4 ft). The bush is vigorous and fairly thorny.
Flowering: Only slightly recurrent
Cultivation: Prune in winter, removing any poorly bearing wood and shortening the remaining stems by one-third.

ZÉPHIRINE DROUHIN

Botanical grouping: Chinensis
Parentage: Unknown
Other names: Thornless Rose
Other varieties: None
Year: 1868
Origin: France
Description: A very popular, tall-growing variety normally grown as a climber and irrevocably associated with cottage gardens so expect no sophistication. A fluttering, summery, semi-double rose of cheerful cerise pink, sweetly fragrant and abundantly generous. It reaches approximately 3 m (10 ft) high and 1.8 m (6 ft) wide.
Flowering: Very repeat flowering over a long period.
Cultivation: Somewhat prone to mildew. Use as a pillar rose or trained along a fence in preference to growing against a wall where it is far more prone to mildew attack. It is also grown pruned as a shrub or hedge.

ZIGEUNERKNABE

Botanical grouping: Chinensis
Parentage: Russelliana x *R. rugosa* hybrid
Other names: Gipsy Boy
Other varieties: None
Year: 1909
Origin: Germany
Description: Takes its name from the spectacular, smouldering dark colour of the roses, a sumptuous mixture of deep red to purple-black with a centre of golden stamens. The individual flowers are not large, but they are sweetly scented and smother the long, arching branches. The foliage is tough and rather coarse
Flowering: Very slightly recurrent
Cultivation: Prune regularly in winter. Remove weak, unproductive growth and prune back some remaining branches by one-third each year to force strong healthy growth. Grown as a shrub or short climber.

Vivid

Zéphirine Drouhin

Zigeunerknabe

Boursault Roses

A small and almost forgotten group of roses, of which only a few still remain in cultivation. Thought to be a cross between *R. chinensis* and *R. pendulina*, they are characterised by generally thornless wood, long spaces between the growth buds on the stems and new growth that is purple-red in colour. There has not been much success in attempts to improve the class by hybridisation.

Pruning is required after flowering to reduce the length of long shoots.

Mme Sancy de Parabère

AMADIS

Botanical grouping: Cassiorhodon
Parentage: Unknown
Other names: Crimson Boursault
Other varieties: None
Year: 1829
Origin: France
Description: Double or semi-double crimson-purple, almost scentless blooms are borne on long arching, thornless canes up to 5 m (16 ft). The foliage is dark green, almost purplish when young.
Flowering: Early spring, with occasional later bloom
Cultivation: Vigorous and healthy when given a warm, sunny position in good soil that is mulched and watered well in summer. Remove old, weak wood after flowering or in winter.

Amadis

BLUSH BOURSAULT

Botanical grouping: Cassiorhodon
Parentage: Unknown
Other names: Calypso
Other varieties: None
Year: 1848
Origin: France
Description: An early flowering climber bearing pendulous, very double blush pink blooms with deeper pink centres that are almost scentless. There is much debate over the parentage of this rose and it is often seen growing in the wild. The arching, thornless canes reach between 2–5 m (6–16 ft) high and retain their dark green leaves well.
Flowering: Early spring, non-repeating
Cultivation: It needs a very good aspect with plenty of sun and water. Prune back after flowering.

L'HÉRITIERANA

Botanical grouping: Cassiorhodon
Parentage: Thought to be derived from *R. pendulina* or some related species and *R. chinensis*
Other names: None
Other varieties: None
Year: Before 1820
Origin: France
Description: This is the original boursault rose. It can be grown as a large shrub or a semi-climbing rose. Densely packed, deep pink-red medium blooms are borne on slender stems on long, arching thornless canes. A well foliated rose that will grow to about 4 m (13 ft).
Flowering: Early spring, non-repeating
Cultivation: Prune laterals back after flowering, quite severely if grown as a bush. It prefers full sun, and good soil that is well mulched and watered.

MME SANCY DE PARABÈRE

Botanical grouping: Cassiorhodon
Parentage: Unknown
Other names: None
Other varieties: None
Year: Before 1845
Origin: France
Description: A well-known and vigorous climber, growing up to 5 m (16 ft), producing elegant and large, flat, rosy pink, semi-double nodding flowers. The blooms are saucer-shaped, up to 13 cm (5 in) across and are sweetly perfumed. The lush, dark green to brownish leaves are coarse toothed.
Flowering: Profusely, once only, in mid-summer
Cultivation: Prefers a sunny, warm position in good soil that is well mulched and watered. Prune back after flowering.

Morlettii

MORLETTII

Botanical grouping: Cassiorhodon
Parentage: Probably a *R. pendulina* hybrid x Plena
Other names: None
Other varieties: None
Year: 1883
Origin: France
Description: A well-shaped bush which will grow up to 3 m (10 ft). It is thornless, a characteristic of Boursaults, with leaves which produce good autumn colouring. Densely packed bright pink semi-double flowers are offset by attractive mid-green serrated leaves.
Flowering: Summer, non-repeating
Cultivation: Thrives in full sun and good soil. It is a vigorous rose that needs pruning back after flowering.

Blush Boursault

China Roses

This group of roses is directly descended from the garden roses of China, which, when imported to Europe, revolutionised the rose world by introducing true recurrency (the ability to flower more than once in a season). Generally small and compact, China roses feature light green foliage tinged with red and a dense, twiggy habit. When planted in a warm, sunny position many will start flowering very early in the season and continue through until winter. Flowers vary considerably, and are in the white, creamy white, salmon pink to scarlet-crimson colour range.

Prune in winter to remove dead or spindly wood, and shorten new stems back by one-half.

Archduke Charles

ANNA MARIA DE MONTRAVAL

Botanical grouping: Chinensis
Parentage: A polyantha x Mme de Tartas
Other names: None
Other varieties: None
Year: 1880
Origin: France
Description: A compact plant growing to a height of 1 m (3 ft) with a tendency to sprawl if not trimmed back. The fully double, pure white flowers are globular, large and fragrant and are borne in profuse clusters.
Flowering: Almost continuously throughout summer
Cultivation: Rich soil and a sunny position will ensure almost continuous flowering. Prune lightly to encourage repeat flowering by removing dead or spindly wood. It can be grown in a glasshouse or in a container.

ARCHDUKE CHARLES

Botanical grouping: Chinensis
Parentage: Unknown
Other names: None

Other varieties: None
Year: Before 1837
Origin: China
Description: Growing to about 1 m (3 ft) with flowers about 7.5 cm (3 in) across, this rose is extremely fragrant. Double rosy pink blooms, sometimes with crimson-red marbled with blush-pink. The colours deepen with age and hot weather develops darker tones throughout the blooms.
Flowering: Repeats throughout summer and autumn.
Cultivation: Prefers a sunny position in humus-enriched soil. Prune laterals back by half once established. Water well during dry weather to prevent mildew.

COMTESSE DU CAYLA

Botanical grouping: Chinensis
Parentage: Unknown
Other names: None
Other varieties: None
Year: 1902
Origin: France
Description: A vigorous, slightly angular shrub growing to about 1 m (3 ft) with dark

copper-coloured foliage. New growth is purple, becoming glossy and dark as it hardens. The blooms are semi-double, bright orange and pink with red highlights. It has a slightly drooping habit, is free-flowering and highly scented.
Flowering: More or less continuously throughout summer to autumn
Cultivation: Grows well in any good soil in a sunny garden position, in pots or a glasshouse. Its slightly twiggy growth requires some pruning. Water well in warm weather.

CRAMOISI SUPÉRIEUR

Botanical grouping: Chinensis
Parentage: Unknown
Other names: Agrippina
Other varieties: None
Year: 1832
Origin: France

Anna Maria de Montraval

Comtesse du Cayla

Cramoisi Supérieur

Description: A compact bush growing to 1 m (3 ft) with a low, spreading habit. Makes a charming informal hedge needing little more than occasional maintenance. Large clusters of semi-double, cupped, clear red blooms with lighter centres are sometimes streaked with white. Faintly perfumed.
Flowering: Summer only
Cultivation: A hardy shrub that flourishes even in poorer soils and pots. Plant in a warm, sunny position and provide adequate water and occasional mulching.

ECHO

Botanical grouping: Chinensis
Parentage: Unknown
Other names: Baby Tausendschön (Thousand Beauties)
Other varieties: None
Year: 1914
Origin: Unknown
Description: Prolific large, semi-double, cupped blooms from almost white to deep pink grow in clusters on a compact bush to about 1 m (3 ft). All of the colour variations appear at once, against glossy green foliage, making this an eye-catching feature in a garden.
Flowering: Summer to autumn
Cultivation: This is a hardy plant and will thrive in most soils given normal rose maintenance.

FABVIER

Botanical grouping: Chinensis
Parentage: Unknown
Other names: None
Other varieties: None
Year: 1832
Origin: France
Description: A popular bedding plant due to its twiggy, compact 50 cm (1 ½ ft) growth and low spreading habit and is well suited to rock gardens. Clusters of scarlet-crimson,

Fabvier

Fortune's Double Yellow

semi-double blooms with occasional white streaks make it an attractive and profuse ground cover. Foliage is dark glossy green tinted with purple.
Flowering: Repeats throughout summer to autumn
Cultivation: Will grow well in poorer soils but will benefit from mulch in drier areas. It needs little attention apart from adequate watering. A sunny position is preferred.

FELLENBERG

Botanical grouping: Chinensis
Parentage: Unknown
Other names: La Belle Marseillaise
Other varieties: None
Year: Before 1842
Origin: Unknown

Fellenberg

Description: An attractive cascading habit makes this an ideal pillar rose, although the stems are thorny unlike most China roses. Cupped, double, cerise to crimson-red blooms are borne in trusses on vigorous spreading canes up to 2 m (7 ft). Flowers prolifically amid generous, mid-green foliage.
Flowering: Almost continuously throughout summer and autumn
Cultivation: Cuttings of this hardy rose will strike readily. It needs little more than sun, water and occasional mulching and will grow in poorer soils.

FORTUNE'S DOUBLE YELLOW

Botanical grouping: Chinensis
Parentage: *R. odorata pseudindica*
Other names: Gold of Ophir, Beauty of Glazenwood
Other varieties: None
Year: 1845
Origin: China
Description: A spectacular and vigorous rose which grows up to 5 m (16 ft). Exquisite buds open to semi-double, fragrant yellow flowers up to10 cm (4 in) across and develop to salmon-orange edged with a flame flush. The long canes can be intergrown with wistaria to dramatic effect.
Flowering: Repeats throughout spring
Cultivation: Requires good soil in a frost free area. It resents pruning and prefers little interference. Old specimens grow to a great height. It requires a sunny position and plenty of space to show its true beauty, although it may be grown in a glasshouse.

Gloire des Rosomanes   *Grüss an Teplitz*   *Hermosa*

Irène Watts

Cultivation: Suited to cooler, shaded walls and even poorer soils but will thrive in the sun and in pots.

GRÜSS AN TEPLITZ

Botanical grouping: Chinensis
Parentage: (Sir Joseph Paxton x Fellenberg) x (Papa Gontier x Gloire des Rosomanes)
Other names: None
Other varieties: None
Year: 1897
Origin: Hungary
Description: A China–bourbon hybrid, it makes a tall shrub or a small climber to 2–4 m (6–13 ft) on a wall or pergola. Scarlet-crimson, velvety textured flowers hang down on weak necks, a feature if grown as a climber. It has abundant, light green foliage.
Flowering: More or less continuously from spring to summer
Cultivation: Suitable as a hedging rose. It is inclined to mildew in dry weather as it needs plenty of water. Cuttings strike easily in good soil.

HERMOSA

Botanical grouping: Chinensis
Parentage: Unknown
Other names: Armosa, Mélanie Lemaire, Mme Neumann
Other varieties: None
Year: 1840
Origin: France
Description: An old bush rose, growing to 1 m (3 ft), well suited to borders and clumps. It produces an almost continuous display of double, very fragrant, light pink blooms, set off by grey-green foliage.
Flowering: Continuously through spring to autumn
Cultivation: To flourish it should be left alone and treated as a flowering shrub. In warmer areas it can be relied on for a good display almost year-round. Partial shade or full sun is suitable and it will grow well in pots.

GLOIRE DES ROSOMANES

Botanical grouping: Chinensis
Parentage: Unknown
Other names: Ragged Robin, Red Robin
Other varieties: None
Year: 1825
Origin: France
Description: Once used in the breeding of Bourbon roses, this vigorous, free-flowering and sweetly scented rose grows to 1.2 m (4 ft). The largish flowers, 13 cm (5 in) across, are double, rich crimson and grow in large clusters. Often used as a hedging rose in California.
Flowering: More or less continuously from spring to summer

IRÈNE WATTS

Botanical grouping: Chinensis
Parentage: Unknown
Other names: None
Other varieties: None
Year: 1896
Origin: France
Description: A good bedding rose, free-flowering and growing to 70 cm (2 ft). The bushy dark green foliage is edged with purple. Pale salmon-pink blooms appear first as pointed buds, opening loosely flat, about 4 cm (nearly 2 in) across.
Flowering: Continuously from spring to autumn

Le Vésuve

Cultivation: Most soils suit this rose. Best results are gained by providing a sunny position in a bed that has been well dug and fertilised. Pot-planting is also suitable.

LE VÉSUVE

Botanical grouping: Chinensis
Parentage: Unknown
Other names: Lemesle
Other varieties: None
Year: 1825
Origin: France

Minima (double form)

Description: A branching, thorny shrub growing to 1.5 m (5 ft) with repeat flowerings of nodding double, pale pink, fragrant blooms that deepen in colour as they age. The foliage is shiny and dark green.
Flowering: Continuously from spring to autumn
Cultivation: The dense twiggy growth and spreading habit make it well suited to use as a hedging plant. It likes hot weather and thrives in a sunny location and can also be cultivated in glasshouses or in pots.

MINIMA

Botanical grouping: Chinensis
Parentage: *R. chinensis minima*
Other names: Miss Lawrance's Rose, Fairy Rose
Other varieties: None
Year: 1815
Origin: China
Description: A single, soft rose pink with pointed petals tinged a deeper shade of pink It has abundant foliage, few thorns, and a dwarf, spreading habit, growing to about 30 cm (1 ft). A parent of modern miniatures.
Flowering: Spring to summer
Cultivation: Prefers full sun and good soil, cultivating well in glasshouses and in pots.

MME LAURETTE MESSIMY

Botanical grouping: Chinensis
Parentage: Rival de Paestum x Mme Falcot
Other names: None
Other varieties: None
Year: 1887
Origin: France
Description: Acknowledged as one of the best Chinese hybrids, it grows to 70 cm (2 ft) and is excellent as a bedding plant. A bushy shrub that is upright with a good display of glossy, grey-green leaves and multitudes of loose, semi-double blooms of soft salmon. The buds are darker and open to copper tones with yellow bases. Very free-flowering.
Flowering: Continuously throughout spring to autumn
Cultivation: Best banked up in beds that are well mulched. It grows in full sun or partial shade, in glasshouses and in pots.

MUTABILIS

Botanical grouping: Chinensis
Parentage: Unknown
Other names: Tipo Ideale, *R. turkestanica*
Other varieties: None
Year: Before 1896
Origin: China
Description: An exceptionally graceful China rose which will grow to a height of

Mme Laurette Messimy

Mutabilis

1 m (3 ft) when established. It bears masses of slender pointed buds of vivid flame-red opening to a soft yellow then changing to copper-pink and finally copper-crimson. A spectacular display.

Flowering: Continuously throughout spring to autumn

Cultivation: An extremely healthy and versatile rose, ideal as a hedging plant and one that will grow in partial shade, poorer soils or in glasshouses and in pots.

OLD BLUSH

Botanical grouping: Chinensis
Parentage: Unknown

Papa Hémeray

Other names: Parson's Pink, Monthly Rose, Pallida, Common Blush
Other varieties: None
Year: To Europe 1752
Origin: China
Description: Considered to be one of the treasures of the rose world. A small bush of up to 70 cm (2 ft) which has been cultivated in China for many centuries. Almost thornless, the free-flowering semi-double blooms of rose pink fading to pale silver, are sweetly scented like sweet peas.
Flowering: Continuously throughout summer to winter
Cultivation: Prefers shade and mulch at root level to retain moisture. It will grow in

Rouletii

Old Blush

poorer soils in cooler, shaded positions. Mildew will result if not given sufficient water. Prune lightly and remove spent flowers. It can be grown as a small climber or as a hedging plant.

PAPA HÉMERAY

Botanical grouping: Chinensis
Parentage: Unknown
Other names: None
Other varieties: None
Year: 1912
Origin: France
Description: A bushy, upright shrub, growing to 1.2 m (4 ft), with masses of dark green foliage and beautiful clusters of small, vivid pink to red flowers that are single with a white centre.
Flowering: Continuously throughout summer.
Cultivation: This is a low-growing rose suitable for bed or border, or for cultivation in a container. This rose prefers full sun and should be pruned lightly in winter.

QUEEN MAB

Botanical grouping: Chinensis
Parentage: Unknown
Other names: None
Other varieties: None
Year: 1896
Origin: England
Description: Extra-full blooms of rosy apricot and a vivid orange base are quartered and flat and when fully open are 5 cm (2 in) across. The foliage is copper red and wiry. It will grow to about 1 m (3 ft).
Flowering: Spring to summer
Cultivation: Bred for massing in beds, this rose is not suited to very wet areas as the heavy petals open poorly in wet weather. A warm, dry position suits it.

ROULETII

Botanical grouping: Chinensis
Parentage: Unknown, thought to be a mutant form of *R. chinensis pumila*
Other names: Pompon de Paris
Other varieties: None
Year: 1922
Origin: Switzerland
Description: This is a parent of many miniature roses. It has many thorns on an almost evergreen bush growing to 30 cm (1 ft). Very free-flowering, fully double, clear pink flowers are borne in clusters.
Flowering: Almost continuously from spring to summer
Cultivation: This is a hardy rose that grows well in a pot, where it was originally discovered. It prefers full sun and can also be grown in a glasshouse.

SANGUINEA

Botanical grouping: Chinensis
Parentage: Unknown, probably a reversion
from *R. chinensis semperflorens*
Other names: Miss Lowe, Bengal Crimson
Other varieties: None
Year: 1887
Origin: China
Description: A twiggy bush growing to 1.2 m
(4 ft) and bearing a succession of single,
5 petal, deep crimson flowers up to 4 cm
(2 in) across, which deepen in colour with
age. It has a slightly angular growth.
Flowering: Continuously throughout spring
to autumn
Cultivation: Grow in full sun. Most garden
conditions are suitable and it can be
cultivated in pots.

Viridiflora

Viridiflora

Semperflorens

SEMPERFLORENS

Botanical grouping: Chinensis
Parentage: Unknown
Other names: Slater's or Miss Wilmott's
Crimson China, Old Crimson China
Other varieties: None
Year: To England *c*.1791
Origin: China
Description: One of the original China
roses. A dwarf, branching, bushy plant up to
1 m (3 ft), with dark green foliage and few
broad, flat thorns. Crimson to scarlet, semi-
double blooms with centres that are some-
times streaked with white.
Flowering: Almost continuously from
spring to summer
Cultivation: Thrives in full sun, in pots or
against a low wall.

VIRIDIFLORA

Botanical grouping: Chinensis
Parentage: Unknown
Other names: The Green Rose,
R. monstrosa
Other varieties: None
Year: 1833
Origin: Unknown
Description: An unusual, clear green rose
with serrated sepals rather than petals.
Bronze and russet tones appear later and the
blooms remain on the bush for many weeks.
Popular in floral arrangements as it does not
wilt or drop. Grows to a height of 1 m (3 ft).
Flowering: Almost continuously from
spring to autumn
Cultivation: A hardy and disease-resistant
rose although it may refuse to flower if given
more than a light pruning. Remove dead
wood and trim into shape. Grows in poorer
soils, in full sun and in pots.

Noisette Roses

Blush Noisette

This group owes its heritage to a cross between a hybrid of *R. chinensis* and *R. moschata* performed by an American gardener in the early 1800s and then exported to France in 1814. The flowers are small to medium in size and very fragrant, often borne in clusters, in the white, pale pink, cream and pale yellow colour range. The foliage is light green and glossy, while the stems are smooth and covered with thorns.

Most varieties flower more than once each season. Many noisettes are vigorous climbers, and as such they need pruning in winter to replace old wood with fresh young growth. Both old and new wood is generally reduced by one quarter.

AIMÉE VIBERT

Botanical grouping: Chinensis
Parentage: Champney's Pink Cluster x *R. sempervirens* hybrid
Other names: Bouquet de la Mariee, Nivea
Other varieties: None
Year: 1828
Origin: France
Description: Almost thornless, this vigorous rose produces large sprays of pure white flowers on the ends of flexible branches. The foliage is dense, dark green with long and narrow leaflets. It can grow up to 3.5 m (12 ft).
Flowering: Late summer. May repeat.
Cultivation: Tolerant of poorer soils, it will grow in partial shade but dislikes frosts. If allowed to climb through a tall tree it will bloom more freely.

Alister Stella Gray

ALISTER STELLA GRAY

Botanical grouping: Chinensis
Parentage: Unknown
Other names: Golden Rambler
Other varieties: None
Year: 1894
Origin: England
Description: A rather angular growth but a very popular rose because of its very fragrant, small, double, egg-yellow buds which open to a paler yellow then deepen to an orange and then fade to a rich cream colour. Almost thorn-free, the foliage is dense and dark green and it will grow to 4.5 m (15 ft).
Flowering: Almost perpetually from summer to autumn
Cultivation: Careful pruning is needed. Vigorous new shoots appear at the base and quickly flower. Suitable for training on a wall, over arches or pergolas or through trees. Plant in a sunny position.

BLUSH NOISETTE

Botanical grouping: Chinensis
Parentage: Seedling from Champney's Pink Cluster, Flesh-coloured Noisette
Other names: None
Other varieties: None
Year: *c.* 1814
Origin: United States
Description: The original noisette rose. The semi-double flowers are deep pink, mauve and blush-pink and appear in loose clusters almost continuously. They are offset by abundant, attractive, dark green foliage with few thorns. It makes a loose bush to 2 m (7 ft) or can be trained on a wall to 5 m (16 ft).
Flowering: More or less continuously from spring to autumn
Cultivation: Remove spindly and dead wood and prune old and young wood back by about a quarter in winter. This rose will grow in partial shade and in poorer soils.

Céline Forestier

Champney's Pink Cluster

Cloth of Gold

Claire Jacquier

CÉLINE FORESTIER

Botanical grouping: Chinensis
Parentage: Unknown
Other names: None
Other varieties: None
Year: 1842
Origin: France
Description: Although slow to establish itself, it rewards with its clusters of large quartered, button-eyed blooms of primrose-yellow, tinged with pink. It has a strong, spicy, tea scent. Fine but vigorous, its growth is inclined to be bushy to 2–4 m (6–12 ft). Profuse light green foliage and darker stems.
Flowering: More or less continuously from spring to autumn.
Cultivation: A good, free-flowering, small climber in a warm situation. It is tolerant of poorer soils and can be grown in a glasshouse or in pots.

CHAMPNEY'S PINK CLUSTER

Botanical grouping: Chinensis
Parentage: *R. chinensis* x *R. moschata*
Other names: None
Other varieties: None
Year: 1802
Origin: United States
Description: One of the finest noisette roses. An arching shrub climber to 4.5 m (15 ft). Clusters of small, cupped, semi-double blooms are soft blush, tinged with lilac and very fragrant. The foliage is mid to dark green.
Flowering: Summer only
Cultivation: Very vigorous unless contained. Spectacular when allowed to climb freely through a large tree. It is tolerant of poorer soils but likes a sunny position.

CLAIRE JACQUIER

Botanical grouping: Chinensis
Parentage: Possibly *R. multiflora* x a tea rose

Other names: None
Other varieties: None
Year: 1888
Origin: France
Description: A surprisingly vigorous climber growing to more than 6 m (20 ft). The flowers are richly scented, butter-yellow fading to cream, and are borne in clusters. The plentiful foliage is light green.
Flowering: Summer. Repeats in most seasons.
Cultivation: Robust new growth emerges from the base of this climber. It requires plenty of space and can be grown over a cooler wall as it will grow in semi-shade. The vigorous growth makes it ideal to grow through a large tree. Plant in a position that is protected from frosts.

CLOTH OF GOLD

Botanical grouping: Chinensis
Parentage: Lamarque seedling
Other names: Chromatella
Other varieties: None
Year: 1843
Origin: France
Description: Large sulphur-yellow blooms are pointed in the bud. Flowers are fragrant and borne on long stems and open to a cupped tea rose shape. The foliage is light green and plentiful. Grows to 3.5 m (12 ft).
Flowering: Repeats in spring and summer.
Cultivation: Will flower well if grown in a sunny sheltered position in rich soil protected from cold and frosts. It can also be grown in a glasshouse or in pots.

CRÉPUSCULE

Botanical grouping: Chinensis
Parentage: Unknown
Other names: None
Other varieties: None
Year: 1904
Origin: France
Description: Masses of semi-double old-gold, fragrant blooms are carried on this almost thornless climber. Flowers and deep green foliage constantly clothe the plant. Generally a shrub rose but it will spread over fences and trees to about 3.5 m (12 ft) and will cover a large area.
Flowering: Constantly throughout spring and autumn
Cultivation: Tender to cold but will spread rapidly in a warm sunny position in good soil. It can also be grown in a glasshouse.

DESPREZ À FLEUR JAUNE

Botanical grouping: Chinensis
Parentage: Blush Noisette x Park's Yellow China
Other names: Jaune Desprez
Other varieties: None
Year: 1830
Origin: France

Gloire de Dijon

Crépuscule

Desprez à Fleur Jaune

Description: Buff-coloured blooms are shaded with warm yellow, peach and apricot tones and have a rich fragrance. Flowers are borne in clusters on long shoots which will grow to 6 m (20 ft) against a wall or fence. Growth is vigorous with light green foliage on dark, mottled stems.
Flowering: Repeats from spring to autumn
Cultivation: As the rich colours will fade quickly in hot sun, plant in a semi-shaded, protected position away from cold, frosts and winds. It will grow in poorer soils or in a glasshouse. The vigorous growth makes it ideal to grow in a tree.

DUCHESSE DE GRAMMONT

Botanical grouping: Chinensis
Parentage: Unknown
Other names: None
Other varieties: None
Year: Unknown
Origin: Unknown
Description: Reminiscent of Blush Noisette, this is not a very well-known hybrid although a very old variety. Low growing to about 2 m (7 ft), it is very proliferous and is covered with large clusters of small, double, soft, blossom-pink, fragrant blooms.
Flowering: Spring to summer
Cultivation: A hardy rose that will thrive in a warm, sunny position in good soil.

GLOIRE DE DIJON

Botanical grouping: Chinensis
Parentage: Unknown tea rose x Souvenir de la Malmaison
Other names: The Old Glory Rose
Other varieties: None
Year: 1853
Origin: France
Description: Very large, double and quartered blooms filled with a heady fragrance are rich deep buff-yellow, amber and sometimes shaded apricot. In warmer climates, pink tones predominate. A favourite in English gardens, it climbs to 3.5 m (12 ft).
Flowering: Repeats throughout spring to summer.
Cultivation: Prefers full sun but is very hardy even in shaded areas. It is prone to black spot after the first flush. Flowers may repeat in autumn in a sunny position.

LAMARQUE

Botanical grouping: Chinensis
Parentage: Blush Noisette x Park's Yellow Tea Scented China
Other names: Thé Maréchal
Other varieties: None
Year: 1830
Origin: France
Description: Large marble-white, double, flat and quartered blooms mass on long,

Lamarque

Maréchal Niel

well-foliated stems that are almost thornless. One of the rose world's favourite white climbers, it grows to 4.5 m (15 ft) and is very fragrant.

Flowering: Recurrent throughout spring and summer.

Cultivation: A vigorous climber, plant in a warm, sunny situation which is protected from cold. It can be trimmed back and grown as a shrub rose in the garden or glasshouse.

LOUISE D'ARZENS

Botanical grouping: Chinensis
Parentage: Unknown
Other names: None
Other varieties: None
Year: Unknown
Origin: Unknown
Description: A rare and little-known hybrid, with masses of cream, blushed pink buds opening to very double, medium-sized pure white blooms. Very fragrant. A restrained climbing rose growing to a height of about 3 m (10 ft).

Flowering: Spring to summer
Cultivation: Plant in full sun in a position that is protected from frosts and cold winds.

MARÉCHAL NIEL

Botanical grouping: Chinensis
Parentage: Seedling from Cloth of Gold
Other names: None
Other varieties: None
Year: 1864
Origin: France
Description: An outstanding, vigorous climber. Butter-yellow double, nodding blooms develop from pointed buds. The heady fragrance is a mixture of wild strawberries and tea rose scent. It will climb to 4.5 m (15 ft) up a trellis or over a pergola and its attractive foliage is dark copper-green.

Flowering: Repeats throughout spring and summer

Cultivation: Thrives in a warm, sheltered position in the garden or in pots but dislikes hot weather. Best grown in a greenhouse in colder climates as extreme conditions do not suit it.

MME ALFRED CARRIÈRE

Botanical grouping: Chinensis
Parentage: Unknown
Other names: None

Other varieties: None
Year: 1879
Origin: France
Description: Masses of milky white, cupped, very fragrant double blooms blushed with pink grow on vigorous canes with few thorns. An exceptional rose, it can be trained as a hedge or allowed to climb a trellis or wall where it will reach to 6 m (20 ft). Large leaves are pale green and abundant.

Flowering: Almost continuously from spring to autumn
Cultivation: Partial shade is suitable although a sunny position will encourage continuous flowering and vigorous growth. Tolerant of poorer soils, it can be grown through a large tree or as an attractive glasshouse specimen.

NASTARANA

Botanical grouping: Synstylae
Parentage: Unknown
Other names: Persian Musk Rose
Other varieties: None
Year: 1879
Origin: Iran
Description: Similar shrub to *R. moschata*

Mme Alfred Carrière

but with smaller leaves and a somewhat more vigorous habit in colder climates. Flowers are white with a pinkish tinge and are produced in clusters.

Flowering: Continuously through summer and autumn

Cultivation: Does well in open, sunny positions but can tolerate poorer soils and some shade, including walls in shade. Useful for places where other roses will not thrive.

PERLE DES BLANCHES

Botanical grouping: Chinensis
Parentage: Unknown
Other names: None
Other varieties: None
Year: Unknown
Origin: France
Description: Pure white, medium-sized blooms gather in clusters and resemble camellias on opening then reflex into a snowball shape. The petals have a waxy appearance. The leaves are thick and dark, setting off the red-tinted plump buds and pale flowers. Grows to 4.5 m (15 ft).
Flowering: Repeats throughout spring to summer
Cultivation: A vigorous climber, well suited

Nastarana

Rêve d'Or

to growing over a pergola or verandah in a warm sunny position. It will tolerate some shade.

RÊVE D'OR

Botanical grouping: Chinensis
Parentage: Mme Schultz seedling
Other names: Golden Chain
Other varieties: None
Year: 1869
Origin: France
Description: Semi-double deep salmon-

buff and yellow flowers, sometimes blushed with pink, bloom continuously amid rich green foliage. Similar in form and fragrance to Gloire de Dijon. Vigorous and free-flowering, it will grow to 3.5 m (12 ft) high.
Flowering: Repeats from spring to autumn.
Cultivation: Requires a sheltered position in full sun for best results. Rather tender, it is best suited to warmer areas and can be cultivated in glasshouses or in pots.

SOLFATERRE

Botanical grouping: Chinensis
Parentage: Lamarque seedling
Other names: Solfa
Other varieties: None
Year: 1843
Origin: France
Description: Free-flowering and very fragrant, this rose has double, pale sulphur-yellow blooms and is similar in habit to its parent Lamarque.
Flowering: Repeats throughout spring and summer.
Cultivation: Grow in full sun. In colder areas it needs a warm, sheltered position or greenhouse to flourish. It may also be grown in pots.

WILLIAM ALLEN RICHARDSON

Botanical grouping: Chinensis
Parentage: Rêve d'Or sport
Other names: None
Other varieties: None
Year: 1878
Origin: France
Description: Very double, medium-sized blooms of rich apricot fading to apricot-gold are very free-flowering and fragrant. The stems are quite thorny and dark with deep green, almost plum-coloured, foliage. It will climb to a height of 4 m (13 ft).
Flowering: Repeats from spring to summer
Cultivation: This climber needs a warm, sheltered position to flourish. It may be grown in a glasshouse or in pots.

William Allen Richardson

Rugosa Roses

A hardy group of old roses distinguished by their rough, dark green, leathery leaves covered with an indented network of veins. Originally from China, Korea and Japan, rugosas were first introduced to Europe in the late 1700s, although they were not as popular as other imported varieties. However, rugosas are prized for their ease of cultivation, even in very difficult situations. The stems are covered with stiff, straight thorns and the large fragrant flowers are single, semi-double or double in a wide range of colours from pure white to deepest red.

Flowers are followed by showy red rosehips, and although the main flowering is in summer, some varieties have sporadic blooms through summer and into autumn. Little pruning is required except to shape old, straggly plants.

Agnes

AGNES

Botanical grouping: Cassiorhodon (Cinnamomeae)
Parentage: *R. rugosa* x *R. foetida persiana*
Other names: None
Other varieties: None
Year: 1922
Origin: Canada
Description: A bushy rose, to 1.8 m (6 ft), with dense growth and a covering of deep green, crinkled foliage borne on thorny stems. Flowers are amber yellow, fully double and strongly scented—this is one of the few yellow rugosas. The flowers fade to white as they mature.
Flowering: Recurrent flowering in summer.
Cultivation: Easily grown in a wide range of soils and conditions, preferring full sun and space to grow. Ideal for the back of a border, bed or shrubbery.

BELLE POITEVINE

Botanical grouping: Cassiorhodon (Cinnamomeae)
Parentage: Unknown

Belle Poitevine

Other names: None
Other varieties: None
Year: 1894
Origin: France
Description: The well-foliaged bush, with thickly growing dark green veined leaves, reaches 2 m (7 ft). Shapely buds open to large, floppy blooms in palest pink, rather like double poppies. Sweet fragrance. Flowering is followed by large scarlet hips and the autumn foliage is outstanding.
Flowering: Several repeat flowerings in a season.
Cultivation: Tolerant of a wide range of soil and weather conditions, and can stand some shade. Pruning not generally required unless the plant becomes straggly, in which case some shaping may be in order.

BLANC DOUBLE DE COUBERT

Botanical grouping: Cassiorhodon (Cinnamomeae)
Parentage: Possibly *R. rugosa* x Sombreuil
Other names: None
Other varieties: None
Year: 1892

Blanc Double de Coubert

Origin: France
Description: This rose is described as 'one of the glories of the late Victorian period'. It is an attractive bushy plant with dark green veined leaves giving good autumn colour. It grows vigorously and may reach over 2 m (7 ft). The large (9 cm, 3 1/2 in) flowers are pure white and semi-double, opening flat and loose around gold stamens, with an overwhelming fragrance. Fruit are large and red though not copious.
Flowering: Recurrent through summer to autumn
Cultivation: Tolerant of shade and will stand most soil and weather conditions. Responds well to container cultivation and can be kept shapely by pruning. Ideal for use in hedging or screening.

CONRAD FERDINAND MEYER

Botanical grouping: Cassiorhodon (Cinnamomeae)
Parentage: *R. rugosa* hybrid x Gloire de Dijon
Other names: None
Other varieties: None
Year: 1899
Origin: Germany
Description: This splendid bush may spread as wide as 3 m (10 ft) and looks truly spectacular with large, unfading silver-pink flowers of slightly blowsy appearance, which are richly scented. The leaves are dark green, borne on thick, thorny stems, and the plant reaches a height of 2.5 m (8 ft). Looks especially good in the autumn.
Flowering: Main flowering in early summer with a late flush in autumn.
Cultivation: A useful hedging specimen, it is a strong grower and tolerant of tough conditions, though it can suffer from rust. Keep the area at the base of the plant free from weed growth, and prune straggly growth if necessary.

Delicata

DELICATA

Botanical grouping: Cassiorhodon (Cinnamomeae)
Parentage: Unknown
Other names: None
Other varieties: None
Year: 1898
Origin: England
Description: Not a very vigorous rugosa, although the flowers are particularly beautiful. Grows to 1.5 m (5 ft) with crinkled mid-green foliage and showy semi-double cerise-pink flowers with yellow stamens. The flowers are very fragrant. Orange hips sometimes appear at the same time as the flowers.
Flowering: Summer
Cultivation: Choose a sunny position and deep, well-drained soil. Not invasive, so can be planted in a mixed bed or border.

F.J. GROOTENDOORST

Botanical grouping: Cassiorhodon (Cinnamomeae)
Parentage: *R. rugosa rubra* x Mme Norbert Levavasseur

F.J. Grootendoorst

Fimbriata

Other names: None
Other varieties: None
Year: 1918
Origin: The Netherlands
Description: Dark green, leathery and very thorny foliage characterises this plant but it is lightened by clusters of small, frilly crimson-red blooms with serrated edges, similar to dianthus or carnation. No scent. Makes a useful protective hedge and grows to 1.5 m (5 ft).
Flowering: Profuse flowering in summer
Cultivation: Can be grown successfully in a container and trimmed to any desired height. It is a robust plant. Tolerates shade.

FIMBRIATA

Botanical grouping: Cassiorhodon (Cinnamomeae)
Parentage: *R. rugosa* x Mme Alfred Carrière
Other names: Phoebe's Frilled Pink, Dianthiflora
Other varieties: None
Year: 1891
Origin: France

Description: The flower of this rose is notable for its similarity to dianthus or carnation, a similarity which arises from the serrated edges of the petals on its small, double blush pink-to-white flowers. The bush is an attractive upright plant with dense light green foliage, growing to 1.5 m (5 ft) and bearing the flowers in clusters.
Flowering: Repeat flowering
Cultivation: An excellent container or hedge specimen. It is hardy and will tolerate shade as well as most soils.

FRAU DAGMAR HASTRUP

Botanical grouping: Cassiorhodon (Cinnamomeae)
Parentage: Unknown
Other names: Fru./Frau Dagmar Hartopp
Other varieties: None
Year: 1914
Origin: Denmark
Description: Compact, moderate grower to 1 m (3 ft) with spreading habit and large, light green, veined leaves. This justly admired rose has large, delicate pink single

Frau Dagmar Hastrup

Grootendoorst Supreme

yellowing leaves. Unscented, like its parent. Reaches 1.5 m (5 ft).
Flowering: Recurrent
Cultivation: Can be grown successfully in a container or trimmed to any desired height. It is a robust plant, and can tolerate some shade. If used as a hedging plant, trim into shape during winter.

HANSA

Botanical grouping: Cassiorhodon (Cinnamomeae)
Parentage: Unknown
Other names: None
Other varieties: None

Hansa

Year: 1905
Origin: The Netherlands
Description: Double, purplish-red flowers with mauve highlights, very heavily petalled and with a strong, clove-like fragrance. Well-foliaged, upright bush bears lovely red hips after the blooms and reaches a height of 1.2 m (4 ft). A good low hedging plant.
Flowering: Free-flowering, summer through to autumn.
Cultivation: Vigorous and hardy, the plant will thrive in most conditions and can be grown in a container. Shade tolerant. Winter is the best time for shaping the bush, especially if used as a hedging plant.

HARVEST HOME

Botanical grouping: Cassiohorodon (Cinnamomeae)
Parentage: Scabrosa seedling
Other names: None
Other varieties: None
Year: 1983
Origin: England
Description: A vigorous, rounded shrub, growing to 1 m (3 ft), with wrinkled green rugosa foliage and masses of mauve-pink, loosely cupped flowers, some followed by large red hips. The flowers have a pleasing fragrance.
Flowering: Summer to autumn.
Cultivation: Ideal for a low-growing hedge, bed or border, this rose prefers full sun and moderately rich, well-drained soil. Prune out dead wood in winter.

Harvest Home

blooms, cup-shaped opening to saucer-shaped. They are very fragrant, with creamy stamens. The blooms are followed by crimson hips as big as small apples, and the autumn colour of the bush is splendid.
Flowering: Free-flowering in summer with some autumn flowers.
Cultivation: Extremely hardy, will tolerate tough conditions and some shade, and will take winter clipping to maintain low height if used as a hedge.

GROOTENDOORST SUPREME

Botanical grouping: Cassiorhodon (Cinnamomeae)
Parentage: Sport of F.J. Grootendoorst
Other names: None
Other varieties: None
Year: 1936
Origin: The Netherlands
Description: Similar characteristics to its parent F.J. Grootendoorst, the only significant difference being in the colour, which is a deeper crimson-red in the sport, and in a less vigorous bush which can exhibit

Lady Curzon

Martin Frobisher

Max Graf

Hunter

HUNTER

Botanical grouping: Cassiorhodon
(Cinnamomeae)
Parentage: *R. rugosa rubra* x Independence
Other names: None
Other varieties: None
Year: 1961
Origin: England
Description: A vigorous, bushy shrub with dark green foliage more like that of a Hybrid Tea, growing to 1.5 m (5 ft)—taller under some conditions—with clusters of double, bright red flowers. Faintly scented.
Flowering: Mid-summer and recurrent in autumn.
Cultivation: This hardy plant responds well in most conditions and can be container grown. Makes a useful hedging plant. Trim back excessive growth in winter, and remove dead wood where necessary.

LADY CURZON

Botanical grouping: Cassiorhodon
(Cinnamomeae)
Parentage: *R. macrantha* x *R. rugosa rubra*
Other names: None
Other varieties: None
Year: 1901
Origin: England
Description: This tall plant can reach 2.5 m (8 ft) in some conditions, and is a very vigorous climber with an arching habit. Its dark green leaves grow on thorny stems. The profuse blooms are large (up to 10 cm, 4 in), single and pale pink, fading to yellow-white near the golden stamens.
Flowering: Flourishes in mid-summer, no recurrence.
Cultivation: Needs plenty of space, but will tolerate a degree of shade and tough conditions generally. Some training may be needed if grown as a climber.

MARTIN FROBISHER

Botanical grouping: Cassiorhodon
(Cinnamomeae)
Parentage: Schneezwerg seedling
Other names: None
Other varieties: None
Year: 1969
Origin: Canada
Description: Masses of double blooms in soft pink with a strong fragrance on bright green foliage. The bush may grow to over 2 m (7 ft).
Flowering: Recurrent
Cultivation: This relatively recent introduction is a good rose for very cold areas, as it is extremely resistant to cold conditions and will also tolerate some shade. Altogether a hardy specimen. Ideal as a backdrop, screen or windbreak.

MAX GRAF

Botanical grouping: Cassiorhodon
(Cinnamomeae)
Parentage: *R. rugosa* x *R. wichuriaiana*
Other names: None
Other varieties: None
Year: 1919
Origin: United States
Description: This modern and very unusual rugosa hybrid is ideal for growing as a ground cover, for example on a bank, as tends to trail along the ground and can spread to 2.5 m (8 ft). The foliage is dense and bright green. The medium-sized flowers

are single, pink shading to white around prominent yellow stamens, and smell of apples. Minimal or no hips.

Flowering: Has only one flowering period, in summer, but this lasts a long time.

Cultivation: An excellent ground cover plant, which will keep weeds at bay, provided it has room to spread.

MME GEORGES BRUANT

Botanical grouping: Cassiorhodon (Cinnamomeae)
Parentage: *R. rugosa* x Sombreuil
Other names: None
Other varieties: None
Year: 1887
Origin: France
Description: A very dense, dark green, thorny bush, this makes an excellent protective hedge, growing to 1.5 m (5 ft). The cream buds open to loose, semi-double, creamy white flowers with yellow-gold stamens and a good scent. Typical rugosa foliage.

Flowering: Free-flowering and recurrent over a long period.

Cultivation: Tolerant of some shade and very hardy in most soils and conditions. Prune back excessive growth if necessary, and mulch well to prevent weed growth at the base of the plant.

MRS ANTHONY WATERER

Botanical grouping: Cassiorhodon (Cinnamomeae)
Parentage: *R. rugosa* x Général Jacqueminot
Other names: None
Other varieties: None
Year: 1898
Origin: England
Description: A very vigorous, spreading bush with coarse-looking leaves and dense growth which can spread to 2 m (7 ft). The

Mme Georges Bruant

colour of the strongly scented and loosely double reddish purple-magenta flowers has been described as 'rather virulent' and is thus not to everyone's taste. Nevertheless, it is a prolific flowerer and placed on its own, this rose can be quite striking.

Flowering: One main flush later in summer, with minimal recurrence.

Cultivation: Will tolerate the toughest conditions. Its dense growth can be useful in suppressing weeds, but it may need to be pegged down.

NOVA ZEMBLA

Botanical grouping: Cassiorhodon (Cinnamomeae)
Parentage: Conrad Ferdinand Meyer sport
Other names: None
Other varieties: None
Year: 1907
Origin: The Netherlands
Description: This sport has similar characteristics to its parent, Conrad F. Meyer,

Mrs Anthony Waterer

except that it is pure white where the parent has silver-pink tones. Vigorous tall plant reaching 3 m (10 ft).

Flowering: Recurrent

Cultivation: An easy to grow and hardy specimen, although it can suffer from rust. Keep weed growth down at the base of the plant, and mulch well.

Nova Zembla

Nyveldt's White

Parfum de l'Hay

Pink Grootendoorst

NYVELDT'S WHITE

Botanical grouping: Cassiorhodon (Cinnamomeae)
Parentage: (*R. rugosa rubra* x *R. majalis*) x *R. nitida*
Other names: None
Other varieties: None
Year: 1955
Origin: The Netherlands
Description: A relatively recent hybrid, this large thorny shrub grows densely and can reach over 2 m (7 ft). The very sweetly scented flowers are single and pure white borne on dark green stems. Attractive autumn foliage and masses of shiny red hips.
Flowering: Virtually continuous throughout summer.
Cultivation: Hardy and shade tolerant. It is well suited for use as hedging. If grown as a hedging plant trim to the desired height in winter, and thereafter only prune back straggly stems.

PARFUM DE L'HAY

Botanical grouping: Cassiorhodon (Cinnamomeae)
Parentage: (*R. damascena* x Général Jacqueminot) x *R. rugosa*
Other names: Rose à Parfum de l'Hay
Other varieties: None
Year: 1901
Origin: France
Description: The rich fragrance of this rose comes from its damask antecedents, and is regarded as one of the greatest rose scents. The large, double, cherry red flowers open flat among dense, dark green foliage, borne on a thorny bush which can grow to 1.5 m (5 ft).
Flowering: Profuse flowers over a long period.
Cultivation: Can be container grown if kept shaped. Will tolerate some shade. Mildew problems may develop later in the season and will require treatment.

PAULII

Botanical grouping: Cassiorhodon (Cinnamomeae)
Parentage: *R. rugosa* x *R. arvensis*
Other names: *R. rugosa repens alba*
Other varieties: None
Year: Prior to 1903
Origin: Unknown
Description: A vigorous trailing or ground covering shrub to 3.5 m (12 ft), very thorny with dark green foliage. The clove-scented flowers are white with gold stamens and are similar to the popular climber clematis in appearance.
Flowering: Summer only
Cultivation: A hardy shrub that does well when fertilised heavily. Prefers an open, sunny position but can make do with some shade.

PAULII ROSEA

Botanical grouping: Cassiorhodon (Cinnamomeae)
Parentage: A sport from *R. paulii*
Other names: *R. paulii rosea*
Other varieties: None
Year: Prior to 1912
Origin: England
Description: A pink form of *R. paulii*. The shrub is more compact and less vigorous than its parent with darker leaves and stems. The flowers are a clear pink but white at the centre around the yellow stamens.
Flowering: Summer only
Cultivation: Prefers an open, sunny position and rich soil but will survive some shade. Use as a ground cover or climber.

PINK GROOTENDOORST

Botanical grouping: Cassiorhodon (Cinnamomeae)
Parentage: F.J. Grootendorst sport
Other names: None
Other varieties: None
Year: 1923
Origin: The Netherlands
Description: One of the rugosa hybrids with carnation or dianthus-like serrated petals on its small, rose pink flowers. No scent. The shrub itself is not notable, being very thorny with rather leathery foliage. It grows upright and reaches 1.5 m (5 ft) or more.
Flowering: Free-flowering constantly through summer to autumn.
Cultivation: As for F.J. Grootendorst, though this sport may perform rather better than its parent. Suited to container cultivation, and can be trimmed to any desired height.

Paulii

Paulii rosea

R. rugosa alba

R. RUGOSA ALBA

Botanical grouping: Cassiorhodon (Cinnamomeae)
Parentage: Species
Other names: None
Other varieties: None
Year: To England *c.* 1870
Origin: Russia, China, Japan
Description: Tall bush which may reach 2 m (7 ft), with glossy deep green foliage, sturdy stems and small thorns. The enormous (10 cm, 4in) flowers are pure white, single, and richly scented, with overlapping petals around a gold heart. The blooms are followed by large, bright red hips and lovely autumn colour, which add to the immense appeal of this superb rose.
Flowering: Recurrent flowering into early winter.
Cultivation: A hardy plant which will tolerate poor soils, some shade, and extreme conditions. Excellent as a hedging specimen. Heavy pruning may be required to control old or straggly growth.

R. RUGOSA RUBRA

Botanical grouping: Cassiorhodon (Cinnamomeae)
Parentage: Species
Other names: *R. rugosa atropurpurea*
Other varieties: None
Year: Unknown
Origin: Japan
Description: General characteristics similar to those for other *R. rugosa* species, including bright green, veined foliage. *R. rugosa rubra* has large, purplish red single blooms which provide a striking counterpoint to the yellow stamens. It is particularly noted for its copious orange-red flattish hips, which are regarded as some of the best among all roses. This plant can reach over 2 m (7 ft).
Flowering: Recurrent over a long season
Cultivation: Will tolerate a degree of shade as well as most soil types. Makes a good hedging specimen.

R. rugosa rubra

ROBUSTA

Botanical grouping: Cassiorhodon (Cinnamomeae)
Parentage: *R. rugosa* x seedling
Other names: None
Other varieties: None
Year: 1979
Origin: Germany
Description: A vigorous bush with dark, leathery leaves and thick thorny stems, growing to 1.5 m (5 ft). Single, scented, rich crimson flowers open in a cup shape, with rather frilly-edged petals around yellow-gold stamens.
Flowering: Very free-flowering, summer through autumn.
Cultivation: A robust plant which will stand most soil and weather conditions, and some shade. Makes an excellent, very dense hedge. When grown as a hedge, winter shaping will be required.

ROSERAIE DE L'HAY

Botanical grouping: Cassiorhodon (Cinnamomeae)
Parentage: Sport of *R. rugosa*
Other names: None
Other varieties: None
Year: 1901
Origin: France
Description: One of the most loved rugosas and very rewarding, for it is in flower almost constantly. The semi-double blooms are strongly scented and open flat and slightly blowsy. Colour is rich velvety wine-red with purplish tinges, very unusual. A very thorny and dense but quite handsome bush, with dark green foliage, reaching 2 m (7 ft). Autumn foliage is splendid, though there are few hips.
Flowering: Constant, over a long period.
Cultivation: Very hardy. Tolerant of all weathers and some shade. Good for hedging.

Robusta

Roseraie de l'Hay

Schneelicht

Scabrosa

Sarah van Fleet

RUSKIN

Botanical grouping: Cassiorhodon
(Cinnamomeae)
Parentage: Souvenir de Pierre Leperdrieux
x Victor Hugo
Other names: VFI, John Ruskin
Other varieties: None
Year: 1928
Origin: United States
Description: A very thorny plant which
makes up for this by producing masses of
large, fully double and very fragrant crimson
flowers on a lushly foliaged bush. Reaches
over 2 m (7 ft) under the right conditions.
Flowering: Recurrent
Cultivation: Although this plant will
tolerate some shade, it flowers most profusely in a sunny situation. It is rather leggy
and floppy in habit and requires suitable
support. Can be used as a cascading
specimen for a container.

SARAH VAN FLEET

Botanical grouping: Cassiorhodon
(Cinnamomeae)
Parentage: *R. rugosa* x My Maryland
Other names: None
Other varieties: None
Year: 1926
Origin: United States
Description: Tall bush bearing clusters of
semi-double blooms in light clear pink, set
around a central clump of creamy gold
stamens. The bush is extremely thorny and
the foliage is dense and spreading. Its
growth is stiffer and more upright than most
rugosas, and it can reach 2.5 m (8 ft). Little
or no fruit.
Flowering: Repeated flushes of flowers
from spring to late summer
Cultivation: An ideal tall hedge specimen.
Can show some bare stems near ground

level and may need pruning from time to
time to encourage more growth from the
base. Can be grown successfully in a
container.

SCABROSA

Botanical grouping: Cassiorhodon
(Cinnamomeae)
Parentage: Unknown, could be a form of *R.
rugosa rubra*
Other names: *R. rugosa scabrosa*
Other varieties: None
Year: 1950
Origin: England
Description: Widely regarded as one of the
finest rugosas because of its beautiful cerise-
pink and sweetly fragrant single flowers
with striking yellow stamens, and the very
large, tomato-shaped, bright red fruit which
follows, enhancing the superb autumn
colour. The name 'scabrosa' refers to the
roughness of the foliage, but in fact the
foliage is quite attractive: clear green and
deeply veined. Can reach 2 m (7 ft).
Flowering: Profuse and virtually continuous through summer.
Cultivation: This is a vigorous, spreading
bush and is best used in a larger garden,
where it can be a good hedge specimen. It is
tolerant of a wide range of climate and soil
conditions, and can stand some shade.

SCHNEELICHT

Botanical grouping: Cassiorhodon
(Cinnamomeae)
Parentage: *R. rugosa* x *R. phoenicia*
Other names: None
Other varieties: None
Year: 1896
Origin: Hungary
Description: Clusters of large, single white
fragrant flowers with attractive gold stamens
are carried on a densely foliaged and
extremely thorny shrub. Grows to 2 m (7 ft).

Flowering: Long flowering season
Cultivation: A very hardy plant which can withstand almost any conditions. Makes an impenetrable hedge where security is needed.

SCHNEEZWERG

Botanical grouping: Cassiorhodon (Cinnamomeae)
Parentage: *R. rugosa* x a white polyantha rose or *R. bracteata*
Other names: Snow Dwarf
Other varieties: None
Year: 1912
Origin: Germany
Description: This is distinguished from other rugosas by its smaller leaves and hips. The flowers, which open flat, are scented, semi-double and medium sized, clear white in colour with prominent pale yellow stamens. Attractive apple-green foliage makes a pleasant contrast with the flowers and orange hips (which appear simultaneously). The bush reaches 1.5 m (5 ft) and has dense growth.
Flowering: Recurrent and profuse over several months into autumn.
Cultivation: Hardy and tolerant of all weathers. Makes an excellent hedge.

SOUVENIR DE PHILÉMON COCHET

Botanical grouping: Cassiorhodon (Cinnamomeae)
Parentage: Blanc Double de Coubert sport
Other names: None
Other varieties: None
Year: 1899
Origin: France
Description: Very similar to its parent, the superb, large, double white flower has a densely packed blush-pink centre. The bush is well-foliaged and grows to 1.5 m (5 ft).
Flowering: Continuous flowering over a long period.
Cultivation: As for Blanc Double de Coubert. May be pruned from time to time to encourage leaf growth and eliminate bare stems at ground level.

THERÉSÈ BUGNET

Botanical grouping: Cassiorhodon (Cinnamomeae)
Parentage: (*R. acicularis* x *R. rugosa kamtchatica*) x (*R. amblyotis* x *R. rugosa plena*) x Betty Bland
Other names: None
Other varieties: None
Year: 1950
Origin: Canada

Description: The complex ancestry of this rose means that it is not instantly recognisable as a rugosa. It is a vigorous bush with long stems, which can reach over 2 m (7 ft), and bears large double fragrant flowers in bright red fading to pink.
Flowering: Constant flowering over a long season.
Cultivation: Very hardy, withstanding poor soils and shaded conditions.

WHITE GROOTENDOORST

Botanical grouping: Cassiorhodon (Cinnamomeae)
Parentage: Sport of Pink Grootendoorst
Other names: None
Other varieties: None
Year: 1962
Origin: United States
Description: Except for its white colour, this rose is identical to the other Grootendoorsts (see F.J. Grootendoorst, Grootendoorst Supreme, Pink Grootendoorst), with the same clusters of small, slightly scented dianthus-like flowers.
Flowering: Continuous flowering over a long period.
Cultivation: Can be grown successfully in a container and trimmed to any desired height. It is a robust plant and tolerates some shade.

Souvenir de Philémon Cochet

White Grootendoorst

Schneezwerg

Tea Roses

Tea roses originated in the Orient, and are thought to have evolved as a cross between *R. gigantea* and *R. chinensis*. The first tea roses arrived in England in the ships of the East India Company carrying cargoes of tea, and this is why the name tea rose was attributed to these roses, not for their fragrance as was commonly thought. Although not totally hardy, tea roses were valued for their simple beauty. The blooms have distinctive pointed buds, and are borne on rather slender, weak stems. One of the most famous tea roses is Parks' Yellow, named after its collector John Parks. Eventually, tea roses were crossed with hybrid perpetuals to produce the famous hybrid teas that are so popular today.

Baronne Henriette de Snoy

Bon Silène

Anna Olivier

ANNA OLIVIER

Botanical grouping: Chinensis
Parentage: Unknown
Other names: None
Other varieties: None
Year: 1872
Origin: France
Description: Elegant, high-centred blooms are apricot-cream with a deep rose flushed reverse. Their full heads hanging down on weak stems give a nodding appearance. The bush, well foliated with mid-green leaves, will grow to 1 m (3 ft).
Flowering: Almost continuously throughout spring to autumn.

Cultivation: A vigorous, branching bush rose, it requires only light pruning. Likes a position with full sun in the garden or in pots.

BARONNE HENRIETTE DE SNOY

Botanical grouping: Chinensis
Parentage: Gloire de Dijon x Mme Lombard
Other names: None
Other varieties: None
Year: 1897
Origin: France
Description: Deep pink to crimson on the reverse of the petals and creamy pink, large, fully double, very fragrant blooms with shapely centres, make this an attractive and free-flowering rose. It makes an angular but vigorous bush to 1.5 m (5 ft), with large, mid-green leaves.
Flowering: Repeats from spring to autumn
Cultivation: Remove twiggy growth when flowering is completed. Plant in a warm, sunny position, either in a garden bed or in pots.

BON SILÈNE

Botanical grouping: Chinensis
Parentage: Unknown
Other names: None
Other varieties: None
Year: 1839
Origin: France
Description: Well-formed buds, large, fully double, deep pink to rosy crimson flowers are produced in profusion. A sweetly scented, compact but vigorous plant that grows to 1.5 m (5 ft). Thorny, with mid-green foliage.
Flowering: Repeats throughout spring and summer
Cultivation: Plant in full sun and water well in warmer weather. It may also be cultivated in a glasshouse or in pots.

Catherine Mermet

CATHERINE MERMET

Botanical grouping: Chinensis
Parentage: Unknown
Other names: None
Other varieties: None
Year: 1869
Origin: France
Description: Considered one of the finest tea roses of its day, it produced many sports. A sweetly scented, full, pale pink rose with a creamy yellow base, it is sometimes flushed with lavender. The long stems and high-pointed buds make it ideal as a cutting rose. It can grow to a height of 2 m (7 ft).
Flowering: Summer to autumn
Cultivation: An old rose that likes to ramble over hedges or trees. It is a sun-lover although the colour will fade as the blooms mature. Suited to glass house cultivation in colder climates.

DEVONIENSIS

Botanical grouping: Chinensis
Parentage: Unknown
Other names: Magnolia Rose
Other varieties: None

Year: 1838
Origin: England
Description: A popular old tea rose, it produces large, double and beautifully formed blooms of creamy-white tinged with pink at the centre. They open flat and ruffled, are richly fragrant and perpetual. Foliage is light green and plentiful with relatively few thorns. The climbing form will grow to 3.5 m (12 ft). (The bush form was superseded by a climbing sport and is little grown.)
Flowering: Freely from spring to autumn
Cultivation: Although vigorous, this rose needs a very warm, sheltered position in order to thrive. Cultivation in a glasshouse is recommended in colder climates.

DUCHESSE DE BRABANT

Botanical grouping: Chinensis
Parentage: Unknown
Other names: Comtesse de Laberthe, Comtesse Ouwaroff
Other varieties: None
Year: 1857
Origin: France
Description: An Old World favourite with its translucent pearl-pink, cupped and nodding blooms, clustered and tea-scented, borne on a medium, twiggy bush that grows up to 1.2 m (4 ft). In older gardens it has been used successfully as a hedging rose, growing to about 2.5 m (8 ft) in warmer climates. It has a spreading habit and is well foliated.
Flowering: Continuously throughout spring to winter
Cultivation: Plant in good soil enriched with humus, in full sun or partial shade. It will grow well in a glasshouse or in pots.

GÉNÉRAL GALLIÉNI

Botanical grouping: Chinensis
Parentage: Souvenir de Thérése Levet x

Reine Emma des Pays-Bas
Other names: None
Other varieties: None
Year: 1899
Origin: France
Description: A robust rose with a unique 'square' look due to the way the cupped and quartered flowers have their petals folded. It has an extraordinary colour range, changing dramatically with the temperature, from rosy red, strawberry-pink overlaid with cream, through buff-yellow and wine-red, and is tea scented. A vigorous, wiry bush, relatively thorn-free, it grows to 1.2 m (4 ft) and is densely foliated with with glossy, mid-green leaves.
Flowering: Recurrent flowerings from spring to summer
Cultivation: Once popular as a large standard rose. It prefers full sun and needs pruning back to curb its growth in warmer areas. It can be grown in a glasshouse or in containers.

GÉNÉRAL SCHABLIKINE

Botanical grouping: Chinensis
Parentage: Unknown
Other names: None
Other varieties: None
Year: 1878
Origin: France
Description: Abundant double, almost quartered blooms of cherry red flushed with salmon and buff, grow erect on well-spaced sprays. The sweetly scented flowers make good cut flowers for indoors. The foliage is fresh blue-green on healthy stems. Grows to approximately 1 m (3 ft).
Flowering: Profusely from spring to autumn
Cultivation: This compact plant is disease resistant and needs minimal pruning. It withstands hot weather and requires a sunny, warm position to thrive. It can also be grown in a glasshouse.

Duchesse de Brabant

Général Galliéni

Général Schablikine

Hugo Roller

Hume's Blush

Jean Ducher

R. gigantea

Other names: *R. odorata*, Hume's Blush Tea-Scented China
Other varieties: None
Year: 1810
Origin: China
Description: The first tea rose introduced from China and a parent of many hybrids. Semi-double to occasional single, tea-scented blooms, varying in colour from off-white cream to blush-pink, sometimes a brownish pink. This is a vigorous but erratic rose with glossy, mid-green foliage growing to a height of 1.5 m (5 ft).
Flowering: Recurrently from spring to summer
Cultivation: It can be grown under glass or in a warm position in full sun in well-mulched, rich soil.

JEAN DUCHER

Botanical grouping: Chinensis
Parentage: Unknown
Other names: None
Other varieties: None
Year: 1873
Origin: France
Description: Richly tea-scented, the globular soft peach-salmon double flowers change to peach-pink and blend well with the young foliage. The stems and branches seldom have thorns but the leaves may carry small thorns on the reverse. Grows to a height of up to 2 m (7 ft).
Flowering: Prolifically, repeats through spring and summer
Cultivation: Its neat low spreading habit makes it ideal for growing in larger pots. Vigorous and hardy, it has no special requirements other than a warm position in full sun.

KAISERIN AUGUSTE VIKTORIA

Botanical grouping: Chinensis
Parentage: Coquette de Lyon x Lady Mary Fitzwilliam
Other names: Sometimes known as KAV
Other varieties: None
Year: 1891
Origin: Germany
Description: A fragrant white rose, fully double and cream at the centre of the bloom when fully open. The buds are long and pointed and are set off by rich green foliage on a bush that grows to 1.5 m (5 ft).
Flowering: Spring to summer
Cultivation: A strong and compact bushy rose which responds well to a warm position in full sun or partial shade. Prune lightly to shape the bush and remove spent flower heads to encourage growth and prolific flowering.

HUGO ROLLER

Botanical grouping: Chinensis
Parentage: Unknown
Other names: None
Other varieties: None
Year: 1907
Origin: England
Description: One of the finest garden tea roses which can carry hundreds of blooms at a time when established. A compact, bushy, low variety of moderate growth. Double, large and fragrant, creamy yellow blooms are often edged with a ruby-red shading which spreads down the petals. Although the heads are carried on weak stems, the bush has very few thorns and small, rich green foliage.
Flowering: Repeats continuously from spring to summer
Cultivation: Grow in full sun or partial shade.

HUME'S BLUSH

Botanical grouping: Chinensis
Parentage: Thought to be *R. chinensis* x

Lady Hillingdon

LADY HILLINGDON

Botanical grouping: Chinensis
Parentage: Papa Gontier x Mme Hoste
Other names: None
Other varieties: None
Year: 1910
Origin: England
Description: A consistently popular rose since its introduction. Long, copper-apricot buds open to large, loosely filled double blooms with a heady fragrance of fruit and tea scent. The thin arching stems produce attractive foliage of dark purple to brownish-red and it is a relatively thornless bush growing to 1 m (3 ft).
Flowering: Continuously until mid-winter
Cultivation: Can be grown in a glasshouse in colder climates. In the garden it prefers a sunny, protected position in well-mulched soil. It can also be grown in pots.

LADY ROBERTS

Botanical grouping: Chinensis
Parentage: Sport of Anna Olivier
Other names: None
Other varieties: None
Year: 1902
Origin: France
Description: Long, pointed, apricot buds open to double blooms of rich apricot-orange flushed with coppery-red, although the colour may vary considerably. The bush is vigorous but the rose stems are weak, producing a nodding effect. It grows to a height of 3 m (10 ft).
Flowering: Repeats throughout spring and summer
Cultivation: Hardy and vigorous, this is a rose for growing in pots, in the glasshouse or in a garden bed where it will thrive in full sun. Prune back after flowering.

LORRAINE LEE

Botanical grouping: Chinensis
Parentage: Thought to be Jessie Clark (a

Lorraine Lee

seedling of *R. gigantea*) x Capitaine Miller (a seedling of General Schlablikine)
Other names: None
Other varieties: None
Year: 1924
Origin: Australia
Description: A vigorous, Australian-bred rose producing elegant, semi-double, open and cupped blooms in shades of rosy-apricot and pink. The foliage is rich green and glossy with plum-coloured stems overlaid with silver. The fragrance is fruity.

Flowering: Early spring to late summer. In milder climates it also flowers through winter.
Cultivation: A healthy hedging rose which may flower in winter if pruned hard in late summer. Best kept as a shrub as it may be too rampant in some gardens. Not hardy enough for northern Europe.

MARIE VAN HOUTTE

Botanical grouping: Chinensis
Parentage: Mme de Tartas x Mme Falcot
Other names: None
Other varieties: None
Year: 1871
Origin: France
Description: Very graceful and nodding flowers have high centres suffused with cream and are blushed at the edges with bright pink tinged with orange. The foliage is glossy and rich dark green on a bush growing to 1 m (3 ft).
Flowering: Continuously throughout spring and summer
Cultivation: Free-flowering and vigorous but inclined to sprawl. Best grown against a warm wall where it may grow to 2 m (7 ft). It can also be grown in pots or in a glasshouse.

Marie van Houtte

Mme Lombard

Monsieur Tillier

Mrs Dudley Cross

Mrs B.R. Cant

Niphetos

MME LOMBARD

Botanical grouping: Chinensis
Parentage: Mme de Tartas seedling
Other names: Mme Lambard
Other varieties: None
Year: 1878
Origin: France
Description: Carmine-pink in the bud, it opens to large, double blooms of rich pink-salmon, deeper in the centre. The colours are much stronger in cooler weather. Flowers are profuse and tea-scented. A vigorous bush with dark green foliage growing to 1 m (3 ft)
Flowering: Continuously throughout spring and summer
Cultivation: Susceptible to mildew in dry weather. Plant in full sun and water well in summer. It can also be grown in pots.

MONSIEUR TILLIER

Botanical grouping: Chinensis
Parentage: Unknown
Other names: None
Other varieties: None
Year: 1891
Origin: France

Description: A tall and vigorous bush with a lax habit and a good covering of mid-green foliage. The double flowers are a deep, rich red tinged with violet.
Flowering: Continuously throughout summer.
Cultivation: Easy to cultivate in a wide range of soils, however may need some protection in very cold climates. Often grown under glass.

MRS B.R. CANT

Botanical grouping: Chinensis
Parentage: Unknown
Other names: None
Other varieties: None
Year: 1901
Origin: England
Description: The very full, double, cupped blooms, are deep rosy-pink merging to silver-rose in the centre and buff-yellow at the base. The outstanding fragrance and long stems make this a very good cutting rose. It grows to a height of 2 m (7 ft).
Flowering: Very floriferous throughout spring and summer.
Cultivation: A vigorous trouble-free rose

that thrives in a warm sunny position. Remove dead-heads to prolong flowering.

MRS DUDLEY CROSS

Botanical grouping: Chinensis
Parentage: Unknown
Other names: None
Other varieties: None
Year: 1907
Origin: England
Description: Large, perfectly formed double blooms of creamy yellow, sometimes flushed with pink, this is a favourite with rose growers because of its autumn flowering when the blooms may turn to crimson. It is almost thornless and has a distinctive, rich and exotic fruit and tea fragrance, making it a good cutting rose. It normally grows to a 1.2 m (4 ft) high, more in a favoured site.
Flowering: Spring to autumn.
Cultivation: A vigorous and attractive bush that likes a protected situation that is warm and sunny. Prune lightly after flowering.

NIPHETOS

Botanical grouping: Chinensis
Parentage: Unknown
Other names: None
Other varieties: None
Year: 1843
Origin: France
Description: An old favourite for bridal bouquets, the elegant, tapering buds open to large, tulip-shaped, lemon-cream flowers. The central paper-white petals remain closed over the centre for some time, creating an effect similar to a camellia. It has a sweet, tea perfume and the vigorous bush grows to 1.5m (5 ft) with light green foliage.
Flowering: Repeats throughout spring and summer
Cultivation: Once cultivated extensively in glasshouses for florists, where it creates the best blooms, this rose can also be grown in pots or in the garden in full sun.

PAPA GONTIER

Botanical grouping: Chinensis
Parentage: Unknown
Other names: None
Other varieties: None
Year: 1883
Origin: France
Description: Slightly scented and very floriferous, this is a popular old rose. The large semi-double, loosely cupped blooms of rose-pink have a carmine reverse. It was once grown mostly under glass for florists and is a good cutting rose. The bush can be wiry and thorny with sparse glossy, dark green leaves. Grows to 1 m (3 ft) and more in warmer areas.
Flowering: Almost continuously through spring and summer, and even into winter in warmer climates
Cultivation: Hardy and reliable, and versatile enough to thrive in full sun against a trellis or wall, in a glasshouse or in pots.

RIVAL DE PAESTUM

Botanical grouping: Chinensis
Parentage: Unknown
Other names: None
Other varieties: None
Year: 1848
Origin: England
Description: An uncommon old-fashioned rose, the pale pink buds open to creamy white, loosely double, nodding and scented blooms. They are well set off by a densely foliated bush growing to 1 m (3 ft) of dark bronze-green leaves.
Flowering: Almost continuously throughout spring and summer
Cultivation: Plant in a warm sunny position in rich soil. Several bushes can be massed to create an informal hedge. It will also grow in a glasshouse or in pots.

ROSETTE DELIZY

Botanical grouping: Chinensis
Parentage: Général Galliéni x Comtesse Bardi
Other names: None
Other varieties: None
Year: 1922
Origin: France
Description: Cadmium-yellow edged with bronze-red double blooms flower profusely on a quite branchy bush that grows to 1 m (3 ft) with good foliage. A very fragrant rose.
Flowering: Continuously from spring to summer
Cultivation: A very vigorous and healthy bush requiring little more than full sun, occasional mulching and light pruning at the end of summer. It can be cultivated in a glasshouse or in pots.

SAFRANO

Botanical grouping: Chinensis
Parentage: Unknown
Other names: None
Other varieties: None
Year: 1839
Origin: France
Description: This is one of the oldest tea roses and is very effective when grown in groups. Elegant, long, saffron-yellow buds open to pale buff-coloured flowers that are

Rosette Delizy

Safrano

semi-double, large, loose and tea-scented. It is very proliferous, even into winter in warmer climates. The foliage is mid-green and dense and the bush grows to 1 m (3 ft).
Flowering: Almost continuously from spring to summer
Cultivation: Grow in groups or in pots in full sun and in a protected position. It may be grown in a glasshouse. In warmer climates it can grow up to 2 m (7 ft).

SNOWFLAKE

Botanical grouping: Chinensis
Parentage: Possibly a sport of Mme Bravy
Other names: Marie Lambert
Other varieties: None
Year: 1886
Origin: France
Description: Closely resembling its parent, the blooms are fully double and the cupped petals have a pointed centre. It is pure white and fragrant with good foliage on a healthy bush growing to 2 m (7 ft).
Flowering: Repeats throughout spring and summer
Cultivation: Plant in a warm, sunny position protected from cold and winds in ground that has been well worked with mulch and organic matter.

Snowflake

SOUVENIR D'UN AMI

Botanical grouping: Chinensis
Parentage: Unknown
Other names: None
Other varieties: None
Year: 1846
Origin: France
Description: An old favourite with rose growers and one which merits a prominent position in the garden. The large, slightly cupped flowers, almost circular, are of a soft salmon-rose colour with a deeper tone on the outer petals. The colour deepens in autumn to a rosy carmine. It is highly perfumed. The foliage can grow quite leathery with age, rolling slightly at the edges with a deep port-wine sheen on the reverse. A vigorous plant to 2.5 m (8 ft).
Flowering: Repeats throughout spring to autumn
Cultivation: A sturdy, healthy bush that can be grown in the garden, a glasshouse or in pots. It requires a light pruning after each flowering and will continue flowering well into winter in warmer climates. Water well and mulch occasionally.

Souvenir d'un Ami

WHITE DUCHESSE DE BRABANT

Botanical grouping: Chinensis
Parentage: Thought to be a sport of Duchesse de Brabant
Other names: None
Other varieties: None
Year: Unknown
Origin: Unknown
Description: Like its parent except that it is pearly white with a pale apricot-pink centre. The elegant buds are pale pink and the blooms have a rich fragrance. Grows to 2.5 m (8 ft), has a spreading habit and is well foliated.
Flowering: Continuously from spring to winter
Cultivation: Plant in full sun or partial shade in good soil in the garden, in pots or in a glasshouse.

WHITE MAMAN COCHET

Botanical grouping: Chinensis
Parentage: Sport of Maman Cochet
Other names: None
Other varieties: None
Year: 1896

Origin: United States
Description: The strongly fragrant, white blooms are large, about 10 cm (4 in) across, heavy, and may show a blush pink overtone in cooler weather. They are borne profusely on a bushy plant, with dark green, leathery foliage, to about 1 m (3 ft).
Flowering: Continuously throughout spring and summer
Cultivation: Treat in the same way as its parent. Plant in full sun in the garden or in pots. Can also be grown in a glasshouse.

White Maman Cochet

Hybrid Perpetual Roses

This rose is often described as the bridge between old and new roses, having evolved from four hybrid groups (noisettes, bourbons, Portlands and hybrid Chinas). In form, many hybrid perpetuals resemble modern roses—stiff and leggy with sparse foliage, although there is a great variety of shapes and forms, including some climbers. The flowers, classically cupped and quartered, are in the white through pink, crimson, purple and maroon colour range, with some outstanding striped varieties.

Flowering is recurrent, although the second flowering is less vigorous. Most varieties need a good pruning back each year at the end of flowering, with long shoots shortened and dead or weak growth removed.

American Beauty

AMERICAN BEAUTY

Botanical grouping: Chinensis
Parentage: Unknown
Other names: Mme Ferdinand Jamin
Other varieties: None
Year: 1875
Origin: France
Description: Long-stemmed variety, suited to arrangements and bouquets, with double, rounded carmine-pink flowers and crimson shades. Extremely fragrant. Compact bush to 1 m (3 ft).
Flowering: Repeat flowering
Cultivation: Well suited to growing in a pot or tub; was traditionally grown as a glasshouse rose. Cut back long shoots, and remove dead or weak stems after flowering.

ANNA DE DIESBACH

Botanical grouping: Chinensis
Parentage: La Reine x seedling
Other names: Gloire de Paris
Other varieties: None
Year: 1858
Origin: France
Description: A slightly leggy but leafy shrub which grows to 1.5 m (5 ft), bearing rich pink, strongly fragrant flowers shaded with deeper pink. Blooms initially show a cup shape but later flatten out.
Flowering: Recurrent flowering
Cultivation: Suited to container growing as well as use in the garden. If the plant is weak, or not doing well, a hard cut-back may restore health. Do this when all flowering has finished in late summer or autumn.

ARDS ROVER

Botanical grouping: Chinensis
Parentage: Unknown
Other names: None
Other varieties: None

Year: 1898
Origin: Northern Ireland
Description: Excellent climbing rose for situations where very prolific growth is not required. Spreads to a moderate 3 m (10 ft) high and 2 m (6 ft) wide, with rich crimson, strongly fragrant and shapely flowers and abundant dark green foliage.
Flowering: Repeat flowering
Cultivation: Should be carefully inspected for mildew on the new growth each season. Unless long shoots are being tied down, prune back strongly after flowering.

BARON GIROD DE L'AIN

Botanical grouping: Chinensis
Parentage: Sport of Eugène Fürst
Other names: None

Other varieties: None
Year: 1897
Origin: France
Description: Appealing, unusual rose with white tips to its crimson petals, giving the appearance of slightly ragged edges, with a good scent. Double, cupped blooms borne in clusters on stems with substantial thorns and thick dark green leaves, giving the shrub a slightly untidy look, but it is a vigorous grower to 1.5 m (5 ft).
Flowering: Repeat flowering
Cultivation: A hardy plant which will tolerate poorer soil conditions. Prune back hard at the end of summer to control vigorous growth.

Baron Girod de l'Ain

BARONESS ROTHSCHILD

Botanical grouping: Chinensis
Parentage: Sport of Souvenir de la Reine d'Angleterre
Other names: Baronne Adolphe de Rothschild
Other varieties: None
Year: 1868
Origin: France
Description: Beautiful bush with strong, thick stems and grey-green foliage, growing to 1.5 m (5 ft). Double cup-shaped flowers with broad outer petals curling around the inner ones, in a delightful light rose pink. Deeply scented.
Flowering: Prolific flowering during the season, when the bush will be nearly covered in blooms, and some later flowering.
Cultivation: Ideally suited to growing as a border or bedding specimen, or in a container. Will tolerate quite poor soils. Prune back long shoots, and remove any weak stems or dead wood after flowering has finished.

BARONNE PRÉVOST

Botanical grouping: Chinensis
Parentage: Unknown
Other names: None
Other varieties: None
Year: 1842
Origin: France
Description: Very pretty buds open flat to large double blooms in deep rose pink with lighter shading toward the edges. The flowers are a mass of petals around a button eye, and are richly fragrant. The vigorous bush is upright and shrubby with stout thorns, growing to 1.5 m (5 ft).
Flowering: Recurrent flowering during summer, with some later flowers.
Cultivation: This is a long-lived rose which can be seen in many old gardens. It will tolerate a degree of neglect and relatively poor soil.

Baroness Rothschild

Baronne Prévost

BLACK PRINCE

Botanical grouping: Chinensis
Parentage: Unknown
Other names: None
Other varieties: None
Year: 1866
Origin: England
Description: A strong grower, reaching 1.5 m (5 ft) with attractive foliage and buds. The flowers are very dark crimson to virtually black in colour, opening to an attractive cup shape, with a sweet fragrance.
Flowering: Repeat flowering
Cultivation: Should be carefully watched for signs of mildew. To keep the plant growing vigorously, prune back strongly each year after flowering has finished.

CROWN PRINCE

Botanical grouping: Chinensis
Parentage: Unknown
Other names: None
Other varieties: None
Year: 1880
Origin: England
Description: A neat, compact bush with dark green leaves, growing to 1 m (3 ft). The flower is fully double and attractively coloured in shades of crimson and purple.
Flowering: Repeat flowering
Cultivation: Can be grown as a container specimen. Little or no pruning required apart from the routine removal of dead wood or weak stem growth.

Dembrowski

Eclair

DEMBROWSKI

Botanical grouping: Chinensis
Parentage: Unknown
Other names: None
Other varieties: None
Year: 1864
Origin: France
Description: A medium-sized bush of vigorous habit and clear green foliage, growing to 1.5 m (5 ft). The flowers are attractively shaped double blooms in red with purple tones.
Flowering: Prolific repeat flowering throughout summer.
Cultivation: Hardy plant requiring no special treatment. Prefers full sun, and a good pruning after flowering has finished.

DR ANDRY

Botanical grouping: Chinensis
Parentage: Unknown
Other names: None
Other varieties: None
Year: 1864
Origin: France
Description: Attractive dark green bush with strong growth to 1.5 m (5 ft). Double flowers are only mildly scented, and are coloured an appealing clear red with slightly darker tones in the middle.
Flowering: Repeat flowering
Cultivation: Suitable for container as well as garden cultivation. Remove dead wood annually.

DUKE OF EDINBURGH

Botanical grouping: Chinensis
Parentage: Général Jacqueminot x unknown
Other names: None
Other varieties: None
Year: 1868
Origin: England
Description: Formerly a lanky grower, this

rose appears to have lost vigour, and makes a small bushy shrub, growing as wide as it is high—60 cm x 60 cm (2 ft x 2 ft). Semi-double flowers are richly scented and coloured clear scarlet blushing to crimson.
Flowering: Recurrent during summer
Cultivation: Requires rich soil if it is to bloom successfully. Mulch and feed routinely, and prune back at the end of the flowering season.

DUPUY JAMAIN

Botanical grouping: Chinensis
Parentage: Unknown
Other names: None
Other varieties: None
Year: 1868

Origin: France
Description: A vigorous, upright shrub with attractive grey-green foliage and few thorns, reaching 1.5 m (5 ft). The large flowers are strongly scented and shapely, coloured a rich cerise with red tones.
Flowering: Repeat flowers, good late in season
Cultivation: Will tolerate relatively poor soil conditions and can be grown in a container in a sunny position. Annual pruning keeps the plant in good shape.

ECLAIR

Botanical grouping: Chinensis
Parentage: Général Jacqueminot x unknown
Other names: None
Other varieties: None
Year: 1833
Origin: France
Description: Upright bush growing to 1.5 m (5 ft) with relatively scant foliage. The flowers are very dark red with tightly packed petals opening flat from a central whorl, and fragrant.
Flowering: Recurrent
Cultivation: Can be used as a container specimen. Requires good soil and careful mulching and watering for successful results.

ELISA BOËLLE

Botanical grouping: Chinensis
Parentage: Unknown
Other names: None

Elisa Boëlle

Other varieties: None
Year: 1869
Origin: France
Description: A neat, compact, leafy bush which grows strongly to reach 1.5 m (5 ft). The flowers are deep pink and well scented, forming a cup shape.
Flowering: Recurrent during summer
Cultivation: Can be grown successfully in a container as well as in the garden. In both cases, full sun is required, and a regular pruning at the end of the flowering season.

EMPEREUR DU MAROC

Botanical grouping: Chinensis
Parentage: Géant de Batailles seedling
Other names: Emperor of Morocco
Other varieties: None
Year: 1858
Origin: France
Description: The flower is a portwine colour, a mixture of maroon and crimson, and the medium-sized double blooms, which have a prominent centre, open flat and are carried in large clusters. The bush can grow to 2 m (7 ft) and growth is vigorous on thorny branches. Strong, rich fragrance.
Flowering: Some recurrent flowering after the main flush.
Cultivation: This rose is susceptible to black spot and mildew. The heavy clusters of flowers may weigh down the branches, and judicious pruning or support may be needed. Needs to be in light shade during the very hottest part of summer.

EUGÈNE FÜRST

Botanical grouping: Chinensis
Parentage: Baron de Bonstetten x unknown
Other names: None
Other varieties: Général Korolkov
Year: 1875
Origin: Luxembourg
Description: Large double cup-shaped flowers in deep crimson red with purple tones and a lighter reverse. Rich fragrance. The upright bush grows to 1.5m (5 ft), with prolific, dark green leaves.
Flowering: Recurrent
Cultivation: A valuable garden plant which can also be grown in a pot. Keep the area around the base of the plant free from weeds, and prune at the end of summer.

FERDINAND PICHARD

Botanical grouping: Chinensis
Parentage: Unknown
Other names: None
Other varieties: None
Year: 1921

Empereur du Maroc

Origin: France
Description: Often mistakenly classed as bourbon, this rose carries tight clusters of semi-double fragrant flowers striped in carmine, pink and white which open to a cup shape, and is regarded as one of the very best striped roses. The flowers will fade somewhat as they open, but the stripes remain clear. The shrub is a vigorous grower, reaching as high as 2 m (7 ft) with bushy, light green foliage.
Flowering: Repeat flowering mid-summer through autumn.
Cultivation: This rose can be used for hedging. Will tolerate relatively poor soil conditions. It has a somewhat lanky habit and should be pegged down.

FISHER HOLMES

Botanical grouping: Chinensis
Parentage: Possibly Maurice Bernardin seedling

Ferdinand Pichard

Fisher Holmes

Frau Karl Druschki

Other names: Fisher and Holmes
Other varieties: None
Year: 1865
Origin: France
Description: A vigorous, upright bush with fragrant double blooms in scarlet shading to crimson. Grows quite strongly to reach a height of 1.5 m (5 ft) and displays attractive foliage. Fisher Holmes was a popular rose in Victorian times.
Flowering: Flowers for a long period during summer
Cultivation: Unfortunately, this rose can be prone to disease and needs careful tending. Good container specimen, however, if positioned in full sun.

FRAU KARL DRUSCHKI

Botanical grouping: Chinensis
Parentage: Merveille de Lyon x Madame Caroline Testout
Other names: Reine des Neiges, Snow Queen, White American Beauty
Other varieties: Climbing form which grows to 4.5 m (15 ft).
Year: 1901
Origin: Germany

Description: One of the most justifiably admired white roses. Pink-tinted buds open to splendid, high-centred, pure white flowers with many petals, which hold up well as cut flowers. Unscented. The shrub grows vigorously to 1.5 m (5 ft) on arching stems with dull, rather leathery leaves. Some believe this rose is really a hybrid tea, but it is correctly classified as a hybrid perpetual.

Flowering: Prolific blooms of excellent quality, recurrent.

Cultivation: This rose reacts badly to rain which causes the flowers to close into brownish balls, but it will tolerate quite poor soil and loves dry climates. Pegging down the long shoots will encourage profuse flowering on the side stems. Pruning should be minimal.

GÉNÉRAL JACQUEMINOT

Botanical grouping: Chinensis
Parentage: Gloire des Rosomanes seedling (possibly x Géant de Batailles)
Other names: General Jack, Jack Rose, La Brillante
Other varieties: None
Year: 1853
Origin: France
Description: This lovely rose played a role in the breeding of many modern red roses. Long-stemmed blooms, richly scented, in deep crimson with scarlet touches. A vigorous bush with attractive bright green leaves, which grows to 1.5 m (5 ft).
Flowering: Recurrent
Cultivation: Can suffer from rust later in the summer. Useful border rose. Keep the area at the base of the plant free from weeds, and avoid watering the foliage during summer.

Georg Arends

Général Jacqueminot

GEORG ARENDS

Botanical grouping: Chinensis
Parentage: Frau Karl Druschki x La France
Other names: Fortuné Besson
Other varieties: None
Year: 1910
Origin: Germany
Description: Splendid, soft pink rose with pink-cream shades on the reverse, and very fragrant. Ideal specimen for flower arrangements, with a lovely 'cabbage rose', over-blown quality. A strong, vigorous grower, almost thornless, with abundant blooms, reaching a height of 2 m (7 ft).
Flowering: Produces flowers throughout most of the summer
Cultivation: Tolerant of poorer soil conditions. The nature of its growth makes it eminently suited to use as a hedging plant. Remove dead wood or weak shoots annually.

GLOIRE DE BRUXELLES

Botanical grouping: Chinensis
Parentage: Souvenir de William Wood x Lord Macaulay
Other names: Gloire de l'Exposition
Other varieties: None
Year: 1889

Origin: Luxembourg
Description: Superb, multi-petalled large blooms are scented and open to a rosette shape. The colour is deep crimson with purple touches. The quality of the flowers makes up for the deficiencies of the bush which is small, reaching only 1.2 m (4 ft), but rather floppy.
Flowering: Recurrent flowering.
Cultivation: May need training to contain its unruliness. Prefers an open, sunny position and moderately rich garden soil.

Gloire de Bruxelles

Gloire de Ducher

Henry Nevard

John Hopper

GLOIRE DE DUCHER

Botanical grouping: Chinensis
Parentage: Unknown
Other names: Germania
Other varieties: None
Year: 1865
Origin: France
Description: A strong bush which can grow to over 2 m (7 ft), with arched branches and dark green leaves. Beautiful, loosely arranged, very large and fragrant double blooms of rich crimson-purple with maroon touches, velvety in texture, showing button eyes when fully open.
Flowering: Flowers freely during summer, and bears magnificent late blooms in autumn.
Cultivation: This tall, arching bush needs to be attached to a wall or pillar. It will tolerate less than perfect soil conditions, but can be susceptible to mildew.

GLOIRE LYONNAISE

Botanical grouping: Chinensis
Parentage: Baroness Rothschild x Mme Falcot
Other names: None
Other varieties: None
Year: 1885
Origin: France
Description: Very large, cup-shaped creamy white blooms open from plump pink buds. The flowers are sweetly scented. Healthy, vigorous bush with few thorns and strong stems, leathery foliage. The bush shows an upright habit, though it is relatively small (1.2 m, 4 ft).
Flowering: Reliable repeat flowering throughout summer.
Cultivation: This rose will respond well to cultivation in a pot, or can be grown as an effective hedge. It will stand poor soil conditions. If growing as a hedge, trim back weak growth annually to encourage a bushier habit.

HENRY NEVARD

Botanical grouping: Chinensis
Parentage: Unknown
Other names: None
Other varieties: None
Year: 1924
Origin: England
Description: The leaves are dark green and of tough texture on a strong, compact bush growing to 1.2 m (4 ft). Very large, double blooms in a cup shape, richly fragrant and crimson-scarlet in colour.
Flowering: Recurrent
Cultivation: A robust bush requiring no special treatment. Prune back strongly at the end of each summer to control growth if necessary.

HER MAJESTY

Botanical grouping: Chinensis
Parentage: Mabel Morrison x Canary
Other names: None
Other varieties: None
Year: 1885
Origin: England
Description: The shrub bears large greyish leaves and is a strong grower, though

Gloire Lyonnaise

reaching only 1 m (3 ft). The double flowers are very large and coloured a glorious clear pink.
Flowering: Recurrent
Cultivation: Makes a good container as well as garden specimen. It is generally a robust shrub but can be prone to mildew. Keep the area at the base of the plant free from weeds to prevent this problem.

HUGH DICKSON

Botanical grouping: Chinensis
Parentage: Lord Bacon x Grüss an Teplitz
Other names: None
Other varieties: None
Year: 1905
Origin: Northern Ireland
Description: Large, double, scented flowers in bright crimson, shaped similarly to a hybrid tea. The blooms are borne in clusters on long shoots, and the foliage is dark green with a reddish tinge. Lanky growth, reaching 3 m (10 ft).
Flowering: Repeat flowering
Cultivation: This rose will flower only at the tips unless supported, and is in fact an ideal pillar specimen. Old shoots can be cut out at the end of flowering.

Hugh Dickson

JOHN HOPPER

Botanical grouping: Chinensis
Parentage: Jules Margottin x Mme Vidot
Other names: None
Other varieties: None
Year: 1862
Origin: England
Description: An upright plant of neat but thorny habit, growing strongly to 1.2 m (4 ft). Bears large clear pink flowers showing lavender shades as they fade. Good fragrance. This is an outstanding specimen.
Flowering: Recurrent
Cultivation: This rose will tolerate most soil conditions, and will perform well in a container or when used as a hedge. Pruning should only be necessary to remove dead wood.

LA REINE

Botanical grouping: Chinensis
Parentage: Unknown
Other names: Reine des Francais, Rose de la Reine
Other varieties: None
Year: 1842
Origin: France
Description: Large globular blooms opening to a cup shape of massed petals coloured silvery pink with a hint of lilac. Very fragrant. Upright, bushy shrub with good foliage reaching about 1 m (3 ft).
Flowering: Continued flowering during summer
Cultivation: An excellent choice where space is limited, or as a container specimen. Very hardy and easy to cultivate in a wide range of soils and conditions.

La Reine

Le Havre

LE HAVRE

Botanical grouping: Chinensis
Parentage: Unknown
Other names: None
Other varieties: None
Year: 1871
Origin: France
Description: Dense, double, perfectly shaped flowers in very deep red. Scented. The bush reaches 1.5 m (5 ft) and is a strong, vigorous grower with dark green, leathery leaves.
Flowering: Good repeat flowering
Cultivation: A hardy rose which will grow well in a container. If growth is too vigorous, prune back after flowering. Mulch around the base of the plant to suppress weed growth.

MABEL MORRISON

Botanical grouping: Chinensis
Parentage: Baroness Rothschild sport
Other names: None
Other varieties: None
Year: 1878
Origin: England
Description: This is a delightful white version of the outstanding light pink Baroness Rothschild , and shows similar characteristics, though it differs in having no scent. The flowers begin as a very pale pink, fading to pure white, though a few flushes of pink may emerge in some weather conditions. Makes an excellent cut flower. The well-foliaged shrub reaches 1.5 m (5 ft).
Flowering: Free-flowering and recurrent.
Cultivation: A good border or pot-plant. Will tolerate a wide range of soils. Prune back dead wood or weak stems only.

MME ALFRED DE ROUGEMONT

Botanical grouping: Chinensis
Parentage: Blanche Lafitte x Sappho
Other names: None
Other varieties: None
Year: 1862
Origin: France
Description: A rare hybrid with clusters of rose-pink buds opening to sweetly perfumed, pink and white, medium-sized double flowers. Vigorous growth to 4 m (13 ft).
Flowering: Spring to summer
Cultivation: Plant in rich soil in a warm sunny position, sheltered from frosts and cold winds.

MME VICTOR VERDIER

Botanical grouping: Chinensis
Parentage: Sénateur Vaisse x unknown
Other names: None
Other varieties: None
Year: 1863
Origin: France
Description: Large, deep crimson double blooms with a silvery pink underside. The flowers open flat to a 'cabbage rose' shape and have a rich fragrance. A sturdy and vigorous shrub (although flower stems are weak), with good foliage. Reaches 1.5 m (5 ft).
Flowering: One major flowering with some recurrence.
Cultivation: A hardy rose which will tolerate most soil conditions. Makes a good hedging specimen. Prune back weak stems in late summer or when flowering has finished.

MRS HARKNESS

Botanical grouping: Chinensis
Parentage: Sport of Heinrich Schultheis
Other names: Paul's Early Blush
Other varieties: None
Year: 1893
Origin: England
Description: A bushy, upright grower to 1 m (3 ft). Bears blush pink flowers of a good size and cupped form, well filled with petals, and with sweet fragrance. Light green foliage.
Flowering: Repeat flowering.
Cultivation: Will tolerate most soil conditions. Cut longer shoots by one-third to one-half in autumn, or peg them down to encourage extra flowering side shoots.

MRS JOHN LAING

Botanical grouping: Chinensis
Parentage: François Michelin seedling
Other names: None
Other varieties: None
Year: 1887
Origin: England
Description: This rose is regarded as one of the very best hybrid perpetuals. It is justly admired for its elegantly symmetrical flowers, which open to an almost blowsy shape from pointed buds, and its attractive light green foliage. The blooms are rich silvery pink in colour and well scented. Long stemmed and ideal for picking, they will hold their shape for several days. The vigorous bush can grow as high as 2 m (7 ft), but is more usually around 1.5 m (5 ft).
Flowering: Free-flowering and recurrent
Cultivation: Makes an appealing bushy shrub, ideal for use in containers or as hedging. It is hardy and will stand a wide range of soil conditions.

Mme Victor Verdier

Mrs Harkness

PAUL NEYRON

Botanical grouping: Chinensis
Parentage: Victor Verdier x Anna de Diesbach
Other names: None
Other varieties: None
Year: 1869
Origin: France
Description: This shrub bears enormous lightly scented flowers; which have been described as the largest of any rose (up to 17.5 cm/ 7in). The blooms are warm rose pink flushed lilac with ruffled petals, hold their colour well and have an appearance of

Mrs John Laing

Paul Ricault

Paul Neyron

charming disarray when fully open. The rose gave its name to a once-fashionable colour, Neyron pink. It is a vigorous bush which can grow to 2 m (7 ft) with long stems and leathery but glossy dark green leaves. Good cut flower.
Flowering: Constant repeat flowers in summer with some autumn flowering.
Cultivation: A hardy plant tolerant of quite poor soils. A good container or hedge specimen. Vigorous growth can be controlled by hard pruning at the end of summer.

PAUL RICAULT

Botanical grouping: Chinensis
Parentage: Unknown
Other names: None
Other varieties: None
Year: 1845
Origin: France
Description: The large, deep pink flower is similar to a centifolia. It is fully double, saucer-shaped, high centred, borne in clusters, and has a good fragrance. The shrub has lanky, arching stems with strong thorns and good foliage. Grows to 1.5 m (5 ft).
Flowering: Free-flowering during summer with some recurrence in autumn
Cultivation: A hardy plant tolerant of most soils. Prune back after flowering, removing all dead wood and spindly growth.

PRINCE CAMILLE DE ROHAN

Botanical grouping: Chinensis
Parentage: Possibly Général Jacqueminot x Géant de Batailles
Other names: La Rosière
Other varieties: None
Year: 1861
Origin: France
Description: The full double flowers are noted for their unusual formation and colour, comprising many closely packed overlapping petals in a colour combination of very dark maroon/purple with orange-brown touches. The bush reaches 1.5 m (5 ft), and the flowers are borne on spindly stems.
Flowering: Not a reliable repeat flowerer.
Cultivation: Susceptible to disease, should be kept separate from other roses. Generally grown only by enthusiasts.

REINE DES VIOLETTES

Botanical grouping: Chinensis
Parentage: Seedling of Puis IX
Other names: Queen of the Violets
Other varieties: None
Year: 1860
Origin: France
Description: This virtually thornless upright shrub has glossy grey-green foliage and bears splendid, richly fragrant quartered flowers, opening flat, with button eyes. They are coloured deep red-violet and pass through every shade of purple, lavender and violet with greyish touches as they mature. They do not last long after opening, but in full flush they are superb, and resemble a bourbon or gallica. Grows up to 1.5 m (5 ft)
Flowering: Profuse recurrent blooming, with an especially good show in autumn.
Cultivation: Needs plenty of nourishment and good soil, and in hot areas constant watering, if it is to perform successfully. Judicious, fairly hard pruning will also reap rewards.

ROGER LAMBELIN

Botanical grouping: Chinensis
Parentage: Sport of Prince Camille de Rohan, or less probably of Fisher Holmes
Other names: None
Other varieties: None
Year: 1890
Origin: France
Description: A striking deep scarlet double flower with a narrow white line on the edge of the petals giving it a carnation-like appearance. Extremely fragrant. Grows to 1.2 m (4 ft).
Flowering: Summer flowering with some later blooms.
Cultivation: This rose requires good soil

conditions, and in dry areas should be heavily mulched and well watered. Because of its tendency to develop rust and mildew it should be kept away from other roses.

SIDONIE

Botanical grouping: Chinensis
Parentage: Unknown
Other names: Sydonie
Other varieties: None
Year: 1847
Origin: France
Description: This small bush (1 m, 3 ft) bears clusters of bright pink, double medium-sized flowers. The flowers are scented, and the plant is a strong grower. The foliage, though not particularly attractive, forms a neat bush.
Flowering: Prolific recurrent flowering through the summer.
Cultivation: Enjoys most kinds of soil, including quite poor conditions, and can be successfully grown in a container. Susceptible to black spot, so keep the area at the base of the plant weed-free.

SOUVENIR DU DOCTEUR JAMAIN

Botanical grouping: Chinensis
Parentage: Général Jacqueminot x Charles Lefèbvre
Other names: None
Other varieties: None
Year: 1865
Origin: France
Description: Velvety port-wine coloured rose with a rich fragrance. Its semi-double flowers open cupped on virtually thornless stems, and the bush can grow to 3 m (10 ft).
Flowering: Repeat flowering
Cultivation: This rose reacts badly to very hot sun. Its flowers may burn and it should therefore be grown in semi shade. Requires careful feeding to give its best.

SPENCER

Botanical grouping: Chinensis
Parentage: Merveille de Lyon sport
Other names: None
Other varieties: None
Year: 1892
Origin: England
Description: Rounded pink buds open flat to full double blooms in soft white-pink with a white reverse. Neat, dark foliage and strong growth to 1.5 m (5 ft).
Flowering: Recurrent flowering
Cultivation: May be grown in a container as well as in the garden. Prune only to remove dead wood or weak stem growth.

Sidonie

Reine des Violettes

Souvenir du Docteur Jamain
Roger Lambelin

SURPASSING BEAUTY

Botanical grouping: Chinensis
Parentage: Unknown
Other names: Woolverstone Church Rose, Surpassing Beauty of Woolverstone
Other varieties: None
Year: Rediscovered by Brooke, and reintroduced in 1980 by Beales.
Origin: England
Description: Vigorous old climbing rose of unknown origin, rediscovered in an English churchyard. Dark red and very fragrant flowers opening to a lovely loose, overblown shape. Will reach 2.5 m (8 ft).
Flowering: From spring through summer
Cultivation: Will flourish even in poor conditions. Excellent for areas where other roses are difficult to cultivate.

ULRICH BRUNNER FILS

Botanical grouping: Chinensis
Parentage: Possibly Paul Neyron or Anna de Diesbach sport
Other names: Ulrich Brunner
Other varieties: None
Year: 1882
Origin: France

Ulrich Brunner Fils

Description: Richly fragrant large and loose-cupped flowers in rose-red, shading to carmine. Vigorous, upright bush with good dark foliage and few thorns, which will reach 2 m (7 ft). A good cut flower.
Flowering: Numerous flowers in the early growing period, fewer in the summer, with another flush in the autumn.
Cultivation: Should be kept in shape by pruning which also aids growth. Does best in clay soil but will tolerate most conditions.

VICK'S CAPRICE

Botanical grouping: Chinensis
Parentage: Archduchesse Elizabeth d'Autriche sport
Other names: None
Other varieties: None
Year: 1891
Origin: United States
Description: Striking and unusual blooms combining stripes of rose-pink, lilac-pink, white and carmine. Sweetly scented. The upright bush grows to a modest height of around 1 m (3 ft), and has attractive light green leaves and few thorns.
Flowering: Profuse flowers over a long period

Vick's Caprice

Cultivation: Suitable for use in a container or for hedging. Will tolerate most soil conditions. Little pruning required, except for the removal of dead wood.

VICTOR VERDIER

Botanical grouping: Chinensis
Parentage: Jules Margottin x Safrano
Other names: None
Other varieties: None
Year: 1859
Origin: France
Description: Some believe this rose may be the first hybrid tea, though the classification was not used at the time of its introduction. The large double blooms are a strong rose-pink in colour and sweetly fragrant. The thorny bush, which grows to 1.5 m (5 ft), has an upright habit, with sturdy stems.
Flowering: Recurrent
Cultivation: A hardy rose which will stand most soil conditions. Successfully grown in a container. Prune back leggy growth, and remove dead wood annually.

YOLANDE D'ARAGON

Botanical grouping: Chinensis
Parentage: Unknown
Other names: None
Other varieties: None
Year: 1843
Origin: France
Description: Large double flowers which open flat. The colour is a mix of pink and purple tones, and the blooms are scented. The plant is a strong, healthy grower with attractive light-coloured foliage, and reaches 1.5 m (5 ft).
Flowering: Recurrent
Cultivation: Can be successfully grown as a container specimen as well as in the garden. Hardy, requires no special treatment. Remove dead or diseased wood annually.

Polyantha and Dwarf Polyantha Roses

An interesting small group, thought to have originated from an accidental cross between *R. multiflora* and *R. chinensis*. The foliage resembles that of *R. multiflora*, while the flowers are semi-double or double, appearing in clusters for long periods during summer and autumn. Polyanthas are the predecessor of the modern floribunda (cluster-flowered) roses and they fell from favour when this new, improved group was introduced. However, for the sake of nostalgia there are several worthwhile polyanthas and dwarf polyanthas that can be incorporated into the landscape.

Baby Faurax

BABY FAURAX

Botanical grouping: Dwarf polyantha
Parentage: Unknown
Other names: None
Other varieties: None
Year: 1924
Origin: France
Description: A free-flowering, small growing plant which produces clusters of violet blooms with white centres and yellow stamens. Foliage is large, serrated and mid-green. Grows to 50 cm (1½ ft).
Flowering: Continuously throughout summer
Cultivation: Twiggy and spindly dead wood should be removed. Can be grown successfully in a container.

BALLERINA

Botanical grouping: Polyantha
Parentage: Unknown
Other names: None
Other varieties: None
Year: 1937
Origin: England
Description: This justly popular rose bears masses of small, dainty, light pink flowers with a white centre and a paler underside, followed by tiny orange fruit. The bush, which grows to 1.2 m (4 ft), is of pleasing shape, and the flowers are set off to effect against dense mid-green foliage. Can be cut for use in arrangements.
Flowering: Flowers prolifically over a long period, through summer into autumn.
Cultivation: This delightful rose is well suited to container cultivation, provided the pot is of adequate size, and for hedging purposes. It will tolerate poor soil and some shade, and in the right conditions, such as a large bed, will spread to fill a substantial space.

Ballerina

BLOOMFIELD ABUNDANCE

Botanical grouping: Chinensis
Parentage: Sylvia x Dorothy Page-Roberts
Other names: None
Other varieties: None
Year: 1920
Origin: United States
Description: Grows to 1.8 m (6 ft) high and 1.2 m (4 ft) wide with large pyramidal sprays of small, double, salmon-pink, hybrid tea-like flowers. Young growth sprays out in a fern-like fashion. Foliage is small, leathery and semi-glossy. It is sparse on younger plants but increases with age. The wood is brown when young, but becomes greenish brown with age.
Flowering: Continuously throughout summer
Cultivation: Tolerates poorer soils. Can be used for hedging and for growing in containers.

CAMEO

Botanical grouping: Polyantha
Parentage: Orléans Rose sport
Other names: None
Other varieties: None
Year: 1932
Origin: The Netherlands
Description: Bright green, dense bush to 30 cm (1 ft) high and the same in width. The semi-double flowers are clear orange-pink, are cupped and occur in large trusses.
Flowering: Continuously throughout summer
Cultivation: This is a hardy plant which tolerates poorer soils and light shade. It can be useful as a low hedge, for bedding, or as a container plant. May be difficult to obtain. Remove dead flower heads during the summer, and in winter take out some older stems, and shorten others in order to promote new growth.

CÉCILE BRUNNER

Botanical grouping: Chinensis
Parentage: A polyantha rose x Mme de Tartas
Other names: The Sweetheart Rose, Maltese Rose, Mignon
Other varieties: Climber, White
Year: 1881
Origin: France
Description: A charming and very well-known rose. Small, compact blooms of shell pink are produced freely in huge, well-spaced clusters, on a lengthy stalk. The wood is smooth, brownish purple, sometimes spindly, with few thorns. Foliage is dark green and smooth. The flowers have a faint but distinctive scent. Grows to 1.2 m (4 ft) high and 70 cm (2 ft) wide.
Flowering: Continuously throughout summer
Cultivation: Suitable for growing under glass as well as outdoors. Can also be successfully grown in containers.

CHINA DOLL

Botanical grouping: Dwarf polyantha
Parentage: Mrs Dudley Fulton x Tom Thumb
Other names: None
Other varieties: None
Year: 1946
Origin: United States
Description: China-pink blooms, ruffled and open-cupped, are massed on very large trusses on this delightful old border rose which only grows to a height of 50 cm (1½ ft). The bush is well foliated with light green leaves.
Flowering: Spring to early winter
Cultivation: A healthy border rose providing a good display when massed in full sun or planted in pots. Trim into shape after flowering.

China Doll

Cécile Brunner

GLORIA MUNDI

Botanical grouping: Polyantha
Parentage: Sport from Superb
Other names: None
Other varieties: None
Year: 1929
Origin: The Netherlands
Description: Rounded shrub to 70 cm (2 ft) high and the same in width. Large clusters of semi-double flowers are bright orange-red.
Flowering: Continuously throughout summer
Cultivation: A fairly hardy plant, tolerating poorer soils and light shade. Suitable as a hedge or bedding plant, and as a container specimen. May be difficult to obtain. Remove dead flower heads during the summer, and in winter take out some older stems, and shorten others in order to promote new growth.

KATHARINA ZEIMET

Botanical grouping: Polyantha
Parentage: Etoile de Mai x Marie Pavie
Other names: White Baby Rambler
Other varieties: None
Year: 1901
Origin: Germany
Description: This rose has remained deservedly popular, bearing a multiplicity of white, double blooms in trusses against a background of small, dark green leaves. It is a delightful inclusion in any bed or border, especially if planted in a group. It grows to 50 cm (20 in) high and wide.
Flowering: Flowers reliably over a long period.
Cultivation: A hardy, healthy plant which can withstand weather extremes.

Katharina Zeimet

Little White Pet

Little White Pet

Marie Pavié

flowers with delicate pink tinges, which are attractively displayed against clear green foliage. The plant is bushy and relatively high for a polyantha at 75 cm (2½ ft).
Flowering: Flowers well over a long period.
Cultivation: A useful plant which will tolerate poor soil conditions and also some shade. An ornament to any bed, it also makes an attractive low hedge.

LITTLE WHITE PET

Botanical grouping: Dwarf Sempervirens
Parentage: Probably a seedling of Félicité-Perpétue
Other names: White Pet, Belle of Tehran, Little Dot
Other varieties: None
Year: 1879
Origin: United States
Description: Large clusters of small, tightly packed, creamy flowers provide a continuous display throughout the season. Growing to a height of 80 cm (2½ ft), this dwarf perpetual flowering rose can also be grown as a standard or rock garden rose.
Flowering: Summer to autumn

Cultivation: Fairly hardy and prolific even when planted in a position that is not well aspected. Sun or partial shade suit it equally well provided it receives normal rose maintenance.

MARIE-JEANNE

Botanical grouping: Polyantha
Parentage: Unknown
Other names: None
Other varieties: None
Year: 1913
Origin: France
Description: This charming rose produces substantial clusters of cup-shaped cream

MARIE PAVIÉ

Botanical grouping: Synstylae
Parentage: Unknown
Other names: Marie Pavic
Other varieties: None
Year: 1888
Origin: France
Description: A delightful cluster-flowered bush, growing to 40 cm (1¼ ft) in height, with rich green foliage and an abundance of small, blush white flowers. The flowers are very fragrant.
Flowering: Summer to autumn
Cultivation: Prefers full sun and moderately rich, well-drained soil. Suitable for a low border. Prune out dead wood in winter.

Marjorie Fair

Mignonette

Perle d'Or

MARJORIE FAIR

Botanical grouping: Polyantha
Parentage: Baby Faurax x Ballerina
Other names: Red Ballerina, Red Yesterday
Other varieties: None
Year: 1978
Origin: England
Description: Dense, spreading shrub to 1.2 m (4 ft) high and wide, with very prolific and shiny foliage. Small, fragrant, dark red flowers have white centres, and are borne in enormous clusters, making the shrub a seasonal focal point.
Flowering: Continuously throughout summer
Cultivation: A hardy shrub, but needs full sun. Useful as a specimen or for mass planting in borders and hedges. Dead-head the plant after flowering, and prune in winter, removing all dead and diseased wood. Reduce the length of healthy stems, and encourage new shoots from the base by removing some older canes.

MIGNONETTE

Botanical grouping: Polyantha
Parentage: Possibly *R. multiflora* x *R. chinensis*
Other names: None
Other varieties: None
Year: 1880
Origin: France
Description: Low growing, 50 cm–1 m (1½–3 ft), this is a very useful small rose for edging as well as for rock gardens. Very free-flowering, it bears small, double, blush-pink to white blooms borne in clusters.
Flowering: Spring to autumn
Cultivation: A hardy plant requiring little more than a good sunny position and moisture. Mulch during summer.

MISS EDITH CAVELL

Botanical grouping: Polyantha
Parentage: Sport of Orléans Rose
Other names: Edith Cavell, Nurse Cavell
Other varieties: None
Year: 1917
Origin: The Netherlands
Description: A well-foliaged, bushy plant reaching 70 cm (2 ft) and producing substantial clusters of attractive semi-double blooms in scarlet with crimson flushes.
Flowering: Long flowering season, into autumn

Cultivation: This useful rose will stand some shade and is also tolerant of most soil conditions. Suitable as a hedge or border rose and can be grown in containers.

PERLE D'OR

Botanical grouping: Chinensis
Parentage: Possibly *R. multiflora* seedling x Mme Falcot
Other names: Yellow Cécile Brunner
Other varieties: None
Year: 1884
Origin: France
Description: This vigorous and dense plant can be temperamental. In good situations it will reach over 1.8 m (6 ft) in height, but normally is only 1.2 m (4 ft) or less. It is very similar to Cécile Brunner except for the colour. Its flowers are small, beautifully shaped, creamy buff-yellow with hints of pink. It has a soft perfume. Foliage is dark green with twiggy, almost thornless stems.
Flowering: Continuously throughout summer
Cultivation: This rose is suitable for growing under glass as well as in the garden. Prune out dead or spindly wood in winter.

SPRING SONG

Botanical grouping: Polyantha
Parentage: Gartendirektor O. Linne
seedling
Other names: Unknown
Other varieties: None
Year:1954
Origin: Australia
Description: A semi-double, fragrant, rich
carmine-pink rose that blooms profusely on
a vigorous, arching bush, growing to 1 m (3 ft).
Flowering: Profusely throughout summer
Cultivation: Can be grown in a glasshouse
or a warm position in mixed borders or a
large tub. Plant in fertile soil that is composted
and well drained. Mulch in dry weather.

Spring Song

White Cécile Brunner

THE FAIRY

Botanical grouping: Polyantha
Parentage: Paul Crampel x Lady Gay
Other names. None
Other varieties: None
Year: 1932
Origin: England
Description: This versatile and pretty rose
produces large trusses of small, double
flowers in great abundance. The pink, softly
fragrant blooms are good for cut flowers.
Foliage is small, mid-green and glossy. It has
a spreading, bushy habit to 70 cm (2 ft) high
and up to 1.2 m (4 ft) wide.
Flowering: Very free-flowering; it starts
later than most roses and is then rarely out
of bloom until forced into winter dormancy.
Cultivation: A good specimen for bedding
or planting in groups. It can also be used for
partial ground cover or planted in containers. Will tolerate poorer soils and shade.

WHITE CÉCILE BRUNNER

Botanical grouping: Chinensis
Parentage: Cécile Brunner sport
Other names: None
Other varieties: None
Year: 1909
Origin: France
Description: A sport with the same
attributes and characteristics as its parent,
but is quite rare nowadays. The flowers are
white with a hint of yellow and peach. Grows
to 1.2 m (4 ft) high and 70 cm (2 ft) wide.
Flowering: Continuously throughout summer
Cultivation: Suitable for growing under
glass as well as out of doors. Also suitable
for containers.

YVONNE RABIER

Botanical grouping: Dwarf polyantha
Parentage: *R. wichuraiana* x a polyantha
Other names: None

The Fairy

Yvonne Rabier

Other varieties: None
Year: 1910
Origin: France
Description: Clusters of pure white,
double, fragrant flowers are produced amid
glossy green foliage on a compact bush to
70 cm (2 ft).
Flowering: Very free-flowering throughout
summer
Cultivation: An ideal border rose giving a
good display when massed. Plant in full sun
in soil that has been enriched with humus
and water well.

Climbing and Rambling Roses (old)

Some of the most delightful garden roses are old-fashioned climbers and ramblers, some of them growing to a great size if space permits. They vary from species roses with the simple five-petalled flower form, to some really spectacular semi-double and double flower forms. The wild roses from which they are descended are *R. moschata, R.multiflora, R. gigantea, R. wichuraiana* and *R. chinensis*. Generally, climbers have evolved as hybrids of teas and noisettes, or as sports from hybrid perpetuals and the earlier forms of hybrid teas. Ramblers, on the other hand, appear to have been more deliberately bred. Climbers and ramblers can be used to cover an unsightly wall or fence, or trained successfully onto a trellis, pergola or garden archway.

Adélaide d'Orléans

Achievement

ACHIEVEMENT

Botanical grouping: Rambler
Parentage: Sport from Dorcas
Other names: None
Other varieties: None
Year: 1925
Origin: England
Description: Produces deep, rose pink flowers in large clusters. Foliage is variegated green, cream and pink.
Flowering: Summer only
Cultivation: Cut out dead and spindly wood to keep a good shape. Prefers full sun.

ADÉLAIDE D'ORLÉANS

Botanical grouping: Sempervirens climber
Parentage: *R. sempervirens* hybrid
Other names: None
Other varieties: None
Year: 1826
Origins: France

Adélaide d'Orléans

Description: A well-foliated semi-evergreen. Produces a cascade of small, semi-double, powder pink to white flowers in clusters. Quite vigorous growth to 4.5 m (15 ft) high and 3 m (10 ft) wide.
Flowering: Summer only
Cultivation: Tolerates poorer soils. Suitable for growing up into trees or for hedging.

Albéric Barbier

Albertine

Albéric Barbier

Albertine

ALBÉRIC BARBIER

Botanical grouping: Wichuraiana rambler
Parentage: *R. wichuraiana* x Shirley Hibberd
Other names: None
Other varieties: None
Year: 1900
Origin: France
Description: A superb older variety. Growth is pliable, with dark green wood and few thorns. The flowers start as yellowish buds which open to large, double and semi-double, creamy white blooms. It has a moderate fragrance. The foliage is dark green and very glossy. Grows to 4.5 m (15 ft) high and 3 m (10 ft) wide.
Flowering: Basically summer only, but with some intermittent late blooms
Cultivation: Can be grown on colder walls and will tolerate poorer soils and some shade. Also good for growing up into trees.

ALBERTINE

Botanical grouping: Wichuraiana rambler
Parentage: *R. wichuraiana* x Mrs Arthur Robert Waddell
Other names: None
Other varieties: None
Year: 1921
Origin: France
Description: Flowers, which are very fragrant, appear in small clusters. Buds are

Albertine

shapely, then open to large, loosely double, full blooms of coppery pink with a touch of gold deep down in the base. Foliage is dark green, burnished coppery red. Stems are barbed with hooked thorns. Growth is angular and vigorous but is not as rampant

as many other ramblers. Grows to 4.5 m (15 ft) high and 3 m (10 ft) wide.
Flowering: Long mid-summer
Cultivation: Can be grown up into trees or developed as a lax, sprawling bush. Tolerates poorer soils and is susceptible to mildew.

ALEXANDRE GIRAULT

Botanical grouping: Wichuraiana rambler
Parentage: *R. wichuraiana* x Papa Gontier
Other names: None
Other varieties: None
Year: 1909
Origin: France
Description: Produces fragrant, fully double flowers, opening flat with muddled centres of bright light crimson with hints of yellow. Foliage is dark and glossy and the plant will grow vigorously, though prostrate unless trained. Reaches 3.5 m (12 ft) high and wide.
Flowering: Repeats throughout summer
Cultivation: A useful rambler that can tolerate poorer soils and some shade. Prune out dead wood during winter.

AMERICAN PILLAR

Botanical grouping: Setigera climber
Parentage: (*R. wichuraiana* x *R. setigera*) x Red Letter Day
Other names: None
Other varieties: None
Year: 1902
Origin: United States
Description: A robust plant growing to 4.5 m (15 ft) high and 3 m (10 ft) wide, with single flowers that are produced in clusters. They are reddish pink with off-white centres paling to rose pink with age. Rain tends to mottle them. Foliage is deep green and glossy.
Flowering: Summer only
Cultivation: Tolerates poorer soils and shade. Suitable for growing into trees.

ANEMONE

Botanical grouping: Laevigata climber
Parentage: *R. laevigata* x a tea rose
Other names: Anemone Rose, *R. anemonoides*
Other varieties: None
Year: 1895
Origin: Germany
Description: Produces large, single, papery, medium-pink blooms with a touch of mauve. A vigorous climber with branching shoots of darkish brown armed with hooked thorns. Foliage is dark green and glossy. Grows to 3 m (10 ft) high and 2.5 m (8 ft) wide.
Flowering: Repeats in spring and summer
Cultivation: Prefers a sunny position, but will tolerate sheltered shade and poorer soils. Can be grown on colder walls.

American Pillar

Anemone

Aviateur Blériot

Black Boy

Alexandre Girault

AVIATEUR BLÉRIOT

Botanical grouping: Wichuraiana rambler
Parentage: *R. wichuraiana* x William Allen Richardson
Other names: None
Other varieties: None
Year: 1910
Origin: France
Description: A vigorous, relatively thornless and upright plant growing to 3.5 m (12 ft) high and 1.8 m (6 ft) wide. Produces large trusses of fragrant, double, orange-yellow buds which, when open, become pale to creamy yellow with age. Foliage is dark and glossy.
Flowering: Summer only
Cultivation: Suitable for growing into trees and can be cultivated in poorer soils.

BELLE OF PORTUGAL

Botanical grouping: Gigantea climber
Parentage: *R. gigantea* x Reine Marie Henriette
Other names: Belle Portugaise

Other varieties: None
Year: 1903
Origin: Portugal
Description: Produces semi-double flowers with loosely arranged petals of pale pink with deeper shadings. Flowers profusely and grows vigorously to 4.5 m (15 ft) high and 3 m (10 ft) wide. Has dark green slightly crumpled foliage.
Flowering: Summer only
Cultivation: Requires a warm sheltered position, but will tolerate some shade. Ideal for growing up into trees.

BLACK BOY

Botanical grouping: Large-flowered climber
Parentage: Etoile de France x Bardou Job
Other names: None
Other varieties: Moss rose registered in Germany in 1958
Year: 1919
Origin: Australia
Description: A beautiful, blackish crimson, recurrent hybrid not seen very often nowadays. The flowers are medium-sized and fragrant. Foliage is light in growth and the plant is very vigorous.
Flowering: Repeats throughout summer
Cultivation: Strong shoots should be reduced by about half their length to encourage laterals.

BLAIRII NO. 2

Botanical grouping: Bourbon climber
Parentage: Unknown
Other names: None
Other varieties: None
Year: 1845
Origin: England
Description: The blooms on this rose are particularly beautiful. They are large, flattish and pale pink, with deeper shadings towards the centre and have a delightful fragrance. The young leaves have

mahogany-red tints. Growth is vigorous, if somewhat coarse, to 3.5 m (12 ft) high and 1.8 m (6 ft) wide.

Flowering: Long summer only

Cultivation: Particularly good if grown on a tripod or a similar structure. Slightly prone to mildew late in the season, so keep the ground free from weed growth.

BLEU MAGENTA

Botanical grouping: Polyantha rambler
Parentage: Unknown
Other names: None

Other varieties: None
Year: *c.* 1900
Origin: Unknown
Description: Produces clusters of small, rich purple flowers with muddled petals and golden stamens. Lightly scented. Foliage is mid-green and glossy. Wood is mid-green. Growth is lax and high, reaching 3.5 m (12 ft) high and 3 m (10 ft) wide.

Flowering: Summer only

Cultivation: Can be grown on colder walls and will tolerate poorer soils and shade. Is susceptible to mildew, and therefore needs space around it to maintain air circulation.

Bleu Magenta

Blairii No. 2

Bloomfield Courage

BLOOMFIELD COURAGE

Botanical grouping: Cluster-flowered climber
Parentage: Unknown
Other names: None
Other varieties: None
Year: 1925
Origin: Australia/United States
Description: Single, deep, velvety red flowers appear in clusters. They have white centres and yellow stamens. Foliage is dark and glossy. Grows to 6 m (20 ft).
Flowering: Summer only
Cultivation: Suitable for growing up into trees. Not suitable for cultivation in cold climates.

BLUSH RAMBLER

Botanical grouping: Polyantha climber
Parentage: Crimson Rambler x The Garland
Other names: None
Other varieties: None
Year: 1903
Origin: England
Description: With its cascading clusters of fragrant, double rosette-like, blush-pink blooms and light green foliage this rose was quite popular as a cottage rambler in past decades. It is a vigorous and almost thornless plant, growing to 3.5 m (12 ft) high and 3 m (10 ft) wide.
Flowering: Summer only
Cultivation: A useful rambler that will tolerate poorer soil conditions and can be grown in full sun or semi-shade.

BONFIRE

Botanical grouping: Polyantha climber
Parentage: Crimson Rambler x *R. wichuraiana*
Other names: None
Other varieties: None
Year: 1928
Origin: France
Description: Produces clusters of very

Blush Rambler

double, small flowers which are deep crimson. Plant is hardy and vigorous to 5 m (17 ft).
Flowering: Summer only with some intermittent blooms later
Cultivation: A fast-growing rose that is suitable for growing up into trees and will tolerate some shade and variable soil conditions.

CÉCILE BRUNNER CLIMBER

Botanical grouping: Polyantha climber
Parentage: Cécile Brunner sport
Other names: None
Other varieties: White Cécile Brunner
Year: 1894
Origin: United States
Description: A very vigorous sport, with flowers identical to the bush form, beautifully shaped, shell pink with a reasonable fragrance. These are freely produced but are sometimes hidden by dense, bright green

Cécile Brunner Climber

Blush Rambler

foliage. Grows to 7.5 m (25 ft) high and 6 m (20 ft) wide.
Flowering: Repeats throughout summer
Cultivation: Ideal for growing into trees or covering buildings. Tolerant of most soils and some shade. Will grow on colder walls.

COLONIAL WHITE

Botanical grouping: Tea climber
Parentage: Unknown
Other names: None
Other varieties: None
Year: 1959
Origin: Unknown
Description: A vigorous hybrid with long canes, healthy foliage and large prickles. It produces a dull white, quartered, fragrant flower which opens flat.
Flowering: Repeats throughout summer
Cultivation: Prefers full sun and good growing conditions. Prune back if growth is too vigorous.

Cooper's Burmese Rose

Cupid

COOPER'S BURMESE ROSE

Botanical grouping: Laevigata climber
Parentage: Possibly a spontaneous hybrid of *R. gigantea* x *R. laevigata*
Other names: *R. gigantea cooperi, R.* x *cooperi*
Other varieties: None
Year: 1921
Origin: Burma
Description: Very vigorous climber to 10 m (33 ft) with attractive glossy foliage and purplish brown stems. Large, solitary flowers are white, later developing pink hues and spots. Scented.
Flowering: Spring only
Cultivation: Sensitive to hard frosts and very cold temperatures. Needs a warm, sunny position to do well but can tolerate poorer soils. Suited to training through trees.

CUPID

Botanical grouping: Large-flowered climber
Parentage: Unknown
Other names: None
Other varieties: None
Year: 1915
Origin: England
Description: Produces beautiful, large, sweetly smelling, single blooms. The petals are a soft, peachy pink and the flower has pronounced stamens. Also produces large round orange-red fruit. Foliage is large, greyish green and matt. Growth is upright and stiff to 3.5 m (12 ft) high and 1.8 m (6 ft) wide.
Flowering: Repeats throughout summer
Cultivation: A versatile rose that tolerates poorer soils and some shade. Prune back after flowering if growth is too vigorous.

DÉBUTANTE

Botanical grouping: Wichuraiana rambler
Parentage: *R. wichuraiana* x Baroness Rothschild
Other names: None

Other varieties: None
Year: 1902
Origin: United States
Description: A pretty rose with a light scent. It produces clusters of small, fully double blooms of soft rose pink. Foliage is dark green and glossy. A vigorous plant of slightly spreading habit. Grows to 3.5 m (12 ft) high and 3 m (10 ft) wide.
Flowering: Summer only, but does have a few late blooms
Cultivation: Can be grown as a ground covering rose, or trained to grow up into trees. A hardy specimen, it will tolerate poorer soils and shady conditions.

DEVONIENSIS CLIMBER

Botanical grouping: Tea climber
Parentage: Devoniensis sport
Other names: None
Other varieties: Devoniensis shrub from England, 1841
Year: 1858
Origin: England
Description: A graceful plant, producing very large, creamy white, very fragrant flowers with the occasional blush of pink. Has light green foliage. Grows to 3.5 m (12 ft).
Flowering: Repeats throughout summer
Cultivation: Needs a warm, sunny position to thrive.

DOROTHY PERKINS

Botanical grouping: Wichuraiana rambler
Parentage: *R. wichuraiana* x Mme Gabriel Luizet
Other names: None
Other varieties: None
Year: 1901
Origin: United States
Description: A very free-flowering rose. Blooms cascade in profusion from a vigorous and pliable plant. The flowers are double, rosette-like, small and clear rose pink. Foliage is glossy, dark to mid-green. Grows to 3 m (10 ft) high and 2.5 m (8 ft) wide.

Débutante

Flowering: Summer only

Cultivation: Tolerates poorer soils. Makes a good ground cover but is susceptible to mildew. Keep the area around the base free from weeds or other overcrowding plants.

DR W. VAN FLEET

Botanical grouping: Wichuraiana rambler
Parentage: (*R. wichuraiana* x Safrano) x Souvenir du Président Carnot
Other names: None
Other varieties: None
Year: 1910
Origin: United States
Description: A vigorous plant to 4.5 m (15 ft) high and 3 m (10 ft) wide, with thorny stems and well-foliated, dark green leaves. The flowers are perfumed, double, medium-sized and a soft blush pink.
Flowering: Summer only
Cultivation: Tolerates poorer soils and shade. Can be used for growing into trees and on colder walls.

Dr W. van Fleet

EASLEA'S GOLDEN RAMBLER

Botanical grouping: Large-flowered climber
Parentage: Unknown
Other names: Golden Rambler
Other varieties: None
Year: 1932
Origin: England
Description: Produces medium to large, lovely, apricot-yellow, fully double flowers in small clusters. They appear on long, strong stems and are good flowers for cutting. Foliage is rich, dark green and glossy. Growth is vigorous and rambling to 6 m (20 ft) high and 4.5 m (15 ft) wide.
Flowering: Summer only
Cultivation: Tolerates poorer soils and shade. Can be grown up into trees and on colder walls.

Dorothy Perkins

Easlea's Golden Rambler

EMILY GRAY

Botanical grouping: Wichuraiana rambler
Parentage: Jersey Beauty x Comtesse du Cayla
Other names: None
Other varieties: None
Year: 1918
Origin: England
Description: A beautiful, semi-double bloom of rich yellow, with golden stamens set off by the dark, plum-coloured, young foliage which ages to glossy dark green. Growth is wide and relatively thornless to 4.5 m (15 ft) high and 3 m (10 ft) wide.
Flowering: Summer only
Cultivation: Tolerates poorer soils and shade and will grow on a colder wall.

Emily Gray

Excelsa

EXCELSA

Botanical grouping: Wichuraiana rambler
Parentage: Unknown
Other names: Red Dorothy Perkins
Other varieties: None
Year: 1909
Origin: United States

Description: Produces small bright crimson flowers in large clusters. Foliage is dark green and matt. Grows to 4.5 m (15 ft) high and 3.5m (12 ft) wide, and is relaxed and pliable.
Flowering: Summer only
Cultivation: A versatile plant suitable for colder walls, growing as a ground cover or up into trees. Tolerates poorer soils and shade.

Fortuneana

Félicité Perpétue

FÉLICITÉ PERPÉTUE

Botanical grouping: Synstylae
Parentage: Unknown
Other names: None
Other varieties: Dwarf form, White Pet
Year: 1827
Origin: France
Description: A vigorous, relatively thornless climber which bears clusters of small red buds opening to fully double, cupped, creamy white, rosette-shaped flowers. It is well scented. Foliage is dark green and glossy.
Flowering: Summer only
Cultivation: Suitable for growing next to water or up into trees. Tolerates poorer soils and shade.

FORTUNEANA

Botanical grouping: Banksian climber
Parentage: Obscure but thought to be a cross between *R. banksiae* and *R. laevigata*
Other names: *R.* x *fortuniana*, Fortuniana
Other varieties: None
Year: 1850
Origin: China
Description: An evergreen with beautiful foliage growing to 3.5 m (12 ft) high and 2.5 m (8 ft) wide. It has large, scented, double white flowers with a hint of cream. It is almost thornless.
Flowering: Summer only
Cultivation: Requires a sheltered, warm position to flourish. Prune out dead or spindly wood in winter.

FRANCOIS JURANVILLE

Botanical grouping: Wichuraiana rambler
Parentage: *R. wichuraiana* x Mme Laurette Messimy
Other names: None
Other varieties: None
Year: 1906
Origin: France

Félicité Perpétue

Francois Juranville

Francois Juranville

Goldfinch

Description: Sometimes mistaken for Albertine, this rose has beautiful flowers in clusters which are a tangle of clear, silky pink petals surrounded by dark green, burnished bronze, semi-glossy foliage. Growth is dense and pliable with very few thorns to 4.5 m (15 ft) high and 3 m (10 ft) wide.
Flowering: Summer only
Cultivation: Can be used for ground cover or on colder walls. Will tolerate poorer soils and shade.

GARDENIA

Botanical grouping: Wichuraiana rambler
Parentage: *R. wichuraiana* x Perle des Jardins
Other names: None
Other varieties: None
Year: 1899
Origin: United States
Description: A very beautiful rose with the scent of green apples. It produces yellow buds which open to fully double creamy white flowers. Rich, dark, glossy green foliage complements the blooms. Growth is relaxed and vigorous with few thorns to 6 m (20 ft) high and 4.5 m (15 ft) wide.
Flowering: Summer only
Cultivation: Excellent for growing into trees or for ground cover. Tolerates poorer soils and shade.

GERBE ROSE

Botanical grouping: Wichuraiana rambler
Parentage: *R. wichuraiana* x Baroness Rothschild
Other names: None
Other varieties: None
Year: 1904
Origin: France
Description: A vigorous climber with abundant large, glossy foliage which grows

to 3 m (10 ft) high and 2.5 m (8 ft) wide. It produces a sweetly fragrant, large, loose and quartered, soft, rosy pink flower.
Flowering: Summer only
Cultivation: Can be grown on colder walls or into trees. Will tolerate some shade.

GOLDFINCH

Botanical grouping: Polyantha climber
Parentage: Hélène x Unknown
Other names: None
Other varieties: None

Gerbe Rose

Year: 1907
Origin: England
Description: A bushy plant which grows to 2.5 m (8 ft) high and 1.2 m (4 ft) wide. It produces tightly packed clusters of small, cupped, semi-double flowers which are golden yellow on opening, but fade to cream in hot sun. They will hold their colour on a cloudy or dull day. Foliage is mid-green, glossy and almost thornless.
Flowering: Summer only
Cultivation: Can be grown on a colder wall and will tolerate poorer soils and some shade.

Hiawatha

HIAWATHA

Botanical grouping: Polyantha climber
Parentage: Crimson Rambler x Paul's Carmine Pillar
Other names: None
Other varieties: None
Year: 1904
Origin: United States
Description: A bushy, spreading plant which produces clusters of single, small, scarlet flowers with a white eye. They have no fragrance. Foliage is dark green and semi-glossy. Grows to 4.5 m (15 ft) high and 3.5 m (12 ft) wide.
Flowering: Summer only with a few later blooms
Cultivation: Can be grown up into trees and on colder walls. Will tolerate poorer soils and some shade.

JERSEY BEAUTY

Botanical grouping: Wichuraiana rambler
Parentage: *R. wichuraiana* x Perle des Jardins
Other names: None
Other varieties: None
Year: 1899
Origin: United States
Description: A fragrant hybrid which is very vigorous and grows to 5 m (16 ft). It produces single, creamy yellow flowers with prominent yellow stamens. Foliage is dark and glossy.
Flowering: Summer only
Cultivation: Requires a warm, sheltered situation and moderately rich, well drained soil conditions. Prune out dead wood during winter.

KEW RAMBLER

Botanical grouping: Soulieana rambler
Parentage: *R. soulieana* x Hiawatha
Other names: None
Other varieties: None
Year: 1912

Kew Rambler

Lady Gay

Origin: England
Description: An unusual and vigorous plant which is thorny and stiffish but still pliable. It grows to 5.5 m (18 ft) high and 3.5 m (12 ft) wide and produces large clusters of small, sweetly scented, single, pink flowers with a white eye and yellow stamens. It also has orange hips in the autumn. Foliage is small, plentiful and greyish green.
Flowering: Summer only
Cultivation: A versatile plant, suitable for growing in woodlands, up into trees or on colder walls. Will tolerate shade and is suitable for growing adjacent to water.

LADY GAY

Botanical grouping: Wichuraiana rambler
Parentage: *R. wichuraiana* x Bardou Job
Other names: None
Other varieties: None
Year: 1905
Origin: United States
Description: Produces sprays of small to medium-sized, salmon-pink flowers which are fragrant. A hardy and strong growing plant.
Flowering: Summer only with some later blooms
Cultivation: Similar to Dorothy Perkins, but blooms later and is more resistant to mildew. Prune out dead wood or spindly growth during winter.

LADY HILLINGDON CLIMBER

Botanical grouping: Tea climber
Parentage: Sport from bush form, Papa Gontier x Mme Hoste
Other names: None
Other varieties: Shrub
Year: 1917
Origin: England
Description: A lovely plant for cutting. It has semi-double, blowsy flowers of rich, yolk-yellow which are very fragrant. The

Lady Hillingdon Climber

Lady Hillingdon Climber

LAURÉ DAVOUST

Botanical grouping: Multiflora rambler
Parentage: Seedling x *R. multiflora*
Other names: Marjorie W. Lester
Other varieties: None
Year: 1834
Origin: France
Description: A sweetly scented rambler with small, double, lilac-pink flowers which open flat and are quartered. They have a green pointel in the centre.
Flowering: Summer only
Cultivation: Remove older wood to keep the plant in shape. Prefers full sun and some protection from prevailing winds.

LAWRENCE JOHNSTON

Botanical grouping: Large-flowered climber
Parentage: Mme Eugène Verdier x *R. foetida persiana*
Other names: Hidcote Yellow, *R. foetida* Lawrence Johnston
Other varieties: None
Year: 1923
Origin: France
Description: A vigorous climbing rose to 7.5 m (25 ft) with abundant, glossy foliage. The semi-double clusters of flowers are medium yellow and very fragrant.
Flowering: Flowers early and repeatedly

Lawrence Johnston

throughout the season.
Cultivation: Like all *R. foetida* varieties, dislikes pruning and is prone to black spot. Will tolerate a shady position.

LÉONTINE GERVAIS

Botanical grouping: Wichuraiana rambler
Parentage: *R. wichuraiana* x Souvenir de Catherine Guillot
Other names: None
Other varieties: None
Year: 1903
Origin: France
Description: A vigorous, pliable plant, to

stems are plum coloured with relatively few thorns. Foliage is very dark greyish green. It grows in an upright and branching manner to 4.5 m (15 ft) and 2.5 m (18 ft).
Flowering: Repeats throughout summer
Cultivation: Although this plant will tolerate poorer soils, it requires a sunny position and needs protection in colder climates. It is good for forcing or for growing under glass.

LADY WATERLOW

Botanical grouping: Large-flowered climber
Parentage: La France de '89 x Mme Marie Lavalley
Other names: None
Other varieties: None
Year: 1903
Origin: France
Description: Produces a very pretty, semi-double flower of soft pink with deeper undertones and veining. The flower is fragrant. The plant is well foliated and grows to 3.5 m (12 ft) high and 2.5 m (8 ft) wide.
Flowering: Summer only
Cultivation: A useful rose that will tolerate poorer soils and shade, and can be grown on colder walls.

Lady Waterlow

Léontine Gervais

6 m (20 ft), which produces clusters of medium-sized, fully double, flat flowers. In the bud, they are red-orange, but when open are muddled deep salmon with yellow, red and orange highlights. Foliage is dark green and glossy.

Flowering: Summer only

Cultivation: A useful rambler that is happy in poorer soils and suitable to train up into trees. Prune in winter, removing dead or spindly wood.

LEUCHTSTERN

Botanical grouping: Polyantha climber
Parentage: Daniel Lacombe x Crimson Rambler
Other names: None
Other varieties: None
Year: 1899
Origin: Germany
Description: Produces clusters of medium-sized, deep pink, sweetly perfumed flowers paling to white centres. The foliage is mid-green. It also carries heavy fruit. Grows to 3 m (10 ft) high and 2.5 m (8 ft) wide.
Flowering: Summer only
Cultivation: A hardy specimen that will grow on colder walls and tolerates poorer soils and shade.

LORRAINE LEE CLIMBER

Botanical grouping: Tea climber
Parentage: Sport from bush form of Jessie Clarke x Captain Millet
Other names: None
Other varieties: Shrub from Australia, 1924
Year: 1932
Origin: Australia
Description: A very vigorous climber. Produces double, fragrant, rosy pink flowers with lush green, very glossy foliage. Will grow to 6 m (20 ft) or more.

Lorraine Lee Climber

May Queen

May Queen

Flowering: Continuously throughout summer
Cultivation: This hardy rose may need pruning back if stems become too rampant. Can be grown in quite difficult situations and will withstand hot, relatively dry conditions.

MAY QUEEN

Botanical grouping: Wichuraiana rambler
Parentage: *R. wichuraiana* x Champion of the World
Other names: None
Other varieties: None

Year: 1898
Origin: United States
Description: A vigorous and useful rambler which grows to 4.5 m (15 ft) high and 2.5 m (8 ft) wide. Free-flowering and produces semi-double, lilac-pink flowers which are fragrant and appear in clusters. Has dark green foliage and darkish thorns.
Flowering: Summer only with some repeat blooms
Cultivation: Good for use as a ground cover, for growing up into trees or on colder walls. Will also tolerate shade.

MERMAID

Botanical grouping: Bracteata climber
Parentage: *R. bracteata* x Double Yellow Tea Rose
Other names: *R. bracteata*
Other varieties: None
Year: 1918
Origin: England
Description: A very vigorous shrub capable of climbing to 6 m (20 ft) with attractive dark green foliage and thorny brown branches. The flowers are single, very large (10–15 cm/4–6 in across) and pale yellow with amber stamens. It is scented.
Flowering: Continuously throughout summer
Cultivation: Very difficult to propagate but once established it is extremely vigorous and hardy. It does not require pruning. Prefers sunny walls although it can tolerate some shade. May die back after severe frosts.

MINNEHAHA

Botanical grouping: Wichuraiana rambler
Parentage: *R. wichuraiana* x Paul Neyron
Other names: None
Other varieties: None
Year: 1905
Origin: United States
Description: Foliage is small, and greyish green on a relaxed and vigorous rambler. Produces clusters of cascading, double, rich pink flowers with a light fragrance. Grows to 4.5 m (15 ft) high and 2.5 m (8 ft) wide.
Flowering: Summer only, though will repeat in sheltered areas.
Cultivation: Tolerates poorer soils and shade but is susceptible to mildew. Can be used as a ground cover, for growing up into trees and on colder walls.

MME CAROLINE TESTOUT CLIMBER

Botanical grouping: Hybrid tea climber
Parentage: Mme de Tartas x Lady Mary Fitzwilliam
Other names: None

Other varieties: Mme Caroline Testout (bush),1890
Year: 1901
Origin: France
Description: A vigorous, well-shaped plant that grows to 4.5 m (15 ft) with grey-green foliage and a profusion of large, rounded silvery-pink blooms tinged with carmine. The flowers are strongly fragrant.
Flowering: Summer to autumn
Cultivation: Prefers full sun and a moderately rich, well-drained soil. Mulch around the base to keep weed growth down.

MME GRÉGOIRE STAECHELIN

Botanical grouping: Large-flowered climber
Parentage: Frau Karl Druschki x Château de Clos Vougeot
Other names: Spanish Beauty
Year: 1927
Origin: Spain
Description: This superb variety produces very fragrant pale pink, large, almost double flowers which have a deeper pink reverse and edge to the petals. After its one long flowering season, it will, if not dead-headed, produce a prolific crop of large, urn-shaped hips in autumn. Foliage is matt, dark green. Growth is vigorous to 4.5 m (15 ft) high and 3 m (10 ft) wide.
Flowering: Summer only
Cultivation: Tolerates poorer soil and shade and can be used on colder walls.

Mermaid

Mme Caroline Testout Climber

Mme Grégoire Staechelin

Mrs Herbert Stevens Climber

New Dawn

Mrs Herbert Stevens Climber

MRS HERBERT STEVENS CLIMBER

Botanical grouping: Large-flowered climber
Parentage: Sport from shrub form Frau Karl Druschki x Niphetos
Other names: None
Other varieties: Bush from Northern Ireland, 1910
Year: 1922
Origin: France
Description: Very vigorous grower to 3.5 m (12 ft) high and 2.5 m (8 ft) wide. The flowers, which are very fragrant, are pure white with long buds and are excellent for cutting. They are produced singly in profusion. Foliage is mid-green and matt. Growth is upright and branching.
Flowering: Repeats throughout summer
Cultivation: Can be used on colder walls and will tolerate poorer soils and shade.

NEW DAWN

Botanical grouping: Wichuraiana rambler
Parentage: Sport from Dr W. Van Fleet, (*R. wichuraiana* x Safrano) x Souvenir du Président Carnot
Other names: Everblooming Dr W. van Fleet, The New Dawn
Other varieties: None
Year: 1930
Origin: United States
Description: This plant is valuable for cutting. It produces clusters of semi-double blooms of silver-pink and has a moderate fragrance. Foliage is greyish-green and semi-glossy on a bushy plant. It grows to 3 m (10 ft) high and 2.5 m (8 ft) wide.
Flowering: Continuously throughout summer
Cultivation: Will tolerate poorer soils and shade and can be used on colder walls.

PARADISE

Botanical grouping: Rambler
Parentage: Unknown
Other names: None
Other varieties: Not to be confused with the 1978 hybrid tea
Year: 1907
Origin: Unknown
Description: A beautiful rambler with medium-sized, single fragrant, rose pink flowers with a white centre. Has attractive mid-green foliage and will grow to 5 m (16 ft).
Flowering: Summer only with some late blooms
Cultivation: Remove older wood to keep plant in shape. In winter prune out dead or spindly wood.

PAUL'S SCARLET CLIMBER

Botanical grouping: Polyantha climber
Parentage: Paul's Carmine Pillar x Rêve d'Or
Other names: None
Other varieties: None
Year: 1916
Origin: England
Description: Produces semi-double, medium-sized scarlet flowers in clusters. The blooms are initially cupped and have only a

Paul's Scarlet Climber

Phyllis Bide

Polyantha Grandiflora

touch of fragrance. Growth is upright, sparsely thorned with dark green matt foliage. Grows to 3 m (10 ft) high and 2.5 m (8 ft) wide.
Flowering: Summer only
Cultivation: Will tolerate poorer soils, colder walls and shade.

PHYLLIS BIDE

Botanical grouping: Polyantha climber
Parentage: Perle d'Or x Gloire de Dijon
Other names: None

Purity

Other varieties: None
Year: 1923
Origin: England
Description: Produces small dainty flowers in yellow, cream, pink and red which deepen in colour with age. They have a delicate scent. Growth is upright and vigorous, although it can also be twiggy. Foliage is light green and plentiful. Grows to 3 m (10 ft) high and 1.8 m (6 ft) wide.
Flowering: Repeats throughout summer
Cultivation: Tolerates poorer soils and shade. Remove dead and spindly wood. Can be grown on colder walls.

POLYANTHA GRANDIFLORA

Botanical grouping: Gentiliana rambler
Parentage: *R. gentiliana*
Other names: *R. gentiliana*
Other varieties: None
Year: 1907
Origin: China
Description: A vigorous climbing plant which produces single to semi-double, creamy white flowers with orange stamens in dense, cascading clusters. They are extremely fragrant. In the autumn a good crop of small, orange hips appears. Foliage is light green and glossy with coppery overtones. Stems, which are a similar colour, have a mixture of broad, hooked thorns and smaller bristles. Grows to 6 m (20 ft) high and 3 m (10 ft) wide.
Flowering: Summer only
Cultivation: Worth growing just for its pretty autumn foliage and fruit. Will tolerate poorer soils and shade. Can be used for growing up into trees, for woodland areas and for growing adjacent to water.

PURITY

Botanical grouping: Large-flowered climber
Parentage: Unnamed seedling x Mme Caroline Testout
Other names: None
Other varieties: None
Year: 1917
Origin: United States
Description: Produces large, pure white, shapely flowers which are loose and semi-double. They have an attractive fragrance. Foliage is glossy, light green on a vigorous, thorny plant. Size is 3.5 m (12 ft) high and 2.5 m (8 ft) wide.
Flowering: Summer only with some late blooms
Cultivation: A versatile rambler that tolerates poorer soils and some shade. Prune out dead or spindly wood in winter.

Ramona

Rose-Marie Viaud

Russelliana

Sander's White Rambler

RAMONA

Botanical grouping: Laevigata climber
Parentage: Sport from Anemone Rose
Other names: Red Cherokee
Other varieties: None
Year: 1913
Origin: United States
Description: A beautiful, large, single, rose of deep cerise-pink with prominent yellow stamens. Foliage is dark green and glossy. A vigorous grower, to 3 m (10 ft) high and 2.5 m (8 ft) wide, with branching shoots of darkish brown.
Flowering: Repeats throughout summer
Cultivation: Tolerates some shade and poorer soils but prefers a sunny, sheltered position.

ROSE-MARIE VIAUD

Botanical grouping: Polyantha climber
Parentage: Veilchenblau seedling
Other names: None
Other varieties: None
Year: 1924
Origin: France
Description: Produces clusters of double, rosette-like flowers of lavender-purple. There is only a slight fragrance. Foliage is light green on almost thornless wood. Grows to 3.5 m (12 ft) high and 1.8 m (6 ft) wide.
Flowering: Late summer only
Cultivation: Can be grown in poorer soils and on colder walls as it tolerates some shade. Susceptible to mildew, so the area at the base of the plant should be kept weed-free.

RUSSELLIANA

Botanical grouping: Polyantha climber
Parentage: Obscure, probably a cross between *R. multiflora* and *R. setigera*
Other names: Old Spanish Rose, Russell's Cottage Rose, Scarlet Grevillei, Souvenir de la Bataille de Marengo
Other varieties: None
Year: 1840

Origin: Spain
Description: Bears fragrant, fully double, small flowers of crimson-purple in clusters. The colour fades with age. Foliage is dark green and the stems are thorny. Grows to 3 m (10 ft) high and 3 m (10 ft) wide.
Flowering: Summer only
Cultivation: A fast-growing and hardy rose that can be grown up into trees and against colder walls.

SANDER'S WHITE RAMBLER

Botanical grouping: Wichuraiana rambler
Parentage: Unknown
Other names: Sander's White Rambler
Other varieties: None
Year: 1912
Origin: England
Description: Growth is vigorous and relaxed, making it useful for a variety of locations. Produces an abundant supply of pinkish buds, followed by rosette-shaped, white, sweetly scented flowers. Foliage is mid-green and semi-glossy. Grows to 3.5 m (12 ft) high and 2.5 m (8 ft) wide.
Flowering: Continuously from late summer
Cultivation: Can be used as a ground cover or grown up into trees. Also works as a weeping standard. Will tolerate poorer soils and shade, and can be grown on colder walls.

SEVEN SISTERS

Botanical grouping: Polyantha climber
Parentage: *R. multiflora platyphylla*
Other names: *R. multiflora grevillei*, Seven Sisters Rose
Other varieties: None
Year: 1816
Origin: China
Description: The flowers are borne in very big clusters. They are scented and appear in shades of soft pink, mauve and purple. Foliage is large, dark green and appears on stiff, dark green stems. Grows to 6 m (20 ft) high and 3 m (10 ft) wide.
Flowering: Summer only
Cultivation: Will tolerate poorer soils and shade, but prefers some shelter from extreme cold and protection from wind.

SILVER MOON

Botanical grouping: Laevigata climber
Parentage: Obscure, but probably (*R. wichuraiana* x Devoniensis) x *R. laevigata*
Other names: None
Other varieties: None
Year: 1910
Origin: United States
Description: Produces fragrant, very large, pure white, loose, single flowers with golden stamens. Foliage is dark green and semi-glossy.

Silver Moon

Growth is very strong, wide and branching, to 4.5 m (15 ft) high and 2.5 m (8 ft) wide.
Flowering: Repeats throughout summer
Cultivation: Fast-growing and vigorous, this rose is excellent for growing up into trees.

SOMBREUIL CLIMBER

Botanical grouping: Tea climber
Parentage: Sport of bush form, seedling of Gigantesque
Other names: None
Other varieties: Bush, 1845
Year: 1850
Origin: France
Description: A treasure from the past, this rose has fully double, flattish, pure white flowers with just a hint of cream towards the centre. It has a delightful fragrance. Foliage is ample and lush green. Grows into a dense shrub or small climber to 2.5 m (8 ft) high and 1.5 m (5 ft) wide.
Flowering: Repeats throughout summer
Cultivation: Suitable for growing under glass as well as in the garden. Prune out dead wood in winter.

SOUVENIR DE LA MALMAISON CLIMBER

Botanical grouping: Bourbon climber
Parentage: Sport from bush form, Mme Desprez x a tea rose
Other names: None
Other varieties: Shrub from France, 1843
Year: 1893
Origin: England
Description: One of the most beautiful bourbons. Flowers are blush-white with pink shadings and are fragrant. Blooms open to a flat, quartered shape. Grows to 3.5 m (12 ft) high and 2.5 m (8 ft) wide.
Flowering: Generously in summer but only repeats in good years.
Cultivation: Will do best if planted in a warm, sheltered situation; it hates wet weather. Prune out dead or spindly wood in winter.

Sombreuil Climber

Tausendschön

TAUSENDSCHÖN

Botanical grouping: Polyantha climber
Parentage: Daniel Lacombe x Weisser Herumstreicher
Other names: Thousand Beauties
Other varieties: None
Year: 1906
Origin: Germany
Description: Bears large, double, loose clusters of pink flowers with white towards the centre. Lightly fragrant. The plant is thornless and has mid-green foliage. Grows to 3.5 m (12 ft) high and 2.5 m (8 ft) wide.
Flowering: Summer only
Cultivation: A hardy rose that will tolerate poorer soils and a wide range of soil conditions. Prune out dead wood in winter.

TEA RAMBLER

Botanical grouping: Polyantha climber
Parentage: Crimson Rambler x a tea rose
Other names: None
Other varieties: None
Year: 1904
Origin: England
Description: Produces full, fragrant, medium-sized blooms of soft pink with brighter highlights. A vigorous plant which grows to 3.5 m (12 ft) high and 2.5 m (8 ft) wide, with mid-green foliage.

Tea Rambler

The Garland

Violette

Veilchenblau

Wedding Day

Flowering: Long early summer with some later blooms.
Cultivation: This fast-growing rose can be trained to grow up into trees and will tolerate some shade and poorer soils.

THE GARLAND

Botanical grouping: Moschata climber
Parentage: *R. moschata* x *R. multiflora*
Other names: None
Other varieties: None
Year: 1835
Origin: England
Description: A vigorous, spreading climber. It produces masses of small, very fragrant, semi-double flowers of creamy white blushed with pink. Has stout, hooked thorns and mid to dark green, smaller foliage. Grows to 4.5 m (15 ft) high and 3 m (10 ft) wide.
Flowering: Summer only
Cultivation: Tolerates poorer soils and some shade. Will grow up into trees, on colder walls, and is suitable for growing adjacent to water.

VEILCHENBLAU

Botanical grouping: Polyantha climber
Parentage: Crimson Rambler x Erinnerung an Brod
Other names: Violet Blue, Blue Rambler, Blue Rosalie
Other varieties: None
Year: 1909
Origin: Germany
Description: A loose, semi-double, lavender-purple rose with flecks of white and pale to lilac-grey. The flowers are fragrant and have prominent yellow stamens. Foliage is glossy and mid-green. Growth is bushy and upright to 4.5 m (15 ft) high and 3.5 m (12 ft) wide.

Flowering: Summer only
Cultivation: A hardy rose that will grow up into trees and against colder walls. Prune out dead or spindly wood in winter.

VIOLETTE

Botanical grouping: Polyantha climber
Parentage: Unknown
Other names: None
Other varieties: None
Year: 1921
Origin: France
Description: Produces clusters of deep, purple-crimson, small flowers, with rich golden stamens. A good flower for cutting. Growth is bushy and wide. Foliage is dark green.
Flowering: Summer only
Cultivation: A versatile rose that tolerates some shade and is vigorous enough to grow up into trees. Some pruning, to remove dead or spindly growth, can be done in winter.

WEDDING DAY

Botanical grouping: Sinowilsonii rambler
Parentage: *R. sinowilsonii* x unknown
Other names: None
Other varieties: None
Year: 1950
Origin: England
Description: Produces very large clusters of fragrant, single, white flowers, with orange-yellow stamens. Foliage is bright green and glossy. Has a good crop of small to medium, yellow fruit. Growth is spreading and vigorous to 9 m (30 ft) high and 4.5 m (15 ft) wide.
Flowering: Summer only
Cultivation: A fast-growing rose that can be grown as a ground cover or trained up into trees. Will tolerate shade and can be grown against colder walls.

Climbing and Rambling Roses (modern)

This group covers a wide range of roses grouped together because of their climbing or rambling growth habit. Modern climbers and ramblers are hybrids, and their foliage and flowers vary considerably according to their ancestry. Many of the most popular bush roses have been later developed as climbers, including Iceberg, Peace and Queen Elizabeth. In general, it is advisable to allow plenty of space for these roses to grow and spread, as they can be very invasive in the wrong location. Most benefit from pruning and shaping, and support should be provided in the form of a fence, wall, trellis or pillar.

Alchemist

ALCHEMIST

Botanical grouping: Synstylae
Parentage: Golden Glow x *R. eglanteria* hybrid
Other names: None
Other varieties: None
Year: 1956
Origin: Germany
Description: This vigorous but rather stiff shrub-climber grows to 3.5 m (12 ft) high and 2.5 m (8 ft) wide. The flowers are large, fully double, quartered and fragrant. Their colour is yellow, deepening to apricot and gold. Stems are well arched with a rich, green leathery foliage.
Flowering: Summer only
Cultivation: Can be grown in poorer soils and will tolerate shade. It is suitable for growing up into trees. Shorten back strong laterals and remove dead and spindly wood.

ALOHA

Botanical grouping: Large-flowered climber
Parentage: Mercedes Gallart x New Dawn

Aloha

Other names: None
Other varieties: Can be grown as a free-standing shrub
Year: 1949
Origin: United States
Description: It grows 3 m (10 ft) tall and 1.8 m (6 ft) wide with very fragrant, tightly filled flowers that are rose pink with a deeper reverse, and copper-pink shadings. Foliage is lush dark green with a bronzy overlay.
Flowering: Continuously throughout summer
Cultivation: Tolerant of poorer soils and can also be grown successfully in tubs. Its flowers are good for cutting. A slow grower that requires moderate pruning.

ALTISSIMO

Botanical grouping: Cluster-flowered climber
Parentage: Tenor x Unknown
Other names: None
Other varieties: None
Year: 1966
Origin: France
Description: A spectacular climbing

Altissimo

floribunda, with beautifully shaped, huge, single flowers, about 12.5 cm (5 in) across, in brilliant red shaded with crimson and golden yellow stamens. The deep green, ample, healthy foliage provides an excellent background for the flowers. The individual flowers are long lasting.
Flowering: Repeat flowers and is floriferous.
Cultivation: This is a fully hardy rose and can be used either as a shrub to 2.5 m (8 ft) or a climber to 4 m (13 ft). It should be given a sunny aspect. It offers no difficulties in cultivation.

ASH WEDNESDAY

Botanical grouping: Cluster-flowered climber
Parentage: Reputedly *R. eglanteria* hybrid x Ballet
Other names: Aschermittwoch
Other varieties: None
Year: 1955
Origin: Germany
Description: The colour of this rose is extraordinary. The clusters of double blooms are a mixture of slate, ash grey, and lilac with a buff-brown suffusion. The flowers are large, fully double, beautifully formed, and are borne in profusion in one flowering burst during most seasons. It is a strong grower, well foliated, vigorous and faintly thorny. It reaches 3 m (10 ft) high and 1.8 m (6 ft) wide.
Flowering: Summer
Cultivation: This rose is easy to establish, growing rapidly with reasonable care. Training the long stems sideways encourages breaking of dormant shoots, each side branch adding to the summer display. It can be used as a pillar rose or against a pergola provided the thorns will not impede passers-by.

Bantry Bay

Bantry Bay

Bobbie James

BANTRY BAY

Botanical grouping: Cluster-flowered climber
Parentage: New Dawn x Korona
Other names: None
Other varieties: None
Year: 1967
Origin: Northern Ireland
Description: This is a healthy, strong grower to 4.5 m (15 ft) or more, bearing small clusters of large, semi-double, informal, sweetly scented blooms of rich pink, gently blending to an innocent white eye with golden stamens. The flowers are borne freely on strong healthy canes. The foliage is lush, dark and glossy. It is very free flowering and will reach a width of 2.5 m (8 ft).
Flowering: Repeat flowering and is also markedly free-flowering for a modern climber.
Cultivation: A hardy rose. It is a good choice where good coverage is required, for training on a wall or against an unsightly structure. Prune in winter if required and tie in the new growth regularly.

BOBBIE JAMES

Botanical grouping: Multiflora rambler
Parentage: Unknown, presumed to involve *R. multiflora* breeding.
Other names: None
Other varieties: None
Year: 1960
Origin: England
Description: Named for the Honorable Robert James who owned a beautiful garden of roses at St Nicholas, in Richmond, Yorkshire. This rose is an enormously vigorous climber to 7.5 m (25 ft) high and 3 m (10 ft) wide. It has large heads of creamy white flowers with two to three rows of petals which are richly fragrant. The fresh green, glossy foliage is ample.
Flowering: Summer
Cultivation: An exceptionally vigorous rose which should be grown only where a really

Breath of Life

Bobbie James

large rose will comfortably fit. It can be used to grow up and through a tree or to disguise an ugly wall. With its profuse foliage it needs particular attention to support as it grows. This hardy rose is suitable for cold climates.

BREATH OF LIFE

Botanical grouping: Large-flowered climber
Parentage: Red Dandy x Alexander
Other names: Harquanne
Other varieties: None
Year: 1982
Origin: England

Description: A stiff, upright shrub to 3 m (10 ft) which is classed as a climber but which may be trimmed to a tall shrub if desired. The large, full-petalled flowers are apricot when young, ageing to a more pinkish tone, especially when cut. It is moderately fragrant.
Flowering: Summer to autumn
Cultivation: Suitable for planting against a fence or wall, as a pillar rose, or as a tall bedding or border plant if kept trimmed. A healthy plant with no particular requirements to keep it blooming well.

CASINO

Botanical grouping: Large-flowered climber
Parentage: Coral Dawn x Buccaneer
Other names: Gerbe d'Or
Other varieties: None
Year: 1963
Origin: Northern Ireland
Description: This is a particularly lovely rose with a strong resemblance in the flower to a tea-noisette rose. The flowers are large, very double, globular, opening flat. They are clear primrose yellow, lightly fragrant and grow in small clusters. It is a vigorous, healthy rose with light green, glossy foliage and grows to a modest 3 m (10 ft) with a spread of 2.5 m (8 ft) if trained outward. It is less free-flowering than some but the colour is rare, the old-fashioned formation charming, and its restrained growth useful in smaller gardens.
Flowering: Repeat flowering
Cultivation: This makes a good pillar rose or for use against a verandah or pergola. Prune in winter if required.

CHINATOWN

Botanical grouping: Cluster-flowered climber
Parentage: Columbine x Cläre Grammerstorf
Other names: Ville de Chine

Chinatown

Other varieties: None
Year: 1963
Origin: Denmark
Description: Upright vigorous growth to 1.2 m (4 ft) high and 1 m (3 ft) wide. Its very large, fully double deep yellow fragrant flowers are often flushed pink and are displayed in clusters. It has lush, light green foliage.
Flowering: Continuously throughout summer
Cultivation: Tolerates poorer soils. Good for bedding, growing in groups or for hedging. Can be espaliered. Should only be lightly pruned.

CITY OF YORK

Botanical grouping: Cluster-flowered climber
Parentage: Prof Gnau x Dorothy Perkins
Other names: Direktor Benschop
Other varieties: None
Year: 1945
Origin: Germany
Description: A vigorous, beautiful rambler with attractive dark green foliage. Produces cupped, creamy white, semi-double flowers with lemon centres. Flowers are fragrant and appear individually. They are produced very freely to give a lovely overall effect.
Flowering: Summer only
Cultivation: Suitable for woodland planting or for growing up into trees. Tolerates poorer soils and shade.

Chinatown

Casino

City of York

Cocktail

Cocktail

Other varieties: None
Year: 1957
Origin: France
Description: Produces a very bright, single, red flower with a primrose-yellow centre and yellow stamens on large, upright trusses. Flowers have a moderate fragrance and are surrounded by dark green, glossy foliage. The stems are reddish brown. Grows to 1.8 m (6 ft) high and 1.2 m (4 ft) wide.
Flowering: Continuously throughout summer
Cultivation: Tolerates poorer soils. Use as a climber, a pillar rose or for hedging.

Clair Matin

CLAIR MATIN

Botanical grouping: Cluster-flowered climber
Parentage: Fashion x [(Independence x Orange Triumph) x Phyllis Bide]
Other names: Meimont
Other varieties: None
Year: 1960
Origin: France
Description: A beautiful, light pink rose with deeper, sometimes bronzy highlights, produced in large clusters. It is moderately fragrant with dark green, glossy foliage and dark wood. Growth is relaxed and upright to 2.5 m (8 ft) high and 1.2 m (4 ft) wide. Occasionally the stems arch with the weight of the flowers.
Flowering: Repeats throughout the season from early summer
Cultivation: Tolerates shade and poorer soil. Suitable for hedging or growing as a climber or pillar rose.

COCKTAIL

Botanical grouping: Cluster-flowered climber
Parentage: (Independence x Orange Triumph) x Phyllis Bide
Other names: Meimick

COMPASSION

Botanical grouping: Synstylae
Parentage: White Cockade x Prima Ballerina
Other names: Belle de Londres
Other varieties: None
Year: 1973
Origin: England
Description: This is a climbing hybrid tea with very shapely buds opening to double flowers of soft apricot blushed over with coppery-pink leaving an apricot glow to show through. The flowers are borne singly or in clusters. This is a very vigorous, healthy upright climber with dark, very glossy large leaves. The scent is very pleasing. In most situations this rose will grow to 3 m (10 ft) high and 1.8 m (6 ft) wide.
Flowering: Repeat flowering
Cultivation: This is a healthy, strong climber of restrained dimensions which will suit the smaller garden. Prune in winter if required and tie in new growth.

CONSTANCE SPRY

Botanical grouping: Large-flowered climber or modern shrub
Parentage: Belle Isis x Dainty Maid
Other names: None
Other varieties: None
Year: 1961
Origin: England
Description: One of the most highly prized shrub-climbers with beautiful, large, fully double, cupped, rich-pink blooms that are fragrant. Foliage is rather coarse, mid-green in colour, on a vigorous sprawling plant. The flowers are strongly fragrant. It grows to 6 m (20 ft) high and 3 m (10 ft) wide and needs support when grown as a shrub.
Flowering: Summer only
Cultivation: Can be grown as a climber or pillar rose, or pruned back hard and kept as a shrub. Needs moderately fertile, well-drained soil. It is tolerant of shade.

COPENHAGEN

Botanical grouping: Large-flowered climber
Parentage: Seedling x Ena Harkness
Other names: None
Other varieties: None
Year: 1964
Origin: Denmark
Description: Large, upright and vigorous grower to 3 m (10 ft) high and 1.2 m (4 ft) wide. The dark and glossy foliage has coppery highlights. Mildly scented flowers are bright scarlet, shapely, large and double.
Flowering: Continuously throughout summer
Cultivation: Tolerates poorer soils, but needs full sun. This rose needs support if it is to achieve its full height, and can be

Compassion

Constance Spry

Danse du Feu

trained as a pillar or column. Availability may be limited to specialists. Dead-head the plant after flowering, and prune in winter, removing all dead and diseased wood. Reduce the length of healthy stems, and encourage new shoots from the base by removing some older canes.

DANSE DU FEU

Botanical grouping: Cluster-flowered climber
Parentage: Paul's Scarlet Climber x *R. multiflora* seedling
Other names: Spectacular
Other varieties: None
Year: 1953
Origin: France
Description: This is a rose that, despite its excellence, requires careful placement as the colour is the most brilliant rich scarlet red becoming crimson-purple with age. The flowers, borne in clusters, are medium-sized and double, opening cupped and later flat. They have little fragrance. Grows to 3.5 m (12 ft) high and 2.5 m (8 ft) wide. The foliage is large and dark, and an excellent foil for the flowers.
Flowering: Free flowering and maintains its display throughout the rose season.
Cultivation: Of easy cultivation. This is a hardy rose and will tolerate being grown on the shaded side during the winter months. There is some susceptibility to black spot which should be controlled.

Dortmund

Elegance

Dublin Bay

Dortmund

Dreaming Spires

DORTMUND

Botanical grouping: Cluster-flowered climber
Parentage: Seedling x *R. kordesii*
Other names: None
Other varieties: None
Year: 1955
Origin: Germany
Description: This vigorous and upright plant produces elongated buds which open to large, single, bright red flowers with a white eye. The flowers are produced in clusters and are moderately fragrant. Grows to 2.5 m (8 ft) high and 1.8 m (6 ft) wide.
Flowering: Continuously throughout summer
Cultivation: Tolerates poorer soils. Suitable for hedging, climbing, or as a pillar rose.

DREAMING SPIRES

Botanical grouping: Bush climber
Parentage: Buccaneer x Arthur Bell
Other names: None
Other varieties: None
Year: 1973
Origin: England

Description: An upright, branching climber that reaches 2.8 m (9 ft) in height. The flowers of this climber, bred from two bush roses, are large and fragrant, in a clear, bright yellow colour.
Flowering: Summer to autumn
Cultivation: An excellent rose for a warm, sunny wall, fence or pillar. Quite hardy and suitable for cultivation in a wide range of soils and climates.

DUBLIN BAY

Botanical grouping: Cluster-flowered climber
Parentage: Bantry Bay x Altissimo
Other names: Macdub
Other varieties: None
Year: 1976
Origin: New Zealand
Description: This is a lower growing climbing floribunda used principally as a pillar rose, reaching 2 m (7 ft) high and 1.5 m (5 ft) wide. It bears clusters of medium-sized, rich bright red flowers in generous profusion over a long season making it ideal

for the small garden. The foliage is healthy, glossy and mid-green.
Flowering: Repeat flowering almost constantly over a long season and is floriferous.
Cultivation: This rose, while most commonly used as a pillar rose, can also be used as a large shrub, or as an informal hedging rose.

ELEGANCE

Botanical grouping: Large-flowered climber
Parentage: Glenn Dale x (Mary Wallace x Miss Lolita Armour)
Other names: None
Other varieties: None
Year: 1937
Origin: United States
Description: Very thorny but one of the loveliest roses imaginable. The individual blooms are medium-sized, primrose yellow, slightly deeper in the centre, very double, and of perfect formation. The fragrance is not strong but it is sweet. The foliage is abundant, healthy, glossy and dark green. It can grow to 4.5 m (15 ft) high with a spread of 2.5 m (8 ft).
Flowering: Summer flowering. Occasionally there is a very light flush in autumn.
Cultivation: An extremely hardy rose, very vigorous and healthy and easy to grow, with excellent cold hardiness. Prune in winter if required and tie in regularly and firmly as this is a rapidly growing rose.

FRANCIS E. LESTER

Botanical grouping: Polyantha climber
Parentage: Kathleen x unnamed seedling
Other names: None
Other varieties: None
Year: 1946
Origin: United States
Description: A strong, healthy climber bearing huge trusses of apricot-pink buds opening to single flowers that resemble apple blossom in their milky colour, faintly blushed at the edges, and golden stamens.

The flowers drop cleanly. The scent is free on the air, of the sweet, true musk fragrance often mixed with the intense sweet fragrance of oranges and bananas. The flowers are followed by a mass of bright orange-red hips. The young shoots are stout and covered in fine, prickly thorns; later the thorns are of average size and distribution. Grows to 4.5 m (15 ft) high and 3 m (10 ft) wide. One of the most spectacular climbing roses.

Flowering: Once flowering, fairly late in the season for a summer rose, but then flowering for an extended period.

Cultivation: This is an extraordinarily cold resistant rose. Provide a good strong support as this rose grows rapidly and substantially.

GOLD RUSH

Botanical grouping: Large-flowered climber
Parentage: Unknown
Other names: None
Other varieties: None
Year: 1941
Origin: United States
Description: Large, high-centred, double gold blooms have 24 petals and are very fragrant. A vigorous climbing rose but not dependably recurrent, it has attractive, glossy, ivy-green leaves and grows to more than 3 m (10 ft).
Flowering: Summer
Cultivation: Grow against a warm wall, over a trellis or pergola or through a tall tree that allows sufficient sun. Although it is tolerant of poorer soils, it will do best in fertile soil that is drained and well mulched.

GOLDEN GLOW

Botanical grouping: Synstylae
Parentage: Glenn Dale x (Mary Wallace x a hybrid tea)
Other names: None
Other varieties: None
Year: 1937
Origin: United States
Description: This is a cold hardy rose bearing cupped, almost fully double, clear buttercup yellow, unfading blooms of lovely form with a centre of reddish-gold stamens. The abundant foliage is dark, lush and disease proof, and the climber is vigorous growing to 3.5 m (12 ft) high and 2.5 m (8 ft) wide. This rose was used to introduce yellow colouring into the Kordesii hybrids.
Flowering: Once flowering, but occasionally gives a light autumn flowering. A very floriferous rose.
Cultivation: Very tough and cold hardy, this rose is easily established. It also performs well in hot dry areas. Prune after flowering.

Francis E. Lester

Golden Glow

Golden Showers

GOLDEN SHOWERS

Botanical grouping: Large-flowered climber
Parentage: Charlotte Armstrong x Captain Thomas
Other names: None
Other varieties: None
Year: 1957
Origin: United States
Description: A very popular climber which produces clusters of large, loosely formed, ruffled flowers of deep golden yellow paling to cream. They have a soft fragrance. Foliage is dark green and glossy. Grows in an upright form to 3 m (10 ft) highl and 1.8 m (6 ft) wide.
Flowering: Continuously throughout summer
Cultivation: Tolerates poor soils and shade. In winter remove dead and spindly wood if necessary.

GRAND'MÈRE JENNY CLIMBER

Botanical grouping: Large-flowered climber
Parentage: Sport of the bush form
Other names: None
Other varieties: Bush form bred by Meilland (France), 1950, from a cross Peace x (Julien Potin x Sensation)
Year: 1958
Origin: France
Description: This rose has large elegant buds which open to perfectly formed, high-centred blooms of primrose yellow suffused with coppery pink. The climbing form grows to 5.5 m (18 ft) high, and is well foliated with large, dark green, healthy foliage. It is a reasonably profuse flowerer over a long season but lacks that abundance of bloom typical of the repeat flowering Noisettes and once-flowering Rambler roses.
Flowering: Repeat flowering
Cultivation: This is a good vigorous rose with healthy foliage so that it offers few problems. It is quite cold hardy. Prune at the end of winter.

Golden Showers

GUINÉE

Botanical grouping: Large-flowered climber
Parentage: Souvenir de Claudius Denoyel x Ami Quinard
Other names: None
Other varieties: None
Year: 1938
Origin: France

Guinée

Description: The large flowers, sometimes in clusters of three or four, are a rich, dark, velvety crimson and quite powerfully fragrant, fully double and rather informal when open revealing golden stamens. The dark green foliage is leathery and dull but healthy. This is a rose that will reach to the second story of a house and give good coverage. It reaches 4.5 m (15 ft) high with a spread of 3 m (10 ft).
Flowering: Slightly repeat flowering, the autumn flush usually being much lighter than that of summer.
Cultivation: This is a strong variety performing well in a wide range of climates and soils. Prune in winter if required.

HAMBURGER PHOENIX

Botanical grouping: Cluster-flowered climber
Parentage: *R. kordesii* x seedling
Other names: None
Other varieties: None
Year: 1955
Origin: Germany

Lady Sylvia Climber

this rose has deeper colouring, being pure pink with a deeper suffusion of apricot in its heart. The fragrance is outstanding, rich and very sweet. This is a medium-sized climber reaching 3.5 m (12 ft) high with a spread of 3 m (10 ft). The grey-green foliage is neat and healthy providing an excellent backdrop for the clusters of roses.

Flowering: Repeat flowers reliably throughout the rose season.

Cultivation: An easily grown variety tolerant of a wide range of climates and soils. It has good cold hardiness.

LEVERKUSEN

Botanical grouping: Cluster-flowered climber
Parentage: *R. kordesii* x Golden Glow
Other names: None
Other varieties: None
Year: 1954
Origin: Germany
Description: This hardy, healthy variety produces flowers in profusion which are almost double, light yellow in colour, with attractive ragged edges when open. Foliage is glossy, serrated and light green. It is bushy with some thorns. Grows to 3 m (10 ft) high and 2.5 m (8 ft) wide.
Flowering: Continuously throughout summer
Cultivation: Tolerates poorer soils and shade and will grow on colder walls.

LYKKEFUND

Botanical grouping: Helenae climber
Parentage: *R. helenae* x Zéphirine Drouhin
Other names: None
Other varieties: None
Year: 1930
Origin: Denmark
Description: This is a rambler rose of great and quite spectacular charm with huge clusters of smallish almost single creamy yellow flowers with a pearl-like sheen and lovely sweet scent. It is bushy and sturdy

Lady Sylvia Climber

with smooth thornless canes. The leaves are composed of long elegant mid-green leaflets. It will grow to 6 m (20 ft) or more in height with a spread of 4.5 m (15 ft) and can be trained through a fairly open tree.
Flowering: Once only, but extremely free-flowering
Cultivation: While this is often used as a climber it also makes an outstanding specimen shrub which has the advantage of not catching passers-by in its embrace.

MADELEINE SELZER

Botanical grouping: Polyantha climber
Parentage: Tausendschön x Mrs Aaron Ward
Other names: Yellow Tausendschön

Leverkusen

Other varieties: None
Year: 1926
Origin: France
Description: This is one of the smaller growing rambler roses. Combined with the fact that this rose is almost thornless it is a welcome variety for the smaller garden. It is a spectacular rose with trusses of fragrant double flowers which are lemon, frosting to white. The foliage is bronzed green. Grows to 3 m (10 ft) with a spread of 1.8 m (6 ft).
Flowering: Once flowering
Cultivation: Prune soon after flowering is completed removing unproductive wood. While this is quite restrained in growth, when in heavy flower it will test the support provided which must be strong.

Lykkefund

Maigold

Maigold

Morning Jewel

MAIGOLD

Botanical grouping: Cluster-flowered climber
Parentage: Poulsen's Pink x Frühlingstag
Other names: None
Other varieties: None
Year: 1953
Origin: Germany
Description: This angular, upright climber is one of the first to flower each season. Has clusters of rich, semi-double, golden yellow flowers which are flushed with orange. It has a good fragrance. Foliage is rich mid-green and very glossy. Stems are prickly with reddish thorns. Grows to 3.5 m (12 ft) tall and 2.5 m (8 ft) wide.
Flowering: Summer only
Cultivation: Tolerates poorer soils and shade and can be grown against walls that are partially shaded.

MME JULES GRAVEREAUX

Botanical grouping: Tea climber
Parentage: Rêve d'Or x Viscountess Folkestone
Other names: None

Other varieties: None
Year: 1901
Origin: Luxembourg
Description: A climbing tea rose, seen at Mottisfont Abbey in England. The large, full, fragrant blooms are a gorgeous concoction of peach, apricot and pink lit by gold. The foliage is plentiful, healthy and dark. Specimens in warm areas reach 3 m (10 ft) but in cooler climates it reaches 2.5 m (8 ft) with a width of 1.8 m (6 ft).
Flowering: Repeat flowering
Cultivation: Planted against a warm wall this rose has sufficient hardiness to come through most winters unharmed in cooler areas but it is not recommended for cold climates.

MORNING JEWEL

Botanical grouping: Cluster-flowered climber
Parentage: New Dawn x Red Dandy
Other names: None
Other varieties: None
Year: 1968
Origin: Scotland

Description: A vigorous climber to 4 m (13 ft) with attractive glossy foliage. The scented flowers are of medium size in a clear, bright pink. After the first flush, the plant is without blooms until later in summer.
Flowering: Summer to autumn
Cultivation: Extremely healthy with an excellent resistance to disease. The flowers are also resistant to weather damage. It is excellent as a climber for difficult spots along walls and fences, and is also good as a pillar rose.

NANCY HAYWARD

Botanical grouping: Large-flowered climber
Parentage: Jessie Clark x unknown
Other names: None
Other varieties: None
Year: 1937
Origin: Australia
Description: The blooms have a very striking colour, the shade of ripe tomatoes. They are glowing, large, open and single and are borne on a healthy and robust

Nancy Hayward

Parkdirektor Riggers

Pink Perpetué

climbing bush which grows to 2 m (7 ft).
Flowering: Spring and summer
Cultivation: Prune in late summer for a late winter or spring blooming. Bred in Australia, this is a warm climate-loving rose that prefers full sun and good soil.

PARADE

Botanical grouping: Cluster-flowered climber
Parentage: New Dawn seedling x World's Fair
Other names: None
Other varieties: None
Year: 1953
Origin: United States
Description: A lower growing rose commonly used as a pillar rose. The blooms are a rich cerise, close to crimson, that glowing colour typical of Thai silk. They are fragrant and fully double, borne generously on a healthy plant. Foliage is deep green, glossy and plentiful. Grows to 3 m (10 ft) high and 2.5 m (8 ft) wide.
Flowering: Repeat flowering and very free-flowering
Cultivation: A good healthy rose, hardy, and establishing rapidly. It may also be used as a specimen shrub.

PARKDIREKTOR RIGGERS

Botanical grouping: Cluster-flowered climber
Parentage: *R. kordesii* x Our Princess
Other names: None
Other varieties: None
Year: 1957
Origin: Germany
Description: This popular climber has large, almost single, velvety deep red flowers in clusters. They have almost no fragrance. It grows to 3.5 m (12 ft) high and 1.8 m (6 ft) wide. The foliage is virtually disease free in most situations, and is dark green and healthy.
Flowering: Repeat flowering and floriferous
Cultivation: A hardy climber, easy to grow.

Parkdirektor Riggers

PINK PERPETUÉ

Botanical grouping: Cluster-flowered climber
Parentage: Danse du Feu x New Dawn
Other names: None
Other varieties: None
Year: 1965
Origin: England
Description: Charming, soft pink flowers with golden stamens open from dark pink buds and are offset by small glossy green foliage on long canes that grow up to 3 m (10 ft). It repeat flowers well but has little perfume.
Flowering: Repeats throughout summer
Cultivation: Although tolerant of poorer soils this climber needs full sun and a warm position, preferably against a brick wall, to flower freely.

Parade

Pink Perpetué

RAMBLING RECTOR

Botanical grouping: Polyantha climber
Parentage: Unknown. Possibly *R. multiflora* x *R. moschata*
Other names: None
Other varieties: None
Year: Before 1912
Origin: Unknown
Description: A charming rose with large heads of small, semi-double flowers which are creamy white with golden stamens. They have a delicious fragrance. The Rector rambles quite far and wide, to 6 m (20 ft) high and 4.5 m (15 ft) wide. The flowers are followed by dainty sprays of polished red hips in autumn. The foliage is healthy and plentful. This rose is a beautiful sight in full bloom.
Flowering: Once flowering and very floriferous.
Cultivation: This is a vigorous, healthy, hardy and easy rose to grow showing no susceptibility to disease. It can be used to form a large, dense and spectacular shrub, and can be used to grow through and over a tree, to cover an unsightly structure, or for a substantial pergola. It has shown the ability to adapt to a range of climates.

Rambling Rector

RED GLORY

Botanical grouping: Floribunda
Parentage: Gay Lady x (Pinocchio x Floradora)
Other names: None
Other varieties: None
Year: 1958
Origin: United States
Description: Grows to 2 m (7 ft) tall. Produces semi-double, cherry-crimson, lightly scented flowers, profusely over a long period. Very vigorous.
Flowering: Continuously throughout summer
Cultivation: Suitable for use as a hedge or fence. If used as a hedge prune long growths in summer and winter.

RÉVEIL DIJONNAIS

Botanical grouping: Large-flowered climber
Parentage: Eugène Fürst x Constance
Other names: None
Other varieties: None
Year: 1931
Origin: France

Rosanna

Description: The semi-double, loosely petalled flowers are a stunning mixture of red, gold and orange typical of the Pernetiana roses. It has very shiny, light green, profuse foliage and the stems are thorny. It grows to 3 m (10 ft) high or more, with a spread of 1.8 m (6 ft).
Flowering: Repeat flowering
Cultivation: This rose's chief failing is black spot which should be controlled.

ROSANNA

Botanical grouping: Large-flowered climber
Parentage: Coral Dawn x seedling
Other names: Korinter
Other varieties: None
Year: 1982
Origin: Germany
Description: Large, urn-shaped buds open to well-formed, rich pink blooms that have a wild-rose perfume and are accompanied by abundant mid-green foliage starting at ground level. The plant grows up to 2.5 m (8 ft) high.
Flowering: Spring and summer
Cultivation: A vigorous and healthy climber which will thrive against a warm wall or trellis, over a pergola or trained up a pillar. Plant in full sun, in drained fertile soil that is well watered and mulched in warmer weather.

ROSY MANTLE

Botanical grouping: Large-flowered climber
Parentage: New Dawn x Prima Ballerina
Other names: None
Other varieties: None
Year: 1968
Origin: Scotland
Description: This is a climber of considerable charm with small clusters of large, full, silvery pink flowers which are delightfully fragrant. The plant is a small but vigorous climber growing to 3 m (10 ft) high and 3 m (10 ft) wide. The foliage is glossy and mid-green.

Rosy Mantle

Schoolgirl

Sparkling Scarlet

Softie

Flowering: Repeat flowering and floriferous
Cultivation: A reliable rose with good cold hardiness. It can get out of hand if not regularly tied in. Prune in winter if required.

SCHOOLGIRL

Botanical grouping: Large-flowered climber
Parentage: Coral Dawn x Belle Blonde
Other names: None
Other varieties: None
Year: 1964
Origin: Northern Ireland
Description: A rather sparse, upright plant reaching 3 m (10 ft) in height, with not a very good coverage of foliage. The flowers are outstanding—a rich apricot colour, which is not common in climbers, with a beautiful fragrance.
Flowering: Summer to autumn
Cultivation: Plant in a sunny, sheltered position against a wall, trellis or pillar. Ideal for cultivation in a wide range of soils and conditions. Prune out dead wood in winter.

SOFTIE

Botanical grouping: Cluster-flowered climber
Parentage: Unknown
Other names: None
Other varieties: None
Year: 1991
Origin: Denmark
Description: Very pretty miniature white flowers with pointed petals are blushed with palest lemon. They are borne almost continuously, offset by shining green foliage.
Flowering: Spring and summer
Cultivation: Grow against a sunny wall or trellis or over a pergola. Plant in fertile soil that is well drained and mulched. Prune in summer. If pruned in winter, the flowering wood is cut off.

SPARKLING SCARLET

Botanical grouping: Cluster-flowered climber
Parentage: Danse des Sylphes x Zambra
Other names: Iskra, Meihaiti

Sparrieshoop

Summer Snow Climbing

Summer Wine

Other varieties: None
Year: 1970
Origin: France
Description: This is a floriferous rose making an excellent display. The flowers are semi-double, in a bright clear scarlet, and are borne in quite stiff, long-lasting, unfading clusters. The foliage is mid-green and clothes the plant well. Grows to 3 m (10 ft) with a spread of 1.8 m (5 ft).
Flowering: Repeat flowering
Cultivation: Of easy cultivation, healthy and hardy. Prune in winter if required.

SPARRIESHOOP

Botanical grouping: Cluster-flowered climber

Parentage: Baby Château x Else Poulsen x Magnifica
Other names: None
Other varieties: None
Year: 1953
Origin: Germany
Description: An upright, bushy plant which grows to 1.5 m (5 ft) tall and 1.2 m (4 ft) wide. It produces clusters of large, very fragrant, single, clear pink blooms with seven petals and golden stamens. Foliage is mid-green and leathery.
Flowering: Repeats throughout summer
Cultivation: A hardy specimen that tolerates poorer soils and some shade. Can be grown as a shrub and is suitable for hedging if long stems are pruned in summer and winter.

SUMMER SNOW CLIMBING

Botanical grouping: Cluster-flowered climber
Parentage: Seedling of Tausendschön x unknown
Other names: None
Other varieties: Summer Snow, bush sport from United States, 1938
Year: 1936
Origin: United States
Description: A very reliable and useful rose which bears large clusters of lightly fragrant, semi-double, open, snow white flowers and is very well covered with attractive foliage.
Flowering: Freely throughout summer
Cultivation: This is a very vigorous grower that can cover the side of a barn or house. It can be grown over a trellis or along a verandah and should be given plenty of space in full sun and fertile soil. New growth emerges from basal shoots.

SUMMER WINE

Botanical grouping: Cluster-flowered climber
Parentage: Unknown
Other names: Korizont
Other varieties: None
Year: 1985
Origin: Germany
Description: An upright, bushy plant that will reach 3 m (10 ft) when grown in the right position. The foliage is large, mid-green and slightly glossy, and the large, semi-double flowers are coral pink with red stamens.
Flowering: Summer to autumn
Cultivation: Easy to cultivate in a wide range of soils and conditions. It prefers a warm, sheltered position and some support in the form of a fence, wall, pillar or trellis upon which it can climb.

SUNNY JUNE

Botanical grouping: Cluster-flowered climber
Parentage: Crimson Glory x Captain Thomas
Other names: None
Other varieties: None
Year: 1952
Origin: United States
Description: An upright plant growing to 2.5 m (8 ft). It has single, deep golden yellow fragrant flowers with red stamens.
Flowering: Repeats throughout summer
Cultivation: Compact grower suitable as a pillar or shrub rose. Plant in full sun and prune out dead or spindly wood in winter.

SWAN LAKE

Botanical grouping: Large-flowered
climber
Parentage: Memoriam x Heidelberg
Other names: Schwanensee
Other varieties: None
Year: 1968
Origin: Northern Ireland
Description: This is an exceptionally lovely
climber of the hybrid tea persuasion with
large, full, beautifully formed blooms
opening from shapely buds. The flowers are
pure white, faintly blushed with pink in the
centre and they are produced liberally over
a long season. They have little fragrance. It
is upright growing, to 3 m (10 ft) high and
1.8 m (6 ft) wide, with deep green foliage.
Flowering: Repeat flowering
Cultivation: It can show black spot and this
should be controlled, but its many virtues
should outweigh such a maintenance
problem. Prune in winter. A tidy grower
easily trained against a wall or other support.

WARM WELCOME

Botanical grouping: Miniature climber
Parentage: Seedling of Anna Ford
Other names: Chewizz
Other varieties: None
Year: 1991
Origin: England
Description: Miniature climber to 2 m (7 ft)
with attractive dark green foliage. The semi-
double flowers are a reddish-orange with a
yellow base, borne in clusters along the full
length of the plant.
Flowering: Summer to autumn
Cultivation: Healthy with no particular
requirements, this rose does prefer an open,
sunny position. The blooms are resistant to
weather damage. Suitable for training
against a wall or fence or as a pillar rose.

WHITE SPARRIESHOOP

Botanical grouping: Cluster-flowered
climber
Parentage: Obscure, but believed to be a
white sport from Sparrieshoop
Other names: Weisse aus Sparrieshoop
Other varieties: Sparrieshoop
Year: 1962
Origin: Germany
Description: Produces clusters of large,
single, white blooms with golden stamens
and waxy petals. Foliage is mid-green and
plentiful. It is very fragrant and grows to
1.5 m (5 ft) tall and 1.2 m (4 ft) wide.
Flowering: Repeats throughout summer
Cultivation: A versatile rose that tolerates
poorer soils and shade. Can be used as a
hedging plant if pruned back in winter.

Swan Lake

Warm Welcome

White Sparrieshoop

Hybrid Tea (large-flowered) Roses

Hybrid teas have large and elegant flowers and are easily the most popular garden roses of this century. They owe their characteristics to the best features of the hybrid perpetual and the tea rose, from which they are descended; however, modern hybrid teas now have a much more mixed genealogy. The size and shape of the blooms is the distinguishing feature setting them apart, and it is the reason why they have been reclassified as 'large-flowered bush roses' by the Rose Society. Unlike the old tea roses the stems are sturdy, to support the weight of the blooms. Many thousands of new varieties have been introduced in the past 90 years and while some have come and gone according to fashion, some are so outstanding that they have remained popular many decades after they were originally introduced.

Admiral Rodney

ABBEYFIELD ROSE

Botanical grouping: Large-flowered hybrid tea
Parentage: National Trust x Silver Jubilee
Other names: Cocbrose
Other varieties: None
Year: 1985
Origin: Scotland
Description: Bushy shrub to around 1 m (3 ft) with mid-green leaves and branches. The high-centred flowers are a deep rose pink and lightly scented but are considered by some to be rather sparsely petalled.
Flowering: Continuously throughout summer
Cultivation: Suitable as a bedding or border plant or for massed display. Requires full sun. Flowers are tolerant of rain and sun. Dead-head after flowering.

ACE OF HEARTS

Botanical grouping: Large-flowered hybrid tea
Parentage: Unknown
Other names: Asso di Cuori, Toque Rouge, Korred
Other varieties: None
Year: 1981
Origin: Germany
Description: Upright shrub to 1 m (3 ft) with vigorous, dark green foliage. The well-shaped flowers have stiff petals of crimson to scarlet with a moderate fragrance.
Flowering: Continuously throughout summer
Cultivation: For bed, border or massed display. Prefers full sun and well-drained, rich soil. Prune out dead wood in winter, and shorten new stems by two-thirds to encourage larger blooms.

ADMIRAL RODNEY

Botanical grouping: Large-flowered hybrid tea
Parentage: Unknown
Other names: None
Other varieties: None
Year: 1973
Origin: England
Description: Small, bushy shrub to 70 cm (2 ft) with an abundance of leafy branches. The clear pink flowers are very large and scented and have a good shape.
Flowering: Continuously throughout summer
Cultivation: Not especially vigorous and rather sparsely flowered. Prized as an exhibition plant. Has a tendency to black spot and dislikes wet weather when in flower.

Abbeyfield Rose

Ace of Hearts

Alec's Red

ADOLF HORSTMANN

Botanical grouping: Large-flowered hybrid tea
Parentage: Colour Wonder x Dr A.J. Verhage
Other names: None
Other varieties: None
Year: 1971
Origin: Germany
Description: Neat, upright shrub to 1 m (3 ft) with bright green, glossy foliage. The large flowers are yellow tinged with orange-pink and slightly fragrant and are at their most attractive when nearly open.
Flowering: Almost continuously throughout summer.
Cultivation: Suitable for use as a bedding, border or small hedging plant and is also a good choice as an exhibition rose. Prefers well-drained, rich soil and an open, sunny position. Water well in summer, and prune out dead or diseased wood.

ALEC'S RED

Botanical grouping: Large-flowered hybrid tea
Parentage: Fragrant Cloud x Dame de Coeur
Other names: Cored
Other varieties: None
Year: 1970
Origin: Scotland
Description: Bushy, tree-branching shrub to 1 m (3 ft) with dark green foliage. Rather thorny. The abundant flowers are large and well formed, crimson to deep cherry-red and heavily scented.
Flowering: Continuously throughout summer and early autumn
Cultivation: Tolerant of poorer soils, but needs full sun to thrive. This rose is useful as a cut flower and is considered a good exhibition specimen. May be used as a bedding or border plant as well as for hedging and massed display.

ALEXANDER

Botanical grouping: Large-flowered hybrid tea
Parentage: Super Star x (Ann Elizabeth x Allgold)
Other names: Alexandra
Other varieties: None
Year: 1972
Origin: England
Description: Vigorous, upright shrub to 1.5 m (5 ft) with dark green, glossy foliage. The large, bright vermilion-red flowers are carried on tall stems, making them ideal as cut roses. They should be cut while in bud to ensure a lasting cut specimen. Lightly scented.
Flowering: Continuously from summer to early autumn
Cultivation: Disease resistant and very easy to grow. Late winter pruning of long stems will encourage good flower production. Use for bed, border, hedge or fence plant.

ALPINE SUNSET

Botanical grouping: Large-flowered hybrid tea
Parentage: Dr A.J. Verhage x Grandpa Dickson
Other names: None
Other varieties: None
Year: 1974
Origin: England
Description: Upright, vigorously free-flowering shrub to 75 cm (2½ ft) with mid-green leaves carried on rather short, stumpy stems. The very large peachy yellow flowers are abundant and are extremely fragrant.
Flowering: Continuously from summer through to autumn
Cultivation: Generally quite hardy, although may die off if exposed to severe frosts or very cold winds. Suitable as a bedding or border plant. May be used as an exhibition rose.

Adolf Horstmann

Alexander

Alpine Sunset

Alpine Sunset

Anneka

Apricot Silk

Arianna

ANGÈLE PERNET

Botanical grouping: Large-flowered hybrid tea
Parentage: Bénédicte Seguin x a hybrid tea
Other names: None
Other varieties: None
Year: 1924
Origin: France
Description: Small shrub to 70 cm (2 ft) with glossy, dark green leaves and branches. The flowers are beautifully formed and are a delicate coppery orange and moderately fragrant. Only a few flowers are formed at any one time.
Flowering: Continuously throughout summer
Cultivation: A difficult rose to cultivate with some expertise required. Its size makes it suitable as a potted specimen and it could also be used as a border plant.

ANNA PAVLOVA

Botanical grouping: Large-flowered hybrid tea
Parentage: Unknown
Other names: None

Anna Pavlova

Other varieties: None
Year: 1981
Origin: England
Description: Upright shrub to 1.2 m (4 ft) with glossy, dark green foliage and thick stems. The large flowers are rounded, full and many-petalled, in a delicate pink with deeper pink tones. When fully open some petals are fringed. A very fragrant rose.
Flowering: Continuously throughout summer
Cultivation: Prefers a warm, sunny position. Suitable as a glasshouse rose and is a good cut flower and exhibition rose. May be cultivated in a pot. Flowers tend to ball up in the rain. Do not prune this rose if grown in poor soils.

ANNEKA

Botanical grouping: Large-flowered hybrid tea
Parentage: Goldbonnet x Silver Jubilee
Other names: None
Other varieties: None
Year: 1990
Origin: England
Description: Very vigorous, leafy shrub to 1 m (3 ft) with large yellow flowers, tinged with pink as they open. This rose is very free-flowering and has a slight fragrance.
Flowering: Continuously from summer through to autumn
Cultivation: Disease resistant and very hardy, needing only full sun and well-drained, moderately rich soil. Suitable as a hedging or border plant and is attractive in a massed planting.

APRICOT SILK

Botanical grouping: Large-flowered hybrid tea
Parentage: Unknown x Souvenir de Jacques Verschuren
Other names: None

Other varieties: None
Year: 1965
Origin: England
Description: A moderately vigorous shrub to 70 cm (2 ft). The flowers are large and free-flowering in orange-apricot to red shades. It is moderately fragrant.
Flowering: Continuously throughout summer
Cultivation: Susceptible to black spot, rust and mildew. Requires a very rich and well-prepared soil to flourish. Keep the area around the rose free from weeds. Useful as a potted specimen or as a border plant.

ARIANNA

Botanical grouping: Large-flowered hybrid tea
Parentage: Charlotte Armstrong x (Peace x Michèle Meilland)
Other names: Meidali
Other varieties: None
Year: 1968
Origin: France
Description: Vigorous, upright shrub to 1 m (3 ft) with dark green foliage. The large flowers are high-centred and full, carmine rose in colour and tinged with coral at the edges of the petals. Moderately scented.
Flowering: Continuously throughout summer
Cultivation: Tolerant of poorer quality soil but does best in full sun. Popular as an exhibition plant and useful for bedding, borders and massed displays.

AVON

Botanical grouping: Large-flowered hybrid tea
Parentage: Nocturne x Chrysler Imperial
Other names: None
Other varieties: None
Year: 1961
Origin: United States
Description: A great favourite in Australia

Avon

where it is one of the best-loved red roses. Prolific, elegant, pointed buds open to large and well-formed high-centred blooms 10 cm (4 in) across. Long stems and a sweet fragrance make this an excellent cutting rose. The vigorous, upright bush grows to 1.5 m (5 ft) high and has abundant, leathery green foliage.

Flowering: Spring and summer, repeating in hotter climates

Cultivation: Plant in full sun in soil that has been well mulched and has good drainage. Grows in filtered shade although adequate drainage and good soil are necessary.

BACCARÀ

Botanical grouping: Large-flowered hybrid tea
Parentage: Happiness x Independence
Other names: Meger, Jaqueline
Other varieties: None
Year: 1954
Origin: France
Description: Upright shrub to 1 m (3 ft) with dark green stems and leaves and large, moderately abundant thorns. The flowers are deep red when grown outside, or brighter red when forced under glass. With very long stems, they are excellent as cut flowers. Unscented.
Flowering: Continuously throughout summer
Cultivation: Requires an open, very sunny and warm position with well-drained soil.

BARBARA RICHARDS

Botanical grouping: Large-flowered hybrid tea
Parentage: Unknown
Other names: None
Other varieties: None
Year: 1930
Origin: Northern Ireland
Description: Bushy shrub to 70 cm (2 ft)

with dark green foliage. The shapely, double flowers are yellow, flushed with pink, and very fragrant. The stems are rather too weak to support these large flowers. May be difficult to obtain.

Flowering: Continuously throughout summer
Cultivation: Prefers a sunny aspect, and may be grown in a pot.

BASILDON BOND

Botanical grouping: Large-flowered hybrid tea
Parentage: (Sabine x Circus) x (Yellow Cushion x Glory of Ceylon)
Other names: Harjosine
Other varieties: None
Year: 1980
Origin: England
Description: Bushy, free-flowering shrub to 70 cm (2 ft) with attractive, glossy, reddish green foliage. The large, urn-shaped flowers are apricot with flushes of yellow and red, and are moderately scented.

Baccarà

Basildon Bond

Flowering: Continuously throughout summer until autumn
Cultivation: A hardy rose which requires little other than full sun and a well-drained and mulched soil. Use as a bedding or border plant, in massed displays, or grow in pots.

Bel Air

Berolina

Benson and Hedges Gold

Parentage: Peace x Lorraine
Other names: None
Other varieties: None
Year: 1955
Origin: France
Description: Bushy, upright, rather low-growing shrub, with large, dark green and glossy foliage. The large, double blooms are a deep golden yellow darkening towards the centre and are quite fragrant. It is very floriferous.
Flowering: Continuously from summer to autumn
Cultivation: Less healthy and resilient than its parent, Peace, with a tendency to black spot. Planted in pots or as a bedding plant.

BENSON AND HEDGES GOLD

Botanical grouping: Large-flowered hybrid tea
Parentage: Yellow Pages x (Arthur Bell x Cynthia Brooke)
Other names: Macgem
Other varieties: None
Year: 1979
Origin: New Zealand
Description: Compact, bushy shrub grows to 75 cm (2 1/2 ft). The well-formed flowers are a deep golden yellow with tints of red are and are moderately fragrant.
Flowering: A good repeat flowerer throughout summer and autumn
Cultivation: A hardy and healthy rose. Requires plenty of sun and a well-drained position. Mulch well in summer to retain soil moisture. Suited to planting as a hedge, border, in massed plantings or in pots. The flowers are resistant to weather damage.

BEROLINA

Botanical grouping: Large-flowered hybrid tea
Parentage: Unknown
Other names: Korpriwa, Selfridges
Other varieties: None
Year: 1984
Origin: Germany
Description: Long, pointed buds open to amber yellow, deepening in colour when fully open. Grows to 9 cm (3 in) across. Abundant, high-centred blooms have a sweet tea rose fragrance and are carried along the sides and ends of large canes. Growing to a height of up to 2 m (7 ft), this is a very robust rose with mid-green, semi-glossy foliage.
Flowering: Spring to summer
Cultivation: Large canes develop each year from the ground and will flower the second year. Treat this rose as a shrub and prune more severely if it needs to be contained.

BEL AIR

Botanical grouping: Large-flowered hybrid tea
Parentage: Unknown
Other names: None
Other varieties: None
Year: Unknown
Origin: Unknown
Description: Exquisitely formed and large, rich red blooms flower prolifically on a strong, healthy bush to 1.5 m (5 ft) with good foliage. The long stems and impressive blooms make this a good cutting rose.
Flowering: Freely throughout summer
Cultivation: Will grow in full sun or partial shade if good drainage is provided. Prune back when flowering is finished and mulch soil in hot weather.

BELLE BLONDE

Botanical grouping: Large-flowered hybrid tea

Beryl Bach

Big Chief

Big Purple

BERYL BACH

Botanical grouping: Large-flowered hybrid tea
Parentage: Korresia x Silver Jubilee
Other names: Hartesia
Other varieties: None
Year: 1985
Origin: England
Description: Vigorous shrub to 1 m (3 ft) with a very leafy habit. The abundant flowers are high-centred, well-shaped and many-petalled. The colour varies from creamy white to primrose-yellow with tinges of crimson.
Flowering: Continuously from summer to autumn.
Cultivation: A useful rose for all conditions, it is suited as a bedding, hedge or border plant and also makes a good cut flower. The blooms are weather resistant. A healthy shrub with no special requirements other than plenty of sun and good drainage.

BETTINA

Botanical grouping: Large-flowered hybrid tea
Parentage: Peace x (Mme Joseph Perraud x Demain)
Other names: Mepal
Other varieties: Climbing form with flowers like Bettina
Year: 1953
Origin: France
Description: Low-growing, vigorous shrub to 70 cm (2 ft) with dark green, glossy foliage which is bronze when young. As buds the petals are coppery coloured; on opening the flat, full blooms are yellow-orange with deeper veins of bronze and lightly scented.
Flowering: Continuously throughout summer to autumn
Cultivation: Not completely hardy. It requires full sun to thrive and is prone to black spot. Useful as a potted specimen and may be forced under glass.

BIG CHIEF

Botanical grouping: Large-flowered hybrid tea
Parentage: Ernest H. Morse x Red Planet
Other names: Portland Trailblazer
Other varieties: None
Year: 1975
Origin: Northern Ireland
Description: Very vigorous shrub to around 1.2 m (4 ft) with dull green foliage and very leggy stems. The flowers are very large and high-centred in a deep crimson. Moderately scented. This rose offers scope for the exhibitor but is not considered a good garden specimen as it does not produce many flowers.
Flowering: Repeat flowering throughout summer
Cultivation: Not especially hardy and may die back. Best grown under glass.

Bettina

BIG PURPLE

Botanical grouping: Large-flowered hybrid tea
Parentage: Unknown
Other names: Nuit d'Orient, Stebigpu, Stephens' big purple
Other varieties: None
Year: 1987
Origin: New Zealand
Description: Sturdy shrub to 1 m (3 ft) with a branching habit and dark foliage. The large flower has an attractive, well-formed shape and is a very striking, deep beetroot-purple. It is quite fragrant.
Flowering: Continuously throughout summer to autumn
Cultivation: A hardy and disease-resistant rose with no special requirements other than a sunny position with well-drained soil. Its colour might limit its use in the average garden but it is suited as a bedding or border plant.

Bing Crosby

Blessings

Blue River

BING CROSBY

Botanical grouping: Large-flowered hybrid tea
Parentage: Candy Apple x First Prize
Other names: None
Other varieties: None
Year: 1981
Origin: United States
Description: An excellent exhibition and cut flower specimen, with consistently fine, though scentless, blooms of vivid, persimmon-red. The attractive buds are ovoid amid dark, glossy foliage on a bush which grows to 1.2 m (4 ft).
Flowering: Spring to summer
Cultivation: Prefers day-long sun in good fertile soil that is well drained, watered and mulched. It will tolerate partial shade.

BLESSINGS

Botanical grouping: Large-flowered hybrid tea
Parentage: Queen Elizabeth x seedling
Other names: None
Other varieties: None
Year: 1967
Origin: England
Description: Strong-growing, upright and dense shrub to around 75 cm (2½ ft) with medium green foliage on dark stems. The large, double flowers grow in clusters and are a soft coral-pink with a slight fragrance. It is very free-flowering, and provides an attractive cut flower.
Flowering: Continuously throughout summer
Cultivation: Tolerant of poorer soil quality and is reasonably hardy and disease resistant. May be used in borders and looks particularly good in massed displays.

BLUE MOON

Botanical grouping: Large-flowered hybrid tea
Parentage: Sterling Silver seedling x seedling

Other names: Blue Monday, Sissi, Mainzer Fastnacht, Tannacht
Other varieties: None
Year: 1964
Origin: Germany
Description: Upright and vigorous shrub reaches around 75 cm (2½ ft) with glossy, bright green foliage. The flowers are large and high-centred, in shades ranging from silvery lilac to lilac-purple on long stems. The sun will bring out the blue tones.
Flowering: Continuously throughout summer
Cultivation: Grown in pots or as a bedding plant, it also provides beautiful, very fragrant, cut flowers. Often grown as an exhibition rose. Hardy and in general reasonably healthy, but may occasionally die back. Prefers a little shade and needs rich, well-drained soil. Water thoroughly in hot, dry months.

BLUE RIVER

Botanical grouping: Large-flowered hybrid tea
Parentage: Blue Moon x Zorina
Other Names: Korsicht
Other varieties: None
Year: 1984
Origin: Germany
Description: A well-formed, large, mauve rose edged with deep magenta, with 40–45

Blue Moon

petals and a rich fragrance. Blooms are offset by glossy, attractive foliage. Grows to 1.2 m (4 ft) high.
Flowering: Very free blooming throughout summer
Cultivation: A vigorous, upright sun-lover that responds well to regular maintenance, good soil enriched with humus and adequate water. Mulch in dry weather.

BOBBY CHARLTON

Botanical grouping: Large-flowered hybrid tea
Parentage: Royal Highness x Prima Ballerina
Other names: None
Other varieties: None
Year: 1974
Origin: England
Description: A vigorous and upright shrub with dark green, leathery foliage, inclined to legginess. The flowers are large and very double and occur either singly or in clusters. They are deep pink with a paler, silvery reverse and are very fragrant. While often grown as an exhibition rose it is not at all free-flowering, which reduces its usefulness as a garden rose.
Flowering: Continuously from early summer to autumn
Cultivation: A healthy and hardy rose with

Bobby Charlton

no particular requirements. Richer soil will tend to increase flower size. Rain will damage the blooms.

BONNIE SCOTLAND

Botanical grouping: Large-flowered hybrid tea
Parentage: Wendy Cussons x Percy Thrower
Other names: None
Other varieties: None
Year: 1976
Origin: Scotland
Description: An upright shrub of medium height to around 75 cm (2½ ft) with glossy, medium green foliage. The flowers are large, full and high-centred in a rose pink to red with a moderate fragrance. It is very free-flowering and free-growing.
Flowering: Continuously throughout summer
Cultivation: A hardy rose which requires a well-drained soil and plenty of water in summer. Suited to massed plantings.

BONSOIR

Botanical grouping: Large-flowered hybrid tea
Parentage: Seedling x seedling
Other names: None
Other varieties: None
Year: 1968
Origin: Northern Ireland
Description: A strong growing and upright shrub reaching 75 cm (2½ ft) with dark green, glossy foliage. The double flowers have a perfect shape and are peach-pink with darker pink shadings. They have a good fragrance. The shrub is not very free-flowering and is therefore best suited to exhibition or glasshouse cultivation.
Flowering: Repeat flowering from early summer until autumn
Cultivation: A sensitive rose that dislikes wet weather and is best grown under glass in controlled conditions. May be grown in a pot.

BROADWAY

Botanical grouping: Large-flowered hybrid tea
Parentage: (First Prize x Golden Glow) x Sutter's Gold
Other names: Burway
Other varieties: None
Year: 1985
Origin: United States
Description: Elegant and sweetly perfumed, this is an excellent rose for cutting as well as garden display. Large yellow flowers, brushed pink and orange at the edges, are set off by lush mid-green foliage on a plant growing to 1.2 m (4 ft).

Bonsoir

Broadway

Flowering: Spring to summer
Cultivation: A good exhibition rose deserving a prominent position in the garden. Plant in full sun in rich soil that has been mulched and is well drained.

BUCCANEER

Botanical grouping: Large-flowered hybrid tea
Parentage: Golden Rapture x (Max Krause x Captain Thomas)
Other names: None
Other varieties: None
Year: 1952
Origin: United States
Description: An upright and fairly vigorous shrub to 1.2 m (4 ft) with few branches, long stems and matt green foliage. The flower is considered one of the best yellow roses, with urn-shaped long buds opening to loosely double, medium large blooms of pure golden yellow which does not fade as the flower ages. It is very free-flowering and moderately fragrant.
Flowering: Continuously throughout summer
Cultivation: A fine cut flower and excellent grown in large beds or against walls. Best grown up a strong post to provide support. Tolerates poorer soils. Prune lightly after flowering and water well in summer.

Buccaneer

CAN CAN

Botanical grouping: Large-flowered hybrid tea
Parentage: Just Joey x (Superior x Mischief)
Other names: Legglow
Other varieties: None
Year: 1982
Origin: England
Description: A sturdy, bushy shrub reaching 70 cm (2 ft) with attractive foliage. The flowers are large and deep orange-red and are moderately scented. It is very free-flowering.
Flowering: Continuously throughout summer
Cultivation: Healthy, disease-resistant plant with no special requirements. Water well in summer and provide a sunny spot and well-drained soil.

CANDLELIGHT

Botanical grouping: Large-flowered hybrid tea
Parentage: Shirley Laugharn x (Bewitched x King's Ransom)
Other names: Arowdye
Other varieties: None
Year: 1982
Origin: United States
Description: High-centred, large, double, soft lemon blooms are tinged with pink on a deeper yellow base. The overall colour of the rose deepens in hot weather. Delightfully fragrant, the glossy, well-foliated plant grows to a height of about 1 m (3 ft).
Flowering: Spring and summer
Cultivation: Will tolerate partial shade but prefers a sunny position in good soil that has been mulched and enriched with humus.

CANDY STRIPE

Botanical grouping: Large-flowered hybrid tea
Parentage: A sport of Pink Peace
Other names: None

Can Can

Other varieties: None
Year: 1963
Origin: United States
Description: Plump, ovoid buds open to large, 60-petalled flowers almost 15 cm (6 in) across. The blooms are cupped, highly fragrant and dusty pink striped with a creamy almost white pink reminiscent of a carnation, and are ideal for cutting. Leathery, dark green foliage is plentiful on a bush growing to 1.2 m (4 ft) high.
Flowering: Very freely throughout summer
Cultivation: A good exhibition rose making an especially fine display when massed. Needs full sun and good soil that is mulched and well drained. It is not tolerant of shade.

CENTURY TWO

Botanical grouping: Large-flowered hybrid tea
Parentage: Charlotte Armstrong x Duet
Other names: None
Other varieties: None
Year: 1971
Origin: United States
Description: Graceful, long, pointed buds, borne on long stems, open to carmine-pink, cupped blooms. Their holding habit and sweet perfume make this an excellent cutting rose. Attractive leathery green foliage is disease-resistant and abundant on a bush which grows to 1.2 m (4 ft).

Candlelight

Candy Stripe

Century Two

Flowering: Repeats throughout summer
Cultivation: A shapely bush with a healthy constitution requiring only little maintenance. It will tolerate a sandy soil and will grow in full sun or filtered shade.

CHAMPION

Botanical grouping: Large-flowered hybrid tea
Parentage: Grandpa Dickson x Whisky Mac
Other names: None
Other varieties: None
Year: 1976
Origin: England
Description: The shrub is bushy and short, reaching 70 cm (2 ft), with light green foliage. The large, full flowers are creamy yellow, flushed with red and pink and have an attractive shape. They are moderately fragrant. The rose is only really suitable for exhibition since the petals are too delicate to withstand the normal weather fluctuations that occur in the average garden.
Flowering: Repeat flowering from early summer to autumn
Cultivation: Prone to black spot. The blooms are very susceptible to rain damage. May be planted in pots.

CHAMPS-ELYSÉES

Botanical grouping: Large-flowered hybrid tea
Parentage: Monique x Happiness
Other names: None
Other varieties: None
Year: 1957
Origin: France
Description: A strong and bushy shrub to 70 cm (2 ft) with matt, medium green foliage. The flowers are large and fully double with a velvety feel to the petals which are a rich crimson-red. It has only a slight scent.
Flowering: Continuously throughout summer

Cheshire Life

Cultivation: Able to tolerate poorer soil quality and is also healthy, hardy and reasonably disease resistant. May be planted in pots or in beds for a massed display.

CHESHIRE LIFE

Botanical grouping: Large-flowered hybrid tea
Parentage: Prima Ballerina x Princess Michiko
Other names: None
Other varieties: None
Year: 1972
Origin: England
Description: Upright shrub with bushy foliage reaching around 75 cm (2½ ft). The medium-sized rose is a rich vermilion-red, very free-flowering with a slight fragrance.
Flowering: Continuously throughout summer
Cultivation: A healthy, hardy rose which requires moderately rich soil, good drainage and a sunny spot. It is best suited as a bedding plant in massed displays or will form an attractive hedge. The blooms tolerate wet weather very well.

CHICAGO PEACE

Botanical grouping: Large-flowered hybrid tea
Parentage: Sport from Peace
Other names: None
Other varieties: None
Year: 1962
Origin: United States

Champion

Champs-Elysées

Chicago Peace

Christian Dior

CLEO

Botanical grouping: Large-flowered hybrid tea
Parentage: Perfecta x Prima Ballerina
Other names: Beebop
Other varieties: None
Year: 1981
Origin: England
Description: A bushy and upright, very free-flowering shrub growing to around 75 cm (2½ ft) with abundant medium green foliage. The flowers are large and very full in a delicate rose pink. It is lightly scented.
Flowering: Continuously throughout summer until autumn
Cultivation: A hardy and disease-resistant rose without any special requirements except a sunny position and well-drained and mulched soil. Best suited as a bedding plant or for massed displays. Can also be used as an exhibition rose.

COLORAMA

Botanical grouping: Large-flowered hybrid tea
Parentage: Suspense x Confidence
Other names: Dr R. Maag, Meirigalu
Other varieties: None
Year: 1968
Origin: France
Description: A medium-sized shrub of strong growth and upright habit to around 75 cm (2½ ft) with very glossy foliage. The large flower has a cupped shape and is very double. The petals are crimson-red with a yellow reverse streaked with salmon tones. It is unscented.
Flowering: Continuously from early summer to autumn
Cultivation: A hardy and healthy rose, with no particular requirements except adequate sun and heavy waterings during summer. The shrub does well as a bedding plant or in a pot.

Description: A strong growing, well-branched shrub to 1.2 m (4 ft) with glossy, leathery foliage. The flower is identical to its parent except for the colour which ranges from deep yellow to primrose, veined with copper and orange. It is slightly scented.
Flowering: Continuously throughout summer
Cultivation: It has many uses, from exhibition rose to cut flower and as well as for bedding and hedging. Can tolerate poorer soil quality and is hardy and healthy. Water well in hot months and mulch the beds well.

CHRISTIAN DIOR

Botanical grouping: Large-flowered hybrid tea
Parentage: (Independence x Happiness) x (Peace x Happiness)
Other names: Meilie
Other varieties: None
Year: 1959
Origin: France
Description: A strong and upright, very free-flowering shrub to 1 m (3 ft) with glossy, dark foliage. The large flowers are very double and full, a velvety crimson-red with paler exterior petals and unscented. The blooms are held on strong stems and are therefore good as cut flowers and are also suitable for exhibition.
Flowering: Continuously throughout summer
Cultivation: The blooms are not tolerant of rain and the shrub is very susceptible to mildew. In general it is a shrub that needs special attention to do well.

CHRYSLER IMPERIAL

Botanical grouping: Large-flowered hybrid tea
Parentage: Charlotte Armstrong x Mirandy
Other names: None
Other varieties: None
Year: 1952
Origin: United States
Description: A bushy and vigorous shrub reaching around 75 cm (2½ ft) with glossy, medium green foliage. The flowers are large and very double in a deep glowing crimson with quite a good fragrance.
Flowering: Continuously throughout summer until autumn
Cultivation: Suited as an exhibition rose or as a bedding plant. Not an especially hardy rose with a tendency to deteriorate after a few years. It is prone to die-back.

Chrysler Imperial

Colorama

Colour Wonder

Congratulations

Country Lady

COLOUR WONDER

Botanical grouping: Large-flowered hybrid tea
Parentage: Perfecta x Super Star
Other names: Queen of Roses, Königen der Rosen, Reine des Roses, Korbico
Other varieties: None
Year: 1964
Origin: Germany
Description: A bushy, vigorous and free-flowering shrub to 75 cm (2½ ft) with bronze-green, leafy foliage. The very large flowers have a perfect shape and are held on long stems making them suitable as cut flowers. The petals are streaked with orange, salmon-pink and yellow with a creamy reverse and the rose is lightly scented.
Flowering: Continuously from early summer to autumn
Cultivation: Hardy and disease resistant, this rose does well with little special care. Plant it in a sunny position in well-drained and mulched soil. Plant in pots, in borders or beds, or use as an exhibition rose.

CONGRATULATIONS

Botanical grouping: Large-flowered hybrid tea
Parentage: Carina x a seedling
Other names: Sylvia, Korlift
Other varieties: None
Year: 1978
Origin: Germany
Description: An upright, tall shrub reaching around 1.2 m (4 ft) with attractive, glossy foliage. The medium-sized, delicate rose pink flowers are fully double with a good shape and are lightly scented.
Flowering: Continuously from early summer to autumn
Cultivation: Healthy, disease resistant plant that has no special requirements. It will tolerate poorer soils but thrives in a sunny position. This rose is suitable for exhibition and may also be used as a bedding rose, particularly for massed displays.

CORDON BLEU

Botanical grouping: Large-flowered hybrid tea
Parentage: Basildon Bond x Silver Jubilee
Other names: Harubasil
Other varieties: None
Year: 1992
Origin: England
Description: An upright bush with dark green, glossy foliage and a good display of apricot flowers, shaded in red, with a strong fruity fragrance. The flowers have an unusual shape, with reflex outer petals and a conical centre.
Flowering: Summer to autumn
Cultivation: Ideal for a bed or border, or as a hedging rose. Can be grown in most soils and conditions, but prefers full sun.

Cordon Bleu

COUNTRY LADY

Botanical grouping: Large-flowered hybrid tea
Parentage: Alexander x Bright Smile
Other names: Hartsam
Other varieties: None
Year: 1988
Origin: England
Description: A handsome shrub, reaching 1 m (3 ft) in height, clothed in a mass of red-green foliage. The unusual flowers are borne on long, slender stems, with soft salmon-pink petals.
Flowering: Summer to autumn
Cultivation: A useful rose for bed, border or as a distinctive hedge. Quite hardy and suited to a wide range of soils and climates. Prune out dead wood in winter.

Crimson Glory

CRIMSON GLORY

Botanical grouping: Large-flowered hybrid tea
Parentage: Catherine Kordes seedling x W.E. Chaplin
Other names: None
Other varieties: Climbing sport
Year: 1935
Origin: Germany
Description: A medium-sized, upright and very free-flowering shrub to around 75 cm (2½ ft) with dark green, rather sparse foliage. The spectacular flowers are large and double in a velvety deep crimson-red. It is strongly scented. Unfortunately the blooms are carried on rather weak stems.
Flowering: Continuously from early summer to autumn
Cultivation: May be grown as a bedding or border plant, but this rose dislikes rain when in flower and is therefore best grown under glass.

CRYSTALLINE

Botanical grouping: Large-flowered hybrid tea
Parentage: Unknown
Other names: Arobipy
Other varieties: None
Year: 1987
Origin: United States
Description: Long-stemmed and multi-headed, this is a clear white rose that lasts well when cut. Although only slightly scented, it is very floriferous and has light green foliage on a bushy plant growing to 1.2 m (4 ft).
Flowering: Freely throughout summer
Cultivation: Grow in full sun or partial shade in well mulched soil with good drainage. Prune lightly when flowering finishes, harder once the plant is established.

Crystalline

DAINTY BESS

Botanical grouping: Large-flowered hybrid tea
Parentage: Ophelia x Kitchener of Khartoum
Other names: None
Other varieties: None

Dainty Bess

Year: 1925
Origin: England
Description: An old-fashioned hybrid tea rose evocative of the 1920s. A single, five-petalled rose of soft pink with a central cluster of wine-coloured stamens, produced in clusters amid dark green foliage. A prolific and upright bush, to 1 m (3 ft).
Flowering: Continuously throughout summer
Cultivation: Requiring little more than occasional maintenance and good soil this rose will make a fine informal hedging rose. Best grown under glasshouse conditions in colder climates.

DAME EDITH HELEN

Botanical grouping: Large-flowered hybrid tea
Parentage: Unknown
Other names: None
Other varieties: None
Year: 1926
Origin: England
Description: An upright shrub with few branches to 75 cm (2½ ft) with bushy, medium-green foliage. The very fragrant

flowers are large and double in a rich silvery pink. The blooms sometimes open quartered in the old-fashioned style. The shrub is not at all free-flowering and its use as a garden rose is somewhat limited.

Flowering: Repeat flowering throughout the summer

Cultivation: It may be grown in a pot or as a bedding or border plant. It dislikes the rain when in flower.

DARLING

Botanical grouping: Large-flowered hybrid tea
Parentage: Pink Princess x Charlotte Armstrong
Other names: None
Other varieties: None
Year: 1958
Origin: United States
Description: A modern hybrid with fragrant, large, shell pink blooms which are produced on a vigorous plant amid dark and glossy foliage.
Flowering: Spring to summer
Cultivation: Plant in a warm sunny position in soil that has been well dug and enriched with humus. Water well during hot and dry weather.

DIAMOND JUBILEE

Botanical grouping: Large-flowered hybrid tea
Parentage: Maréchal Niel x Feu Pernet-Ducher
Other names: None
Other varieties: None
Year: 1947
Origin: United States
Description: A bushy, medium-sized and free-flowering shrub to 1 m (3 ft) with leathery, dark green and glossy foliage. The double flowers are large and cupped, creamy buff coloured with apricot shadings. The rose is lightly scented. It is one of the

classic hybrid tea roses and therefore used often as an exhibition plant.
Flowering: Continuously throughout summer
Cultivation: A hardy and healthy rose, it will tolerate poorer soils. For best results plant in an open, sunny position in well-drained soil. It may also be grown in a pot or under glass as well as in garden beds.

DIORAMA

Botanical grouping: Large-flowered hybrid tea
Parentage: Peace x Beauté
Other names: None
Other varieties: None
Year: 1965
Origin: The Netherlands
Description: An upright and vigorous shrub to 1 m (3 ft) with bushy, mid-green foliage. The double flowers are large and well-shaped in an intense yellow flushed reddish apricot. The blooms are moderately fragrant. Good as a cut flower.
Flowering: Continuously throughout summer
Cultivation: Tolerant of poorer soils and generally healthy. Thrives in a sunny position. Water well in summer and mulch the surface soil. May be planted in pots or used as bedding or border shrubs.

DOLLY PARTON

Botanical grouping: Large-flowered hybrid tea
Parentage: Fragrant Cloud x Oklahoma
Other names: None
Other varieties: None
Year: 1983
Origin: United States
Description: Large, shapely buds open to huge, many-petalled orange-red blooms which are heavily scented. A vigorous bush, it is well foliated and grows to 1.5 m (5 ft) high.
Flowering: Spring and summer
Cultivation: Full sun is preferred although it will tolerate partial shade. Well dug soil enriched with humus, mulched in warmer weather, will ensure healthy growth.

DOUBLE DELIGHT

Botanical grouping: Large-flowered hybrid tea
Parentage: Granada x Garden Party
Other names: Andeli
Other varieties: Climbing sport from United States, 1985
Year: 1977
Origin: United States
Description: A spreading, very bushy shrub to 1 m (3 ft) with glossy, abundant foliage.

Dolly Parton

Double Delight

Dame Edith Helen

Diamond Jubilee

Diorama

The large, very fragrant flowers are high-centred and double in a creamy white with red streaks around the edges of the petals. A free-flowering shrub.

Flowering: Continuously throughout summer

Cultivation: Not an easy rose to grow, although it is very mildew resistant. It requires an open, very sunny position and the blooms do not tolerate wet weather. Best suited to cultivation under glass, although it may also be grown in a pot.

DR A.J. VERHAGE

Botanical grouping: Large-flowered hybrid tea

Parentage: Tawny Gold x (Baccarà x a seedling)

Other names: Golden Wave

Other varieties: None

Year: 1963

Origin: The Netherlands

Description: A compact, bushy shrub to 75 cm (2 ½ ft) with dark green, abundant foliage. The attractively shaped flowers have long, slightly frilled petals of a deep yellow, darkening toward the centre and paling along the edges of the petals in sunlight. Often used as a glasshouse variety, it provides fragrant cut flowers.

Flowering: Continuously from summer to autumn

Cultivation: Will tolerate poorer soils, but does best under glass. It may also be cultivated in a pot. While not as good out-of-doors, it may be used as a hedging or border plant.

DR MCALPINE

Botanical grouping: Large-flowered hybrid tea

Parentage: Unknown

Other names: Peafirst

Other varieties: None

Year: 1983

Origin: England

Dr A.J. Verhage

Electron

Description: A short, rather sprawling shrub to 50 cm (1 ½ ft) with bushy, abundant foliage. The rose pink flowers are large and borne in clusters, hence its classification in the United States as a floribunda. It is very fragrant.

Flowering: Continuously from summer to autumn

Cultivation: A hardy, disease-resistant plant with no special requirements. Its flowers are very resistant to rain damage. Cultivate as a small border shrub or use in massed plantings where height is not required.

EDEN ROSE

Botanical grouping: Large-flowered hybrid tea

Parentage: Peace x Signora

Other names: None

Other varieties: None

Year: 1950

Origin: France

Description: A strong, upright shrub to around 1.2 m (4 ft) with glossy foliage and little branching. The double flowers are an intense pink with deeper shadings and a lighter, silver-pink reverse. The blooms are very fragrant. It is used as an exhibition rose.

Flowering: Continuously from early summer to autumn

Cultivation: Is tolerant of poor soil quality but likes a sunny position. It has no special cultivation requirements and is quite disease-resistant. Can be forced under glass.

ELECTRON

Botanical grouping: Large-flowered hybrid tea

Parentage: Paddy McGredy x Prima Ballerina

Other names: Mullard Jubilee

Other varieties: None

Year: 1970

Origin: New Zealand

Description: An elegant, classic-formed, long-lasting rose on long, strong stems, ideal for cutting. The high-centred, deep rose pink blooms are very fragrant, 13 cm (5 in) across and have 32 petals. This is a good choice for areas prone to wet weather as it holds the form well even in rain.

Flowering: Spring and summer

Cultivation: Tolerant of sandy soils and partial shade although it prefers day-long sun. Suitable as a hedging plant. Grow in fertile soil that is well drained and mulched.

ELINA

Botanical grouping: Large-flowered hybrid tea
Parentage: Nana Mouskouri x Lolita
Other names: Peaudouce, Dicjana
Other varieties: None
Year: 1985
Origin: Northern Ireland
Description: A bushy rose, growing to 1 m (3 ft), with large dark green leaves and very large, well formed white blooms with lemon yellow centres. A particularly beautiful specimen, ideal for cut flowers.
Flowering: Continuously throughout summer
Cultivation: A useful rose for both bed and border, suitable for growing in a wide range of soil types and climates. Cut roses frequently to encourage further growth.

ELIZABETH HARKNESS

Botanical grouping: Large-flowered hybrid tea
Parentage: Red Dandy x Piccadilly
Other names: None
Other varieties: Climbing sport from England, 1975
Year: 1969
Origin: England
Description: Bushy, upright shrub to 75 cm (2½ ft) with abundant mid-green foliage. The flowers are very attractive and well-shaped in an ivory to cream colour, flushed with pink tonings toward the centre. The blooms are abundant with a slight scent.
Flowering: Continuously from summer to autumn
Cultivation: A hardy and healthy shrub with no particular requirements. Will tolerate poorer soils. Plant in a massed display or as a border plant. It is popular as an exhibition rose.

ELLEN WILLMOTT

Botanical grouping: Large-flowered hybrid tea
Parentage: Dainty Bess x Lady Hillingdon
Other names: None
Other varieties: None
Year: 1936
Origin: England
Description: A charming product of two rose world favourites. Single cream blushed pink, wavy petals centred with bright golden stamens. Dark glossy green foliage is produced on a bushy plant to 1.5 m (5 ft).
Flowering: More or less continuously throughout summer
Cultivation: A vigorous bushy plant that requires a warm, sheltered position either in a garden bed or in a pot.

Elina

Elizabeth Harkness

ENA HARKNESS

Botanical grouping: Large-flowered hybrid tea
Parentage: Crimson Glory x Southport
Other names: None
Other varieties: Climbing sport from England, 1954
Year: 1946
Origin: England
Description: A strong-growing, free-flowering shrub to 70 cm (2 ft) with rather sparse, mid-green foliage. The flowers are large and very double in a velvety scarlet to crimson shade and moderately scented. The stems are weak and the blooms have a tendency to nod.
Flowering: Continuously from early summer to autumn
Cultivation: Tolerates poor soil but needs a sunny position to thrive. Probably best raised in a glasshouse as the flowers dislike rain.

Ena Harkness

Ellen Willmott

Eroica

EROICA

Botanical grouping: Large-flowered hybrid tea
Parentage: Unknown
Other names: Erotika
Other varieties: None
Year: 1968
Origin: Germany
Description: An upright, sturdy shrub to 1 m (3 ft) with dark green, glossy foliage and purple new growth. The flowers are velvety dark red to crimson and very large and are held singly on long stems, making them a good cut flower with a very strong scent.
Flowering: Continuously from summer to autumn
Cultivation: Healthy and reasonably hardy, it has no special cultivation requirements but does best with a well-drained, rich soil with plenty of sun. May be used as a bedding plant or as a medium-sized border or hedging shrub.

ETOILE DE HOLLANDE

Botanical grouping: Large-flowered hybrid tea
Parentage: General MacArthur x Hadley
Other names: None
Other varieties: Climbing sport from The Netherlands, 1931
Year: 1919
Origin: The Netherlands
Description: Medium-sized, bushy shrub to 70 cm (2 ft) with dark green, matt foliage. The double flowers are a deep red with a strong fragrance and are well shaped.
Flowering: Continuously from summer to autumn
Cultivation: Has a sickly constitution with a tendency to mildew. Requires special care but may still not thrive. Does well under glass, and may be used as a cut flower. The climbing form is very vigorous and well worth growing.

Etoile de Hollande

FELICITY KENDALL

Botanical grouping: Large-flowered hybrid tea
Parentage: Fragrant Cloud x Mildred Reynolds
Other names: Lanken
Other varieties: None
Year: 1985
Origin: England
Description: Bushy, branching shrub to around 1 m (3 ft). The vermilion flowers are carried above the plant on strong stems and are large and well-formed. They are lightly scented. A good exhibition rose or cut flower.
Flowering: Continuously from summer to autumn
Cultivation: The blooms deteriorate on exposure to rain, but the shrub is otherwise very healthy and hardy, requiring only a sunny position to thrive. Does well as a bedding or border plant.

FIRST LOVE

Botanical grouping: Large-flowered hybrid tea
Parentage: Charlotte Armstrong x Show Girl
Other names: Premier Amour
Other varieties: None
Year: 1951

Origin: United States
Description: Upright, free-flowering shrub to 1 m (3 ft) with light green, leathery foliage. The pointed buds open to semi-double flowers of deep pink to with some fragrance, which are attractive when cut.
Flowering: Continuously from summer to autumn
Cultivation: Will tolerate poorer soils but does best in well-drained, moderately rich soil. Makes a good potted specimen. Also suitable as a glasshouse shrub.

First Love

First Prize

Fragrant Cloud

Fragrant Dream

FIRST PRIZE

Botanical grouping: Large-flowered hybrid tea
Parentage: Enchantment seedling x Golden Masterpiece seedling
Other names: None
Other varieties: None
Year: 1970
Origin: United States
Description: Deep rose pink, urn-shaped buds, almost 10 cm (4 in) long, have silvery reverses. They open to very large, high-centred, flesh pink with deep rose pink on the outer edges of waxy-textured petals. A good cutting and exhibition rose but has very little scent. The bush grows to 1.2 m (4 ft).
Flowering: Spring and summer
Cultivation: A vigorous plant giving a spectacular display of blooms. It prefers full sun and good soil. Prune lightly after flowering, once the plant is established.

FRAGRANT CLOUD

Botanical grouping: Large-flowered hybrid tea
Parentage: Seedling x Prima Ballerina
Other names: Duftwolke, Nuage Parfumé, Tanellis
Other varieties: None
Year: 1963
Origin: Germany
Description: Upright shrub to 75 cm (2½ ft) with abundant, deep green, leathery foliage. The flowers range in colour from coral-red to purplish-red and as the name suggests, are very fragrant. Its large petals make it suitable as an exhibition rose.
Flowering: Continuously from early summer through to autumn
Cultivation: Exposure to rain can cause the flowers to ball and lose colour. It is other-wise healthy and hardy. Looks good in a massed planting.

FRAGRANT DREAM

Botanical grouping: Large-flowered hybrid tea
Parentage: Unknown
Other names: Dicodour
Other varieties: None
Year: 1989
Origin: Northern Ireland
Description: Vigorous, upright bush to 1 m (3 ft), with flowers in the typical hybrid tea mould, high-centred and large-petalled. The blooms are clear apricot with salmon-pink tones and are moderately fragrant.
Flowering: Summer to autumn
Cultivation: Disease resistant and hardy, this rose has no special cultivation requirements Best suited as a bedding plant, it may also be used for cut flowers or as a hedging bush.

FRAGRANT PLUM

Botanical grouping: Large-flowered hybrid tea
Parentage: Unknown
Other names: Aroplumi
Other varieties: None
Year: Unknown
Origin: United States
Description: A headily perfumed, high-centred rose of deep lilac, with edges of rich purple set off by mid-green foliage. The bush grows to about 1.2 m (4 ft).
Flowering: Spring and summer
Cultivation: This is a rose for a prominent position in the garden where its rich perfume can be enjoyed. Plant in a warm position in full sun or partial shade and in fertile soil.

Fragrant Plum

FREEDOM

Botanical grouping: Large-flowered hybrid tea
Parentage: (Eurorose x Typhoon) x Bright Smile
Other names: Dicjem
Other varieties: None
Year: 1984
Origin: Northern Ireland
Description: Free-flowering, vigorous shrub to around 75 cm (2½ ft) with attractive glossy foliage. The plant tends to send out shoots from its base. The flowers are small to medium size in a bright yellow and are moderately fragrant. Its neat habit makes it suitable for almost any situation.
Flowering: Summer to autumn
Cultivation: Hardy and healthy, this rose enjoys moderately rich and well-drained soil. Prune in winter, reducing long stems and removing dead wood.

FRIENDSHIP

Botanical grouping: Large-flowered hybrid tea
Parentage: Fragrant Cloud x Miss All America Beauty
Other names: Linrick
Other varieties: None
Year: 1978
Origin: United States
Description: Very fragrant, giant pink blooms develop from pointed buds. The flowers are cupped to flat, have 25 to 30 petals and are almost 15 cm (6 in) across. This is a decorative rose indoors or in the garden and holds its form well. The bush, well foliated with large, dark green leaves, can grow to almost 2 m (7 ft).
Flowering: Spring and summer
Cultivation: Grow in sun and soil that is well mulched, drained and watered. Summer pruning is necessary to induce good flowering.

Friendship

Freedom

FULTON MACKAY

Botanical grouping: Large-flowered hybrid tea
Parentage: Silver Jubilee x Jana
Other names: Cocdana
Other varieties: None
Year: 1988
Origin: Scotland
Description: Shapely, high-centred, apricot blooms are borne on a vigorous, bushy plant with glossy foliage, reaching 75 cm (2½ ft). Fragrant.
Flowering: Consistent flowers through summer and autumn.
Cultivation: Hardy, will tolerate most conditions. Regularly cut flowers to keep up the production of new blooms.

GIVENCHY

Botanical grouping: Large-flowered hybrid tea
Parentage: Gingersnap x Double Delight
Other names: Arodousna, Paris Pink
Other varieties: None
Year: 1986
Origin: United States

Givenchy

Fulton Mackay

Description: High-centred, luminous and strongly perfumed, this is a rose for cutting. Its beautiful two-toned, deep magenta-pink petals blend to a softer, light pink on the inner petals. The bush is well foliated and grows to a height of 1.2 m (4 ft).
Flowering: Spring and summer
Cultivation: Grow in full sun or partial shade. In shaded areas it will need rich soil boosted with organic material and good drainage. Mulch in warmer weather.

GOLD CROWN

Botanical grouping: Large-flowered hybrid tea
Parentage: Peace x Spek's Yellow
Other names: Corona de Oro, Couronne d'Or, Goldkrone
Other varieties: None
Year: 1960
Origin: Germany
Description: Upright shrub to 1 m (3 ft) with glossy, dark green foliage. The large, lightly scented flowers are an intense yellow with some outer petals blotched red. When fully open the petals are sometimes quartered in the style of old roses. Long stems

Gold Crown

make this rose ideal for cut flowers although its habit is rather lanky as a garden specimen.

Flowering: Continuously from summer to autumn

Cultivation: A hardy shrub which can tolerate poor soils but which thrives in an open, sunny position.

GOLDEN JUBILEE

Botanical grouping: Large-flowered hybrid tea
Parentage: Peer Gynt x Gay Gordons
Other names: Cocagold
Other varieties: None
Year: 1981
Origin: Scotland
Description: Upright, free-flowering shrub to 75 cm (2½ ft) with attractive, crisp foliage. The yellow, lightly scented flowers have a touch of pink and are large and well-shaped.
Flowering: Continuously from summer to autumn
Cultivation: A healthy plant requiring little attention to thrive. The shrub looks good as a hedging or border plant or in a massed display.

GOLDEN MELODY

Botanical grouping: Large-flowered hybrid tea
Parentage: Mme Butterfly x (Lady Hillingdon x Souvenir de Claudius Pernet)
Other names: Irene Churruca
Other varieties: None
Year: 1934
Origin: Spain
Description: Angular, upright shrub to 75 cm (2½ ft) with dark green foliage and purplish stems. The flowers are considered to be very beautiful, high-centred and full in a delicate buff-yellow flushed with pink and darkening toward the centre. They are very fragrant. A good cut flower, suitable for exhibition.
Flowering: Continuously from summer to autumn
Cultivation: Not fully hardy and requires special attention to do well. Useful as a bedding or border plant.

GOLD MEDAL

Botanical grouping: Large-flowered hybrid tea
Parentage: Yellow Pages x (Granada x Garden Party)
Other names: Aroyqueli
Other varieties: None
Year: 1982
Origin: United States
Description: Gold blooms are tinged with copper and although scentless, it is a good

Golden Jubilee

Golden Melody

Gold Medal

Goldstar

cutting rose and free-flowering on a compact bush to more than 1.2 m (4 ft). The foliage is attractive and light green.
Flowering: Freely throughout summer
Cultivation: Prefers day-long sun but is tolerant of filtered shade. The soil should be drained, fertile, well mulched and enriched with humus especially if sandy.

GOLDSTAR

Botanical grouping: Large-flowered hybrid tea
Parentage: Yellow Pages x Dr A.J. Verhage
Other names: Point du Jour, Candide, Goldina
Other varieties: None
Year: 1983
Origin: England
Description: Upright, free-flowering shrub to 75 cm (2½ ft) with dark green, glossy foliage. The urn-shaped flowers are a deep yellow, slightly fragrant and last well when cut.
Flowering: Continuously from summer to autumn
Cultivation: A hardy and largely disease-free rose whose blooms are also resistant to rain. Use as a bedding or border plant or for cut flowers. Plant in an open, sunny spot and water well in summer.

Granada

GRANADA

Botanical grouping: Large-flowered hybrid tea
Parentage: Tiffany x Cavalcade
Other names: Donatella
Other varieties: None
Year: 1963
Origin: United States
Description: Urn-shaped buds open to reveal large, high-centred flowers almost 13 cm (5 in) across with 18 to 25 petals. A richly fragrant, multi-coloured rose, nasturtium red, rose-pink and lemon-yellow

Grande Amore

shadings, almost 'everblooming'. A good cutting rose. The slightly spreading bush grows to a height of 1.2 m (4 ft) with unusually crinkled, paper-thin foliage.
Flowering: Repeats throughout autumn
Cultivation: Full sun or partial shade is suitable if adequate drainage if provided, especially in winter. It can be grown as an informal hedge.

GRANDE AMORE

Botanical grouping: Large-flowered hybrid tea
Parentage: Prima Ballerina x Detroiter
Other names: Korliegra
Other varieties: None
Year: 1968
Origin: Germany
Description: Flowers are classic-shaped, rosy red, many-petalled and large, almost 13 cm (5 in) across. Evocatively perfumed, this rose blooms freely and is suitable for cutting. Dark green, leathery foliage is abundant on a compact bush growing to 1.2 m (4 ft) high.
Flowering: Freely and repeatedly throughout summer
Cultivation: A good bedding rose suitable for massed plantings. Plant in full sun in well-drained, fertile soil that has been mulched.

GRANDPA DICKSON

Botanical grouping: Large-flowered hybrid tea
Parentage: (Perfecta x Gov. Braga de Cruz) x Piccadilly
Other names: Irish Gold
Other varieties: None
Year: 1966
Origin: Northern Ireland
Description: An upright shrub, growing to 75 cm (2½ ft), with sparse foliage but a fantastic display of large flowers that are light yellow, tinged with pink flushes during warm weather.

Grandpa Dickson

Flowering: Freely through summer to autumn
Cultivation: A wonderful rose for the garden and highly prized for exhibition. Position in full sun in well-drained soil, and mulch well to keep weed growth down. Water well at ground level during hot weather.

GRÜSS AN COBURG

Botanical grouping: Large-flowered hybrid tea
Parentage: Alice Kaempff x Souvenir de Claudius Pernet
Other names: None
Other varieties: None
Year: 1927
Origin: Germany
Description: Very fragrant, globular flowers of apricot-yellow and copper reverse on the petals. A vigorous plant with glossy green foliage.
Flowering: Spring to summer. May recur in other seasons.
Cultivation: Rich soil, well dug and composted and a warm position with adequate water will ensure good flowering.

GWYNNE CARR

Botanical grouping: Large-flowered hybrid tea
Parentage: Unknown
Other names: None
Other varieties: Climbing sport from England, 1928
Year: 1924
Origin: Northern Ireland
Description: A little known, double, silvery pink, hybrid tea rose.
Flowering: Spring to summer
Cultivation: Plant in a warm, sheltered position in full sun in soil that has been well prepared with organic material.

HARMONIE

Botanical grouping: Large-flowered hybrid tea
Parentage: Fragrant Cloud x Uwe Seeler
Other names: Kortember
Other varieties: None
Year: 1981
Origin: Germany
Description: An especially lovely and large rose with unusually shaded coral-salmon blooms of 20 to 25 petals. Strongly perfumed. A good cutting rose. The bush has an upright habit with few thorns and grows to 1.2 m (4 ft).
Flowering: Spring and summer
Cultivation: This rose deserves a prominent position in the garden. Plant in full sun in fertile soil that is drained and well mulched during warmer weather.

Harry Wheatcroft

HARRY WHEATCROFT

Botanical grouping: Large-flowered hybrid tea
Parentage: Piccadilly sport
Other names: Caribia
Other varieties: Climbing sport from United States, 1981
Year: 1972
Origin: England
Description: Upright shrub to 75 cm (2½ ft) with abundant coppery-green, semi-glossy foliage. The lightly scented flowers are well formed, orange-red and striped with yellow—a very striking combination. The colour deepens when fully open.
Flowering: Continuously throughout summer until autumn
Cultivation: While generally hardy and strong growing, it is susceptible to rust. Suited both as a potted specimen or for bedding or borders. Plant in a sunny spot with well-drained soil.

HECTOR DEANE

Botanical grouping: Large-flowered hybrid tea
Parentage: McGredy's Scarlet x Lesley Dudley
Other names: None
Other varieties: None

Harmonie

Honor

Year: 1938
Origin: Northern Ireland
Description: Bushy, compact shrub to 70 cm (2 ft) with glossy, deep green foliage. The flowers are full and high-centred in pink and orange with darker tonings. A very free-flowering and fragrant specimen.
Flowering: Continuously throughout summer until autumn
Cultivation: A healthy and hardy plant. Plant in a position with adequate sun and a well-drained and moderately rich soil. Watch for rust. Use in borders or in beds for a massed display. Also suitable for containers.

HOLTERMANN'S GOLD

Botanical grouping: Large-flowered hybrid tea
Parentage: Unknown
Other names: None
Other varieties: None
Year: 1989
Origin: Australia
Description: Nicely textured, medium to full blooms of rich golden yellow have long stems and are sweetly perfumed, making this an excellent cut flower. A strong growing bush to 1.5 m (5 ft) with shining dark green foliage.
Flowering: Spring and summer
Cultivation: A healthy and vigorous bush

Holtermann's Gold

which thrives in fertile soil and a sunny garden position. Prune back lightly after flowering.

HONOR

Botanical grouping: Large-flowered hybrid tea
Parentage: Unknown
Other names: Jacolite, Michèle Torr
Other varieties: None
Year: 1980
Origin: United States
Description: Long elegant buds open to luminous satin white double blooms, almost 13 cm (5 in) across, that are highly perfumed and supported by long, strong stems. Excellent as a cut flower. Dark olive green foliage is produced on a healthy bush growing to 1.2 m (4 ft).
Flowering: Spring and summer
Cultivation: Fertile soil and full sun or light to filtered shade is preferred. Prune lightly once flowering has ceased. Remove spent blooms to encourage growth. May need winter protection in cold areas.

INGRID BERGMAN

Botanical grouping: Large-flowered hybrid tea
Parentage: Precious Platinum x a seedling
Other names: Poulman
Other varieties: None
Year: 1986
Origin: Denmark
Description: Upright, free-flowering shrub to 70 cm (2 ft) with dark green, leathery foliage. The double flowers are a deep red with no hint of blue and are produced above the plant on long stems, making them good for cutting.
Flowering: Continuously from summer until autumn
Cultivation: A hardy rose, reasonably disease-resistant with no special demands. Use as a bedding plant or plant in pots.

Ingrid Bergman

INTERMEZZO

Botanical grouping: Large-flowered hybrid tea
Parentage: Grey Pearl x Lila Vidri
Other names: None
Other varieties: None
Year: 1963
Origin: Spain
Description: A compact, bushy shrub to 50 cm (1½ ft) with abundant, shiny foliage. The flowers are double and produced in clusters, the petals sometimes quartered in a silvery, greyish-lavender with a pink sheen. They are moderately scented.
Flowering: Continuously from summer until autumn
Cultivation: The plant will tolerate poorer soils but likes a fair amount of sun. Water well in summer. Use in beds for a massed display or as a low hedge or in pots.

IRISH FIREFLAME

Botanical grouping: Large-flowered hybrid tea
Parentage: Unknown
Other names: None
Other varieties: Climbing sport from Northern Ireland, 1916
Year: 1914
Origin: Northern Ireland
Description: An uncommon, five-petalled single rose of autumnal colouring. Large petals of pale apricot to soft orange have golden centres and deepen in intensity toward the outer edges. The blooms are sometimes veined with citrus-yellow and crimson and are very fragrant. Dark green foliage covers the shrub which grows to 1 m (3 ft).
Flowering: Repeats during throughout summer
Cultivation: A vigorous and healthy bush that thrives in full sun and rich soil. Prune lightly after flowering.

ISOBEL HARKNESS

Botanical grouping: Large-flowered hybrid tea
Parentage: McGredy's Yellow x Phyllis Gold
Other names: None
Other varieties: Climbing sport from United States, 1959
Year: 1957
Origin: England
Description: A compact shrub to 70 cm (2 ft) with dark green, leathery foliage. The double, very large flowers in a pure yellow fade slightly on opening. They are quite fragrant and are carried on strong stems making them a good cut flower.
Flowering: Continuously from summer to autumn

Jenny Brown

Cultivation: Best suited as a bedding plant. Susceptible to black spot but otherwise quite hardy. Grow in a sunny spot and avoid watering the foliage, especially in the evening.

JEMA

Botanical grouping: Large-flowered hybrid tea
Parentage: Helen Traubel x Lolita
Other names: None
Other varieties: None
Year: 1982
Origin: United States
Description: Large, upright shrub to 1.2 m (4 ft) with pale green foliage. The flowers are well formed and full in a delicate apricot shade and have a moderate scent. They are good as cut flowers.
Flowering: Continuously from summer to autumn
Cultivation: Suitable as bedding plants for massed display or hedges and borders. Healthy, hardy and strong growing, it likes full sun and a moderately rich soil.

JENNY BROWN

Botanical grouping: Large-flowered hybrid tea
Parentage: (Pink Favourite x Dorothy Peach) x Dainty Bess
Other names: None
Other varieties: None
Year: 1974
Origin: Australia
Description: Long pointed buds open to large single blooms of salmon-pink fading to paler centres. The flowers are profuse and very fragrant and are good cut roses. Glossy foliage is produced on a bush which grows to about 1.2 m (4 ft).
Flowering: Freely throughout summer
Cultivation: The bush has a vigorous and upright habit and prefers a position in full sun or partial shade in soil that is fertile, well drained and mulched in warmer weather.

JESSIKA

Botanical grouping: Large-flowered hybrid tea
Parentage: Königen der Rosen x Piccadilly
Other names: Tanjeka, Jehoca
Other varieties: None

Jessika

Year: 1971
Origin: Germany
Description: Elegant long pointed buds open to reveal large, double, salmon-pink to apricot flowers that are sweetly perfumed, free-blooming and attractive in the vase or garden. Healthy mid-green foliage abounds on the bush which grows to about 1.2 m (4 ft) tall.
Flowering: Spring and summer
Cultivation: Full sun or partial shade in a warm position in soil that has been well dug with humus and mulched, suits this vigorous and upright bush. Good drainage is essential, particularly if planted in shade.

JOHN WATERER

Botanical grouping: Large-flowered hybrid tea
Parentage: King of Hearts x Hanne
Other names: None
Other varieties: None
Year: 1970
Origin: Northern Ireland
Description: Free-flowering, upright shrub to 1 m (3 ft) with attractive deep green foliage. The flowers are large with long petals in a deep crimson and are moderately scented.
Flowering: Continuously from summer to autumn
Cultivation: A healthy and disease-resistant plant whose flowers are resistant to rain damage. Good for massed displays or as a border plant and often used as an exhibition rose.

JULIA'S ROSE

Botanical grouping: Large-flowered hybrid tea
Parentage: Blue Moon x Dr A.J. Verhage
Other names: None

John Waterer

Other varieties: None
Year: 1976
Origin: England
Description: An upright, medium-sized shrub to 70 cm (2 ft) with dark green foliage with reddish tints. The flowers are an unusual colour, coppery-tan with pinkish tints, and have an attractive form with delicately frilled petals opening wide to reveal golden stamens. It is lightly scented. It is a long-lasting rose and provides good cut flowers.
Flowering: Continuously from summer to autumn
Cultivation: Needs special attention to do well, the soil being rich and very well drained and the site chosen to provide maximum sun. May also be grown in a glasshouse.

JULIE

Botanical grouping: Large-flowered hybrid tea
Parentage: Unknown:
Other names: None
Other varieties: None
Year: 1970

Julia's Rose

Origin: Germany
Description: Plump, ovoid buds open to well-formed double, cupped, fragrant flowers of deepest red. It blooms freely amid abundant soft, dark green foliage on a smallish plant to less than 1 m (3 ft).
Flowering: Freely throughout summer
Cultivation: A moderate grower, it may be planted as a border, massed in garden beds or in large pots. Full sun is preferred and fertile, well-drained soil that is mulched.

Julie

Keepsake

Just Joey

Kardinal

KARDINAL

Botanical grouping: Large-flowered hybrid tea
Parentage: Seedling x Flamingo
Other names: Korlingo
Other varieties: None
Year: 1985
Origin: Germany
Description: An excellent cut flower that has very long stems, is long lasting and highly perfumed. Large, rich, cardinal red flowers of 25 to 30 petals bloom on this very robust plant which grows to 1.2 m (4 ft) high.
Flowering: Freely throughout summer
Cultivation: This is a vigorous rose which is very resistant to fungus diseases. Plant in full sun or partial shade in fertile soil that is well drained and mulched in warm weather.

KEEPSAKE

Botanical grouping: Large-flowered hybrid tea
Parentage: Seedling x Red Planet
Other names: Esmeralda, Kormalda
Other varieties: None
Year: 1981
Origin: Germany
Description: A vigorous, upright but rather untidy shrub to 75 cm (2½ ft) with dark green, very dense foliage. The flowers are full petalled and well formed in deep pinks ranging from carmine to blush and are moderately scented. The outer petals are reflexed when open. Often seen at exhibitions.
Flowering: Continuously from summer to autumn
Cultivation: Suitable as a bedding plant or for borders and hedges. Will tolerate poorer soils and is reasonably hardy. The flowers can withstand wet weather.

JUST JOEY

Botanical grouping: Large-flowered hybrid tea
Parentage: Fragrant Cloud x Dr A.J. Verhage
Other names: None
Other varieties: None
Year: 1973
Origin: England
Description: Medium-sized shrub reaching 75 cm (2½ ft) with dark green, rather sparse foliage. The flowers are full-petalled and large in tones of fawn, copper and buff and are moderately fragrant. In warm weather the blooms develop to an extremely large size.
Flowering: Summer to autumn
Cultivation: Attractive as a cut flower, it also looks good in beds or borders. Has no special requirements and is quite disease resistant and hardy.

KAN-PAI

Botanical grouping: Large-flowered hybrid tea
Parentage: [Yu-ai x (Happiness x American Beauty)] x Pharaoh
Other names: None
Other varieties: None
Year: 1980
Origin: Japan
Description: Medium-sized, upright shrub to around 75 cm (2½ ft) with dark green foliage. The dark red flower is well shaped and high-centred and carried on a strong stem. A good cut flower. Moderately scented.
Flowering: Continuously from summer to autumn
Cultivation: Use as a bedding plant in massed displays or for hedges and borders. Tolerates poorer soils and is generally hardy and healthy with no special requirements.

KENTUCKY DERBY

Botanical grouping: Large-flowered hybrid tea
Parentage: John S. Armstrong x Grand Slam
Other names: Aroder
Other varieties: None
Year: 1972
Origin: United States
Description: A superb red rose with a heady fragrance that is eye-catching in the garden or in a vase. Huge heads, 15 cm (6 in) across, are high centred and dark velvet-red, with even darker red shadings. Generous leathery foliage is produced on an almost rampant bush growing more than 1.2 m (4 ft) high.
Flowering: Repeats throughout summer
Cultivation: Regular maintenance and good soil will reward with spectacular blooms. Plant in full sun or partial shade.

Kentucky Derby

King's Ransom

La France

KING'S RANSOM

Botanical grouping: Large-flowered hybrid tea
Parentage: Golden Masterpiece x Lydia
Other names: None
Other varieties: None
Year: 1961
Origin: United States
Description: Upright, very free-flowering shrub to 75 cm (2½ ft) with leathery, pale green foliage. The flowers are double, flat when open in a rich, golden yellow with darker veins carried on long, strong stems, making them ideal as cut flowers. They are moderately fragrant.
Flowering: Continuously from summer to autumn
Cultivation: A hardy shrub which grows well when given adequate sun and water. It may be grown in pots or under glass.

LADY BEAUTY

Botanical grouping: Large-flowered hybrid tea
Parentage: Lady x Princess Takamatsu
Other names: None
Other varieties: None
Year: 1984
Origin: Japan
Description: Vigorous and upright shrub to 1 m (3 ft) with abundant, medium green and glossy foliage. The lightly scented flowers are pale pink with a hint of yellow, with a somewhat deeper reverse. Suitable in pots or under glass as well as outdoors as bedding or border shrubs.
Flowering: Continuously from summer to autumn
Cultivation: Will tolerate poorer soils and is a hardy rose with no special requirements.

LADY ROSE

Botanical grouping: Large-flowered hybrid tea
Parentage: Seedling x Träumerei

La France

Lady Rose

Other names: Korlady
Other varieties: None
Year: 1979
Origin: Germany
Description: A bushy shrub, growing to 75 cm (2½ ft), with shiny mid-green foliage and a good display of slender buds opening to high-centred, orange-salmon-coloured flowers. The flowers are very fragrant.
Flowering: Continuously throughout summer
Cultivation: A beautiful bedding or border plant that prefers full sun and well-drained soil. Prune out dead wood in winter.

LA FRANCE

Botanical grouping: Large-flowered hybrid tea
Parentage: Probably a seedling of Mme Falcot, or possibly Mme Victor Verdier x

Mme Bravy
Other names: None
Other varieties: None
Year: 1867
Origin: France
Description: Historically, this rose is thought to be the first hybrid tea. The blooms are large, double, well shaped with a tendency to ball and are silvery pink with a deeper pink reverse. Richly fragrant. Grows to 1–1.5 m (3–5 ft).
Flowering: Very free-flowering throughout summer.
Cultivation: Plant in a warm, sunny position in a garden bed that is well mulched and watered. It can also be cultivated in a glasshouse and in pots.

LAKELAND

Botanical grouping: Large-flowered hybrid tea
Parentage: Fragrant Cloud x Queen Elizabeth
Other names: None
Other varieties: None
Year: 1976
Origin: England
Description: An upright, free-growing and free-flowering shrub to 1 m (3 ft) with medium green foliage. The double flowers are a pale shell pink with a slight fragrance and are produced singly or in small clusters. It makes a good exhibition rose.
Flowering: Continuously from summer to autumn
Cultivation: Prefers a well-drained and mulched soil and plenty of sun to thrive. May be grown in a pot.

LIMELIGHT

Botanical grouping: Large-flowered hybrid tea
Parentage: Peach Melba x seedling
Other names: Golden Medaillon, Korikon
Other varieties: None

Limelight

Lincoln Cathedral

Year: 1985
Origin: Germany
Description: Medium yellow, double (35 petals), high centred, large, very fragrant, bushy, with plentiful, dark semi-glossy foliage.
Flowering: Freely throughout summer
Cultivation: It suits bed and border. It prefers a warm, sunny position and fertile, well-drained soil preferably enriched with organic matter and mulched in dry weather.

LINCOLN CATHEDRAL

Botanical grouping: Large-flowered hybrid tea
Parentage: Silver Jubilee x Royal Dane
Other names: Glanlin
Other varieties: None
Year: 1985
Origin: England
Description: A free-flowering, bushy shrub to 75 cm (2½ ft) with thorny branches and medium-green foliage. The flowers are a mix of orange and pink with a yellow reverse and are lightly scented.
Flowering: Continuously from summer to autumn
Cultivation: Can tolerate poorer soil quality but does best in an open, sunny position with a moderately rich, well-drained soil.

Suitable as a bedding or border plant and may also be grown in a pot.

LOLITA

Botanical grouping: Large-flowered hybrid tea
Parentage: Dr A.J. Verhage x Colour Wonder
Other names: Litakor, Korlita
Other varieties: None
Year: 1972
Origin: Germany
Description: A strong, upright shrub to around 1 m (3 ft) with abundant foliage that

Lolita

is purple when young. The double flowers are large in a coppery orange shade with a moderately strong fragrance. The blooms are long-lasting and make good cut flowers.

Flowering: Continuously from summer to autumn

Cultivation: Likes a rich, well-drained and mulched soil in a sunny position. Make sure the plant is well watered in summer. Plant in pots or garden beds, for border or hedge.

L'ORÉAL TROPHY

Botanical grouping: Large-flowered hybrid tea
Parentage: Sport from Alexander
Other names: Harlexis, Alexis
Other varieties: None
Year: 1982
Origin: England
Description: Upright and bushy shrub to 1.8 m (6 ft) with medium-green, glossy foliage. The flowers are light orange-salmon with a slight fragrance, the petals are somewhat untidy when fully open. The blooms make good cut flowers if cut early.
Flowering: Continuously from summer to autumn
Cultivation: This rose will tolerate poorer soils and may also be cultivated in a pot with good results. Makes a useful hedging plant and looks good in large beds.

LOVELY LADY

Botanical grouping: Large-flowered hybrid tea
Parentage: Silver Jubilee x (Eurorose x Anabel)
Other names: Dickson's Jubilee, Dicjubell
Other varieties: None
Year: 1986
Origin: Northern Ireland
Description: An upright, spreading shrub up to 75 cm (2½ ft) with mid-green foliage and a dramatic display of large, well-formed, double flowers in a warm rosy pink tone. Blooms can weigh down the branches in mid-summer, but make beautiful cut flowers.
Flowering: Summer through to autumn
Cultivation: A useful bedding rose that can be grown in a wide range of soils and conditions, preferably in full sun. Prune well in winter to prevent leggy stem growth.

LOVERS' MEETING

Botanical grouping: Large-flowered hybrid tea
Parentage: Seedling x Egyptian Treasure
Other names: None
Other varieties: None
Year: 1980
Origin: England

L'Oréal Trophy

Lovely Lady

Loving Memory

Description: An upright bush to 75 cm (2½ ft) with mid-green foliage. The slender buds open to loosely double flowers in a warm orange-red hue, with large petals that make each bloom quite weighty.
Flowering: Summer to autumn
Cultivation: A useful rose that can be cultivated successfully in most soils and climates, in a bed or border. It prefers full sun and well-drained soil. Excellent for cut flowers.

LOVING MEMORY

Botanical grouping: Large-flowered hybrid tea
Parentage: Seedling x Red Planet seedling
Other names: Red Cedar, Burgundy '81, Korgund '81
Other varieties: None
Year: 1981
Origin: Germany
Description: Upright and bushy shrub to around 1 m (3 ft) with glossy, medium green foliage. The flowers are high-pointed, fully double and are a bright crimson-red with a moderately strong scent. With strong, long stems they make ideal cut flowers. The colour tends to become dull in cooler climates.
Flowering: Continuously from summer to autumn

Lovers' Meeting

Cultivation: Thrives in moderately rich soil, well drained and mulched, in a sunny, open position. Grow under glass as an exhibition rose, or in large beds.

LUIS BRINAS

Botanical grouping: Large-flowered hybrid tea
Parentage: Mme Butterfly x Federico Casas
Other names: None
Other varieties: None
Year: 1934
Origin: Spain
Description: A slightly drooping but nonetheless vigorous shrub to 1 m (3 ft) with limp-looking foliage. The cupped flowers are orangey-pink with a very strong fragrance and are carried on strong stems, making them ideal as cut flowers.
Flowering: Repeats from early summer to autumn
Cultivation: A hardy rose with no special requirements to do well. May be grown under glass or outdoors for massed display.

Lyon Rose

Maestro

Malcolm Sargent

Maria Callas

MAESTRO

Botanical grouping: Large-flowered hybrid tea
Parentage: Picasso seedling x a seedling
Other names: Mackinju
Other varieties: None
Year: 1980
Origin: New Zealand
Description: Free-flowering, upright shrub to 75 cm (2½ ft) with prickly stems and dark green foliage. The slightly fragrant flowers are very eye-catching in crimson with white and cream markings with a 'hand-painted' appearance.
Flowering: Continuously from summer to autumn
Cultivation: A hardy rose with no special requirements. The flowers are quite weather resistant. Does well as a bedding plant or in pots.

MALCOLM SARGENT

Botanical grouping: Large-flowered hybrid tea
Parentage: Herbstfeuer x Trumpeter
Other names: Harwharry, Natascha
Other varieties: None
Year: 1988
Origin: England
Description: Dense, rounded shrub to 1 m (3 ft) high and wide, with prolific dark shiny leaves. Warm, shiny red flowers begin as urn-shaped buds.
Flowering: Summer
Cultivation: Hardy, but needs full sun. Suitable for cut flowers. Used for mass planting in beds and borders, or as a hedge. Dead-head the plant after flowering, and prune in winter, removing all dead and diseased wood. Reduce the length of healthy stems, and encourage new shoots from the base by removing some older canes.

MARIA CALLAS

Botanical grouping: Large-flowered hybrid tea
Parentage: Chrysler Imperial x Karl Herbst
Other names: Miss All-American Beauty, Meidaud
Other varieties: Climbing sport from France, 1969
Year: 1965
Origin: France
Description: Huge cupped blooms 13–15cm (5–6 in) across are packed with up to 60 petals and hold their shape while becoming full-blown. Headily scented, dark pink and generous, just two blooms will fill a vase. A medium bush growing to 1.2 m (4 ft).
Flowering: Abundantly throughout summer
Cultivation: A versatile rose to grow as a hedge, along a trellis or pergola or against a wall. Plant in full sun and in fertile soil that is well drained, mulched and composted.

LYON ROSE

Botanical grouping: Large-flowered hybrid tea
Parentage: Mélanie Soupert x Soleil d'Or seedling
Other names: None
Other varieties: Climbing sport from Luxembourg, 1924
Year: 1907
Origin: France
Description: A bushy shrub to 70 cm (2 ft) with attractive foliage. The very double flowers are a combination of coral-pink and red with yellow centres and are very fragrant.
Flowering: Repeats from early summer to autumn
Cultivation: A hardy rose that does well with minimal intervention from the gardener. It grows well under glass or in a pot.

MARION HARKNESS

Botanical grouping: Large-flowered hybrid tea
Parentage: [(Manx Queen x Prima Ballerina) x (Chanelle x Piccadilly)] x Piccadilly
Other names: Harkantabil
Other varieties: None
Year: 1979
Origin: England
Description: Bushy, upright shrub to 75 cm (2½ ft) with dark green foliage. The cupped flowers are deep yellow, brushed with orangey red at the petal edges which become darker with age. A slightly fragrant rose, it makes a useful cutting rose.
Flowering: Continuously from summer to autumn
Cultivation: Tolerant of poorer soils, and the flowers are resistant to rain damage. May be grown in pots or outdoors, for massed display or borders.

MARMALADE

Botanical grouping: Large-flowered hybrid tea
Parentage: Arlene Francis x Bewitched
Other names: None
Other varieties: None
Year: 1977
Origin: United States
Description: Tea-scented blooms of bright orange on the inner petals with deep butter-yellow on the reverse are flushed with amber. Large heads almost 13 cm (6 in) across and long, elegant buds are carried on tall stems making this an excellent cut flower. Light to medium-green foliage and a healthy bush which grows to 1.2 m (4 ft).
Flowering: Spring and summer, and will repeat if pruned.
Cultivation: Tolerant of sandy soil but prefers a warm sunny position in drained, fertile and mulched soil. Suitable for hedging or mass planting. Prune throughout summer.

MCGREDY'S YELLOW

Botanical grouping: Large-flowered hybrid tea
Parentage: Mrs Charles Lamplough x (The Queen Alexandra Rose x J.B. Clark)
Other names: None
Other varieties: Climbing sport from United States, 1937
Year: 1934
Origin: Northern Ireland
Description: Upright bush to 70 cm (2 ft) with bronze-green, glossy foliage. The pointed buds open to large, double, well-shaped flowers in a bright primrose-yellow. They are lightly scented. The colour is long-lasting making them good cut flowers.

Marion Harkness

Marmalade

Message

Flowering: Continuously from summer to autumn
Cultivation: This rose will tolerate poorer soils but it should be planted in full sun for best results. Use as a bedding plant or grow in pots.

MESSAGE

Botanical grouping: Large-flowered hybrid tea
Parentage: (Virgo x Peace) x Virgo
Other names: White Knight, Meban
Other varieties: None

Year: 1955
Origin: France
Description: A consistently good white rose with long-pointed buds carried on long stems. Usually pure white but it may sometimes show an attractive pale green hue and is a good cut flower. A healthy, tall bush growing to more than 1.2 m (4 ft) with light green, strong foliage.
Flowering: Spring and summer
Cultivation: Will grow in full sun or in light or partial shade. If grown in shade extra nutrients are needed in the soil. Mulch during warm weather and prune back after flowering.

Michelle Joy

Mischief

Mission Bells

MICHELLE JOY

Botanical grouping: Large-flowered hybrid tea
Parentage: Unknown
Other names: None
Other varieties: None
Year: 1991
Origin: United States
Description: Masses of large, light pink to deep peach high-centred blooms are produced on a tall, upright, bushy plant to more than 1.2 m (4 ft) with mid-green foliage. Although almost scentless it is very attractive in the vase or garden.
Flowering: Spring and summer
Cultivation: Plant in full sun in soil that is fertile, well drained and composted. Water well in hot weather and mulch.

MINNIE WATSON

Botanical grouping: Large-flowered hybrid tea
Parentage: Dickson's Flame x Dickson's Flame
Other names: None
Other varieties: None
Year: 1965
Origin: Australia
Description: An Australian-bred rose

Minnie Watson

producing globular buds which open to semi-double, open, fragrant blooms of apricot to pale pink. They are set amid glossy, light green foliage on a bush growing to 1.2 m (4 ft).
Flowering: Spring and summer
Cultivation: A free-blooming, compact, bushy plant which can be grown as an informal hedge or massed in a border, in full sun to partial shade. Prune lightly until established.

MISCHIEF

Botanical grouping: Large-flowered hybrid tea
Parentage: Peace x Spartan
Other names: Macmi
Other varieties: None
Year: 1961
Origin: Northern Ireland
Description: A vigorous, upright, free-flowering shrub to 1 m (3 ft) with free branching and light green foliage. The flower is a rich salmon-pink which deepens in autumn and is lightly scented.
Flowering: Continuously from summer to autumn
Cultivation: Very susceptible to black spot but is otherwise healthy. Will tolerate poorer soil conditions. May be grown as a cutting rose or in garden beds or pots.

MISSION BELLS

Botanical grouping: Large-flowered hybrid tea
Parentage: Mrs Sam McGredy x Malar-Ros
Other names: None
Other varieties: None
Year: 1949
Origin: United States
Description: The buds are long and pointed, opening to a large, double, high-centred bloom, almost 13 cm (5 in) across and packed with 40 to 45 rich-pink petals. It blooms profusely, is very fragrant and a

good cut flower. The foliage is dark and soft.
Flowering: Freely throughout summer
Cultivation: A very vigorous and healthy bush which responds well to a warm position in full sun and fertile soil. Remove spent blooms to stimulate repeat flowering. Mulch in warmer weather.

MISTER LINCOLN

Botanical grouping: Large-flowered hybrid tea
Parentage: Chrysler Imperial x Charles Mallerin
Other names: None
Other varieties: None
Year: 1964
Origin: United States
Description: One of the most internationally popular of all roses, greatly prized as a cut flower. Upright shrub to 1 m (3 ft) with leathery, dull green foliage. The dark red buds open to cupped flowers in the same colour and are very fragrant. The blooms are carried on strong stems making them ideal for cutting, although the shrub itself is not particularly attractive and therefore not so good as a bedding plant.
Flowering: Continuously from summer to autumn
Cultivation: May be grown under glass. It

Mister Lincoln

Mme Abel Chatenay

will tolerate poorer soil conditions and is quite hardy.

MME ABEL CHATENAY

Botanical grouping: Large-flowered hybrid tea
Parentage: Dr Grill x Victor Verdier
Other names: None
Other varieties: None
Year: 1895
Origin: France
Description: One of the oldest roses that have remained consistently popular. The blooms have a modern shape with high centres and reflexing petals of soft, silky pink with a dark silver reverse. It is strongly tea-scented. The dark green foliage is small and dense with an angular growth that is quite thorny. Grows to 3 m (10 ft).
Flowering: Repeats throughout summer.
Cultivation: A large open bush, it resents pruning other than removing spent wood. Hardy, although it prefers full sun.

MME BUTTERFLY

Botanical grouping: Large-flowered hybrid tea
Parentage: Sport from Ophelia
Other names: None
Other varieties: Climbing sport from England, 1926
Year: 1918
Origin: United States
Description: Upright, bushy shrub to 70 cm (2 ft) with medium green, somewhat sparse foliage and few branches. The well-shaped flower is blush-pink with a darker centre and a yellow cast at the base and is very fragrant. The flowers are often borne in clusters.
Flowering: Continuously from summer to autumn
Cultivation: Can tolerate poor soils but does best in an open, sunny position with well-drained beds. It is best as a border

plant with shorter plants grown in front. It can also be grown under glass or in pots.

MODERN ART

Botanical grouping: Large-flowered hybrid tea
Parentage: Unknown
Other names: Poulart
Other varieties: None
Year: 1984
Origin: Denmark
Description: A very different rose that almost looks hand-painted and is dramatic in a vase. Nicely formed buds open to large, double, 25-petalled, salmon-pink and white blooms that have dark red markings on the petals. The colours fade prettily as the flowers age. The well-foliated bush has an upright habit and reddish young shoots. It grows to 1 m (3 ft) high.
Flowering: Spring and summer
Cultivation: Plant in full sun or partial shade, in fertile soil that is well drained and mulched.

MON CHERI

Botanical grouping: Large-flowered hybrid tea
Parentage: (White Satin x Bewitched) x Double Delight
Other names: Arocher
Other varieties: None
Year: 1982
Origin: United States
Description: Huge, many-petalled blooms almost 15 cm (6 in) across open from plump pink buds and develop into deep red with a lemon base. Grows to 1.2 m (4 ft) high. A good cutting rose, free-flowering, fragrant and one of the first to bloom in the season.
Flowering: Freely throughout summer
Cultivation: May be grown as a hedge or massed in beds. Prefers day-long sun and fertile soil that is well drained and well mulched. Will tolerate light to filtered shade.

Mme Butterfly

Modern Art

Modern Art

Mon Cheri

Montezuma

My Choice

Mrs Oakley Fisher

MONIQUE

Botanical grouping: Large-flowered hybrid tea
Parentage: Lady Sylvia x a seedling
Other names: None
Other varieties: None
Year: 1949
Origin: France
Description: Upright, strong-growing shrub to 75 cm (2½ ft) with light-green, matt foliage. The large, double flowers are salmon-pink, fading with age, with a strong fragrance. They make good cut flowers.
Flowering: Continuously from summer to autumn
Cultivation: Plant in a moderately rich soil in an open, sunny spot. Mulch the soil and water well in summer. Suitable for growing in pots or in beds for massed display.

MONTEZUMA

Botanical grouping: Large-flowered hybrid tea
Parentage: Fandango x Floradora
Other names: None
Other varieties: None
Year: 1955
Origin: United States
Description: Bushy, upright shrub to 1.5 m (5 ft) with leathery, red-green foliage. The flower is large and high-centred in a salmon-pink shade with a somewhat metallic quality which it loses as it ages, to become rather dull in appearance.
Flowering: Continuously from summer to autumn
Cultivation: Very resistant to most diseases, particularly black spot. Unfortunately, rain will easily damage the blooms. Plant only in warm climates or where protection from the rain is possible. It works well as a bedding plant and may also be grown in pots or under glass.

MORIAH

Botanical grouping: Large-flowered hybrid tea
Parentage: Fragrant Cloud x seedling
Other names: Ganhol
Other varieties: None
Year: 1983
Origin: Israel
Description: Bushy, upright shrub to 75 cm (2½ ft) with dull, dark green foliage. The flowers are large, delicate orange with a darker reverse, and are very fragrant.
Flowering: Continuously from summer to autumn
Cultivation: A hardy rose with no special conditions. Does well in a pot or as a bedding plant. The blooms dislike rain so avoid planting where there are wet summers.

MRS OAKLEY FISHER

Botanical grouping: Large-flowered hybrid tea
Parentage: Unknown
Other names: None
Other varieties: None
Year: 1921
Origin: England
Description: A shrub of around 75 cm (2½ ft) with bronze-green foliage and purple stems. The flowers are of the five-petalled variety in an orange-yellow flushed red and are moderately fragrant.
Flowering: Continuously from summer to autumn
Cultivation: While it appears fragile, this rose is actually quite hardy and may be cultivated without difficulty. Provide moderately rich soil and a sunny position for best results. It may be grown either in pots or in garden beds.

MRS SAM MCGREDY

Botanical grouping: Large-flowered hybrid tea
Parentage: (Donald McDonald x Golden Emblem) x (seedling x The Queen Alexandra Rose)
Other names: None
Other varieties: Climbing variety (Geneviève Genest)
Year: 1929
Origin: Northern Ireland
Description: Sparse, angular shrub to 1 m (3 ft) with bronze, glossy foliage, dark red when young. The flower is very attractive, high-centred and well-shaped opening slowly to reveal coppery orange petals, yellow at the base and streaked with red in the young flower. It has no scent.
Flowering: Repeat flowers from summer to autumn
Cultivation: A hardy and healthy rose which does well in rich soil and a sunny spot. The flowers are resistant to rain damage. The plant would look best as a border with smaller shrubs in front to hide the rather bare, thin stems. Vigorous and easy to grow, it also makes a superb climber.

MY CHOICE

Botanical grouping: Large-flowered hybrid tea
Parentage: Wellworth x Ena Harkness
Other names: None
Other varieties: None
Year: 1958
Origin: England
Description: An upright shrub to 75 cm (2½ ft) with matt, grey-green foliage. The large, high-centred flowers are a soft salmon-pink with a delicate yellow reverse and are very fragrant.
Flowering: Continuously from summer to autumn
Cultivation: Hardy with no special requirements and will perform well even in poor soils. Plant as an exhibition rose or for beds and borders.

Desciption: Well-formed buds open to large, cerise-red flowers striped with white, almost scentless but providing a dramatic, free-flowering display in the garden or indoors. The bush is strong growing to 1.2 m (4 ft) and is well foliated with light green leaves.

Flowering: Freely throughout summer

Cultivation: A hardy and vigorous bush that will flourish in fertile soil and full sun, although it will tolerate some shade. Good drainage is essential as is mulching in warmer weather.

PAPA MEILLAND

Botanical grouping: Large-flowered hybrid tea

Parentage: Chrysler Imperial x Charles Mallerin

Other names: Meisar

Other varieties: Climbing sport from Australia, 1970

Year: 1963

Origin: France

Description: Upright shrub to 1 m (3 ft) with leathery, darkish-green foliage. The very fragrant flowers at their best are superb, with high-centred, dark crimson petals. A very good exhibition rose and wonderful cut flower.

Flowering: Repeat flowers throughout summer to autumn

Cultivation: Very susceptible to mildew and black spot and tends to die back in winter. May be used as a border plant or for massed displays. Not an easy rose to grow.

Papa Meilland

PARADISE

Botanical grouping: Large-flowered hybrid tea

Parentage: Swarthmore x seedling

Other names: Burning Sky, Wezeip

Other varieties: None

Year: 1978

Origin: United States

Description: A beautiful bush, growing to 1 m (3 ft) in height, and spreading to 70 cm (2 ft) with mid-green foliage and an abundance of silvery lilac blooms edged in ruby red. The long, slender buds are particularly graceful.

Flowering: Summer to autumn

Cultivation: Prefers warmer climates and

Paradise

light, well-drained soil. Does not thrive in cold, wet conditions. Prune back in winter, removing dead and spindly wood.

PASCALI

Botanical grouping: Large-flowered hybrid tea

Parentage: Queen Elizabeth x White Butterfly

Other names: Blanche Pasca, Lenip

Other varieties: None

Year: 1963

Origin: Belgium

Description: An upright plant, growing to 1 m (3 ft) high, with dark green, semi-matt foliage, and well-formed, almost pure white flowers with a cream base. Only slightly fragrant.

Flowering: Continuously throughout summer

Cultivation: A useful white rose for a wide range of soils and conditions, planted in a bed or border. The flowers are excellent for cutting. Quite disease and pest resistant.

Papageno

Pascali

Paul Shirville

Perfecta

Piccadilly

Peace

Perfume Delight

PAUL SHIRVILLE

Botanical grouping: Large-flowered hybrid tea
Parentage: Compassion x Mischief
Other names: Harqueterwife, Heart Throb
Other varieties: None
Year: 1983
Origin: England
Description: Slightly spreading shrub to 75 cm (2½ ft) with dark green, glossy foliage. The salmon-pink flowers are high centred in the typical hybrid tea fashion and are nicely scented. Suitable as a bedding or border plant.
Flowering: Summer to autumn
Cultivation: Reasonably healthy and hardy, this rose requires a sunny position and moderately rich, well-drained and mulched soil.

PEACE

Botanical grouping: Large-flowered hybrid tea
Parentage: [(George Dickson x Souvenir de Claudius Pernet) x (Joanna Hill x Charles P. Kilham)] x Margaret McGredy
Other names: Gioia, Gloria Dei, Mme A. Meilland
Other varieties: Climbing sport from

Germany, 1951
Year: 1945
Origin: France
Description: Bushy, vigorous shrub to 1.2 m (4 ft) with glossy, dark green foliage. The very large flowers are bright yellow, flushed pinkish-red at the edges, and are lightly scented. A deservedly famous and popular rose which looks good even when not in flower.
Flowering: Continuously from summer to autumn
Cultivation: A healthy and hardy rose which is reasonably easy to grow. Plant for beds, borders, hedges or as an exhibition or cutting rose.

PERFECTA

Botanical grouping: Large-flowered hybrid tea
Parentage: Spek's Yellow x Karl Herbst
Other names: Kordes Perfecta, Koralu
Other varieties: None
Year: 1957
Origin: Germany
Description: Upright and thorny shrub to 75 cm (2½ ft) with dark green, glossy foliage. The large flowers are deep cream,

flushed with pink and edged with reddish pink with a trace of yellow at the base. They are moderately scented. Cut the flowers when half open for long-lasting results.
Flowering: Continuously from summer to autumn
Cultivation: The blooms tend to spoil in rainy weather so it is best planted in sheltered conditions or in dry summer climates. Plant in beds or pots or as a hedging plant.

PERFUME DELIGHT

Botanical grouping: Large-flowered hybrid tea
Parentage: Peace x [(Happiness x Chrysler Imperial) x El Capitan]
Other names: None
Other varieties: None
Year: 1973
Origin: United States
Description: Very fragrant and free-flowering, the long elegant buds open to double blooms of deepest rose pink, making this a good cutting rose. They are borne on a medium bush to about 1.2 m (4 ft) accompanied by large, leathery, dark green leaves.
Flowering: Freely throughout summer
Cultivation: A good exhibition rose that merits a special place in the garden. It will thrive in full sun and fertile soil that is well drained and mulched. Prune back after each flush to encourage free flowering.

PICCADILLY

Botanical grouping: Large-flowered hybrid tea
Parentage: McGredy's Yellow x Karl Herbst
Other names: None
Other varieties: None
Year: 1959
Origin: Northern Ireland
Description: A bushy, upright shrub, reaching 75 cm (2½ ft), with attractive glossy dark green leaves and a wonderful display

of large, bright scarlet flowers with yellow undersides. A very prolific bloomer.

Flowering: Summer through to autumn.

Cultivation: A useful rose for bed or border, and can also be grown as an exhibition plant. Can withstand a wide range of soils and conditions, and requires winter pruning.

PICTURE

Botanical grouping: Large-flowered hybrid tea
Parentage: Unknown
Other names: None
Other varieties: None
Year: 1932
Origin: Northern Ireland
Description: Bushy, compact shrub to 45 cm (1½ ft) with matt, greyish-green foliage. The flowers are a clear pink with scrolled petals when half open. They are lightly scented.
Flowering: Continuously from summer to autumn
Cultivation: May be cultivated under glass but does well in the garden, even in poorer soils. Suitable as a potted specimen or for low-growing borders, hedges or massed displays.

PINK FAVOURITE

Botanical grouping: Large-flowered hybrid tea
Parentage: Juno x (Georg Arends x New Dawn)
Other names: None
Other varieties: None
Year: 1956
Origin: United States
Description: Free-flowering, bushy shrub to 75 cm (2½ ft) with unusual, long, pale green leaves. The cupped flowers are large, clear pink and have a very slight fragrance. A good exhibition rose.
Flowering: Continuously from summer to autumn

Pink Favourite

Pink Peace

Cultivation: A very healthy, disease-resistant rose with a liking for moderately rich, well-drained soil and plenty of sun. Looks attractive in beds or borders.

PINK PEACE

Botanical grouping: Large-flowered hybrid tea
Parentage: (Peace x Monique) x (Peace x Mrs John Laing)

Pink Peace

Other names: Meibil
Other varieties: None
Year: 1959
Origin: France
Description: An upright, free-flowering shrub to around 1 m (3 ft) with matt, medium green foliage.. The flowers are very large and double in a rich, rosy pink with obvious veining. They are very fragrant.
Flowering: Continuously from summer to autumn
Cultivation: While this rose will tolerate poor soil, it has a tendency to rust. The blooms are also very prone to rain damage. Plant as a hedge or tall border, as well as for exhibition.

Picture

Polar Star

Polo Club

Polly

Precious Platinum

PINTA

Botanical grouping: Large-flowered hybrid tea
Parentage: Ena Harkness x Pascali
Other names: None
Other varieties: None
Year: 1973
Origin: England
Description: A free-flowering, hardy shrub to around 1 m (3 ft) with matt, medium-green foliage. The well-shaped flowers are creamy white and very fragrant with the scent of eglantine. A good rose for exhibition.
Flowering: Continuously from summer to autumn
Cultivation: Not an easy rose to grow due to its susceptibility to rust and the sensitivity of the blooms to wet weather. It will, however, tolerate poor soil quality. Use in the garden as a hedging plant or grow in a pot.

POLAR STAR

Botanical grouping: Large-flowered hybrid tea
Parentage: Unknown
Other names: Polastern, Tanlarpost
Other varieties: None
Year: 1982
Origin: Germany
Description: A medium-sized, free-flowering shrub to 1 m (3 ft) with pale

green, rather sparse foliage and quite prickly stems. The flowers are very large in a creamy white, borne on strong necks. They are unscented.
Flowering: Continuously from summer to autumn
Cultivation: A healthy plant which will tolerate poorer soils and which has no special requirements to do well. Plant for exhibition, beds or borders or for cutting.

POLLY

Botanical grouping: Large-flowered hybrid tea
Parentage: Ophelia seedling x Mme Colette Martinet
Other names: None
Other varieties: None
Year: 1927
Origin: England
Description: Branching, rather spindly shrub to 70 cm (2 ft) with somewhat sparse foliage cover. The moderately scented flowers are of the floribunda type in a creamy blush with a yellowish tint in the centre of the rose and are carried in large sprays.
Flowering: Summer to autumn
Cultivation: Not fully hardy, this rose needs special attention to do well. May be useful as a border shrub, but because of its sparse foliage it is probably best raised in a glasshouse.

POLO CLUB

Botanical grouping: Large-flowered hybrid tea
Parentage: Unknown
Other names: None
Other varieties: None
Year: 1986
Origin: United States
Description: A compact bush to 1.2 m (4 ft) with plentiful, healthy, disease-resistant foliage. Iridescent, bright yellow blooms are bordered with vivid red and appear double although technically they are semi-double. Although scentless, this is a spectacular, colourful rose for vase or garden.
Flowering: Spring and summer
Cultivation: This makes an excellent, low-growing hedge and needs only full sun or partial shade and fertile soil that is drained and mulched to flourish. It is unequalled for colour and merits a special place in the garden.

PRECIOUS PLATINUM

Botanical grouping: Large-flowered hybrid tea
Parentage: Red Planet x Franklin Englemann
Other names: Red Star, Opa Pötschke
Other varieties: Noen
Year: 1974
Origin: Northern Ireland
Description: A bushy, vigorous shrub to 1 m (3 ft) with medium-green, glossy foliage. The flowers are bright crimson with a very attractive sheen to the petals. The rose is very fragrant and is held on strong stems.
Flowering: Continuously from summer to autumn
Cultivation: Healthy and generally easy to grow. Tolerates poorer soils. A good rose for cutting and exhibition. May be cultivated in pots or under glass; also does well in massed displays or for borders and hedges.

PRIMA BALLERINA

Botanical grouping: Large-flowered hybrid tea
Parentage: Seedling x Peace
Other names: Première Ballerine
Other varieties: None
Year: 1957
Origin: Germany
Description: Vigorous, bushy shrub to 75cm (2½ ft) with bronze-green foliage and thorny stems. The very fragrant, double flowers are large in a clear rose pink, tinged with yellow which fades with age.
Flowering: Continuously from summer to autumn
Cultivation: While the bloom is resistant to weather damage, the plant has a tendency to mildew. Plant in an open, sunny position. Use for beds or for small borders or hedges.

PRINCESSE DE MONACO

Botanical grouping: Large-flowered hybrid tea
Parentage: Ambassador x Peace
Other names: Meimagarmic, Preference, Princess Grace
Other varieties: None
Year: 1982
Origin: France
Description: Upright, strong-growing shrub to 1 m (3 ft) with dark green, glossy foliage. The large, full blush flowers are edged with pinky red and very fragrant.
Flowering: Continuously from summer to autumn
Cultivation: The blooms require warm, dry weather to open, so the plant should be cultivated in areas where there is not a lot of rain in the flowering season. Makes a good bedding or border plant.

PRINCESS MARGARET OF ENGLAND

Botanical grouping: Large-flowered hybrid tea
Parentage: Queen Elizabeth x (Peace x Michèle Meilland)
Other names: None
Other varieties: Climbing sport from France, 1969
Year: 1968
Origin: France
Description: Upright, vigorous shrub to 75 cm (2½ ft) with dark green leathery foliage. The large, double flowers are high-centred in a soft crimson-pink with a delicate fragrance.
Flowering: Continuously from summer to autumn
Cultivation: This is a hardy, healthy rose whose blooms are very weather resistant. It may be grown as a potted plant or in garden beds for massed display.

Prima Ballerina

Princess Margaret of England

Princesse de Monaco

Princesse de Monaco

Queen Beatrix

Remember Me

Rose Gaujard

Pristine

Queen Charlotte

PRISTINE

Botanical grouping: Large-flowered hybrid tea
Parentage: White Masterpiece x First Prize
Other names: Jacpico
Other varieties: None
Year: 1978
Origin: United States
Description: Very free-flowering, upright shrub to around 1 m (3 ft) with deep green, dense foliage. The large flowers are creamy white with pale pink tints and are very fragrant. Makes a good cut flower.

Flowering: Continuous, but much more profuse in spring than summer.
Cultivation: The plant is very healthy and disease resistant. It will also tolerate poor soils. Grow it under glass or in the garden.

QUEEN BEATRIX

Botanical grouping: Large-flowered hybrid tea
Parentage: Seedling x Patricia
Other names: Königin Beatrix, Hetkora
Other varieties: None
Year: 1982
Origin: Germany
Description: Pointed buds of copper-yellow open to well formed blooms of a luminous peach-copper shade which have a strong, wild rose perfume. The blooms, grouped on good stems, are well displayed in a vase surrounded by their rich and shiny, deep green foliage. The bush grows to 1.2 m (4 ft).
Flowering: Abundantly throughout summer
Cultivation: The bush has a sturdy, upright habit, well branched, with quick re-growth throughout the season. It prefers full sun and rich, fertile soil, mulched in summer.

QUEEN CHARLOTTE

Botanical grouping: Large-flowered hybrid tea
Parentage: Basildon Bond x Silver Jubilee
Other names: Harubondee
Other varieties: None
Year: 1989
Origin: England
Description: A medium-sized, vigorous shrub to 1 m (3 ft) with dark green, abundant foliage. The high-centred flowers are a pale salmon-pink with darker tonings. There is a slight fragrance.
Flowering: Continuously from summer to autumn
Cultivation: The flowers are resistant to weather damage and the plant is healthy and hardy with no special requirements. Plant it

in beds for massed display or for borders or hedges.

REMEMBER ME

Botanical grouping: Large-flowered hybrid tea
Parentage: Alexander x Siver Jubilee
Other names: Cocdestin
Other varieties: None
Year: 1984
Origin: Scotland
Description: A bushy and upright shrub to 1 m (3 ft) with plenty of small, dark green leaves and a good display of shapely orange and copper flowers. The flowers are only slightly fragrant.
Flowering: Continuously throughout summer
Cultivation: Easy to grow in many situations and soil types. Choose full sun and provide some wind protection. Prune out dead wood in winter.

ROSE GAUJARD

Botanical grouping: Large-flowered hybrid tea
Parentage: Peace x Opéra seedling
Other names: Gaumo
Other varieties: Climbing sport from Japan, 1964
Year: 1957
Origin: France
Description: Vigorous, upright shrub to 1.2 m (4 ft) with glossy, dark green foliage. The very double flowers are carmine-red with a silvery white to blush reverse, giving a bicolour effect. The petals are sometimes split or quartered when open. This is a good rose for exhibition and for cutting.
Flowering: Continuously from summer to autumn
Cultivation: This plant is tolerant of poor soils and the blooms are very weather resisitant, making it a useful rose for a variety of conditions. Its height makes it suitable as a hedging rose.

ROSEMARY HARKNESS

Botanical grouping: Large-flowered hybrid tea
Parentage: Compassion x (Basildon Bond x Grandpa Dickson)
Other names: Harrowbond
Other varieties: None
Year: 1985
Origin: England
Description: The flowers are a mixture of orange-yellow and salmon which fade as the blooms age. They are sweetly scented, and this rose has won prizes for its fragrance. Grows to 75 cm (2½ ft) with a spreading habit and glossy dark foliage.
Flowering: Summer to autumn
Cultivation: A hardy rose which prefers full sun and rich soil. The blooms are resistant to rain damage. Suitable as a plant for massed display or for borders and hedges.

ROUNDELAY

Botanical grouping: Large-flowered hybrid tea
Parentage: Charlotte Armstrong x Floradora
Other names: None
Other varieties: None
Year: 1954
Origin: England

Description: Upright shrub to 1.2 m (4 ft) high and 1 m (3 ft) wide with dark, shiny foliage The fragrant flowers begin as pointed buds, then open to dark crimson flowers which are flat and double, and occur in medium-sized clusters.
Flowering: Continuously throughout summer
Cultivation: This rose tolerates poorer soils, but requires full sun. It is considered excellent for mass planting, in beds or hedges, also as a cut flower and a container specimen. Remove dead flower heads during the summer, and in winter take out some older stems, and shorten others in order to promote new growth.

ROYAL ALBERT HALL

Botanical grouping: Large-flowered hybrid tea
Parentage: Fragrant Cloud x Postillon
Other names: None
Other varieties: None
Year: 1972
Origin: Scotland
Description: Bushy, upright shrub to 70 cm (2 ft) with abundant, dark green foliage which is purple when young. The very double flowers are deep cherry-red with a primrose-yellow reverse and are very fragrant.

Flowering: Continuously from summer to autumn
Cultivation: This rose is very prone to black spot and rust and therefore needs extra care and attention to do well. If cared for, it is useful for beds for massed displays and for cutting.

ROYAL WILLIAM

Botanical grouping: Large-flowered hybrid tea
Parentage: Feuerzauber x seedling
Other names: Duftzauber '84, Korzaun, Fragrant Charm
Other varieties: None
Year: 1984
Origin: Germany
Description: Vigorous, free-flowering shrub to 75 cm (2½ ft) with dark green, semi-glossy foliage. The large flowers are high-centred and well-formed in a deep, crimson-red with a moderate fragrance. The quality of the blooms is variable across the seasons. Makes an excellent cut flower.
Flowering: Continuously from summer to autumn
Cultivation: A healthy, disease-resistant rose. Prefers a sunny position and well-drained, moderately rich soil. A good bedding or border plant, which also does well in a pot.

Rosemary Harkness

Royal Albert Hall

Royal William

Sandringham Centenary

Savoy Hotel

Sharon Louise

Shire County

SANDRINGHAM CENTENARY

Botanical grouping: Large-flowered hybrid tea
Parentage: Queen Elizabeth x Baccarà
Other names: None
Other varieties: None
Year: 1981
Origin: England
Description: Free-flowering, vigorous shrub to 1.2 m (4 ft) with abundant, medium-green foliage. The large flower begins as a rich, dark orange, fading to salmon-pink with age. It is lightly scented and makes a lovely cut flower.

Flowering: Continuously from summer to autumn
Cultivation: May be cultivated under glass and is able to tolerate poorer soils. It is a healthy plant and the blooms are weather resistant. Its height makes it a useful hedging plant.

SAVOY HOTEL

Botanical grouping: Large-flowered hybrid tea
Parentage: Silver Jubilee x Amber Queen
Other names: Harvintage, Integrity

Other varieties: None
Year: 1989
Origin: England
Description: A bushy grower to 1 m (3 ft) with plentiful dark green foliage. The flowers are light pink with deeper pink on the petal reverse, very large and full, and beautifully formed.
Flowering: Freely through summer and autumn
Cultivation: Best in an open position on fertile, well-drained soil. Excellent for beds and cutting, and a useful exhibitor's rose.

SHARON LOUISE

Botanical grouping: Large-flowered hybrid tea
Parentage: Queen Elizabeth x Virgo
Other names: None
Other varieties: None
Year: 1968
Origin: Australia
Description: Blush-pink blooms of medium size open from shapely ovoid buds on this compact Australian-bred rose which grows to a height of 1 m (3 ft). The slightly fragrant flowers bloom profusely and are suitable for cutting. The foliage is dark green and leathery.
Flowering: Spring and summer
Cultivation: A vigorous rose for a warm and sunny climate, it makes a neat hedge or border and likes full sun and good soil that is well mulched and watered in drier weather.

SHIRE COUNTY

Botanical grouping: Large-flowered hybrid tea
Parentage: Amy Brown x Bonfire Night
Other names: Harsamy
Other varieties: None
Year: 1989
Origin: England
Description: Spreading shrub to 75 cm (2½ ft) with dark green, leathery foliage. The large, full flowers are cupped when open and are an attractive blend of yellow, apricot and salmon-pink which becomes darker

with age. They are moderately scented.
Flowering: Continuously from summer to autumn
Cultivation: A healthy and vigorous plant whose blooms are very weather resistant. Plant in rich, well-drained soil in a position with plenty of sun. A good border or bedding plant.

SHOT SILK

Botanical grouping: Large-flowered hybrid tea
Parentage: Hugh Dickson seedling x Sunstar
Other names: None
Other varieties: None
Year: 1924
Origin: Northern Ireland
Description: A popular old hybrid tea, noted for its silky petals and rich fragrance. It is a short, upright bush, growing to 50 cm (1½ ft), and the petals are a distinctive integration of orange, pink, salmon and yellow hues. The flowers contrast beautifully with the glossy green foliage.
Flowering: Summer to autumn
Cultivation: A hardy rose that can withstand a wide range of soils and climates. Prune well to keep a compact shape.

SHOWTIME

Botanical grouping: Large-flowered hybrid tea
Parentage: Kordes Perfecta x Granada
Other names: None
Other varieties: None
Year: 1969
Origin: United States
Description: An exhibition rose with a fruity fragrance, it is beautifully high-centred, true pink and the buds and blooms hold their shape well for long periods making this an ideal cutting rose. The foliage is glossy, good-looking and leathery on a stocky bush which grows to 1.2 m (4 ft).
Flowering: Freely throughout summer
Cultivation: This is a sturdy, free-blooming bush. To increase bloom production remove spent flowers. It can be grown as a hedge, in mass plantings or as a standard. It prefers full sun, drained and fertile soil that is well watered and mulched.

SILVER JUBILEE

Botanical grouping: Large-flowered hybrid tea
Parentage: [(Highlight x Colour Wonder) x (Parkdirektor Riggers x Piccadilly)] x Mischief
Other names: None

Other varieties: None
Year: 1978
Origin: Scotland
Description: A bushy, upright shrub to around 1 m (3 ft) with glossy, medium-green foliage. This rose is famous for its large size and perfect form. The lightly scented flowers are salmon-pink and apricot and produced in clusters. If the plant is disbudded, the flowers that remain will grow very large.
Flowering: Continuously from summer to autumn
Cultivation: It makes a wonderful cut flower. May be grown in the garden, under glass or for exhibition. This plant will tolerate poorer soils and will do well even in a pot. A very hardy rose.

SIMBA

Botanical grouping: Large-flowered hybrid tea
Parentage: Korgold x a seedling
Other names: Goldsmith, Helmut Schmidt, Korbelma
Other varieties: None

Year: 1981
Origin: Germany
Description: A medium-sized shrub to 75 cm (2½ ft) with attractive foliage. The bright yellow flowers are beautifully formed and are held on strong stems, making them suitable for cutting.
Flowering: Continuously from summer to autumn
Cultivation: A healthy rose that likes full sun and moderately rich, well-drained soil. The flowers are resistant to rain damage. Plant in garden beds and borders or under glass.

SOLITAIRE

Botanical grouping: Large-flowered hybrid tea
Parentage: Freude x Benson and Hedges Gold
Other names: Macyefre
Other varieties: None
Year: 1987
Origin: New Zealand
Description: An upright, vigorous rose, growing up to 2 m (7 ft), with a good

Shot Silk

Showtime

Silver Jubilee

Simba

Solitaire

Sonia

Summer Sunshine

covering of mid-green foliage. The flowers are very large and beautiful, similar to the famous Peace rose, although a little more yellow, and the pink flush more pronounced. Has a beautiful fragrance.
Flowering: Continuously throughout summer
Cultivation: Plant in an open sheltered position for best results. Prune back long growths to keep the bush in shape. Ideal for use behind shorter plants in a border.

SONIA

Botanical grouping: Large-flowered hybrid tea
Parentage: Zambra x (Baccarà x Message)
Other names: Sweet Promise, Sonia

Meilland, Meihelvet
Other varieties: Climbing sport from France, 1976
Year: 1974
Origin: France
Description: Free-flowering, upright, rather dense shrub to 75 cm (2½ ft) with deep green foliage. The flowers are semi-double, rosette-shaped in a light pink with a delicate fragrance and are produced either singly or in small clusters.
Flowering: Continuously from summer to autumn
Cultivation: A very good glasshouse variety, it also does well in the garden in beds or pots. The flowers do not like rain and the plant prefers full sun and rich soil.

STELLA

Botanical grouping: Large-flowered hybrid tea
Parentage: Horstmann's Jubiläumsrose x Peace
Other names: None
Other varieties: None
Year: 1958
Origin: Germany
Description: A vigorous, free-flowering shrub to 75 cm (2½ ft) with dark green, leathery foliage. The lightly scented flowers are very full and high-centred, creamy yellow at the centre with the outer petals deepening pink to light crimson. A good cut flower.
Flowering: Continuously from summer to autumn
Cultivation: The plant is susceptible to black spot but is otherwise reasonably healthy and hardy. Does well in a pot.

SUMMER SUNSHINE

Botanical grouping: Large-flowered hybrid tea
Parentage: Buccaneer x Lemon Chiffon
Other names: Soleil d'Eté
Other varieties: Climbing sport
Year: 1962
Origin: United States
Description: Spreading, untidy shrub to 1 m (3 ft) with medium-green, sparse, leathery foliage. The intensely yellow flower is very attractive and has a good scent.
Flowering: Continuously from summer to autumn
Cultivation: Good for cutting and for glasshouse cultivation, it is not so useful in the garden due to the nature of the plant. It will tolerate poor soils, but it is not an especially vigorous or hardy plant. The blooms are resistant to rain damage.

SUNBURNT COUNTRY

Botanical grouping: Large-flowered hybrid tea
Parentage: Uwe seeler x Sonia
Other names: Kordes Korav, Ave Maria
Other varieties: None
Year: 1981
Origin: Germany
Description: Well-foliated bush to 1.2 m (4 ft). Unusual, burnt coral-orange blooms are packed with about 40 petals; firm and very free-flowering with a pronounced fragrance. They are borne on long stems making this a very good cut rose.
Flowering: Freely throughout summer
Cultivation: A hardy and unusually coloured rose that provides a good display in a massed border or individually. Grow in full sun and well-drained, fertile soil that is well mulched in warmer weather. Water well.

Sunburnt Country

Talisman

Tequila Sunrise

SUSAN HAMPSHIRE

Botanical grouping: Large-flowered
hybrid tea
Parentage: (Monique x Symphonie) x Maria
Callas
Other names: Meinatac
Other varieties: None
Year: 1972
Origin: France
Description: Vigorous, dense and free-
flowering shrub to 75 cm (2½ ft) with matt,
medium green foliage. The flowers, emerging from very large buds, are very double
and high-centred in a lovely deep pink and
are moderately fragrant. A good cutting rose.
Flowering: Continuously from summer to
autumn
Cultivation: May be grown in the garden or in
pots. Likes a sunny position with well-drained,
rich soil, although it can tolerate poorer soils.

Susan Hampshire

TALISMAN

Botanical grouping: Large-flowered
hybrid tea
Parentage: Ophelia x Souvenir de Claudius
Pernet
Other names: None
Other varieties: None
Year: 1929
Origin: United States
Description: Upright, vigorous shrub to
1 m (3 ft) with pale green, leathery, glossy
foliage. The semi-double flower is a deep
yellow to copper with a moderate fragrance.
Its long stems make it a good cut flower.
Flowering: Continuously from summer to
autumn
Cultivation: A hardy, healthy rose which
will tolerate poorer soil conditions. Plant in
the garden for a massed display or in the
glasshouse in pots.

TEQUILA SUNRISE

Botanical grouping: Large-flowered
hybrid tea
Parentage: Bonfire Night x Freedom
Other names: Dicobey, Beaulieu
Other varieties: None
Year: 1989
Origin: Northern Ireland
Description: Bushy, free-flowering shrub to
75 cm (2½ ft) with medium green, glossy
foliage. The flowers are bright yellow with a
bright red blush at the petal edge. They last
well, making them a good cut flower.
Flowering: Continuously from summer to
autumn
Cultivation: Healthy with no special
requirements apart from a sunny spot and good
soil. Looks good in garden beds as a massed
display or as a border or hedging plant.

TEXAS CENTENNIAL

Botanical grouping: Large-flowered
hybrid tea
Parentage: Sport from President Herbert
Hoover
Other names: None
Other varieties: Climbing sports from
United States, 1936 and 1942
Year: 1935

Texas Centennial

The Doctor

Origin: United States
Description: A vigorous, bushy shrub to 1.2 m (4 ft) with, leathery, matt foliage. The scented, double flowers in a vermilion-red with a tinge of yellow are held on long, strong stems, making them excellent as cut flowers.
Flowering: Continuously from summer to autumn
Cultivation: An attractive bush that can be used as a specimen shrub or hedging plant. Tolerates poorer soils and is quite disease resistant.

THE DOCTOR

Botanical grouping: Large-flowered hybrid tea
Parentage: Mrs J.D. Eisele x Los Angeles
Other names: None
Other varieties: Climbing sport from United States, 1950
Year: 1936
Origin: United States
Description: A bushy grower to 75 cm (2½ ft) with greyish-green foliage. The large, double flowers are a medium, silvery pink with a satiny finish to the petals and are very fragrant. It makes an attractive cut flower and exhibition rose.
Flowering: Continuously from summer to autumn
Cultivation: Rather prone to black spot, its blooms are sensitive to rain and are easily damaged. Plant in a dry, sunny climate. Grow in pots or in garden beds.

THE LADY

Botanical grouping: Large-flowered hybrid tea
Parentage: Pink Parfait x Redgold
Other names: Fryjingo
Other varieties: None
Year: 1985
Origin: England
Description: An upright rose growing to 75 cm (2½ ft), with glossy mid-green foliage and large, shapely, warm yellow flowers with a salmon tinge. The flowers are moderately fragrant.
Flowering: Continuously throughout summer
Cultivation: Suitable for growing in a wide range of soils and conditions, including in a large container. Good as an exhibition rose, or for cut flowers.

TIFFANY

Botanical grouping: Large-flowered hybrid tea
Parentage: Charlotte Armstrong x Girona
Other names: None
Other varieties: Climbing sport from United States, 1958
Year: 1954
Origin: United States
Description: Elegant long buds open to reveal classic, high-centred, rose pink blended flowers on long stems that are suitable for cutting. Strongly scented, the blooms contrast well with their dark green foliage on a bush which grows to about 1.2 m (4 ft).
Flowering: Freely throughout summer
Cultivation: An easy-to-care-for rose that requires little more than fertile soil, good drainage and full sun. Grow against a trellis or wall, as a hedge or a standard.

TROIKA

Botanical grouping: Large-flowered hybrid tea
Parentage: [(Super Star x (Baccarà x Princesse Astrid)] x Hanne
Other names: Royal Dane
Other varieties: None
Year: 1971
Origin: Denmark
Description: An upright, bushy shrub to 75 cm (2½ ft) with dark green, glossy foliage. The large, high-centred flowers are a mix of orange-yellow and pink and are quite fragrant. Use this rose for exhibition or cutting.
Flowering: Continuously from summer to autumn
Cultivation: A reasonably healthy plant which prefers a rich, well-drained soil with plenty of sun. Plant for massed display.

The Lady

Tiffany

Troika

Uncle Walter

UNCLE WALTER

Botanical grouping: Large-flowered hybrid tea
Parentage: Detroiter x Heidelberg
Other names: Macon
Other varieties: None
Year: 1963
Origin: Northern Ireland
Description: Tall, upright shrub reaches 1.5 m (5 ft) high and 1.2 m (4 ft) wide, with dark shiny foliage which is leathery and reddish when young. Medium-sized flowers are shapely and deep scarlet, and can be

improved through disbudding.

Flowering: Continuously throughout summer

Cultivation: Tolerates poorer soils, and is useful as a hedge or bedding plant. Can also be used as a container specimen and, with care, for flower exhibition. Remove dead flower heads during the summer, and in winter take out some older stems, and shorten others in order to promote new growth.

VALENCIA

Botanical grouping: Large-flowered hybrid tea

Parentage: Unknown

Other names: Koreklia

Other varieties: None

Year: 1989

Origin: Germany

Description: A new, fragrant, hybrid tea that should not be confused with the rose of the same name introduced in the late 1960s. Long buds open to reveal large blooms of a rich, old-gold colour. The bush is well foliated and grows to 1.2 m (4 ft).

Flowering: Freely throughout summer

Cultivation: Grow in full sun or partial shade, in fertile soil that is well drained and well mulched. Prune back lightly after each flush and remove spent blooms to promote repeat flowering.

Valencia

Vienna Charm

VIENNA CHARM

Botanical grouping: Large-flowered hybrid tea

Parentage: Chantré x Golden Sun

Other names: Charming Vienna, Wiener Charme, Charme de Vienne, Korschaprat

Other varieties: None

Year: 1963

Origin: Germany

Description: Upright shrub to around 1 m (3 ft) with dark green, glossy foliage. The large flowers are coppery orange with a moderate fragrance.

Flowering: Continuously from summer to autumn

Cultivation: Not fully hardy, this plant needs extra attention to do well. It should be planted in a very sunny position with rich, well-drained soil. Its height makes it a useful hedging plant, but it also looks good in massed display or in pots.

VIOLINISTA COSTA

Botanical grouping: Large-flowered hybrid tea

Parentage: Sensation x Shot Silk

Other names: None

Other varieties: None

Year: 1936

Virgo

Voodoo

Origin: Spain

Description: Angular, free-flowering shrub to 75 cm (2½ ft) with thorny branches and medium green, glossy foliage. The lightly scented flowers are an intense pink with definite orange tones and yellow at the base.

Flowering: Continuously from summer to autumn

Cultivation: A hardy, healthy rose which will tolerate poorer soil conditions. Plant in an open, sunny spot for best results. Suitable for pots or garden beds, for hedges or massed display.

VIRGO

Botanical grouping: Large-flowered hybrid tea

Parentage: Blanche Mallerin x Neige Parfum

Other names: None

Other varieties: None

Year: 1947

Origin: France

Description: An elegant bush, growing to 70 cm (2 ft) with a good covering of mid-green foliage. This rose is valued for its pure white blooms, emerging from slender buds.

Flowering: Over many months, from summer to autumn.

Cultivation: As it is prone to mildew, this rose must be grown in good conditions and protected against damp or overcrowding. Prune out dead or diseased wood in winter.

VOODOO

Botanical grouping: Large-flowered hybrid tea

Parentage: [(Camelot x First Prize) x Typhoo Tea] x Lolita

Other names: Aromiclea

Other varieties: None

Year: 1986

Origin: United States

Description: An award-winning rose with very large blooms displaying a blend of colours ranging from a yellow base to peach, orange and scarlet. An outstanding cut flower with a powerful perfume, the bush grows to 1.5 m (5 ft).

Flowering: Spring and summer

Cultivation: An eye-catching feature rose that merits a special place in the garden. A very robust plant, it prefers full sun, soil that is enriched with organic matter and mulched in dry weather.

WHISKY MAC

Botanical grouping: Large-flowered hybrid tea

Parentage: Seedling x Golden Wave

Other names: Whisky, Tanky

Voodoo

Other varieties: Climbing sport from Scotland, 1985
Year: 1967
Origin: Germany
Description: Vigorous, bushy shrub to 1 m (3 ft) with deep green foliage. The large, double flowers are a golden amber with orange tints and a good fragrance.
Flowering: Summer to autumn
Cultivation: Rather prone to mildew and may die back during cold winters. It makes a good cut flower as well as an attractive plant for bedding or border.

YOUNG AT HEART

Botanical grouping: Large-flowered hybrid tea
Parentage: Unknown
Other names: None
Other varieties: None
Year: 1989

Whisky Mac

Origin: United States
Description: An award-winning rose that is fragrant, high-centred, with peach to apricot-pink, long-lasting blooms that are borne singly or in clusters on strong stems. It has a recurrent blooming habit and glossy foliage and grows

Young at Heart

to 1.2 m (4 ft). A good cut flower.
Flowering: Recurrently throughout summer
Cultivation: Prefers fertile soil and full sun to partial shade. Remove spent blooms to encourage free-flowering, and mulch in warmer weather.

Floribunda (cluster-flowered) Roses

These delightful roses are the result of a cross between a polyantha and a hybrid tea by Danish breeders in 1924. They were initially called hybrid polyanthas, but US growers dubbed them floribundas, and the name has remained as such. Floribundas are distinguished by the way that their flowers are carried in clusters or sprays, often giving a dramatic display. The early floribundas were in the pink and red colour range, however in the 1930s a yellow rose named Fortschritt was introduced in Germany, and more recently, apricot, multi-coloured and 'hand-painted' varieties have been developed. In the garden, floribundas are used as bedding and hedging plants, and some of the smaller varieties can also be grown in containers.

Amber Queen

Allgold

Anisley Dickson

ABUNDANCE

Botanical grouping: Cluster-flowered floribunda
Parentage: Seedling x Firecracker
Other names: None
Other varieties: None
Year: 1974
Origin: England
Description: Dwarf bush, to 50 cm (1½ ft), with dark green leaves, bearing a profusion of full, double, pink blooms in clusters. Lightly scented.
Flowering: Flowers over a long period from early summer.
Cultivation: This attractive small bush makes a good low hedge or foreground specimen, and can also be grown in a container. It is hardy and will tolerate most soils and conditions.

ALLGOLD

Botanical grouping: Cluster-flowered floribunda
Parentage: Goldilocks x Ellinor le Grice
Other names: None
Other varieties: Climbing sport from England, 1961
Year: 1956
Origin: England
Description: Robust, small bush growing to 70 cm (2 ft), with glossy, deep green foliage. The neat, golden yellow, double blooms, which have a slight fragrance, are borne in trusses and make attractive cut flowers, keeping their colour well until the petals drop.
Flowering: Constant throughout the season
Cultivation: Hardy, requiring no special treatment. Hard pruning will help to encourage growth from the base.

AMBER QUEEN

Botanical grouping: Cluster-flowered floribunda
Parentage: Southampton x Typhoon
Other names: Harroony, Prinz Eugen von Savoyen
Other varieties: None
Year: 1984
Origin: England
Description: A handsome shrub growing to 50 cm (1½ ft) with masses of reddish green foliage and very large flowers in a rich amber shade. The flowers are very fragrant, and the shrub develops a spreading habit.
Flowering: Summer through to autumn
Cultivation: A good rose for bed or border or as a low-growing hedge. Suitable for a wide range of soils and conditions.

ANISLEY DICKSON

Botanical grouping: Cluster-flowered floribunda
Parentage: Coventry Cathedral x Memento
Other names: Dicky, Münchner Kindl, Dickimono
Other varieties: None
Year: 1983
Origin: Northern Ireland
Description: Clusters of large, salmon-pink, full, double, slightly scented flowers contrast attractively with glossy dark green foliage. Bushy growth to 1 m (3 ft).
Flowering: Reliable repeat flowering over a long period.
Cultivation: A robust plant which can be grown in a container and also makes a good bedding or hedge specimen.

ANNA LIVIA

Botanical grouping: Cluster-flowered
floribunda
Parentage: Unknown
Other names: Kormetter, Trier 2000
Other varieties: None
Year: 1985
Origin: Germany
Description: Showy clusters of shapely,
clear pink blooms borne on a well-foliaged
bush which grows to 75 cm (2½ ft).
Flowering: Summer to autumn
Cultivation: A very hardy plant tolerant of
most conditions. Makes a good hedge or
bedding specimen.

ANNA WHEATCROFT

Botanical grouping: Cluster-flowered
floribunda
Parentage: Cinnabar seedling x unknown
Other names: None
Other varieties: None
Year: 1959
Origin: Germany
Description: Clusters of large, single,
vermilion flowers which open flat to display
prominent, bright yellow stamens. Lightly
scented. Bushy plant with attractive mid-
green foliage growing to 1 m (3 ft).
Flowering: Repeat flowers from early
summer to autumn.
Cultivation: A vigorous grower and good
hedging specimen. Prune back vigorous
new stems by two-thirds to encourage larger
flowers.

ANNE COCKER

Botanical grouping: Cluster-flowered
floribunda
Parentage: Highlight x Colour Wonder
Other names: None
Other varieties: None
Year: 1970
Origin: Scotland
Description: The clusters of small, closely
packed double flowers, vermilion in colour,
are ideal for cutting, and very long-lasting.
The upright, compact, rather thorny bush
carries handsome darkish green, glossy
leaves and may reach 1 m (3 ft).
Flowering: Flowers throughout summer
and into autumn.
Cultivation: Susceptible to mildew, but will
tolerate poor soil and extremes of weather.
Keep the area around the rose free from
weeds or competing plants.

ANNE HARKNESS

Botanical grouping: Cluster-flowered
floribunda
Parentage: Bobby Dazzler x [(Manx Queen

Anne Cocker

Anne Harkness

x Prima Ballerina) x (Chanelle x Piccadilly)]
Other names: Harkaramel
Other varieties: None
Year: 1980
Origin: England
Description: The full, apricot-yellow
blooms of this rose are carried in attractive
sprays, perfectly spaced and with long
stems, making it a lovely cut flower. Slight
fragrance. A vigorous, upright grower to
1.2 m (4 ft), with good foliage.
Flowering: Flowers later than most, in mid-
summer, but continues through to autumn.
Cultivation: Hardy and weatherproof, this
rose does not mind rain. It benefits from
hard pruning to contain growth.

Apricot Nectar

Ards Beauty

(2 ft) in height, with a good coverage of mid-green foliage. The prolific, medium-sized canary yellow flowers are borne on short, stiff stems and have a strong fragrance. In hot climates some flowers may develop with green centres.
Flowering: Summer to autumn
Cultivation: Prefers full sun and well-drained, moderately rich soil. Ideal for bed or border, and makes a pretty hedge.

ARTHUR BELL

Botanical grouping: Cluster-flowered floribunda
Parentage: Cläre Grammerstorf x Piccadilly
Other names: None
Other varieties: None
Year: 1965
Origin: Northern Ireland
Description: Large clusters of bright yellow, richly fragrant semi-double flowers with long petals, fading as they mature to paler yellow. Lovely cut flower or button-hole. Dense light green foliage on a neat, upright bush growing to 1 m (3 ft).
Flowering: Reliable flowering through summer to autumn.
Cultivation: Use this rose for bedding, hedge or container. It is tolerant of most weather conditions and a wide range of soils.

Arthur Bell

APRICOT NECTAR

Botanical grouping: Cluster-flowered floribunda
Parentage: Seedling x Spartan
Other names: None
Other varieties: None
Year: 1965
Origin: United States
Description: Large, rounded, very fragrant apricot blooms with pink tints, shaped like peonies. Compact bush to 70 cm (2 ft) with light green leaves and strong stems. Lovely flower in arrangements.
Flowering: Constant flowering summer through to autumn.
Cultivation: A warm climate rose that does not like wet or cold conditions. New stems can be pruned back by two-thirds to encourage larger blooms.

ARDS BEAUTY

Botanical grouping: Cluster-flowered floribunda
Parentage: (Eurorose x Whisky Mac) x Bright Smile
Other names: Dicjoy
Other varieties: None
Year: 1986
Origin: Northern Ireland
Description: An upright bush to 70 cm

AUGUST SEEBAUER

Botanical grouping: Cluster-flowered floribunda
Parentage: Break o'Day x Else Poulsen
Other names: The Queen Mother
Other varieties: None
Year: 1944
Origin: Germany
Description: Large clusters of shapely, pink, double blooms with prominent centres, lightly scented. The bush, which reaches 75 cm (2½ ft), is well-foliaged with small, bright green, glossy leaves.

August Seebauer

Avignon

Beautiful Britain

Bernina

Flowering: Constant flowering throughout summer, into autumn.

Cultivation: Good hedging, bedding or container specimen. A vigorous grower, tolerant of difficult soil conditions. Prune back new stems by two thirds.

AVIGNON

Botanical grouping: Cluster-flowered floribunda
Parentage: Zambra x Allgold
Other names: None
Other varieties: None
Year: 1974
Origin: England
Description: Trusses of bright yellow double flowers with a light fragrance are borne on an upright, sturdy bush which may exceed 1 m (3 ft) in height.
Flowering: Continuous flowers through summer to autumn
Cultivation: Grow as a hedge or bedding rose. Vigorous and tolerant of poor soil conditions. Responds well to hard pruning.

BEAUTIFUL BRITAIN

Botanical grouping: Cluster-flowered floribunda
Parentage: Red Planet x Eurorose
Other names: Dicfire
Other varieties: None
Year: 1983
Origin: Northern Ireland
Description: Large clusters of attractive orange-red blooms, opening from neat buds. Slightly scented, the flowers are useful in arrangements and for buttonholes. The plant, which grows to 75 cm (2½ ft), is upright and bushy, with clear green glossy leaves.
Flowering. Reliable flowering summer through to autumn.
Cultivation: Can be used as a bedding, hedge or container specimen. A hardy rose, requiring no special treatment except for pruning of vigorous new stem growth.

BERNINA

Botanical grouping: Cluster-flowered floribunda
Parentage: Unknown
Other names: None
Other varieties: None
Year: 1988
Origin: The Netherlands
Description: Massed clusters of sweetly scented, petite, high-pointed, white blooms with attractive reflexed petals are produced on a small to medium bush up to 1.2 m (4 ft).
Flowering: Spring to summer
Cultivation: Full sun, good soil and water and light pruning to tidy the bush after flowering is all that this rose needs to flourish. An excellent border rose.

BONFIRE NIGHT

Botanical grouping: Cluster-flowered floribunda
Parentage: Tiki x Variety Club
Other names: Bonfire
Other varieties: None
Year: 1971
Origin: Northern Ireland
Description: A handsome, well-shaped bush growing to 75 cm (2½ ft) with a good covering of dark green foliage. The flowers make an excellent display in large clusters, with deep yellow petals overlaid with orange and scarlet.
Flowering: Summer to autumn
Cultivation: A versatile rose that can be grown in a wide range of climates and conditions. Ideal for bed, border or hedge. Prune out dead wood in winter.

BRIDAL PINK

Botanical grouping: Cluster-flowered floribunda
Parentage: Summertime seedling x Spartan seedling
Other names: None
Other varieties: None
Year: 1967

Bridal Pink

Bonfire Night

Origin: United States
Description: Clusters of pale pink, ovoid pointed buds, opening to large, high-centred double blooms that are well formed, mass very freely on this robust bush. The flowers are very fragrant and make an excellent display in the garden or vase. Leathery dark green foliage. Grows to 1.2 m (4 ft).
Flowering: Abundant blooms throughout summer
Cultivation: This is a very vigorous, upright and bushy rose. Prune lightly when flowering is finished to encourage repeat flowerings. Prefers full sun or partial shade and good drainage and watering.

By Appointment

Chanelle

Bright Smile

Centenaire de Lourdes

BRIGHT SMILE

Botanical grouping: Cluster-flowered floribunda
Parentage: Eurorose x seedling
Other names: Dicdance
Other varieties: None
Year: 1980
Origin: Northern Ireland
Description: Neat but bushy floribunda growing to 45 cm (1½ ft) with attractive shiny foliage. Long, slim buds open flat to reveal buttery yellow flowers with light fragrance.
Flowering: Summer to autumn
Cultivation: A healthy and hardy rose, whose flowers are resistant to rain damage and make good cut flowers. Plant in a sunny spot to show off the foliage and flowers to best effect. A very useful shrub for low hedges, small spaces and beds and borders.

BY APPOINTMENT

Botanical grouping: Cluster-flowered floribunda
Parentage: Anne Harkness x Letchworth Garden City
Other names: Harvolute
Other varieties: None
Year: 1990
Origin: England
Description: Clusters of creamy blooms with touches of apricot borne on long stems, which make superb cut flowers. Upright bush to 75 cm (2½ ft), with dark green leaves providing a delightful counterpoint to the blooms.
Flowering: Constant flowering, summer through to autumn.
Cultivation: Hardy and tolerant of all weathers. Prune out dead wood in winter, and shorten new stem growth by two-thirds.

CENTENAIRE DE LOURDES

Botanical grouping: Cluster-flowered floribunda
Parentage: (Frau Karl Druschki x seedling) x seedling
Other names: Mrs Jones, Delge
Other varieties: None
Year: 1958
Origin: France
Description: One of the most widely admired modern roses with many clusters of double, cup-shaped flowers in clear satin pink, set against handsome, dark green, glossy foliage. Slight fragrance. Upright bush which in the right conditions can grow to 1.8 m (6 ft), but is usually around 1 m (3 ft).
Flowering: Consistent flowers through summer to autumn.
Cultivation: Will not tolerate very cold conditions. Excellent as a bedding or hedging rose. Prune dead wood in late winter, and shorten stem growth by two-thirds.

CHANELLE

Botanical grouping: Cluster-flowered floribunda
Parentage: Ma Perkins x (Fashion x Mrs William Sprot)
Other names: None
Other varieties: None
Year: 1959
Origin: Northern Ireland
Description: Attractive buds open to cup-shaped, creamy pink flowers, shading to apricot at the base, which grow in large clusters. Fragrant. Bushy, vigorous grower to 75 cm (2½ ft), with glossy dark green leaves.
Flowering: Constant flowers over a long period.
Cultivation: Use for beds or hedging. This is a hardy rose that will grow in a wide range of soils and conditions.

CHARLESTON

Botanical grouping: Cluster-flowered floribunda
Parentage: Masquerade x (Radar x Caprice)
Other names: Meiridge
Other varieties: Climbing sport from Australia, 1966
Year: 1963
Origin: France
Description: Large semi-double blooms in clusters, yellow with crimson flushes turning deeper crimson with maturity. Bushy, vigorous plant to 75 cm (2½ ft) with glossy, medium green leaves.
Flowering: Flowers summer through to autumn.
Cultivation: Needs careful attention for signs of black spot. Keep the area at the base of the plant free from weeds, and avoid overhead watering.

CHORUS

Botanical grouping: Cluster-flowered floribunda
Parentage: Tamango x (Sarabande x Zambra)
Other names: Meijulito, Meimore
Other varieties: None
Year: 1975
Origin: France
Description: A sturdy bush of vigorous habit to 75 cm (2½ ft) with medium green, shiny leaves. Clusters of large, double, clear red flowers with a slight scent.
Flowering: Reliable flowers over a long period.
Cultivation: Good hedge specimen, and tolerant of poor soil conditions. Pick the first flush of flowers to encourage further growth.

CHRISTINGLE

Botanical grouping: Cluster-flowered floribunda
Parentage: Bobby Dazzler x Alexander
Other names: Harvalex
Other varieties: None
Year: 1987
Origin: England
Description: A leafy, free-branching bush that grows to 75 cm (2½ ft) with a good covering of mid-green foliage. The large sprays of full-petalled flowers are a rich orange-red shade, with red veins on the outer petals.
Flowering: Summer to autumn
Cultivation: An ideal rose for bed or border, or as a colourful hedge. Makes an excellent cut flower. Can be grown in a wide range of soils and climate.

Charleston

Christingle

Chorus

223

CIRCUS

Botanical grouping: Cluster-flowered floribunda
Parentage: Fandango x Pinocchio
Other names: None
Other varieties: Climbing sport from United States, 1961
Year: 1956
Origin: United States
Description: Clusters of cup-shaped double flowers, predominantly yellow, with flushes of pink and scarlet/orange. Slight fragrance. Bushy and vigorous, grows to 75 cm (2½ ft).
Flowering: Early summer through to autumn.

City of Belfast

Circus

Cultivation: A good hedging or border specimen, which will tolerate poor soil conditions. Prune out dead wood in late winter and shorten new stem growth by two-thirds.

CITY OF BELFAST

Botanical grouping: Cluster-flowered floribunda
Parentage: Evelyn Fison x (Korona x Circus)
Other names: Macci
Other varieties: None
Year: 1968

City of Leeds

Origin: Northern Ireland
Description: Rich, clear scarlet, full blooms with slightly frilled edges, borne in well-spaced clusters. These striking blooms contrast with the glossy, leafy bush, which is of upright habit, growing to 70 cm (2 ft).
Flowering: Consistent flowering over a long period.
Cultivation: Good hedge specimen. Hardy and robust, will tolerate poor soils and most weather conditions. Dead-head spent flower stems in summer, and prune out dead wood in winter.

CITY OF LEEDS

Botanical grouping: Cluster-flowered floribunda
Parentage: Evelyn Fison x (Spartan x Red Favourite)
Other names: None
Other varieties: None
Year: 1966
Origin: Northern Ireland
Description: Lovely bedding rose with well-spaced clusters of salmon-pink, cupped flowers. Neat, compact bush to 75 cm (2½ ft), with large, dark green leaves.
Flowering: Constant flowering, summer through to autumn.
Cultivation: Tolerant of all climates and less than perfect soil conditions. Prune back hard in the first year; from then onwards a moderate pruning should suffice.

CITY OF LONDON

Botanical grouping: Cluster-flowered floribunda
Parentage: New Dawn x Radox Bouquet
Other names: Harukfore
Other varieties: None
Year:1988
Origin: England
Description: The sweet, lasting fragrance and appealing shape of this rose makes it an ideal cut flower. The blooms open wide

City of London

from neat buds and, as they mature, take on a lovely loose effect. The clear green foliage is glossy and plentiful. The bush can exceed 1 m (3 ft) and, if supported, can be grown as a climber.

Flowering: Constant flowering over a long period.

Cultivation: While the growth can be somewhat uneven, the bush should be allowed free rein and not cut back if it is to flower to its full capacity.

CONQUEROR'S GOLD

Botanical grouping: Cluster-flowered floribunda

Parentage: Amy Brown x Judy Garland

Other names: Donauwalzer, Hartwiz

Other varieties: None

Year: 1986

Origin: England

Description: Floribunda, cluster-flowered rose with a bushy habit to around 1 m (3 ft). The lightly scented flowers begin as yellow but gradually become suffused with pinkish tones, deepening to red and with many flowers in each cluster, the colour effect is very striking.

Flowering: Summer to autumn

Cultivation: Suitable as a bedding plant for massed display or for hedges and borders. Healthy and hardy, this rose will do well with a minimum of special attention. Plant in full sun and provide rich, well-drained soil.

DAME OF SARK

Botanical grouping: Cluster-flowered floribunda

Parentage: (Pink Parfait x Masquerade) x Tabler's Choice

Other names: None

Other varieties: None

Year: 1976

Origin: England

Description: The double blooms are an unusual, attractive mixture of orange-gold

Dame of Sark

Disco Dancer

and yellow with scarlet flushes, and are borne in clusters. Glossy dark green leaves on an upright, vigorous bush to 1 m (3 ft).

Flowering: Continued flowering over a long period.

Cultivation: This rose will stand a certain amount of shade. Pick flowers regularly to encourage further flowering, and prune out dead wood in winter.

DAME WENDY

Botanical grouping: Cluster-flowered floribunda

Parentage: English Miss x Memento

Other names: Canson

Other varieties: None

Year: 1990

Origin: England

Description: Clusters of warm pink, shapely, many-petalled flowers carried on a slightly leggy plant with attractive, grey-green leaves, growing to 70 cm (2 ft).

Flowering: Flowers from summer through to autumn.

Cultivation: Makes a good low hedge or border rose. It is hardy and tolerant of extremes of weather. Prune back stem growth by two-thirds to encourage larger blooms.

DISCO DANCER

Botanical grouping: Cluster-flowered floribunda

Parentage: Coventry Cathedral x Memento

Other names: Dicinfra

Other varieties: None

Year: 1984

Origin: Northern Ireland

Description: The well-shaped, semi-double flowers of this popular rose are a striking, bright scarlet with orange touches, and are carried in clusters. Slightly scented. The

Dame Wendy

Dreamland

Escapade

English Miss

foliage is dense and glossy and the bush grows vigorously to 1 m (3 ft).

Flowering: Flowers consistently through summer to autumn.

Cultivation: A hardy plant, tolerant of various climates and soil conditions. Can be successfully grown in a container if pruned into shape.

DREAMLAND

Botanical grouping: Cluster-flowered floribunda

Parentage: Cinnabar Improved x Fashion

Other names: Traumland

Other varieties: None

Year: 1958

Origin: Germany

Description: Large clusters of peach-pink, slightly scented double flowers are borne on a low-growing (50 cm/1½ ft), well-foliaged bush.

Flowering: Continued flowering through summer and autumn.

Cultivation: This makes an excellent border or low hedge specimen and also responds well to container cultivation. Prune back stems growth by two-thirds and remove dead wood in winter.

EDITH HOLDEN

Botanical grouping: Cluster-flowered floribunda

Parentage: Unknown

Other names: Chewlegacy, Edwardian Lady

Other varieties: None

Year: 1988

Origin: England

Description: This rose is noted for its very unusual colour of russet shot through with gold. The flowers are modest in size and semi-double, opening to a cup shape. Sturdy stems make them ideal cut flowers. The upright bush grows to 75 cm (2½ ft), with dark green leaves.

Flowering: Consistent flowers summer through to autumn.

Cultivation: A hardy plant requiring no special attention. Cut flowers frequently as this will encourage further flowering.

ENGLISH MISS

Botanical grouping: Cluster-flowered floribunda

Parentage: Dearest x Sweet Repose

Other names: None

Other varieties: None

Year:1978

Origin: England

Description: The tight clusters of blush pink flowers open to a wide, even shape and have an attractive but slight fragrance. The blooms are attractively set off against the dark green foliage, which grows thickly on an upright bush to 75 cm (2½ ft).

Flowering: Continued flowers through summer to autumn.

Cultivation: Hardy and tolerant of different soils and weather conditions. Will grow well in a container, or as a hedge or border.

ESCAPADE

Botanical grouping: Cluster-flowered floribunda

Parentage: Pink Parfait x Baby Faurax

Other names: Harpade

Other varieties: None

Year: 1967

Origin: England

Description: Striking, rose-violet, semi-double flowers with mauve tinges and a white centre are carried in well-spaced clusters. Fragrant, and suited for use as a cut flower. Attractive, leafy shrub growing to 1 m (3 ft).

Flowering: Flowers through summer into autumn.

Cultivation: Hardy and vigorous, requires no special treatment. Prune out dead or diseased wood in winter.

Europa

Europeana

Evening Star

EUROPA

Botanical grouping: Cluster-flowered floribunda
Parentage: Unknown
Other names: Feurop, Kortexung
Other varieties: None
Year: 1987
Origin: Germany
Description: Well-formed, double pink blooms blushed with salmon. Free-flowering with good keeping qualities, this is a lightly fragrant rose suitable for cutting. The deep green foliage has reddish tints on an upright bush of medium height to 1.2 m (4 ft).
Flowering: Freely through summer
Cultivation: A healthy and vigorous plant which prefers full sun in soil that has been well dug and mulched. May also be grown in a glasshouse in colder climates.

EUROPEANA

Botanical grouping: Cluster-flowered floribunda
Parentage: Ruth Leuwerik x Rosemary Rose
Other names: None
Other varieties: None
Year: 1963
Origin: The Netherlands
Description: A superb combination of large, deep crimson double blooms and dense red-green foliage. The flowers, which have a slight scent, are carried in heavy trusses and the bush is a vigorous grower, with some thorns. Height to 70 cm (2 ft).
Flowering: Flowers consistently through summer into autumn.
Cultivation: Needs attention when there is heavy rain, as the flower clusters can weigh down the branches, and mildew may develop. Keep the base of the plant free from weeds.

EVENING STAR

Botanical grouping: Cluster-flowered floribunda
Parentage: White Masterpiece x Saratoga

Other names: None
Other varieties: None
Year: 1974
Origin: United States
Description: Clear white, globular, double flowers with tinges of yellow are carried in clusters. The bush is upright, growing to 75 cm (2½ ft), with dark green leaves.
Flowering: Continued flowers over a long period.
Cultivation: Will tolerate poor soil conditions, and responds well to container cultivation. Prune out dead wood in winter.

EYEPAINT

Botanical grouping: Cluster-flowered floribunda
Parentage: Seedling x Picasso
Other names: Eye Paint, Tapis Persan, Maceye
Other varieties: None
Year: 1975
Origin: New Zealand
Description: A very rewarding, low-growing bush, ideal as a hedge or border. Grows vigorously to 1 m (3 ft), and bears copious, scarlet, single flowers with a white centre and prominent yellow stamens.

Eyepaint

Flowering: Continued flowers over a long period, summer to autumn.
Cultivation: A hardy plant tolerant of harsh weather and poor soil. Pick flowers to encourage further production of blooms. Prune out dead wood in winter.

FASHION

Botanical grouping: Cluster-flowered floribunda
Parentage: Pinocchio x Crimson Glory
Other names: None
Other varieties: Climbing sport from United States, 1951
Year: 1949
Origin: United States
Description: Clusters of peach-pink buds open to elegant double flowers in a delightful combination of coral and salmon-pink, similar to some geraniums. The colour was innovative at the time it was introduced, and this rose became very popular. Bushy, glossy dark green growth to 70 cm (2 ft).
Flowering: Copious flowering over a long season.
Cultivation: Tendency to rust. Remove and burn affected foliage and spray with rust-control formula.

Fashion

FIRECRACKER

Botanical grouping: Cluster-flowered floribunda
Parentage: Pinocchio seedling x Numa Fay seedling
Other names: None
Other varieties: None
Year: 1956
Origin: United States
Description: Large clusters of semi-double flowers in scarlet with yellow base. Slightly scented. The upright bush is compact, growing to 70 cm (2 ft), with attractive light green leaves.
Flowering: Reliable flowers over a long period.
Cultivation: Grows well in a container. Also useful as a border or hedging plant which can be trimmed into shape annually in winter.

Firecracker

FRAGRANT DELIGHT

Botanical grouping: Cluster-flowered floribunda
Parentage: Chanelle x Whisky Mac
Other names: None
Other varieties: None
Year: 1978
Origin: England
Description: Vigorous bush growing to 1 m (3 ft). The light orange-salmon flowers are carried in generous sprays along the branches and are moderately scented.
Flowering: Summer to autumn
Cultivation: A healthy and hardy plant, suited as a bedding plant for massed display or as a border or hedging bush. The flowers are resistant to weather damage and are good for cutting. Plant in well-drained,well mulched, moderately rich soil. Water well in summer.

Fragrant Delight

FRENZY

Botanical grouping: Cluster-flowered floribunda
Parentage: (Sarabande x Dany Robin) x Zambra
Other names: Prince Igor, Meihigor
Other varieties: None
Year: 1970
Origin: France
Description: This leafy, small bush is an ideal low hedging plant or container specimen, reaching 70 cm (2 ft). Its small, orange-red blooms display a yellow underside and contrast attractively with the dark foliage. Slight fragrance.
Flowering: Long flowering period through summer and autumn.
Cultivation: Hardy, requires no special attention. Can be grown in a container or used as an attractive hedging plant.

GARNETTE

Botanical grouping: Cluster-flowered floribunda
Parentage: (Rosenelfe x Eva) x Heros
Other names: None
Other varieties: A group of similar Garnette roses includes a pink sport named Carol (Amling), Garnette Apricot and White Garnette.
Year: 1947
Origin: Germany
Description: This rose has deepish red, double flowers that open to a rosette shape and are borne in clusters. Widely used as a cut flower because of its ability to hold its shape for many days. The bush has dark green leaves and grows to 70 cm (2 ft).
Flowering: Flowers over a long period.
Cultivation: This is a very popular cut flower, and is normally grown under glass for this purpose. It is not well suited to garden cultivation, and may develop mildew. Grow in a separate bed.

GERALDINE

Botanical grouping: Cluster-flowered floribunda
Parentage: Seedling x a seedling
Other names: Peahaze
Other varieties: None
Year: 1983
Origin: England
Description: A bushy, well-shaped plant reaching 70 cm (2 ft) in height, with glossy mid-green foliage and clusters of yellow-orange flowers. The flowers are frequently used for floral arrangements.
Flowering: Summer to autumn
Cultivation: Excellent for a bed or border, or as as a medium-size hedge. Prefers full sun and well-drained soil.

Frenzy

Geraldine

GLAD TIDINGS

Botanical grouping: Cluster-flowered floribunda
Parentage: Unknown
Other names: Tantide
Other varieties: None
Year: 1988
Origin: Germany
Description: Dark, velvety crimson blooms in well-spaced clusters. The bush is compact and upright, growing to 75 cm (2½ ft), with glossy dark green leaves.
Flowering: Continued flowering over a long period.
Cultivation: A hardy variety; useful border or hedging specimen. Dead-head the bush after flowering, then prune again in late winter.

GLENFIDDICH

Botanical grouping. Cluster-flowered floribunda
Parentage: Arthur Bell x (Sabine x Circus)
Other names: None
Other varieties: None
Year: 1976
Origin: Scotland
Description: An upright bush growing to 1 m (3 ft) with deep green, glossy foliage. The large flowers are outstanding—well-shaped in a rich amber-yellow.
Flowering: Summer to autumn
Cultivation: This rose prefers a moderate climate, and must be sheltered from cold winds and frosts. Prune out dead wood in winter and mulch to keep weed growth from the base of the plant.

GOLD BUNNY

Botanical grouping: Cluster-flowered floribunda
Parentage: Poppy Flash x (Charleston x Allgold)
Other names: Gold Badge, Meigronuri, Rimosa 79

Glad Tidings

Glenfiddich

Other varieties: Climbing sport, 1986
Year: 1978
Origin: France
Description: An attractive hedge or border rose with its large, well-petalled flowers in bright yellow, borne in sizeable clusters amid clear green foliage. Slightly scented. Compact, bushy growth to 70 cm (2 ft).
Flowering: Reliable flowering through summer and autumn.
Cultivation: Prone to black spot. Remove all fallen leaves in winter, and spray to prevent recurrence. Mulch well after pruning.

Gold Bunny

GOLDEN SLIPPERS

Botanical grouping: Cluster-flowered floribunda
Parentage: Goldilocks x seedling
Other names: None
Other varieties: None
Year:1961
Origin: United States
Description: Bright, orange-gold, double flowers with a golden reverse open flat, and fade paler as they mature. Fragrant. Low-growing plant to 70 cm (2 ft), sturdy and

Greensleeves

Golden Slippers

Goldmarie

Golden Years

bushy, with glossy leaves.
Flowering: Flowers over a long period in summer and autumn.
Cultivation: Good container or hedge specimen. Prune back hard the first year after planting, then lightly prune every winter.

GOLDEN YEARS

Botanical grouping: Cluster-flowered floribunda
Parentage: Sunblest x Amber Queen
Other names: Harween
Other varieties: None
Year: 1990
Origin: England
Description: Clusters of large, well-petalled, cup-shaped golden blooms with bronze touches are borne on a compact, bushy plant with dark green, glossy leaves. Fragrant. Grows to 75 cm (2½ ft).
Flowering: Flowers consistently through summer to autumn.
Cultivation: Vigorous and hardy, tolerant of

harsh weathers. Mulch the ground well to keep weed growth down, and avoid overcrowding.

GOLDMARIE

Botanical grouping: Cluster-flowered floribunda
Parentage: Masquerade x Golden Main
Other names: None
Other varieties: None
Year: 1958
Origin: Germany
Description: Large yellow, bronze-edged flowers of about 20 petals, borne in clusters, are sweetly fragrant. A profuse blooming rose, it grows to 1.2 m (4 ft) and the deep green, glossy foliage is disease resistant.
Flowering: Spring and summer
Cultivation: A very healthy and vigorous rose with an upright, bushy habit, it prefers full sun and rich fertile soil to produce its best blooms. Prune back lightly after flowering to encourage growth.

GREENSLEEVES

Botanical grouping: Cluster-flowered floribunda
Parentage: (Rudolph Timm x Arthur Bell) x [(Pascali x Elizabeth of Glamis) x (Sabine x Violette Dot)]
Other names: Harlenten
Other varieties: None
Year: 1980
Origin: England
Description: The pink buds of this very unusual rose open to chartreuse-green, unscented blooms. Makes a long-lasting cut flower provided it is picked before the buds open. Rather leggy, upright growth with dark foliage, reaching 1 m (3 ft).
Flowering: Flowers well through summer and autumn.
Cultivation: Susceptible to black spot. Remove fallen leaves from the base of the plant in winter, and spray to break the cycle. Prune out dead wood in winter.

GRÜSS AN AACHEN

Botanical grouping: Cluster-flowered floribunda
Parentage: Frau Karl Druschki x Franz Deegen
Other names: None
Other varieties: None
Year: 1909
Origin: Germany
Description: A low growing plant reaching up to 70 cm (2 ft) high and wide. It produces clusters of fully double, creamy white flowers with soft pink and peachy highlights. Has a soft fragrance. Growth is bushy and upright with matt, dark green foliage.
Flowering: Continuously throughout summer
Cultivation: A good hedging plant. Also useful for bedding and growing in groups. Suitable for growing in containers. Can be forced or grown under glass.

HANNAH GORDON

Botanical grouping: Cluster-flowered floribunda
Parentage: Seedling x Bordure
Other names: Korweiso
Other varieties: None
Year: 1983
Origin: Germany
Description: Sizeable trusses of attractive creamy white full blooms with cherry-pink shadings at the edges, more pronounced in hot weather. Slightly fragrant and good as a cut flower. Large, glossy deep green leaves, bushy upright growth to 1 m (3 ft).
Flowering: Flowers consistently through summer and autumn.
Cultivation: Hardy, tolerant of most weathers and soils. Responds well to container cultivation with appropriatepruning.

HANS CHRISTIAN ANDERSEN

Botanical grouping: Cluster-flowered floribunda
Parentage: Unknown
Other names: America's Choice, Poulander, Touraine
Other varieties: None
Year: 1986
Origin: Denmark
Description: Unfading, dark red, semi-double blooms, 5 cm (2 in) across are produced in clusters of 3 to 10 per stem. Free-flowering and fresh perfumed, it is ideal for cutting. The dark glossy foliage has a reddish shine on young shoots and the bush grows to 1.5 m (5 ft) high.
Flowering: Freely throughout summer
Cultivation: An excellent fence, shrub or border rose because of its bushy, even growth. Plant in full sun in fertile soil, drained, mulched and well watered.

Grüss an Aachen

Hannah Gordon

Hans Christian Andersen

Harkness Marigold

Harold Macmillan

HARKNESS MARIGOLD

Botanical grouping: Cluster-flowered floribunda
Parentage: Judy Garland x Anne Harkness
Other names: Hartoflax
Other varieties: None
Year: 1986
Origin: England
Description: Large, well-spaced clusters of flowers in a striking salmon-peach colour. Compact, vigorous grower to 1 m (3 ft), with glossy mid-green leaves and upright habit.
Flowering: Mid-summer through to autumn
Cultivation: A robust plant tolerant of most conditions and requiring no special treatment. Dead or spindly wood can be removed in winter. Mulch well after pruning.

HAROLD MACMILLAN

Botanical grouping: Cluster-flowered floribunda
Parentage: Avocet x Remember Me
Other names: Hartwestsun
Other varieties: None
Year: 1989
Origin: England
Description: An upright, bushy plant to 75 cm (2½ ft) with a good covering of deep green, glossy foliage. The sprays of orange-red flowers have a distinctive, luminous richness, contrasting well against the dark foliage.
Flowering: Summer to autumn
Cultivation: An outstanding rose for bed or border, and also makes a dramatic hedge. Likes full sun and moderately rich and well-drained soil.

HARVEST FAYRE

Botanical grouping: Cluster-flowered floribunda
Parentage: Seedling x Bright Smile
Other names: Dicnorth
Other varieties: None
Year: 1990
Origin: Northern Ireland
Description: A very attractive border or hedge rose, with trusses of apricot-coloured blooms neatly spaced amid dense, glossy,

Harvest Fayre

Heidesommer

Honeymoon

Iceberg

Iceberg

light green foliage.

Flowering: Flowers through summer and until late autumn.

Cultivation: A hardy plant requiring no special attention. Dead-head after flowering, and prune again in winter.

HEIDESOMMER

Botanical grouping: Cluster-flowered floribunda
Parentage: The Fairy x seedling
Other names: Cevennes, Korlirus
Other varieties: None
Year: 1985
Origin: Germany
Description: Large clusters of creamy white buds open to show centres of rich, golden stamens. The blooms have 20 to 25 petals, are very fragrant and lovely in a vase. A strong and healthy bush growing to 1.5 m (5 ft) with plentiful light green foliage.
Flowering: Spring and summer
Cultivation: A fine, informal hedging rose needing full sun or partial shade. Plant in fertile, well-mulched soil.

HIGHLAND LADDIE

Botanical grouping: Cluster-flowered floribunda
Parentage: National Trust x Dainty Dinah
Other names: Cocflag
Other varieties: None
Year: 1989
Origin: Scotland
Description: Large clusters of scarlet flowers with appealing crumpled petals are carried on an upright bush to 1 m (3 ft). Makes a striking display when used as hedge or border.
Flowering: Flowers consistently over a long period, summer to autumn.
Cultivation: Very hardy, tolerant of harsh weather. Keep the base of the plant free from weeds, and dead-head after flowering.

HONEYMOON

Botanical grouping: Cluster-flowered floribunda
Parentage: Cläre Grammerstorf x Spek's Yellow
Other names: Honigmond
Other varieties: None
Year: 1960
Origin: Germany
Description: A much admired rose for its fragrant, clear yellow flowers with many petals, carried high on the bush in large clusters. The plant itself is densely foliaged with glossy medium-green leaves.
Flowering: Continued flowering summer

through to autumn.
Cultivation: Vigorous and hardy, requires no special attention. Pick flowers frequently to encourage more blooms.

ICEBERG

Botanical grouping: Cluster-flowered floribunda
Parentage: Robin Hood x Virgo
Other names: Schneewittchen, Fée des Neiges, Korbin
Other varieties: Climbing variety, introduced in 1968 to England.
Year: 1958
Origin: Germany
Description: One of the most popular and widely admired roses, and certainly the best known white floribunda. Very free-flowering, with the scented flowers borne in clusters along the full length of the branch. Shapely buds open to double, rounded flowers, which may show pink flushes as they mature, especially in autumn. Excellent cut flower. The bush is upright and shapely, with large, shiny clear green leaves borne on green stems. Depending on how it is pruned, it will reach between 1 m (3 ft) and 1.5 m (5 ft).
Flowering: Copious flowering over a very long period.
Cultivation: Very hardy, can tolerate extreme cold. May develop black spot or mildew if sited too close to other plants.

ICED GINGER

Botanical grouping: Cluster-flowered floribunda
Parentage: Anne Watkins seedling
Other names: None
Other varieties: None
Year: 1971
Origin: Northern Ireland
Description: A lanky, open bush growing to 1 m (3 ft) with mid-green foliage that features a slightly red overlay. The flowers are amongst the largest in the floribunda group, up to 11 cm (4½ in) across when grown correctly. They are well formed in an interesting combination of colours from buff to copper, tinged with ivory and pink. The flowers have only a slight fragrance.
Flowering: Summer to autumn
Cultivation: This rose will need pruning to maintain a reasonable shape. Plant at the back of a border, and mulch to keep weed growth down.

INTRIGUE

Botanical grouping: Cluster-flowered floribunda
Parentage: White Masterpiece x Heirloom

Iced Ginger

Invincible

Intrigue

Other names: Jacum
Other varieties: None
Year: 1984
Origin: United States
Description: This rose is a compact, well-foliaged plant growing to 75 cm (2½ ft), bearing trusses of richly fragrant double flowers in dark red with purple undertones. It should not be confused with another variety sometimes called 'Intrigue', released in Germany in 1979.
Flowering: Prolific flowering over a long period summer to autumn
Cultivation: A rewarding rose to grow as a low hedge or border specimen. It is hardy and easy to cultivate in a wide range of soils and conditions. Prune out dead wood in winter.

INVINCIBLE

Botanical grouping: Cluster-flowered floribunda
Parentage: Rubella x National Trust
Other names: Fennica, Runatru
Other varieties: None
Year: 1983
Origin: The Netherlands
Description: Bright red semi-double flowers which keep their shape well are attractively displayed in clusters on a neat, upright bush to 75 cm (2½ ft) with shiny foliage. Slight fragrance.
Flowering: Continued flowering through summer and autumn
Cultivation: A robust plant tolerant of extremes of weather. Makes a good container or hedging specimen as well as a striking border plant.

Jiminy Cricket

Julischka

Irish Mist

Origin: Northern Ireland
Description: Shapely salmon-pink flowers with a slight scent, borne in clusters against a background of dense foliage. Strong branches with small dark green leaves, height to 75 cm (2½ ft).
Flowering: Reliable flowers over a long period.
Cultivation: Good hedge or border plant which will also grow well in a container. Dead wood should be removed in winter, and vigorous stems reduced by two-thirds.

JIMINY CRICKET

Botanical grouping: Cluster-flowered floribunda
Parentage: Goldilocks x Geranium Red
Other names: None
Other varieties: None
Year: 1954
Origin: United States
Description: Well-shaped buds of orange-red give way to loose double blooms in a striking blend of pink, orange and coral shades. The plant is a vigorous grower, to 75 cm (2½ ft), and is well branched, with dense, glossy foliage.
Flowering: Consistent flowers through summer into autumn.
Cultivation: With its unusual colour combination, this looks attractive planted as a group or used as a low hedge. No special attention required.

JULISCHKA

Botanical grouping: Cluster-flowered floribunda
Parentage: Unknown
Other names: Tanjuka
Other varieties: None
Year: 1974
Origin: Germany
Description: Elegant, long pointed buds develop into brilliant scarlet, semi-double blooms which display a dark metallic, iridescent hue in dull or cloudy weather. An abundant bloomer, this rose bears masses of fragrant flowers on a compact bush which grows to 1.2 m (4 ft), with splendid, bronze, glossy foliage.
Flowering: Freely and prolifically in summer
Cultivation: Plant in full sun or partial shade in well-prepared soil enriched with compost and mulch.

KORP

Botanical grouping: Cluster-flowered floribunda
Parentage: Colour Wonder x Zorina
Other names: Prominent
Other varieties: None

IRENE OF DENMARK

Botanical grouping: Cluster-flowered floribunda
Parentage: Orléans Rose x (Mme Plantier x Edina)
Other names: Irene von Dänemark
Other varieties: None
Year: 1948
Origin: Denmark
Description: Superb, creamy white, fragrant flowers which open from a cup to a flat rosette and hold their shape well, making them ideal as cut flowers. The bush has many clear green, shiny leaves and is upright in habit, growing to 75 cm (2½ ft).

Flowering: Flowers over a long period through summer and autumn.
Cultivation: A hardy plant, tolerant of a wide range of soils and weathers. Also suitable for container cultivation. Prune in late winter and mulch well.

IRISH MIST

Botanical grouping: Cluster-flowered floribunda
Parentage: Orangeade x Mischief
Other names: Irish Summer
Other varieties: None
Year: 1966

Korp

Korresia

La Paloma

Year: 1970
Origin: Germany
Description: Very bright red and shapely blooms, few to a cluster, grow on strong, upright stems. They are ideal for cutting and last well. The profuse foliage is deep green and rather leathery looking, and makes a striking contrast to the flowers. The bush will reach 1 m (3 ft).
Flowering: Consistent flowers through summer and into autumn.
Cultivation: Hardy plant; will tolerate a wide range of weather and soil conditions. Late winter pruning should be followed by a mulching with well-rotted organic matter.

KORRESIA

Botanical grouping: Cluster-flowered floribunda
Parentage: Friedrich Wörlein x Spanish Sun
Other names: Friesia, Fresia, Sunsprite
Other varieties: None
Year: 1974
Origin: Germany
Description: One of the most justly admired yellow roses, which holds both its shape and its clear bright colour, and is thus ideal as a cut flower. The petals unfurl to a loose, wavy shape and the blooms are very fragrant. The bush is neat and compact, with light green leaves, reaching 75 cm (2½ ft).
Flowering: Reliable flowers over a long period.
Cultivation: Vigorous and hardy. Old wood needs to be removed in winter, and new stems shortened by two-thirds. Mulch well after pruning.

LA PALOMA

Botanical grouping: Cluster-flowered floribunda
Parentage: Unknown
Other names: La Paloma '85, Tanamola
Other varieties: None
Year: 1985
Origin: Germany

Description: An upright bush with bright green foliage and large clusters of clear white blooms which open from particularly shapely buds. The plant will grow to 75 cm (2½ ft).
Flowering: Continued flowering through summer into autumn.
Cultivation: Useful as a border or hedging specimen. Dead or diseased wood should be removed in winter.

LAUGHTER LINES

Botanical grouping: Cluster-flowered floribunda
Parentage: (Pye Colour x Sunday Times) x Eyepaint

Other names: Dickerry
Other varieties: None
Year: 1987
Origin: North Ireland
Description: An unusual and decorative plant, growing to 75 cm (2½ ft), with a backdrop of crisp dark green foliage. The flowers make this plant distinctive, with a hand-painted appearance in shades of cherry-red, gold and white on a rosy-pink background.
Flowering: Summer to autumn
Cultivation: A hardy rose that can be grown successfully in a wide range of soils and conditions. Ideal for bed or border, or as an unusual hedge.

Laughter Lines

Letchworth Garden City

Lilac Charm

LETCHWORTH GARDEN CITY

Botanical grouping: Cluster-flowered
floribunda
Parentage: (Sabine x Pineapple Poll) x
(Circus x Mischief)
Other names: Harkover
Other varieties: None
Year: 1979
Origin: England
Description: A handsome bush, growing to
75 cm (2½ ft) with a good covering of mid-
green foliage. Each cluster contains many
slender buds which open to large rose-pink
flowers tinged with shades of peach and orange.
Flowering: Summer to autumn
Cultivation: Can be grown in a wide range
of soils and climate conditions. Ideal for bed
or border, or as a hedging bush. Prune out
dead wood in winter.

Lilli Marlene

LILAC CHARM

Botanical grouping: Cluster-flowered
floribunda
Parentage: Bred from a *R. californica*
seedling
Other names: None
Other varieties: None
Year: 1961
Origin: England
Description: The rather sparsely petalled,

fragrant blooms of this unusual rose are
lilac-mauve with prominent red stamens,
and grow in large clusters. Compact, bushy
plant to 70 cm (2 ft), with dark, matt leaves.
Flowering: Consistent flowers through
summer into autumn.
Cultivation: The flowers fade when
exposed to bright sunlight. In other respects,
hardy and robust. Prune out dead or
diseased wood in winter.

LILLI MARLENE

Botanical grouping: Cluster-flowered
floribunda
Parentage: (Our Princess x Rudolph Timm)
x Ama
Other names: None
Other varieties: None
Year: 1959

Lilli Marlene

Liverpool Echo

Macspice

Majorette

Manx Queen

Origin: Germany
Description: Large trusses of shapely, bright crimson flowers set against dark, slightly bronzed leaves make this a very attractive rose. A vigorous, strongly branched and thorny bush reaching 75 cm (2½ ft).
Flowering: Reliable flowers over a long period.
Cultivation: Useful as a protective hedge as well as a border specimen. Hardy and robust, apart from a tendency to black spot. Keep base of plant free from weed growth or competing plants.

Origin: New Zealand
Description: An unusual modern rose growing more like a delphinium. Long, gently arching stems carry 25 cm (10 in) long fragrant spikes of lavender-pink flowers gently shading to lilac mauve with age. A tall plant growing to more than 1.5 m (5 ft) with a mass of spraying canes like a fountain.
Flowering: Most of the year
Cultivation: The vigorous habit makes this an excellent espalier plant or an interesting bush in bedding or borders. Prefers day-long sun in fertile soil, well mulched and watered.

The flowers are slightly scented, large and semi-double, and are borne on a well-foliaged bush with tough, dark green leaves. Height to 75 cm (2½ ft).
Flowering: Continued flowering through summer and autumn.
Cultivation: Hardy and tolerant of most soil conditions. Prune in late winter and follow with a mulch of organic matter.

LIVERPOOL ECHO

Botanical grouping: Cluster-flowered floribunda
Parentage: (Little Darling x Goldilocks) x München
Other names: None
Other varieties. Ginoby, blush white sport from England, 1983
Year: 1971
Origin: New Zealand
Description: Large, full flowers in a cool salmon-pink, evenly spaced in substantial clusters. Bushy, upright plant with strong stems and light green leaves, reaching 1 m (3 ft). Lightly scented. A good cut flower.
Flowering: Flowers through summer into autumn.
Cultivation: A vigorous grower, tolerant of extremes of weather and most soil conditions. Can be grown in a container or as a hedge. Prune in late winter and mulch well to keep weed growth down.

MACSPICE

Botanical grouping: Cluster-flowered floribunda
Parentage: Anytime x Gartendirektor Otto Linne
Other names: Macspike
Other varieties: None
Year: 1982

MAJORETTE

Botanical grouping: Cluster-flowered floribunda
Parentage: Magic Carrousel x (Grumpy x Scarletta)
Other names: Meipiess
Other varieties. None
Year: 1986
Origin: France
Description: Plentiful trusses of smallish red blooms with creamy yellow centres, the reverse of the petals being a blend of these colours, carried on strong, slender stems. Compact, upright grower to 50 cm (1½ ft).
Flowering: Copious flowers over a long period, summer and autumn.
Cultivation: An ideal plant to fill a small space or for a container, it will tolerate extremes of weather. Prune in late winter.

MANX QUEEN

Botanical grouping: Cluster-flowered floribunda
Parentage: Shepherd's Delight x Circus
Other names: Isle of Man
Other varieties: None
Year: 1963
Origin: Northern Ireland
Description: This rose is notable for its particularly striking colour, a combination of orange-red, yellow and light brown shades.

MA PERKINS

Botanical grouping: Cluster-flowered floribunda
Parentage: Red Radiance x Fashion
Other names: None
Other varieties: None
Year: 1952
Origin: United States
Description: This delightful rose has copious clusters of cup-shaped, fragrant shell-pink flowers with flushes of apricot and cream. A vigorous, compact bush with upright growth to 70 cm (2 ft) and deep green, glossy leaves.
Flowering: Continued flowering over a long season.
Cultivation: A useful border, container or hedging specimen, with lovely cut flowers. No special care required, except for pruning to remove dead or diseased wood.

Margaret Merril

Matangi

Masquerade

Moulin Rouge

tolerant of most weather and soil conditions. Has a tendency to viral infection in some countries, but normally healthy. Hips should be removed.

MATANGI

Botanical grouping: Cluster-flowered floribunda
Parentage: Seedling x Picasso
Other names: Macman
Other varieties: None
Year: 1974
Origin: New Zealand
Description: This superb rose bears double blooms of bright orange-vermilion with a silver-white eye and silver reverse, which are set attractively in a background of shiny dark leaves. The bush is shapely and well-foliaged, reaching 1 m (3 ft).
Flowering: Consistent flowering over a long period
Cultivation: Hardy and robust, requiring no special attention. After pruning mulch with organic matter to suppress weed growth.

MOULIN ROUGE

Botanical grouping: Cluster-flowered floribunda
Parentage: Alain x Orange Triumph
Other names: Sans Souci
Other varieties: Climbing sport from England, 1963
Year: 1952
Origin: France
Description: Large fragrant clusters of semi-double, prettily formed, scarlet blooms are borne on this small bush which grows to 75 cm (2½ ft).
Flowering: Spring and summer
Cultivation: This is an excellent border rose. It will thrive in a warm, sunny and fertile location where adequate drainage and mulching have been provided.

MARGARET MERRIL

Botanical grouping: Cluster-flowered floribunda
Parentage: (Rudolph Timm x Dedication) x Pascali
Other names: Harkuly
Other varieties: None
Year: 1977
Origin: England
Description: This splendid rose produces small clusters of very pale blush pink, almost white, blooms. The elegant buds give way to a flower with wavy petals around a tightly furled centre, which in time opens to reveal prominent gold stamens. The flowers are richly fragrant, and last well after cutting. The bush is a vigorous, upright grower with dark green leaves, reaching 75 cm (2½ ft).
Flowering: Reliable flowering over a long season
Cultivation: Useful border, container or hedge specimen. Tolerant of extremes of weather.

MASQUERADE

Botanical grouping: Cluster-flowered floribunda
Parentage: Goldilocks x Holiday
Other names: None
Other varieties: Climbing variety (introduced to England in 1959), growing to 3 m x 4 m (10 ft x 12 ft).
Year: 1949
Origin: United States
Description: This rose aroused enormous interest when it was introduced because of its changing colours as it matured, a feature till then confined to older and less vigorous varieties. The blooms, which grow in large clusters, begin as a clear yellow, passing through salmon pink to finish a fairly harsh red as they age. The bush is upright growing, to 1 m (3 ft), with small dark leaves.
Flowering: Flowers well through summer and autumn.
Cultivation: Vigorous and free-flowering,

News

New Year

Norwich Castle

NATHALIE NYPELS

Botanical grouping: Cluster-flowered floribunda
Parentage: Orléons Rose x (Comtesse du Cayla x *R. foetida* bicolor
Other names: Mevrouw Nathalie Nypels
Other varieties: None
Year: 1919
Origin: The Netherlands
Description: A sweetly fragrant bushy plant that grows to a height of 1 m (3 ft) with dark glossy leaves, displaying semi-double bright pink flowers.
Flowering: Long flowering season, into autumn
Cultivation: Likes a warm, well-mulched situation. Remove spent blooms to stimulate repeat flowering and prune lightly when flowering is finished.

NEWS

Botanical grouping: Cluster-flowered floribunda
Parentage: Lilac Charm x Tuscany Superb
Other names: Legnews
Other varieties: None
Year: 1968
Origin: England
Description: Large clusters of fullish blooms in a very unusual colour, rich beetroot red-purple. The slightly scented flowers open cupped, flattening out as they age, and can be used as cut flowers. Mid-green, slightly shiny, dense foliage on an upright, compact plant to 75 cm (2½ ft).
Flowering: Flowers over a long period, summer and autumn.
Cultivation: Tolerant of a wide range of weather and soil conditions, and will grow well in a container.

NEW YEAR

Botanical grouping: Cluster-flowered floribunda
Parentage: Mary Sumner x seedling

News

Other names: Arcadian, Macnewye
Other varieties: None
Year: 1982
Origin: New Zealand
Description: An arresting, coppery apricot-toned rose with a slight perfume. Clusters are borne on a medium bush which grows to 1.2 m (4 ft). The flowers are suited to cutting and are offset by attractive, mid-green foliage.
Flowering: Spring and summer
Cultivation: Plant in a warm, sunny location in fertile soil that is drained and well mulched. Prune back lightly when the rose is established.

NORWICH CASTLE

Botanical grouping: Cluster-flowered floribunda
Parentage: (Whisky Mac x Arthur Bell) x seedling
Other names: None
Other varieties: None
Year: 1979
Origin: England
Description: Rich orange blooms flushed with apricot, set against glossy clear green leaves are borne in dense clusters. The flower has the characteristic form of a hybrid

Norwich Union

Old Master

Orange Sensation

Orangeade

tea, opening to a flat rosette, and makes an excellent cut flower. The bush is of upright habit, reaching 75 cm (2½ ft).
Flowering: Consistent flowers over a long season.
Cultivation: Hardy and tolerant of most soil conditions. Useful for border or hedging purposes and can be grown in a container.

NORWICH UNION

Botanical grouping: Cluster-flowered floribunda
Parentage: Arthur Bell x (seedling x Allgold)
Other names: None
Other varieties: None
Year: 1975
Origin: England
Description: A delightful rose in strong yellow which fades attractively as it matures and is ideal for cutting. The richly scented double blooms form a large cup shape and are carried in smallish clusters. The compact, upright plant grows to 50 cm (1½ ft) and has shiny, clear green leaves.
Flowering: Flowers reliably through summer into autumn.
Cultivation: Because of its capacity to tolerate a certain amount of shade, this rose can be used to fill a difficult space, whether in the garden bed or in a container.

OLD MASTER

Botanical grouping: Cluster-flowered floribunda
Parentage: (Maxi x Evelyn Fison) x (Orange Sweetheart x Frühlingsmorgen)
Other names: Macesp
Other varieties: None
Year: 1974
Origin: New Zealand
Description: Loose, fullish blooms in a striking combination of carmine with a silver eye and reverse are carried in medium-sized trusses. Good cut flowers. The well-foliaged bush is upright, growing to 1 m (3 ft).
Flowering: Continued flowers over a long period.
Cultivation: A hardy rose which will tolerate most soil and weather conditions. Prune out dead or diseased wood in winter.

ORANGEADE

Botanical grouping: Cluster-flowered floribunda
Parentage: Orange Sweetheart x Independence
Other names: None
Other varieties: Climbing sport from England, 1965
Year: 1959
Origin: Northern Ireland
Description: Brilliant orange-red in colour and growing darker with age, the single blooms open to reveal gold stamens and grow in large clusters. Lightly scented. Dark, glossy foliage on a vigorous bush which reaches 1 m (3 ft).
Flowering: Flowers through summer and autumn.
Cultivation: Tolerant of less than perfect soil conditions, but not as robust as more recently introduced roses in this colour range.

ORANGE SENSATION

Botanical grouping: Cluster-flowered floribunda
Parentage: Amor x Fashion

Other names: None
Other varieties: None
Year: 1961
Origin: The Netherlands
Description: Large clusters of cup-shaped flowers in orange-vermilion, flushed slightly darker at the edges, with a sweet scent. The plant grows to 75 cm (2½ ft), has spreading habit, and is well covered with lightish green foliage.
Flowering: Reliable flowering over a long period
Cultivation: Normally quite robust and tolerant of most soil and weather conditions. Mulch after pruning, and remove dead wood from the centre of the plant.

ORANGE TRIUMPH

Botanical grouping: Cluster-flowered floribunda
Parentage: Eva x Solarium
Other names: None
Other varieties: None
Year: 1937
Origin: Germany
Description: A vigorous, upright plant growing to 1 m (3 ft) with a plentiful covering of dark green, glossy foliage. The flowers are also plentiful, small and cup-shaped in a shade of deep orange-red. The flowers are borne in large clusters.
Flowering: Continuously throughout summer
Cultivation: A hardy and easy-to-grow rose, useful as a hedge or as part of a border. Can be grown successfully in a wide range of soils and conditions. Prune out dead wood in winter.

PADDY MCGREDY

Botanical grouping: Cluster-flowered floribunda
Parentage: Spartan x Tzigane
Other names: Macpa

Patricia

Other varieties: None
Year: 1962
Origin: Northern Ireland
Description: Large, fragrant, hybrid tea-shaped, globular blooms, grow singly or in large clusters, and are coloured rose pink to carmine. This rose attracted much attention when it was introduced because of its felicitous combination of hybrid tea and floribunda characteristics. The bush is compact, sturdy and low growing, to 75 cm (2½ ft), with tough, dark foliage.
Flowering: Flowers well over a long season.
Cultivation: Careful attention needed for signs of black spot. Pick off and burn worst affected leaves, and spray to avoid recurrence.

PAINT BOX

Botanical grouping: Cluster-flowered floribunda
Parentage: Seedling x St Pauli
Other names: None
Other varieties: None
Year: 1963
Origin: England
Description: An upright shrub with vigorous growth and deep green, matt foliage. The semi-double flowers are large and showy, combining red and yellow colourings, and becoming darker on maturity.
Flowering: Continuously throughout summer
Cultivation: A useful rose for bed, border or hedge. Flowers fade in strong summer sunlight. Can be grown in most soils and climates. Prune to remove dead and spindly growth in winter.

Paddy McGredy

PATRICIA

Botanical grouping: Cluster-flowered floribunda
Parentage: Sport of Elizabeth of Glamis
Other names: Korpatri
Other varieties: None
Year: 1972
Origin: Germany
Description: Beautifully shaped buds open to reveal sweetly scented, well-formed, double blooms, 7.5 cm (3 in) across, of soft coral-pink to apricot. A good cutting rose. The bush has glossy foliage and grows to 1.2 m (4 ft).
Flowering: Freely throughout summer
Cultivation: Mass in garden beds or use as a hedging rose. Plant in full sun to partial shade. Fertile soil is preferred although it will grow in lesser soils that are composted, drained and mulched, especially in hot weather.

PENELOPE PLUMMER

Botanical grouping: Cluster-flowered floribunda
Parentage: Anna Wheatcroft x Dearest
Other names: None
Other varieties: None
Year: 1970
Origin: England
Description: This low-growing (50 cm/ 1½ ft) bush with dark leaves bears small clusters of semi-double flowers in shades of light pink to salmon-pink. Lightly scented.
Flowering: Continued flowering through summer into autumn
Cultivation: Has a tendency to black spot. Avoid warm, humid conditions and remove diseased leaves. Spray to prevent further outbreaks.

PERNILLE POULSEN

Botanical grouping: Cluster-flowered floribunda
Parentage: Ma Perkins x Columbine
Other names: None
Other varieties: None
Year: 1965
Origin: Denmark
Description: Large clusters of fullish, salmon pink blooms which open from well-formed buds and fade slightly with maturity. Good for cutting. Light green, pointed leaves grow densely on the compact (70 cm/2 ft) bush.
Flowering: Very free-flowering, this rose starts flowering early and continues to late autumn.
Cultivation: Tolerant of most soil and weather conditions. Good hedge or border rose.

PICASSO

Botanical grouping: Cluster-flowered floribunda
Parentage: Marlena x Evelyn Fison (Frühlingsmorgen x Orange Sweetheart)
Other names: Macpic
Other varieties: None
Year:1971
Origin: England

Description: A beautiful rose reaching 75 cm (2½ ft) in height, with a bushy habit and small, deep green foliage. The flowers have been described as 'hand-painted', appearing in clusters, semi-double in a deep pink with silvery edges and reverses.
Flowering: Continuously throughout summer
Cultivation: A good rose for hedging or a container, although susceptible to black spot. Keep the area at the base of the plant free from weeds, and mulch well.

PINK PARFAIT

Botanical grouping: Cluster-flowered floribunda
Parentage: First Love x Pinocchio
Other names: None
Other varieties: None
Year:1960
Origin: United States
Description: A glorious mixture of pinks, including shades of rose, salmon, apricot and peach, characterises this splendid rose. Shapely buds open to large blooms which fade to a more uniform pink as they mature, and are lightly scented. Ideal for use as a cut flower. The flowers are carried in clusters on a neat, bushy plant with upright growth to 1 m (3 ft).

Flowering: Free-flowering over a long period
Cultivation: Hardy and robust. Useful as a hedge, border or bedding rose, and can be grown in a container. Prune back new stems by two-thirds.

PRIDE OF MALDON

Botanical grouping: Cluster-flowered floribunda
Parentage: Southampton x Wandering Minstrel
Other names: Harwonder
Other varieties: None
Year: 1991
Origin: England
Description: A striking rose with clusters of semi-double blooms in which the bright orange petals show a yellow reverse and reveal golden stamens when fully open. The glossy dark foliage sets off the flowers perfectly. Grows to 75 cm (2½ ft) high.
Flowering: Continued flowering over a long season
Cultivation: This rose is robust and hardy, requiring no special treatment. Prune out dead wood in winter. Keep the area at the base of the plant free from weeds, and mulch well.

Pernille Poulsen

Picasso

Pink Parfait

Princess Alice

Princess Michael of Kent

Priscilla Burton

Princess Michiko

PRINCESS ALICE

Botanical grouping: Cluster-flowered floribunda
Parentage: Judy Garland x Anne Harkness
Other names: Brite Lites, Hartanna, Zonta Rose
Other varieties: None
Year: 1985
Origin: England
Description: Floribunda rose to 1 m (3 ft) with plentiful and attractive foliage. The flowers are bright yellow, carried in large clusters on strong stems. They make good cut flowers and are ideal for exhibition. Its upright habit makes it useful for borders and hedges as well.
Flowering: Summer to autumn
Cultivation: Hardy and healthy rose whose flowers are resistant to weather damage. Plant in full sun in rich soil for best results.

PRINCESS MICHAEL OF KENT

Botanical grouping: Cluster-flowered floribunda
Parentage: Manx Queen x Alexander
Other names: Harlightly
Other varieties: None
Year: 1981
Origin: England
Description: Small clusters of bright yellow blooms, full and shapely and with a rich fragrance, which make lovely cut flowers. The plant is compact and bushy, with glossy medium green leaves, reaching 50 cm (1½ ft).
Flowering: Reliable flowers over a long period, with a very good autumn show.
Cultivation: A healthy rose; responds well to most uses, including container cultivation.

PRINCESS MICHIKO

Botanical grouping: Cluster-flowered floribunda
Parentage: Spartan x Circus
Other names: None
Other varieties: None

Year: 1966
Origin: England
Description: Compact, upright and vigorous bush bears large clusters of slightly fragrant, semi-double flowers in a copper-orange colour, which redden as they mature. Leaves are dark green and shiny, and the plant grows to 70 cm (2 ft).
Flowering: Flowers through summer into autumn.
Cultivation: Watch closely for signs of black spot. Remove and burn affected foliage, and spray to prevent recurrence.

PRISCILLA BURTON

Botanical grouping: Cluster-flowered floribunda

Parentage: Old Master x seedling
Other names: Macrat
Other varieties: None
Year: 1978
Origin: New Zealand
Description: Wide opening, large, semi-double blooms in an unusual and eye-catching colour combination: white centres flushing to carmine, with deeper colour at the edges. The slightly scented flowers are borne in clusters among dark green glossy leaves on an upright, bushy plant which grows to 75 cm (2½ ft).
Flowering: Flowers well over a long period.
Cultivation: Susceptible to black spot. Allow plenty of space around the rose, and remove and burn any affected foliage. Spray to prevent spread of the disease.

White Queen Elizabeth

Red and White Delight

Queen Elizabeth

Redgold

Year: 1991
Origin: United States
Description: A colourful, striped rose bearing clusters of floribunda-sized, clear red blooms, striped with white and opening almost flat, like a camellia, and scentless. Well clothed in light green foliage, the bush grows to 1.5 m (5 ft) high.
Flowering: Spring and summer
Cultivation: A vigorous rose that is tolerant of poorer soils but prefers a warm position in full sun or partial shade in soil that is fertile, drained and mulched.

REDGOLD

Botanical grouping: Cluster-flowered floribunda
Parentage: [(Karl Herbst x Masquerade) x Faust] x Piccadilly
Other names: Rouge et Or, Dicor
Other varieties: None
Year: 1967
Origin: Northern Ireland
Description: A very prolific and colourful rose showing ovoid buds which open to fragrant, rich gold blooms edged with red and which intensifies in colour as the flowers age. The colours and quantity of blooms carried in large clusters are spectacular. A splendid cut flower. The medium-sized bush grows to 1.2 m (4 ft) with glossy, leathery foliage.
Flowering: Prolifically throughout summer
Cultivation: This prize-winning rose can be grown to exhibit, as a hedge, against a wall or trellis or in a large tub. Grow in a sunny position in fertile soil that is drained, well mulched and watered.

QUEEN ELIZABETH

Botanical grouping: Cluster-flowered floribunda
Parentage: Charlotte Armstrong x Floradora
Other names: The Queen Elizabeth Rose
Other varieties: Sports: White Queen Elizabeth from England, 1965, Yellow Queen Elizabeth from Belgium, 1964, and a climbing sport from United States, 1957
Year: 1954
Origin: United States
Description: This much admired rose was named to mark the accession to the throne in 1952 of Queen Elizabeth II. It is trouble-free and infinitely rewarding, producing from shapely buds many clusters of large, cyclamen-pink blooms to grace any vase.

The bush is tall and vigorous, growing to 2 m (7 ft), though longer, leggier branches may result unless the plant is judiciously pruned. It has glossy, dark green leaves.
Flowering: Reliable flowers over a long season, summer to autumn.
Cultivation: The bush should be pruned fairly hard annually to contain growth to the desired level.

RED AND WHITE DELIGHT

Botanical grouping: Cluster-flowered floribunda
Parentage: Unknown
Other names: None
Other varieties: None

ROSENRESLI

Botanical grouping: Cluster-flowered floribunda
Parentage: (New Dawn x Prima Ballerina) x seedling
Other names: Korresli

Other varieties: Horstmann's Rosenresli (a white variety, 1954)
Year: 1982
Origin: Germany
Description: Deep, salmon-pink buds open to richer, deeper coloured blooms, with the outer, wavy petals verging towards red. When fully open the flowers have a rich, tea rose perfume and are delightful in the garden or vase. The foliage is plentiful, glossy dark green. The bush grows to 1.2 m (4 ft).
Flowering: Very free-flowering throughout summer
Cultivation: Resistant to fungus diseases, this is a healthy bush that requires little more than basic maintenance. Plant in full sun and fertile soil, well drained and watered.

ROSEMARY ROSE

Botanical grouping: Cluster-flowered floribunda
Parentage: Grüss an Teplitz x a Floribunda seedling
Other names: None
Other varieties: None
Year: 1954
Origin: The Netherlands
Description: Small, dense shrub 75 cm (2½ ft) high and 70 cm (2 ft) wide, with dark green to coppery foliage and reddish new stems which are sometimes weighed down with blooms. Large clusters of rose-carmine flowers are fully double and rosette shaped, with a slight fragrance.
Flowering: Continuously throughout summer
Cultivation: Needs good soil and full sun. An excellent bedding plant, can be mass planted, and is used as a cut flower. Will grow in pots and as a low hedge. Prone to mildew, and supply can be limited to specialist growers. Dead-head after flowering, and prune in winter, removing all dead and diseased wood and reducing healthy stems by half.

ROSABELL

Botanical grouping: Cluster-flowered floribunda
Parentage: Seedling x Darling Flame
Other names: Cocceleste
Other varieties: None
Year: 1986
Origin: England
Description: A short, bushy plant, growing to 40 cm (1¼ ft) in height, with a good covering of dark green-maroon foliage. The full flowers are a bright rose-pink colour, and open out like an old-fashioned rose.
Flowering: More or less continuously throughout summer and early autumn
Cultivation: An excellent container plant. Prefers full sun and moderately rich soils. Sometimes grown as a low hedge, pruned into shape in winter.

ROSEROMANTIC

Botanical grouping: Cluster-flowered floribunda
Parentage: Seedling x Tornado
Other names: Korsommer
Other varieties: None
Year: 1985
Origin: Germany
Description: This is a very free-flowering, single rose of shining, delicate pink, borne in clusters and showing golden stamens when open. It has soft, healthy green foliage on a bush which grows to about 1.5 m (5 ft).
Flowering: Freely throughout summer
Cultivation: Suitable as a cut flower or may be grown as a border or hedging rose. Prefers full sun or filtered shade, well-drained and fertile soil. If planting in the shade extra nutrients may be needed in the soil. Mulch in warmer weather and water well especially in summer months.

ROYAL OCCASION

Botanical grouping: Cluster-flowered floribunda
Parentage: Walzertraum x Europeana
Other names: Montana
Other varieties: None
Year: 1974
Origin: Germany
Description: A handsome bush, upright in growth, reaching 1 m (3 ft) in the right conditions. The plentiful foliage is mid-green and glossy, while the large clusters of flowers are semi-double and a vivid orange-scarlet colour.
Flowering: Repeat flowering through summer and early autumn
Cultivation: A versatile rose that can be cultivated in a wider range of conditions, preferring full sun and moderately rich soil. It is sometimes grown as a hedge and is also suitable for container cultivation.

Rosemary Rose

Rosenresli

Roseromantic

RUMBA

Botanical grouping: Cluster-flowered floribunda
Parentage: Masquerade x (Poulsen's Bedder x Floradora)
Other names: None
Other varieties: None
Year: 1958
Origin: Denmark
Description: Dense green, glossy foliage on an upright shrub 70 cm (2 ft) high and wide. Yellow, double blooms are flushed with red and clustered on the stem, fading with age. Old flowers persist on the stem.
Flowering: Continuously throughout summer
Cultivation: Tolerates poorer soils, but needs full sun. Excellent for bedding, mass planting or hedging, and as a container plant. Dead-head during and after flowering, and prune in winter, reducing stems by half.

SALMON SORBET

Botanical grouping: Cluster-flowered floribunda
Parentage: Unknown
Other names: None
Other varieties: None
Year: 1991
Origin: United States
Description: Sweetly fragrant, soft salmon and white striped, high-centred blooms of medium size are borne in generous clusters with strong stems on a small to medium bush, to 1.2 m (4 ft). A good cut flower.
Flowering: Spring to autumn
Cultivation: A robust and easy to grow bush which makes a good border display or feature in the garden. A sunny position is preferred, in fertile soil that is well watered, drained and mulched.

SAMARITAN

Botanical grouping: Cluster-flowered floribunda
Parentage: Silver Jubilee x Dr A.J. Verhage
Other names: Harverag, Fragrant Surprise
Other varieties: None
Year: 1992
Origin: England
Description: A bushy shrub growing to 75 cm (2½ ft), with bright, glossy leaves. The flowers are apricot with yellow and pink tones, with the petals edged in red as the blooms age. The petals are quartered in the old-fashioned style.
Flowering: Summer to autumn
Cultivation: Quite hardy and healthy with no special requirements. The flowers are resistant to rain damage. Suitable for massed plantings or small hedges and borders.

SATCHMO

Botanical grouping: Cluster-flowered floribunda
Parentage: Evelyn Fison x Diament
Other names: None
Other varieties: None
Year: 1970
Origin: New Zealand
Description: A strong-growing, upright bush reaching 70 cm (2 ft) with glossy deep-green foliage and dramatic clusters of bright scarlet flowers.
Flowering: Summer to autumn
Cultivation: Prefers full sun and a moderately rich, well-drained soil.

SCARLET QUEEN ELIZABETH

Botanical grouping: Cluster-flowered floribunda
Parentage: (Korona x seedling) x Queen Elizabeth
Other names: None
Other varieties: None
Year: 1963

Satchmo

Rumba

Salmon Sorbet

Samaritan

Scarlet Queen Elizabeth

Origin: Northern Ireland
Description: Tall, vigorous shrub to 1.2 m (4 ft) high and 70 cm (2 ft) wide, with leathery dark green foliage. Slightly fragrant, the scarlet flowers are loosely globular and double, borne in large clusters.
Flowering: Continuously throughout summer
Cultivation: Tolerates poorer soils, but needs full sun. Excellent for bedding, or mass planting, and hedging. Dead-head the plant after flowering, and prune in winter, removing all dead and diseased wood and reducing healthy stems by half.

SCENTED AIR

Botanical grouping: Cluster-flowered floribunda
Parentage: Spartan seedling x Queen Elizabeth
Other names: None
Other varieties: None
Year: 1965
Origin: Northern Ireland
Description: A sturdy, rounded bush, growing up to 1 m (3 ft), with plenty of healthy mid-green foliage. The relatively large flowers are prolific and fragrant, in a deep shade of salmon pink.
Flowering: Summer to autumn
Cultivation: An excellent rose for bed or border, or as a distinctive hedge. Prefers full sun and moderately rich, well-drained soil.

SCHERZO

Botanical grouping: Cluster-flowered floribunda
Parentage: Tamango x [Sarabande x (Goldilocks x Fashion)]
Other names: Meipuma
Other varieties: None
Year: 1975
Origin: France
Description: Dense, upright shrub to 1 m (3 ft) high and 70 cm (2 ft) wide with dark green shiny foliage. Intense scarlet flowers

Scented Air

Scherzo

Scented Air

have reverses which are off-white, streaked with crimson. Flowers are double and produced in large clusters.
Flowering: Continuously throughout summer
Cultivation: Tolerates poorer soils and cold positions. Excellent for bedding and mass planting, and as a container plant. Dead-head the plant after flowering, and prune in winter, removing all dead and diseased wood and reducing healthy stems by half.

SEA PEARL

Botanical grouping: Cluster-flowered floribunda
Parentage: Perfecta x Montezuma
Other names: Flower Girl
Other varieties: None
Year: 1964
Origin. Northern Ireland
Description: Vigorous and upright shrub to 1 m (3 ft) high and 70 cm (2 ft) wide, with dark green leathery, glossy leaves. Moderately scented flowers are fully double, and soft pink with yellow reverse. Opening wide

Sea Pearl

and flat, the flowers are borne in large clusters.
Flowering: Continuously throughout summer
Cultivation: Tolerates poorer soils, but needs full sun. Excellent as a bedding plant, for mass planting, cut flower or container planting. Dead-head the plant after flowering, and prune in winter, removing all dead and diseased wood and reducing healthy stems by half.

Sexy Rexy

Sheila MacQueen

Sheila's Perfume

Shocking Blue

SHEILA'S PERFUME

Botanical grouping: Cluster-flowered floribunda
Parentage: Peer Gynt x [Daily Sketch x (Paddy McGredy x Prima Ballerina)]
Other names: Harsherry
Other varieties: None
Year: 1985
Origin: England
Description: Abundant, dark green glossy foliage on a vigorous and upright shrub growing to 80 cm (2½ ft) high by 70 cm (2 ft) wide. Small clusters of bright yellow, double flowers edged with red are very fragrant.
Flowering: Continuously throughout summer
Cultivation: Needs good soil and full sun. An excellent bedding plant, for mass or hedge planting, and is suitable for container planting. Used for cut flowers, but supply may be limited to specialist growers. Dead-head the plant after flowering, and prune in winter, removing all dead and diseased wood and reducing healthy stems by half.

SHOCKING BLUE

Botanical grouping: Cluster-flowered floribunda
Parentage: Unknown
Other names: Korblue
Other varieties: None
Year: 1974
Origin: Germany
Description: Double blooms, magenta-crimson in the large bud, open to magenta-mauve. Richly coloured and headily perfumed, this is a rose for cutting. It grows on a well-foliated and very bushy plant to 1.2 m (4 ft) and is very free-flowering.
Flowering: Freely throughout summer
Cultivation: Plant in good soil in full sun to filtered shade. Trim back lightly after each flush and remove spent blooms to encourage flowering.

SHOWBIZ

Botanical grouping: Cluster-flowered floribunda
Parentage: Unknown
Other names: Tanweieke, Ingrid Weibull, Bernard Daneke Rose
Other varieties: None
Year: 1981
Origin: Germany
Description: Bold, scarlet red, wavy-petalled flowers are produced on 'bouquet branches' with 6 to 12 branch clusters of blooms on stems 25–38 cm (10–15 in) long so they can be used for bouquets. The medium-sized bush is well foliated and grows to 70 cm (2 ft).

SEXY REXY

Botanical grouping: Cluster-flowered floribunda
Parentage: Seaspray x Dreaming
Other names: Macrexy, Heckenzauber
Other varieties: None
Year: 1984
Origin: New Zealand
Description: Bushy, compact shrub to 80 cm (2½ ft) high and 70 m (2 ft) wide, with vigorous stems. Large clusters of flowers are held close to the foliage, and are camellia-like, soft rose pink and very double.
Flowering: Continuously throughout summer
Cultivation: Needs good soil and full sun. Can be used as a bedding plant, in mass planting, as a hedge and for container planting. Dead-head the plant after flowering, and prune in winter, removing all dead and diseased wood and reducing healthy stems by half.

SHEILA MACQUEEN

Botanical grouping: Cluster-flowered floribunda
Parentage: Greensleeves x Letchworth Garden City
Other names: Harwotnext
Other varieties: None
Year: 1988
Origin: England
Description: A most unusual rose grown more for the cut flowers than for its appearance in the garden. The growth habit is upright and the foliage rather sparse. The sprays of flowers are a unique chartreuse green, tinged with ginger and apricot.
Flowering: Summer to autumn
Cultivation: This is a hardy rose that can withstand a wide range of climatic conditions and soils. Needs to have other plants around it in the garden to hide its lanky habit.

Showbiz

Sonoma

Southampton

Flowering: Freely throughout summer
Cultivation: A compact, mildew resistant and easy-to-care-for rose that makes a good border or small hedge. It will thrive in full sun where adequate water, drainage and mulching are provided.

SONOMA

Botanical grouping: Cluster-flowered floribunda
Parentage: Sumatra x Circus
Other names: None
Other varieties: None
Year: 1973
Origin: United States
Description: High-centred flowers shaded from soft pink to salmon-pink, fragrant and medium-sized, bloom generously in clusters on a dainty bush to about 75 cm (2½ ft).
Flowering: Repeats throughout summer
Cultivation: A small but vigorous bush that repeats quickly and can be grown in a tub or border or underplanted with standard roses. Grow in sun in soil that is fertile, drained, well mulched and well watered, especially in hot weather.

SOUTHAMPTON

Botanical grouping: Cluster-flowered floribunda
Parentage: (Ann Elizabeth x Allgold) x Yellow Cushion
Other names: Susan Ann
Other varieties. None
Year: 1972
Origin: England
Description: Handsome upright shrub to 1 m (3 ft) high and 75 cm (2½ ft) wide with rich, shiny foliage. Pointed buds open to marmalade coloured flowers flushed with orange and scarlet; lightly fragrant, large and fully double.
Flowering: Continuously throughout summer
Cultivation: A hardy rose tolerant of poorer soils, but requiring full sun. Recommended

St Boniface

as a bedding plant, for mass or hedge planting and as a container specimen. Dead-head the plant after flowering, and prune in winter, removing all dead and diseased wood and reducing healthy stems by half.

ST BONIFACE

Botanical grouping: Cluster-flowered floribunda
Parentage: Diablotin x Träumerei
Other names: Kormatt
Other varieties: None
Year: 1980

Origin: Germany
Description: Short bushy shrub to 70 cm (2 ft) high and wide, with abundant dark, shiny foliage. Neat but fully double flowers are bright orange-red, medium sized, slightly fragrant and carried in large clusters.
Flowering: Continuously throughout summer
Cultivation: Needs good soil and full sun. Can be used as a bedding plant, for mass planting and hedges, and as a container plant. Dead-head the plant after flowering, and prune in winter, removing all dead and diseased wood and reducing the length of healthy stems by half.

Sue Ryder

Sun Flare

Sue Lawley

Sunsilk

centre, with edges of individual petals white and pink, and are clustered on the plant.
Flowering: Continuously throughout summer
Cultivation: Needs good soil and full sun. Makes an excellent bedding or hedge plant, and is suitable for mass planting, for containers and for cut flowers. Dead-head the plant after flowering, and prune in winter, removing all dead and diseased wood and reducing the length of healthy stems by half.

SUE RYDER

Botanical grouping: Cluster-flowered floribunda
Parentage: Southampton x [(Highlight x Colour Wonder) x (Parkdirektor Riggers x Piccadilly)]
Other names: Harlino
Other varieties: None
Year: 1983
Origin: England
Description: Bushy shrub 1 m (3 ft) high by 70 cm (2 ft) wide with plenty of shiny green leaves. The well-formed, salmon red flowers are fully double, tend to yellow on the reverse and occur in large clusters.
Flowering: Continuously throughout summer
Cultivation: Tolerates poorer soils, but needs full sun. An excellent rose for bedding and hedge or mass planting. Suitable as a cut flower, though availability may be limited to specialist growers. Dead-head the plant after flowering, and prune in winter, removing all dead and diseased wood and reducing the length of healthy stems by half.

SUN FLARE

Botanical grouping: Cluster-flowered floribunda
Parentage: Sunsprite x seedling
Other names: Jacjem
Other varieties: Climbing sport from United States, 1989
Year: 1981
Origin: United States
Description: A very floriferous, butter-yellow rose with a darker, golden centre and stamens. The foliage is glossy, dark green and the bush grows to 1.2 m (4 ft) high.
Flowering: Spring and summer
Cultivation: Prefers full sun to filtered shade and drained, fertile soil that is mulched. Remove spent blooms to encourage new growth and prune lightly when flowering is finished.

SUNSILK

Botanical grouping: Cluster-flowered floribunda
Parentage: Pink Parfait x Redgold seedling

SUE LAWLEY

Botanical grouping: Cluster-flowered floribunda
Parentage: [(Little Darling x Goldilocks) x [Evelyn Fison x (Coryana x Tantau's Triumph)]] x [(John Church x Elizabeth of Glamis) x [Evelyn Fison x (Orange Sweetheart x Frühlingsmorgen)]]
Other names: Spanish Shawl, Macspash
Other varieties: None
Year: 1980
Origin: New Zealand
Description: Bushy shrub growing to 70 cm (2 ft) high and wide, with dark green foliage. Slightly fragrant flowers are warm red in the

Tangerine Tango

Taora

The Times

The Times

Other names: None
Other varieties: None
Year: 1974
Origin: England
Description: An upright shrub growing to 1 m (3 ft) with dark green, leathery foliage. The large flowers are fully double and shapely, in a soft yellow, and appear in prolific clusters.
Flowering: Continuously throughout summer
Cultivation: Suitable for cultivation in a wide range of soils and conditions. Often grown for cut flowers and also makes an attractive hedge. Prune out dead wood in winter.

TANGERINE TANGO

Botanical grouping: Cluster-flowered floribunda
Parentage: Unknown
Other names: None
Other varieties: None
Year: 1991
Origin: United States
Description: High-centred, tangerine-striped, white, medium-sized flowers are borne in abundant clusters, offset by light green foliage. The bush grows to 1.2 m (4 ft) high. Although scentless, the blooms give a good display in the vase or garden.
Flowering: Spring and summer
Cultivation: Mass in borders or beds or grow as an informal hedge in full sun and fertile soil that is well watered and drained and mulched in hot weather.

TAORA

Botanical grouping: Cluster-flowered floribun
Parentage: Fragrant Cloud x Schweizer Grüss
Other names: Tanta
Other varieties: None
Year: 1968

Origin: Germany
Description: Dense, shiny foliage on an upright shrub to 1 m (3 ft) high by 70 cm (2 ft) wide. Slightly fragrant flowers are orange-red, double and very shapely.
Flowering: Continuously throughout summer
Cultivation: Needs good soil and full sun. A good rose for mass planting, bedding and container growing. May be limited to specialist growers. Dead-head the plant after flowering, and prune in winter, removing all dead and diseased wood and reducing the length of healthy stems by half.

THE TIMES

Botanical grouping: Cluster-flowered floribunda
Parentage: Tornado x Redgold
Other names: Mariandel, Carl Philip, Christian IV, Korpeahn,
Other varieties: None
Year: 1984. Named in honour of the famous newspaper's bicentenary
Origin: Germany
Description: Dense, compact plant to 70 cm (2 ft) high and the same, or slightly

Tony Jacklin

Trumpeter

more in width, with thick, dark and shiny foliage. The dark crimson flowers are double when fully open, with prominent yellow stamens, and are carried in clusters at the same level as the outer leaves.

Flowering: Continuously throughout summer
Cultivation: Needs good soil and full sun. The flower/leaf contrast makes this an outstanding plant for bedding and mass planting and also as a hedge. Can be used for cut flowers, and as a container specimen. Dead-head the plant after flowering, and prune in winter, removing all dead and diseased wood and reducing the length of healthy stems by half.

TONY JACKLIN

Botanical grouping: Cluster-flowered floribunda
Parentage: City of Leeds x Irish Mist
Other names: None
Other varieties: None
Year: 1972
Origin: New Zealand
Description: A hardy, coral salmon to orange small rose borne in clusters on a medium to tall growing bush of 1.2–1.5 m (4–5 ft). The mid-green foliage is equally small and plentiful and the blooms have very little perfume.

Flowering: Spring and summer
Cultivation: A good hedging or border rose that prefers full sun and fertile soil. It can be massed in garden beds and pruned back lightly to encourage flowering.

TOPSI

Botanical grouping: Cluster-flowered floribunda
Parentage: Fragrant Cloud x Signalfeuer
Other names: None
Other varieties: None
Year: 1972
Origin: Germany
Description: Short, dense and compact shrub to 50 cm (1½ ft) high and wide. Bright orange-red semi-double flowers open very wide, and occur in large clusters.
Flowering: Continuously throughout summer
Cultivation: Needs good soil and full sun. Can be used as bedding or hedge plant, as well as making a compact tub specimen. May be prone to black spot. Dead-head the plant after flowering, and prune in winter, removing all dead and diseased wood and reducing the length of healthy stems by half.

TRUMPETER

Botanical grouping: Cluster-flowered floribunda
Parentage: Satchmo x seedling
Other names: Mactrum
Other varieties: None
Year: 1977
Origin: New Zealand
Description: Neat, compact shrub to 70 cm (2 ft) high and wide, with dense green, glossy foliage. Free-flowering in large clusters with rounded buds opening to fully double, rich red flowers with a slight fragrance.
Flowering: Continuously throughout summer
Cultivation: Reliable, showy plant in good soils and full sun. Excellent for mass planting, bedding or hedge planting, as well as containers. Dead-head the plant after flowering, and prune in winter, removing all dead and diseased wood and reducing the length of healthy stems by half.

VALENTINE HEART

Botanical grouping: Cluster-flowered floribunda
Parentage: Shona x Pot o' Gold
Other names: Dicogle
Other varieties: None
Year: 1990
Origin: Northern Ireland
Description: Neat, compact shrub to 80 cm (21/2 ft) high by 70 cm (2 ft) wide. Pale scarlet buds open to fragrant blush-pink flowers.
Flowering: Continuously throughout summer

Cultivation: A useful, hardy rose that can be grown as a hedge or incorporated into a bed or border. Dead-head after flowering, and prune back in winter.

VIOLET CARSON

Botanical grouping: Cluster-flowered floribunda
Parentage: Mme Léon Cuny x Spartan
Other names: Macio
Other varieties: None
Year: 1964
Origin: Northern Ireland
Description: Vigorous, dense shrub to 70 cm (2 ft) high and wide. The dark glossy foliage has bronze tints. Full, light peach pink flowers are lightly fragrant and produced in large clusters.
Flowering: Continuously throughout summer
Cultivation: Needs good soil and full sun, and makes an excellent bedding and hedge plant, as well as for cut flowers. Dead-head the plant after flowering, and prune in winter, removing all dead and diseased wood and reducing the length of healthy stems by half.

WISHING

Botanical grouping: Cluster-flowered floribunda
Parentage: Silver Jubilee x Bright Smile
Other names: Georgie Girl, Dickerfuffle
Other varieties: None
Year: 1984
Origin: England
Description: An attractive bushy rose that grows to 75 cm (2½ ft), with matt-green, semi-glossy leaves and a showy display of shapely, deep salmon-pink flowers. The flowers have only a slight fragrance.
Flowering: Continuously throughout summer
Cultivation: A useful bedding or border rose, also suitable for cultivation in a container. Prune out dead wood in winter, and shape as desired.

WOBURN ABBEY

Botanical grouping: Cluster-flowered floribunda
Parentage: Masquerade x Fashion
Other names: None
Other varieties: None
Year: 1962
Origin: England
Description: Strong stems on an upright shrub to 1 m (3 ft) high by 70 cm (2 ft) wide, with prolific, small dark and shiny leaves. Loose, double golden-orange flowers begin as tight oval buds, and are slightly fragrant.
Flowering: Continuously throughout summer

Valentine Heart

Violet Carson

Woburn Abbey

Cultivation: Tolerates poorer soils, but needs full sun. Excellent for mass planting in beds, or as a hedge. Also suitable for containers. Makes a good cut flower, but can be prone to rust. Dead-head the plant after flowering, and prune in winter, removing all dead and diseased wood and reducing the length of healthy stems by half.

ZAMBRA

Botanical grouping: Cluster-flowered floribunda
Parentage: (Goldilocks x Fashion) x (Goldilocks x Fashion)
Other names: Meialfi
Other varieties: Climbing sport from France, 1969
Year: 1961
Origin: France
Description: Shiny leathery leaves on a vigorous shrub to 80 cm (2½ ft) high and 70 cm (2 ft) wide. Slightly fragrant flowers begin as rounded buds and open to clear orange with yellow reverse, medium sized and semi-double.
Flowering: Continuously throughout summer
Cultivation: Tolerates poorer soils, but

Wishing

Zambra

needs full sun. Used for massed planting, as bedding and hedging plants, and also in containers. Prone to black spot. Dead-head the plant after flowering, and prune in winter, removing all dead and diseased wood and reducing the length of healthy stems by half.

Shrub Roses

This diverse group includes all those roses, some dating back to the 1860s, which cannot clearly be classified into any of the other hybrid groups. There are many forms, shapes, sizes and colours of shrub roses, including some that flower in summer only, and those that feature recurrent flowering from summer to autumn. Some of the more popular shrubs, including those developed in England by David Austin, have been bred to contain all the best features of the old-fashioned or 'heritage roses', such as the cupped flower shape and strong fragrance.

Allux Symphony

Abraham Darby

ABRAHAM DARBY

Botanical grouping: Modern shrub
Parentage: Aloha x Yellow Cushion
Other names: Auscot
Other varieties: None
Year: 1985
Origin: England
Description: A delightful, old-fashioned looking rose, growing to 1.5 m (5 ft), with the long arching stems reaching 2.5 m (8 ft). The flowers are showy and cup-shaped, apricot-pink with some yellow, and with a rich, fruity fragrance.
Flowering: Continuously throughout summer
Cultivation: Excellent for a wide border, shrubbery, fence or wall. Thrives in well-drained and well-mulched soil. Can be pruned as a shrub, or allowed to spread as desired.

ALLUX SYMPHONY

Botanical grouping: Modern shrub
Parentage: The Friar x seedling
Other names: None

Amy Robsart

Other varieties: None
Year: 1986
Origin: England
Description: A bushy rose, reaching up to 1 m (3 ft) in height. Its slender stems are covered with deep green leaves, while the large, loosely shaped flowers are a rich creamy yellow and produce a light, delicate scent.
Flowering: Continuously throughout summer
Cultivation: A delicate rose, best suited to sheltered conditions with rich, well-drained soil and frequent mulching at the base. Dead-head after flowering and prune back long stems in winter.

AMY ROBSART

Botanical grouping: Sweet briar shrub
Parentage: *R. eglanteria* hybrid
Other names: None
Other varieties: None
Year: 1894
Origin: England
Description: An arching bush with stems

up to 3 m (10 ft) long. It has a semi-double, deep pink, slightly scented flower with a yellow centre, followed by attractive red fruit.
Flowering: Summer only
Cultivation: Tolerant of poor, chalky soil and of some shade. Prune out dead wood annually. Can be pruned as a shrub or trained onto a trellis or fence.

ANNA ZINKEISEN

Botanical grouping: Modern shrub
Parentage: Seedling x Frank Naylor
Other names: Harqühling
Other varieties: None
Year: 1983
Origin: England
Description: Strong, broad shrub to 1.2 m (4 ft) high and wide, with prolific light and glossy foliage. The plump, pale gold buds open to fully double, golden-ivory flowers, which usually occur in clusters and are fairly fragrant.
Flowering: Continuously throughout summer
Cultivation: Will tolerate poorer soil, but needs full sun. Recommended as a border, hedge, or as a container specimen. Dead-head the plant after flowering, and prune in winter, removing all dead and diseased wood. Reduce the length of healthy stems, and encourage new shoots from the base by removing some older canes.

Anna Zinkeisen

AQUARIUS

Botanical grouping: Modern shrub
Parentage: (Charlotte Armstrong x Contrast) x [Fandango x (World's Fair x Floradora)]
Other names: Armaq
Other varieties: None
Year: 1971
Origin: United States
Description: Plump buds open to high-centred, fragrant, 42-petalled blooms of soft to pale pink with darker rose pink edges, carried on long stems. A good cutting rose that is almost luminous, especially in autumn. The foliage is leathery and dark green. Grows to more than 1 m (3 ft).
Flowering: Prolific, repeats from early summer to late autumn
Cultivation: Grow in full sun or light to filtered shade. Good drainage is essential if grown in shade. It prefers fertile soil that has been well mulched.

ARMADA

Botanical grouping: Modern shrub
Parentage: New Dawn x Silver Jubilee
Other names: Haruseful
Other varieties: None
Year: 1988
Origin: England
Description: Dense, upright shrub to 1.5 m (5 ft) high and 1 m (3 ft) wide with bright green shiny leaves. Semi-double flowers are rich pink and borne in large trusses.
Flowering: Continuously throughout summer
Cultivation: Needs good soil, and full sun. High habit makes it a good rose to use as a pillar or scrambler, or as a container specimen. Dead-head the plant after flowering, and prune in winter, removing all dead and diseased wood. Reduce the length of healthy stems, and encourage new shoots from the base by removing some older canes.

ATHENA

Botanical grouping: Grandiflora
Parentage: Unknown
Other names: None
Other varieties: None
Year: Unknown
Origin: Germany
Description: A new white rose with shapely, pointed buds which open to nicely formed fragrant flowers of about 40 petals with edges tinged with pink. A good cutting rose that holds its petals and keeps well. Healthy dark green foliage is produced on a bush to more than 1 m (3 ft).
Flowering: Spring to summer
Cultivation: Likes full sun and well-drained soil that is mulched. Extra feeding is advisable if grown in filtered shade.

Aquarius

Armada

Athena

Autumn Delight

AUTUMN BOUQUET

Botanical grouping: Modern shrub
Parentage: New Dawn x Crimson Glory
Other names: None
Other varieties: None
Year: 1948
Origin: United States
Description: Dense, upright shrub to 1.2 m (4 ft) high and 1 m (3 ft) wide, with leathery dark green foliage. The very fragrant, fully double, red to deep pink flowers are preceded by long pointed buds.
Flowering: Continuously throughout summer
Cultivation: Tolerates poorer soils and light shade. Can be used as a medium-sized hedge, or as a container rose. This is an excellent cut flower when fully open or at bud stage, but availability may be limited to specialists. Dead-head the plant after flowering, and prune in winter, removing all dead and diseased wood. Reduce the length of healthy stems, and encourage new shoots from the base by removing some older canes.

AUTUMN DELIGHT

Botanical grouping: Modern shrub
Parentage: Unknown
Other names: None

Other varieties: None
Year: 1933
Origin: England
Description: Clusters of elegant, dark gold buds open wide to creamy yellow, richly fragrant flowers—somewhere between a single and a semi-double—with prominent gold stamens. The flowers may fade to white as they mature, and give way to green hips. The bush is upright, to 1.2 m (4 ft), with dark green, matt foliage.
Flowering: Bears flowers over a long period throughout summer.
Cultivation: This plant will tolerate less than perfect soil conditions, and can be used to make an attractive hedge of medium height.

BELINDA

Botanical grouping: Modern shrub
Parentage: Unknown
Other names: None
Other varieties: None
Year: 1936
Origin: England
Description: An upright, vigorous shrub, growing to 1.2 m (4ft), with showy trusses of mid-pink, semi-double flowers. The foliage is deep green, and the flowers only slightly fragrant.

Belinda

Flowering: Continuously throughout summer
Cultivation: Can be grown successfully in a wide range of soils and conditions, making an excellent hedging specimen. Also suited to cultivation in a container.

BELLE STORY

Botanical grouping: Modern shrub
Parentage: (Chaucer x Parade) x (The Prioress x Iceberg)
Other names: Auselle
Other varieties: None
Year: 1984
Origin: England
Description: This strong-growing rose will reach up to 1.2 m (4 ft) in height. The stems are sparsely interspersed with small, dark green foliage and are topped by very large and richly scented blooms which are dusk pink at the flower's centre merging into a fine pale pink at the tips of the petals.
Flowering: Intermittently throughout summer
Cultivation: A relatively hardy rose that will survive varied conditions. Best results will be obtained in rich, well-drained soil.

Belle Story

Bonica 82

BERLIN

Botanical grouping: Modern shrub
Parentage: Eva x Peace
Other names: None
Other varieties: None
Year: 1949
Origin: Germany
Description: An attractive shrub rose with showy, single blooms of rich scarlet-crimson flowers displayed in large, erect trusses. The flowers have a slight fragrance and the foliage is dark green and leathery. Grows upright to 1.5 m (5 ft) high and 1 m (3 ft) wide.
Flowering: Continuously throughout summer
Cultivation: Can be used as a climbing or pillar rose and is also suitable for hedging or growing in containers. Tolerant of poorer soil and a wide range of conditions.

BISHOP DARLINGTON

Botanical grouping: Modern shrub
Parentage: Aviateur Blériot x Moonlight
Other names: None
Other varieties: None

Berlin

Year: 1926
Origin: United States
Description: Pink buds open to large semi-double blooms of creamy white with pink and gold touches, particularly notable for their rich musk fragrance. A strong grower, reaching 1.5 m (5 ft), with darkish foliage and a smattering of fruit.
Flowering: Recurrent flowers during the season.
Cultivation: This rose has no special requirements and makes a striking display in a group planting or when used as a hedge.

BONICA 82

Botanical grouping: Modern shrub
Parentage: (*R. sempervirens* x Mlle Marthe Carron) x Picasso
Other names: Meidomonac
Other varieties: None
Year: 1981
Origin: France
Description: A bushy, spreading shrub growing to 1 m (3 ft) with small, glossy deep green leaves. The fully double flowers are borne in large clusters. They are a pleasing clear pink, fading to a soft pink at the edges, and are slightly fragrant.
Flowering: Continuously throughout summer
Cultivation: Can be grown as a ground covering rose, or as a container plant. The flowers are excellent for cutting. Prune out dead wood in winter.

BONN

Botanical grouping: Modern shrub
Parentage: Hamburg x Independence
Other names: None
Other varieties: None
Year: 1950
Origin: Germany
Description: A moderately fragrant, fully double rose with orange-scarlet flowers borne in clusters. Foliage is glossy and light

Bishop Darlington

Bonn

Buff Beauty

green. An upright and bushy plant growing to 1.8 m (6 ft) high and 1.2 m (4 ft) wide.
Flowering: Continuously throughout summer
Cultivation: Tolerant of poorer soil. It is suitable for hedging, growing as a climbing or as a pillar rose and can also be grown successfully in containers.

BREDON

Botanical grouping: Modern shrub
Parentage: Wife of Bath x Lilian Austin
Other names: None
Other varieties: None
Year: 1984
Origin: England
Description: This leggy, arching rose reaches a maximum of 1 m (3 ft) high. It is distinguished by its large and shining dark green foliage, which is relatively dense all along the stems. Blooms are full and compact, and are a delicate creamy pink colour. The fragrance is rich, but not overwhelming.
Flowering: Continuously throughout summer
Cultivation: Quite a hardy rose that will usually continue to flower in varied and unfriendly conditions. Prune back long stem growth in winter to keep the shape tidy.

BUFF BEAUTY

Botanical grouping: Modern shrub
Parentage: Thought to be a seedling of William Allen Richardson
Other names: None
Other varieties: None
Year: 1939 (possibly older)
Origin: England
Description: The spreading habit of this rose can give it the appearance of being weighed down by its heavy trusses of sweetly scented double blooms, whose

Bredon

colour ranges from apricot through gold to creamy yellow according to conditions. A vigorous bush spreading to 1.5 m (5 ft) high and wide, with dark green foliage.
Flowering: Flowers constantly over a long period, into autumn.
Cultivation: Careful shaping is needed to encourage upward growth. Tolerant of some shade and indifferent soil.

CARDINAL HUME

Botanical grouping: Modern shrub
Parentage: Seedling x Frank Naylor
Other names: Harregale
Other varieties: None
Year: 1984
Origin: England
Description: Dense spreading shrub to 1 m (3 ft) by 1 m (3 ft) with dark, matt foliage. Lightly fragrant double flowers open dark maroon and colour deepens with age.
Flowering: Continuously throughout summer
Cultivation: Suitable as a hedge or bedding plant. Dead-head the plant after flowering, and prune in winter, removing all dead and diseased wood. Reduce the length of healthy stems, and encourage new shoots from the base by removing some older canes.

Cardinal Hume

Charles Austin

Charmian

Chaucer

CHARLES AUSTIN

Botanical grouping: Modern shrub
Parentage: Chaucer x Aloha
Other names: None
Other varieties: Yellow Charles Austin
Year: 1973
Origin: England
Description: One of David Austin's finest roses, admired for its large, showy flowers which have a rich, fruity fragrance. A vigorous, bushy grower, reaching 1.5 m (5 ft), with mid-green foliage and creamy yellow flowers washed with warm apricot highlights.
Flowering: Very long flowering, from summer through to autumn.
Cultivation: Plant in full sun in moderately rich soil. To obtain repeat flowering, prune after the first flush. Mulch around the base to suppress weed growth.

CHARMIAN

Botanical grouping: Modern shrub
Parentage: Unnamed seedling x Lilian Austin
Other names: Ausmian
Other varieties: None
Year: 1982
Origin: England
Description: This rose has an arching habit

that will take it to 1.2 m (4 ft) high. It is dense and bushy, with large clusters of mid-green foliage on sturdy stems. The showy blooms are large and cup-shaped, the petals forming thick folds of a glorious light magenta, and giving off a sweet and delicate scent.
Flowering: Continuously throughout summer
Cultivation: Quite hardy, it will survive semi-dry conditions and poor soil. It is important, however to keep this rose in a relatively sheltered environment.

CHAUCER

Botanical grouping: Modern shrub
Parentage: Seedling x Constance Spry
Other names: None
Other varieties: None
Year: 1970
Origin: England
Description: This vigorous and bushy rose will grow up to 1 m (3 ft) high and wide. It has slender, arching stems and dark green, glossy, serrated foliage.The flowers are of medium size, cup-shaped and are a delicate creamy pink. They produce a rich, strong fragrance.
Flowering: Continuously throughout summer
Cultivation: Prefers full sun and moderately rich soil, with some protection from strong wind. Prune back in winter to maintain shape.

CLAIRE ROSE

Botanical grouping: Modern shrub
Parentage: Charles Austin x (seedling x Iceberg)
Other names: Auslight
Other varieties: None
Year: 1986
Origin: England
Description: This bushy rose will grow up to 1.2 m (4 ft) high with sturdy stems covered in dense, shining, dark green foliage. The blooms are delicate in scent, cup-shaped and a soft pink in colour.

Claire Rose

Flowering: Recurrent throughout summer
Cultivation: Very hardy, but prefers a moderately sunny environment with a rich, well-drained soil. Mulching at the base will suppress weed growth.

CORNELIA

Botanical grouping: Modern shrub
Parentage: Unknown
Other names: None
Other varieties: None
Year: 1925
Origin: England
Description: Sprays of small, many-petalled pink flowers with a dash of apricot open from darker pink buds and are sweetly fragrant. The sprays may be cut and used for arrangements. The bush is densely foliaged, with attractive reddish branches, and nicely rounded in shape, growing to 1.5 m (5 ft) high and wide.
Flowering: Flowers reliably over a very long period.
Cultivation: Use this in a large bed or border, or plant against a fence for a lovely display. This robust plant will stand extremes of weather and a range of soil conditions, as well as some shade.

COUNTRY DANCER

Botanical grouping: Modern shrub
Parentage: Prairie Princess x Johannes Boettner
Other names: None
Other varieties: None
Year: 1972
Origin: United States
Description: An attractive rose with deep, rose-pink, semi-double flowers. Grows to

Country Dancer

Cornelia

1.2 m (4 ft) high. The flowers last very well when cut.
Flowering: Repeats throughout summer
Cultivation: This low growing shrub rose is particularly suitable for hedges.

CRESSIDA

Botanical grouping: Modern shrub
Parentage: Seedling x Conrad F. Meyer
Other names: Auscress
Other varieties: None
Year: 1983
Origin: England
Description: A vigorous and thorny rose which can be easily grown as either a shrub up to 1.5 m (5 ft) or a climber up to 4 m (13 ft). It has slender stems and mid-green serrated foliage, matt in appearance. The flowers are of medium size and loosely shaped and range from a rich creamy apricot to a delicate ivory. They produce a rich and strong fragrance.
Flowering: Continuously throughout summer
Cultivation: Quite hardy as a climber, but usually requires a sheltered surround to protect its delicate blooms and slender stems. Provide a rich, well-drained soil.

CYMBELENE

Botanical grouping: Modern shrub
Parentage: Unnamed seedling x Lilian Austin

Other names: Auslean, Cymbeline
Other varieties: None
Year: 1982
Origin: England
Description: A shrubby rose with a spreading and arching habit. Grows up to 1.2 m (4 ft) in height and even more in width. It has quite sturdy stems with a spattering of mid-green serrated foliage. The delicate, cup-shaped blooms are quite large with loose pale pink petals that have a powerful scent.
Flowering: Intermittently throughout summer
Cultivation: A hardy shrub with good disease resistance that will thrive in most conditions, making it a relatively low maintenance plant.

Cymbelene

Ellen

Dapple Dawn

Dove

DAPPLE DAWN

Botanical grouping: Modern shrub
Parentage: Sport of Red Coat
Other names: None
Other varieties: None
Year: 1983
Origin: England
Description: A simple rose, growing to 1.5 m (5 ft) high, with slender stems. Its mid-green leaves are small and curving with a matt appearance. Its blooms form a single layer of petals in a saucer-like arrangement. They are a rich, light magenta with dark stamens studding the centre. They produce a delicate and unobtrusive fragrance.
Flowering: Continuously throughout summer
Cultivation: Relatively easy to look after when established; however, this delicate shrub demands a sheltered surround and a rich well-drained soil. Mulching around the base of the plant is advisable.

DOVE

Botanical grouping: Modern shrub
Parentage: Wife of Bath x Iceberg seedling
Other names: Ausdove, Dovedale
Other varieties: None
Year: 1984
Origin: England
Description: This rose has a wide, spreading growth of about 1 m (3 ft) and will reach up to 1 m (3 ft) in height. Its delicate stems support a thick covering of dark green matt foliage and classic cup-shaped blooms of a delicate cream-pink colour, with a sweet, fragrance.
Flowering: Continuously throughout summer
Cultivation: A sensitive rose that requires a rich well-drained soil and mulching at the base for the best results.

ELLEN

Botanical grouping: Modern shrub
Parentage: Unknown
Other names: Auscup
Other varieties: None
Year: 1984
Origin: England
Description: A vigorous, bushy shrub that reaches about 1.2 m (4 ft) in height. The stems are durable, supporting thick dark green serrated foliage, and enormous apricot coloured blooms, which are so heavy they are pendulous on the stems.
Flowering: Continuously throughout summer
Cultivation: Very hardy, but the blooms must be well cared for. Will survive in poor soil, but the blooms will not be as spectacular without a well-sheltered and tended surround.

ELMSHORN

Botanical grouping: Modern shrub
Parentage: Hamburg x Verdun
Other names: None
Other varieties: None
Year: 1951
Origin: Germany
Description: With vigorous upright growth this plant produces large trusses of medium-sized, pompon-like flowers. These are deep cerise-pink, and have a moderate fragrance. The foliage is glossy mid-green. Grows to 1.8 m (6 ft) high and 1.2 m (4 ft). It is good for use as a cut flower.
Flowering: Continuously throughout summer
Cultivation: Tolerates poorer soils. Suitable for hedging and can also be successfully grown in containers.

EMANUEL

Botanical grouping: Modern shrub
Parentage: (Chaucer x Parade) x (seedling x Iceberg)

Emanuel

English Garden

Eyeopener

Other names: Ausuel, Emmanuelle
Other varieties: None
Year: 1985
Origin: England
Description: Dense mid-green foliage on an upright shrub to 1.2 m (4 ft) high and 1 m (3 ft) wide. Old-fashioned type flowers are a very soft pink with pale yellow bases and extremely fragrant.
Flowering: Continuously throughout summer
Cultivation: Requires full sun and better soil. Can be used as a hedge or container plant, but may only be available through specialist growers. Dead-head the plant after flowering, and prune in winter, removing all dead and diseased wood. Reduce the length of healthy stems, and encourage new shoots from the base by removing some older canes. There is some liability to black spot.

ENGLISH GARDEN

Botanical grouping: Modern shrub
Parentage: Lilian Austin x (seedling x Iceberg)
Other names: Ausbuff
Other varieties: None
Year: 1986
Origin: England
Description: A compact, upright bush growing to 1 m (3 ft) high. Its durable stems are covered in dark green foliage and topped by very large, showy blooms. The golden-cream petals form extensive layers in a complex bowl-shaped layout. They give off a thick, heady scent.
Flowering: Free-flowering over a long period
Cultivation: Relatively hardy but prefers a soil that is rich and well-drained. Trim long stems in winter to keep the shape compact and shrubby.

EUPHRATES

Botanical grouping: Modern shrub
Parentage: *R. persica* x Fairy Changeling
Other names: Harunique

Elmshorn

Other varieties: None
Year: 1986
Origin: England
Description: Low growing, spreading shrub to 70 cm (2 ft) with the bluish-green, serrated foliage typical of *R. persica*. The flowers are five-petalled in an unusual salmon-pink colour with scarlet at the petal bases. It is unscented.
Flowering: Summer only
Cultivation: Healthy and disease resistant, this plant will tolerate poorer soils and some shade. Plant as a bedding or border shrub as well as a low-growing hedge.

EYEOPENER

Botanical grouping: Ground cover shrub
Parentage: (Seedling x Eyepaint) x (seedling x Dortmund)
Other names: Interop, Erica, Tapis Rouge
Other varieties: None
Year: 1987

Euphrates

Origin: The Netherlands
Description: A low-growing rose, to 30 cm (1 ft) high and 1 m (3 ft) wide, forming an unusual pyramid shape. The foliage is bright green and plentiful, and the showy flowers are vivid red with yellow centres.
Flowering: Continuously throughout summer
Cultivation: An excellent rose for a wide range of soils and conditions, planted as a feature, in a bed or as a low border. Also a good rose for a container. Not readily susceptible to pests or diseases.

FAIR BIANCA

Botanical grouping: Modern shrub
Parentage: Unknown
Other names: Ausca
Other varieties: None
Year: 1982
Origin: England
Description: This sturdy, upright rose will grow up to 1 m (3.5 ft) high, displaying

Felicia

Fair Bianca

Fiona

dense mid-green foliage on its slender stems. It bears large saucer-like blooms of a delicate snowy white, whose rich petal folds emit a strong fragrance.

Flowering: Continuously throughout summer

Cultivation: Prefers a well-drained soil with good mulching at the roots. It will survive, however, under varied conditions.

FELICIA

Botanical grouping: Modern shrub
Parentage: Trier x Ophelia
Other names: None
Other varieties: None
Year: 1928
Origin: England
Description: An upright, branching shrub growing to 1.2 m (4 ft), with a good covering of glossy, mid-green foliage and clusters of soft pink fully double flowers. The flowers are moderately fragrant.
Flowering: Continuously throughout summer
Cultivation: Suitable for a wide range of soils and conditions, and can be grown in semi-shade or in a container. The blooms are prized as cut flowers.

FIONA

Botanical grouping: Modern shrub
Parentage: Sea Foam x Picasso
Other names: Meibeluxen
Other varieties: None
Year: 1979
Origin: France
Description: A bushy, spreading shrub reaching 75 cm (2½ ft) high and 1.2 m (4 ft) wide. The dense foliage is a glossy green colour, while the dramatic flowers are blood red and prolific.
Flowering: Summer to autumn
Cultivation: An excellent shrub for a massed planting, or for bed, border or hedge. Prefers full sun and well-drained soil. Prune out dead wood in winter.

FLOWER CARPET

Botanical grouping: Ground cover shrub
Parentage: Immensee x Amanda
Other names: Heidetraum, Noatraum
Other varieties: Apple Blossom Pink
Year: 1991
Origin: Germany
Description: A useful ground covering rose growing to 80 cm (2½ ft) high and 1 m

(3 ft) wide, with mid-green foliage and prolific flowers that have an old-fashioned appearance. The flowers are small and semi-double, deep rose-pink, tinged with white.
Flowering: Over many months from early summer to early winter. The warmer the climate, the longer the flowering period.
Cultivation: This rose is prized for its ease of cultivation and disease-resistance. Prefers full sun and moderately rich soil, and will flower more prolifically if fed frequently. Can be used as a ground cover, border or container plant.

FOUNTAIN

Botanical grouping: Modern shrub
Parentage: Unknown
Other names: Red Prince, Fontaine
Other varieties: None
Year: 1970
Origin: Germany
Description: A very attractive, large and upright shrub to 2 m (7 ft) high and 1.2 m (4 ft) wide with large, dark and shiny leaves. The lightly scented flowers are large, loose and deep red, and occur in clusters.
Flowering: Continuously throughout summer

Fountain

Frank Naylor

Fritz Nobis

Cultivation: Needs good soil and full sun. An excellent rose for a high hedge, for training as a pillar or climber, or for growing in a container. Dead-head the plant after flowering, and prune in winter, removing all dead and diseased wood. Reduce the length of healthy stems, and encourage new shoots from the base by removing some older canes.

FRANK NAYLOR

Botanical grouping: Modern shrub
Parentage: Complex hybrid involving Cläre Grammerstorf and Frühlingsmorgen
Other names: None
Other varieties: None
Year: 1978
Origin: England
Description: Medium, upright shrub to 1.2 m (4 ft) high and 1 m (3 ft) wide, with small, dark foliage. The flowers are reminiscent of a clematis, having five pointed petals in a warm shade of wine-red with pale yellow centres. They are of medium size, and borne freely in eye-catching trusses.
Flowering: Continuous throughout summer
Cultivation: Needs good soil, but will tolerate light shade. Can be used as a hedge or container plant. Dead-head the plant after flowering, and prune in winter, removing all dead and diseased wood. Reduce the length of healthy stems, and encourage new shoots from the base by removing some older canes.

FRITZ NOBIS

Botanical grouping: Modern shrub
Parentage: Joanna Hill x Magnifica
Other names: None
Other varieties: None
Year: 1940
Origin: Germany
Description: This shrub produces sizeable clusters of superbly formed, fully double, lightly fragrant soft rose-pink blooms. Foliage is semi-glossy, leathery and dark

green. Upright branching growth reaches 1.5 m (5 ft) high and 1.2 m (4 ft) wide.
Flowering: Summer only
Cultivation: Tolerates poorer soils and shade. Can be grown in containers and is also suitable for hedges.

FRÜHLINGSANFANG

Botanical grouping: Pimpinellifolia hybrid
Parentage: Joanna Hill x *R. pimpinellifolia altaica* hybrid

Frühlingsanfang

Other names: None
Other varieties: None
Year: 1950
Origin: Germany
Description: A plant of upright growth reaching 3 m (10 ft) high and 1.8 m (6 ft) wide. Produces large, single, ivory-white, slightly fragrant blooms and has dark green foliage.
Flowering: Summer only
Cultivation: Tolerates poorer soils and a degree of shade. Suitable for hedging or as part of a border or shrubbery.

Frühlingsduft

Frühlingsmorgen

Gertrude Jekyll

Frühlingszauber

Frühlingsgold

Frühlingsgold

FRÜHLINGSDUFT

Botanical grouping: Pimpinellifolia hybrid
Parentage: Joanna Hill x *R. pimpinellifolia altaica*
Other names: None
Other varieties: None
Year: 1949
Origin: Germany
Description: Produces a large, fully double, very fragrant flower of ivory-white and golden yellow, sometimes tinged with soft pink. Growth is angular and upright with large, dark green foliage. Grows to 3 m (10 ft) high and 1.8 m (6 ft) wide.
Flowering: Summer only
Cultivation: Tolerates poorer soils and shade and is suitable for hedging.

FRÜHLINGSGOLD

Botanical grouping: Pimpinellifolia hybrid
Parentage: Joanna Hill x *R. pimpinellifolia hispida*
Other names: Spring Gold
Other varieties: None
Year: 1937
Origin: Germany
Description: A popular, well-known hybrid. It has large, initially cupped, clear primrose-yellow flowers. Buds are tinged

Frühlingsgold

red. It is very fragrant. Foliage is mid-green on an upright, branching plant. Grows to 2 m (7 ft) high and 1.8 m (6 ft) wide.
Flowering: Summer only
Cultivation: Tolerates poorer soils and shade. It is suitable for hedging. Only prune to remove dead or spindly wood, and allow plenty of space for growth.

FRÜHLINGSMORGEN

Botanical grouping: Pimpinellifolia hybrid
Parentage: (E.G. Hill x Cathrine Kordes) x *R. pimpinellifolia altaica*
Other names: Spring Morning
Other varieties: None
Year: 1942
Origin: Germany
Description: Produces large, ivory-white to cream, single flowers, heavily brushed with pinky-red, with pronounced golden brown stamens. The fragrance is very strong. Foliage is dark green on an upright, branching plant of 1.8 m (6 ft) high and 1.5 m (5 ft).
Flowering: Spring only
Cultivation: A hardy specimen that tolerates poorer soils and some light shade. Suitable for hedging or for a shrubbery.

FRÜHLINGSZAUBER

Botanical grouping: Pimpinellifolia hybrid
Parentage: (E.G. Hill x Cathrine Kordes) x *R. pimpinellifolia altaica*
Other names: None
Other varieties: None
Year: 1942
Origin: Germany
Description: Produces large, semi-double, lightly fragrant flowers of ivory-white, blushed heavily with deep pink. An upright, rather thorny plant with dark green foliage. Grows to 2 m (7 ft) high and 1.5 m (5 ft) wide.
Flowering: Summer only
Cultivation: Tolerates poorer soils and shade. Suitable for hedging. Susceptible to mildew, so avoid overcrowding and keep good air circulation around the plant.

GERTRUDE JEKYLL

Botanical grouping: Modern shrub
Parentage: Unknown English rose x Comte de Chambord
Other names: Ausbord
Other varieties: None

Year: 1986
Origin: England
Description: This rose's lanky growth can reach up to 1.2 m (4 ft) high. Its thick mid-green foliage is set off by large, cup-shaped, pink flowers, the petals of which are arranged in a spiral fashion. These deep pink blooms are noted especially for their powerful scent.
Flowering: Continuously throughout summer
Cultivation: A hardy rose that will survive in relatively harsh conditions. For best results, however, provide well-drained and mulched soil.

GOLDBUSCH

Botanical grouping: Modern shrub
Parentage: Golden Glow x *Rosa eglanteria* hybrid
Other names: None
Other varieties: None
Year: 1954
Origin: Germany
Description: Sprawling shrub capable of reaching 2.5 m (8 ft) if supported, and 1.5 m (5 ft) wide. Young foliage is yellow-green, becoming prolific, darker and glossy with age. Golden flowers are large and double or semi-double, and begin as coral pink buds.
Flowering: Flowers repeatedly from early summer
Cultivation: Tolerates poorer soils, and light shade. Excellent as a climbing or pillar rose when given support. Dead-head the plant after flowering, and prune in winter, removing all dead and diseased wood. Reduce the length of healthy stems, and encourage new shoots from the base by removing some older canes.

GOLDEN WINGS

Botanical grouping: Modern shrub
Parentage: (Soeur Thérèse x *R. pimpinellifolia altaica*) x Ormiston Roy
Other names: None
Other varieties: None
Year: 1956
Origin: United States
Description: A very free-flowering shrub. Its large blooms are single, occasionally with a few additional petals. They are clear yellow with prominent, golden brown stamens and have a slight, pleasant fragrance. Foliage is light green and glossy, borne on a bushy plant. Stems are dark, rusty-looking, with few thorns. Grows to 1.5 m (5 ft) high and 1.2 m (4 ft) wide.
Flowering: Continuously throughout summer
Cultivation: Tolerates poorer soils and shade. Makes a good hedging specimen.

Goldbusch

Golden Wings

Graham Thomas

Graham Thomas

GRAHAM THOMAS

Botanical grouping: Modern shrub
Parentage: Charles Austin x seedling
Other names: Ausmas
Other varieties: None
Year: 1983
Origin: England
Description: Named in honour of one of England's most esteemed enthusiasts of old roses, this plant features vigorous and bushy growth up to 1.2 m (4 ft). Foliage is mid-green, while the flowers are softly cupped and warm yellow, with a rich tea-scented fragrance.
Flowering: From early summer though to autumn.
Cultivation: Prefers full sun and moderately rich soil. Picking flowers will help to extend the flowering period.

Helen Knight

HELEN KNIGHT

Botanical grouping: Species hybrid shrub
Parentage: Thought to be *R. ecae* x a
Scotch rose
Other names: None
Other varieties: None
Year: 1970
Origin: England
Description: A most unusual rose. It grows
to 2 m (7 ft) and can be grown as a large
shrub or trained against a wall. The foliage is
fern-like, resembling that of *R. ecae*, and the
slender stems are covered with small, clear
yellow, cup-shaped flowers.
Flowering: Early summer
Cultivation: Choose a warm, sheltered
location away from cold winds or frosts.
Mulch well around the base of the plant, and
prune only lightly to remove dead wood.

HERBSTFEUER

Botanical grouping: Modern shrub
Parentage: Unknown
Other names: Autumn Fire
Other varieties: None
Year: 1966
Origin: Germany
Description: Light green and large foliage
on a shrub to 1.8 m (6 ft) high. Fragrant
flowers are large, double and loosely
formed, bright scarlet with dark red tonings.
Ornamental hips are urn shaped and orange.
Flowering: Repeats throughout summer
Cultivation: Tolerates poorer soils and light
shade. Useful as a hedge or in a mixed
shrubbery. Dead-head the plant after
flowering, and prune in winter, removing all
dead and diseased wood. Reduce the length
of healthy stems, and encourage new shoots
from the base by removing some older canes.

HERITAGE

Botanical grouping: Modern shrub
Parentage: Seedling x Iceberg seedling
Other names: Ausblush
Other varieties: None
Year: 1984
Origin: England
Description: A vigorous, bushy plant
reaching 1.2 m (4 ft) in height. Blooms are
large and showy, pale cream-apricot tinged
with darker apricot around the edge of the
petals. Fragrance is strong and lemony.
Flowering: Repeat flowering through
summer into autumn.
Cultivation: Can be grown in a wide range
of conditions, although prefers rich, well-
drained soil and a layer of organic matter at
the base.

HERO

Botanical grouping: Modern shrub
Parentage: The Prioress x unnamed
seedling
Other names: Aushero
Other varieties: None
Year: 1982
Origin: England
Description: This rose features sturdy

Hilda Murrell

Heritage

Hero

growth and will reach up to 1 m (3 ft) in height. Its strong stems support delicate light-green foliage and medium-sized, semi-double blooms. These simple, willowy flowers are a soft pink in colour, and are strongly scented.

Flowering: Continuously throughout summer
Cultivation: A sturdy rose that will thrive in varied surroundings. A well-drained and rich, loamy soil is preferred. Prune long stems in winter to maintain a compact bush.

HILDA MURRELL

Botanical grouping: Modern shrub
Parentage: Seedling x (Parade x Chaucer)
Other names: Ausmurr
Other varieties: None
Year: 1984
Origin: England
Description: A vigorous and bushy rose that will grow up to 1.2 m (4 ft) high. The dark green leaves are large with serrated edges, while the large, double blooms have thick folds of bright pink petals and a creamy yellow centre. Flowers are strongly fragrant.
Flowering: Predominantly early summer
Cultivation: This rose will survive in harsh conditions in many climates. For the best results in flower size, colour and scent, mulch well around the roots.

IMMORTAL JUNO

Botanical grouping: Modern shrub
Parentage: Unknown
Other names: None
Other varieties: Nonc
Year: 1991
Origin: England
Description: Free-flowering, large, full-petalled, cupped and glowing pink, this rose has a powerful perfume and is beautiful in both vase and garden. A vigorous shrub with strong growth and large, deep green leaves, it grows to 1.2 m (4 ft).
Flowering: Recurrent from early summer through to late autumn.
Cultivation: Combining the best of old and new roses, this is a healthy rose that responds well to full sun and fertile soil that is drained and well mulched.

JACQUELINE DU PRÉ

Botanical grouping: Modern shrub
Parentage: Radox Bouquet x Maigold
Other names: Harwanna
Other varieties: None
Year: 1989
Origin: England
Description: Bushy, vigorous shrub to 1.5 m (5 ft) with dark green, glossy foliage. The semi-double, fragrant flowers are ivory

Immortal Juno

Jacqueline du Pré

blush with scalloped petal edges and reddish gold stamens.
Flowering: Recurrent from early summer through to late autumn
Cultivation: A healthy rose that prefers an open, sunny position with plenty of water in summer and a well-drained and mulched soil. Suitable for massed display, borders, hedges or planted against walls or fences.

KATHLEEN FERRIER

Botanical grouping: Modern shrub
Parentage: Gartenstolz x Shot Silk
Other names: None
Other varieties: None
Year: 1952
Origin: The Netherlands
Description: Vigorous spreading shrub to 1.5 m (5 ft) high and about 1.2 m (4 ft) wide, with dense dark shiny leaves. Young stems are bronze. Strongly scented flowers are pink and salmon, paler at edges, semi-double, and carried in small clusters.
Flowers: Continuously throughout summer
Cultivation: Tolerates poorer soils, and needs full sun. Suitable as an informal hedge, container plant and as a cut flower. Dead-head the plant after flowering, and prune in winter, removing all dead and diseased wood. Reduce the length of healthy stems, and encourage new shoots from the base by removing some older canes.

Kathleen Ferrier

Lady Penzance

LADY PENZANCE

Botanical grouping: Sweet briar shrub
Parentage: R. eglanteria x R. foetida bicolor
Other names: None
Other varieties: None
Year: 1894
Origin: England
Description: A vigorous, dense shrub growing to 2 m (7 ft) high and 1.8 m (6 ft) wide. Has strongly scented foliage and is probably the best known of the sweet briars. Produces single, coppery salmon and pink flowers with pronounced yellow stamens, followed by bright red hips.
Flowering: Summer only
Cultivation: Tolerates poorer soils and shade. Suitable for woodland plantings and for hedges. Worth growing for the ornamental value of its fruit.

LAFTER

Botanical grouping: Modern shrub
Parentage: [V for Victory x (Général Jacqueminot x Dr W. Van Fleet)] x Pink Princess
Other names: None
Other varieties: None
Year: 1948
Origin: United States
Description: Upright and vigorous, this shrub can reach 1.5 m (5 ft) high and 1.2 m (4 ft)

Leander

Lilian Austin

La Sevillana

Description: Rich foliage with bronze shadings on a hardy shrub which grows to 1.2 m (4 ft) high and wide. The lightly fragrant flowers are brilliant red, semi-double and borne in trusses.
Flowering: Continuously throughout summer
Cultivation: Tolerates poorer soils, but needs full sun. Useful as a hedge or specimen. Dead-head the plant after flowering, and prune in winter, removing all dead and diseased wood. Reduce the length of healthy stems, and encourage new shoots from the base by removing some older canes.

LAVENDER LASSIE

Botanical grouping: Modern shrub
Parentage: Hamburg x Mme Norbert Levavasseur
Other names: None
Other varieties: None
Year: 1960
Origin: Germany
Description: A pretty rose that produces fully double, lavender-pink flowers in large trusses. Has dark green, glossy foliage. Its upright tidy growth reaches 1.5 m (5 ft) high and 1.2 m (4 ft) wide. Has a moderate fragrance and is good as a cut flower.
Flowering: Continuously throughout summer
Cultivation: Tolerates poorer soils. Suitable for containers, hedging, or as a climber or pillar rose.

LEANDER

Botanical grouping: Modern shrub
Parentage: Charles Austin x seedling
Other names: Auslea
Other varieties: None
Year: 1982
Origin: England
Description: This adaptable rose can be grown either as a shrub, where it will grow up to 2 m (7 ft) high or as a climber where it will reach up to 4 m (14 ft) high. It has a vigorous and open growth with slim stems supporting mid to dark green foliage and small blooms that are a creamy pink colour. The flowers are strongly scented.
Flowering: Continuously throughout summer
Cultivation: A hardy shrub that will thrive in varied conditions. If grown as a climber it can be trained onto a wall or trellis for support.

LILIAN AUSTIN

Botanical grouping: Modern shrub
Parentage: Aloha x The Yeoman
Other names: None
Other varieties: None
Year: 1973

Lavender Lassie

wide, and has shiny pale green foliage. The fragrant and semi-double flowers are shades of salmon and apricot and borne in clusters.
Flowering: Continuously throughout summer
Cultivation: Tolerates poorer soils, but needs full sun. Can be trained as a climbing or pillar rose, if supported. Dead-head the plant after flowering, and prune in winter, removing all dead and diseased wood. Reduce the length of healthy stems, and encourage new shoots from the base by removing some older canes.

LA SEVILLANA

Botanical grouping: Modern shrub
Parentage: [(Meibrim x Jolie Madam) x (Zambra x Zambra)] x [(Super Star x Super Star) x (Poppy Flash x Poppy Flash)]
Other names: Meigekanu
Other varieties: None
Year: 1978
Origin: France

Origin: England
Description: A splendid bush with curved, arching stems and deep green foliage, growing to a height of 1.2 m (4 ft) in the right conditions. The cup-shaped double flowers are showy and sweetly scented, with rich apricot petals.
Flowering: Over many months in summer and autumn
Cultivation: Apply a mulch of well-rotted manure in summer to prevent the soil surface from drying out. Generally quite easy to grow and disease resistant.

LUCETTA

Botanical grouping: Modern shrub
Parentage: Unknown
Other names: None
Other varieties: None
Year: 1983
Origin: England
Description: This rose has a strong and arching growth, making it suitable for cultivation as a shrub growing to 1.2 m (4 ft) high and wide, or as a climber to 3 m (10 ft) high. It displays prolific dark green foliage and enormous, opulent, fragrant blooms, delicate pink in the centre fading almost to white at the tips.
Flowering: Summer
Cultivation: A hardy shrub, but the delicate blooms need a protected environment for best results.

MAGENTA

Botanical grouping: Modern shrub
Parentage: Yellow floribunda seedling x Lavender Pinocchio
Other names: Kordes' Magenta
Other varieties: None
Year: 1954
Origin: Germany
Description: An open and spreading shrub to 1.5 m (5 ft) high and about 1.2 m (4 ft) wide, with dark and leathery foliage. Branches are weighed down by the large

Magenta

Lucetta

clusters of full and double flowers which are purple through to pink, and are very fragrant.
Flowering: Continuously throughout summer
Cultivation: Demanding but rewarding, this rose needs good soil and full sun. Makes an excellent container plant and is suitable for cut flowers. Dead-head the plant after flowering, and prune in winter, removing all dead and diseased wood. Reduce the length of healthy stems, and encourage new shoots from the base by removing some older canes.

MANY HAPPY RETURNS

Botanical grouping: Modern shrub
Parentage: Herbstfeuer x Pearl Drift
Other names: Harwanted, Prima
Other varieties: None
Year: 1991
Origin: England

Many Happy Returns

Description: Dark shiny foliage on a neat and wide shrub reaching 1 m (3 ft) high and 1.2 m (4 ft) wide. Slender, pink buds become blush coloured and slightly cupped, are very prolific and contrast with the dark background.
Flowering: Continuously throughout summer
Cultivation: A hardy shrub needing full sun. A good spreading rose for mass planting, including hedging, mixed shrubbery, or as a specimen. Dead-head the plant after flowering, and prune in winter, removing all dead and diseased wood. Reduce the length of healthy stems, and encourage new shoots from the base by removing some older canes.

MÄRCHENLAND

Botanical grouping: Modern shrub
Parentage: Swantje x Hamburg
Other names: Exception
Other varieties: None
Year: 1951
Origin: Germany
Description: An attractive, bushy shrub with masses of dark green, semi-glossy foliage, reaching 1.5 m (5 ft) in height. The semi-double flowers appear in large trusses and are a vivid shade of pink, tinged with warm salmon.
Flowering: Continuously throughout summer
Cultivation: A useful and easy-to-grow rose that is tolerant of most soils and climates. It prefers a sunny, open position. It can be grown as a hedge, or as a large container specimen.

Mary Rose

Mary Webb

Moonbeam

MARY ROSE

Botanical grouping: Modern shrub
Parentage: Seedling x The Friar
Other names: Ausmary
Other varieties: Red Mary Rose
Year: 1983
Origin: England
Description: A vigorous grower, reaching
1.2 m (4 ft) in height, it has mid-green
foliage and masses of sweetly scented, cup-
shaped, clear pink blooms that darken as
they mature.
Flowering: Through summer and autumn
Cultivation: This variety is prized for its
resistance to disease, and is easy to cultivate
in a wide range of conditions.

MARY WEBB

Botanical grouping: Modern shrub
Parentage: Seedling x Chinatown
Other names: Auswebb
Other varieties: None
Year: 1984
Origin: England
Description: This shrub has a dense and
vigorous growth reaching up to 1.2 m (4 ft)
in height. It has slender stems, dark green
foliage and medium-sized fragrant blooms.
The flowers are a light buttery colour and
are arranged in an open cup-like fashion
revealing clusters of heart-shaped petals.
Flowering: Recurrent through summer and
autumn
Cultivation: Although adaptable, this is a
delicate rose that requires some attention. A
rich, well-fertilised and well-drained soil is
preferred.

MOONBEAM

Botanical grouping: Modern shrub
Parentage: Unknown
Other names: None
Other varieties: None
Year: 1983
Origin: England
Description: This rose has a robust growth
that takes it up to 1.2 m (4 ft) high. It has
slender stems that bear delicate dark green
foliage and simple, understated flowers.
These blossoms are arranged in a star-like
fashion and are a cream colour with the
stamens forming a dramatic circle of black
dots in the centre.
Flowering: Repeat flowering through
summer and autumn
Cultivation: A delicate rose that prefers a

protected and well-maintained environment
in rich well-drained soil.

MOONLIGHT

Botanical grouping: Modern shrub
Parentage: Trier x Sulphurea
Other names: None
Other varieties: None
Year: 1913
Origin: England
Description: Carries clusters of many richly
scented small flowers, shaped between a
single and a semi-double, in creamy white
with hints of yellow, and prominent gold
stamens. The stems are coloured an attrac-
tive dark red and, combined with dark

Moonlight

Moonlight

leaves, set the flowers off to perfection. Bears small orange-red hips. A robust and vigorous bush which reaches 1.5 m (5 ft).
Flowering: Virtually continuous flowering through summer into autumn.
Cultivation: A hardy plant which will stand extremes of weather and a certain amount of shade. May be affected by seasonal mildew. Can be used to good effect as a hedge.

MOUNTBATTEN

Botanical grouping: Modern shrub
Parentage: Peer Gynt x [(Anne Cocker x Arthur Bell) x Southampton)]
Other names: Harmantelle
Other varieties: None
Year: 1982
Origin: England
Description: Very handsome, dense shrub to 1.5 m (5 ft) high and about 1.2 m (4 ft) wide with crisp, rich green, dense and leathery foliage. Yellow buds are round, and open to large and round, clear yellow flowers with reflexed and incurving petals.
Flowering: Continuously throughout summer
Cultivation: Tolerates poorer soils and needs full sun. Excellent as a bedding or container plant, as a specimen, or as a cut flower. Dead-head the plant after flowering, and prune in winter, removing all dead and diseased wood. Reduce the length of healthy stems, and encourage new shoots from the base by removing some older canes.

MOZART

Botanical grouping: Modern shrub
Parentage: Robin Hood x Rote Pharisäer
Other names: None
Other varieties: None
Year: 1937
Origin: Germany
Description: Bushy shrub to 1.2 m (4 ft) high and 1 m (3 ft) wide. The small flowers are carmine and single, with a white centre, and appear in very large trusses.

Mozart

Flowering: Continuously throughout summer
Cultivation: Tolerates poorer soils and needs full sun. Useful as a bedding plant or hedge, and as a container specimen. Dead-head the plant after flowering, and prune in winter, removing all dead and diseased wood. Reduce the length of healthy stems, and encourage new shoots from the base by removing some older canes.

NANCY STEEN

Botanical grouping: Modern shrub
Parentage: Pink Parfait x (Ophelia x Parkdirektor Riggers)
Other names: None
Other varieties: None
Year: 1976
Origin: New Zealand
Description: Produces abundant flowers throughout the season. A healthy, compact plant growing up to 1.5 m (5 ft) high. Flowers are large, fully double, fragrant and borne in clusters. Their colour is a blush pink with hints of salmon. The centre is cream. Foliage is glossy, dark bronzy green.
Flowering: Continuously throughout summer
Cultivation: Tolerates poorer soils and is suitable for growing as a hedge or in groups. Good as a cut flower and also very good for growing in containers.

Mountbatten

Nancy Steen

Nevada

Nur Mahal

Nymphenburg

Nymphenburg

NEVADA

Botanical grouping: Modern shrub
Parentage: Obscure, but may be La Giralda crossed with *R. moyesii* or a hybrid of *R. pimpinellifolia*
Other names: None
Other varieties: None
Year: 1927
Origin: Spain
Description: A superb and popular rose with large, more than single, slightly blowsy flowers. These are soft, creamy yellow flushed pink, with pronounced brown stamens. Has only a slight fragrance. Foliage is dark green and semi-glossy. A vigorous, dense shrub which grows to 2.5 m (8 ft) high and 2 m (7 ft) wide.
Flowering: Repeats throughout summer
Cultivation: Tolerates poorer soils and some shade. Shorten back strong laterals and remove dead and spindly wood.

NIGEL HAWTHORNE

Botanical grouping: Modern shrub
Parentage: *R. persica* x Harvest Home
Other names: Harquibbler
Other varieties: None
Year: 1989
Origin: England
Description: Prickly shrub to 70 cm (2 ft) with wrinkled foliage in the *R. rugosa* style. The five-petalled flowers are pale salmon pink with red markings at the base of each petal.
Flowering: Summer only
Cultivation: Coming from *R. persica* and *R. rugosa,* it is a healthy and hardy rose with good disease resistance. An unusual rose that would be suited as a border plant. Its usefulness is limited by its short flowering season.

NUR MAHAL

Botanical grouping: Modern shrub
Parentage: Château de Clos Vougeot x Hybrid Musk seedling
Other names: None

Other varieties: None
Year: 1923
Origin: England
Description: Deep cerise to crimson semi-double blooms, opening flat, grow in large clusters against good, dark foliage. The flowers are richly fragrant. The bush bears some orange hips and grows to 1.5 m (5 ft).
Flowering: Flowers consistently over a lengthy season, into autumn.
Cultivation: Makes a colourful hedge and can be grown in part shade and indifferent soil.

NYMPHENBURG

Botanical grouping: Modern shrub
Parentage: Sangerhausen x Sunmist
Other names: Nymphenberg
Other varieties: None
Year: 1954
Origin: Germany
Description: An upright and dense shrub which produces large clusters of reasonably large, salmon-pink flowers with a lemon centre. The colour can vary with weather and soil conditions. Has a very light fragrance. Foliage is rich, dark green and glossy. Grows to 1.8 m (6 ft) high and 1.2 m (4 ft) wide.
Flowering: Continuously throughout summer
Cultivation: Can be used as a climbing or pillar rose. Is also suitable for hedging and growing in containers. Tolerates poorer soils.

OHIO

Botanical grouping: Modern shrub
Parentage: *Rosa soulieana* x seedling from Grüss an Teplitz
Other names: None
Other varieties: None
Year: 1949
Origin: United States
Description: Very hardy and dense shrub to 1.2 m (4 ft) high and 1 m (3 ft) wide. Semi-double flowers are vivid red and clustered.
Flowering: Repeatedly from early summer
Cultivation: Tolerates poorer soils and light

shade. This hardy shrub is useful as a hedge or mass planting in difficult locations. Dead-head during summer, and in winter remove some older branches and shorten others to promote new growth. Availability may be limited.

OTHELLO

Botanical grouping: Modern shrub
Parentage: Lilian Austin x The Squire
Other names: None
Other varieties: None
Year: 1987
Origin: England
Description: This rose has a dense, vertical and thorny growth up to 1.2 m (4 ft) high. It has sturdy stems and delicate dark green foliage. The large and showy flowers are a deep blood-red, and turn purple with age. The fragrance is extremely strong.
Flowering: Freely throughout summer
Cultivation: Quite hardy, but the blooms are nowhere near as glorious if not provided with rich fertilisation.

PAX

Botanical grouping: Modern shrub
Parentage: Trier x Sunburst
Other names: None
Other varieties: None

Pax

Year: 1918
Origin: England
Description: A bushy, spreading shrub that reaches 1.8 m (6 ft) high and 1.5 m (5 ft) wide. The leaves are dark green and leathery, and the flowers are white to cream in colour, semi-double and carried on trusses. The flowers are very fragrant.
Flowering: Continuously throughout summer
Cultivation: Useful as a hedging plant, this rose can withstand a wide range of soils and conditions, even some shade. Prune out dead wood in winter.

PENELOPE

Botanical grouping: Modern shrub
Parentage: Ophelia x unnamed seedling
Other names: None
Other varieties: None
Year: 1924
Origin: England
Description: Reliable, handsome and hardy shrub, neat, dense and spreading, to 1.2 m (4 ft) high and wide, with large and semi-glossy leaves. Fragrant flowers are light blush or shell pink, semi-double and cupped. Flowers are very prolific.
Flowering: Continuously throughout summer
Cultivation: Very hardy, this rose tolerates

Penelope

poorer soils and light shade. It is excellent as a hedge, where its reliability and ornamental hips are advantages. May be prone to mildew. Remove dead flower heads during the summer, and in winter take out some older stems, and shorten others in order to promote new growth.

PERDITA

Botanical grouping: Modern shrub
Parentage: Seedling crosses
Other names: None
Other varieties: None
Year: 1983
Origin: England
Description: This rose has a dense, vigorous growth up to 1.2 m (4 ft) high. Its stems bear a dense covering of dark green foliage and large showy blooms. These are

like a deep bowl in shape with the petals arranged in a circular fashion. They range from a delicate ice-pink to a buttery-pink and produce a strong scent.
Flowering: Recurrent through summer
Cultivation: This hardy bush is disease resistant and will thrive and continue to flower in harsh conditions.

PINK BELLS

Botanical grouping: Ground cover shrub
Parentage: Mini-Poul x Temple Bells
Other names: Poulbells
Other varieties: None
Year: 1983
Origin: Denmark
Description: Vigorous, ground-covering shrub to 75 cm (2½ ft) high and 1.5 m (5 ft) wide, with masses of dark green,

Othello

Perdita

Pink Bells

glossy foliage. The flowers are a clear, rosy pink and are unscented.

Flowering: Summer only

Cultivation: A healthy rose whose flowers are resistant to weather damage. Plant in a sunny, open position for best results. This plant is suitable as a ground cover or for training over a small fence or in a border.

POULSEN'S PARK ROSE

Botanical grouping: Modern shrub
Parentage: Great Western x Karen Poulsen
Other names: None
Other varieties: None
Year: 1953
Origin: Denmark
Description: A healthy shrub. Growth is very thorny and tends to sprawl. Flowers are large, full, silvery pink and are borne in clusters. Perfume is moderately fragrant. Has dark green, leathery, rather coarse foliage. Grows to 1.8 m (6 ft) high and wide.
Flowering: Repeats throughout summer
Cultivation: Tolerates poorer soils and shade, but is susceptible to rust. Suitable for use as a hedging plant, climber or pillar rose.

Pretty Jessica

Prospero

PRETTY JESSICA

Botanical grouping: Modern shrub
Parentage: Seedling crosses
Other names: None
Other varieties: None
Year: 1983
Origin: England
Description: This shrub has a dense and compact growth, reaching only 1 m (3 ft) in height. Its slim stems produce light to mid-green foliage, and bear impressive and richly scented blooms. These flowers are bowl-like in shape and the masses of petals are arranged in a random fashion inside the bordering edge of musk-pink.
Flowering: Recurrent throughout summer
Cultivation: Well-drained soil and continuous mulching around the roots is desirable for best results.

PROSPERITY

Botanical grouping: Modern shrub
Parentage: Marie Jeanne x Perle des Jardins
Other names: None
Other varieties: None
Year: 1919
Origin: England
Description: A large and vigorous sprawling shrub, growing to 1.5 m (5 ft) and spreading to 1.2 m (4 ft). The arching stems are covered with rich, deep green foliage, while the fragrant semi-double flowers are a creamy-white colour, borne in large sprays. The weight of the flowers has a tendency to cause the flowering stems to bend, adding to the beauty of the plant.
Flowering: Summer to autumn
Cultivation: A beautiful rose for bed or border It can be allowed to spread and attain its natural shape, or be pruned to maintain a more compact habit. Hardy and suited to a wide range of soils and climates.

Prosperity

PROSPERO

Botanical grouping: Modern shrub
Parentage: The Knight x seedling
Other names: Auspero
Other varieties: None
Year: 1982
Origin: England
Description: Grown more for its richly fragrant flowers than for the overall effect. Quite a small, shrubby plant, reaching only 70 cm (2 ft), with mid-green foliage and masses of wine-red blooms that mature to a deep grape-purple hue.
Flowering: Continuously throughout summer
Cultivation: Prefers full sun and a moderately rich and well-drained soil. Keep the base of the plant free from weeds to avoid black spot.

PROUD TITANIA

Botanical grouping: Modern shrub
Parentage: Unnamed seedlings
Other names: Austania
Other varieties: None
Year: 1982
Origin: England
Description: Robust growth, up to 1.2 m (4 ft) high. It has robust stems and serrated mid-green foliage. The blooms are medium-sized and cupped, in a pale shade of creamy apricot. They are noted for their delicate fragrance
Flowering: Summer
Cultivation: Quite hardy, and will survive in many different conditions. It will only thrive and flower successfully, however, in a relatively protected environment with a well-mulched and well-drained soil.

RAUBRITTER

Botanical grouping: Modern shrub-climber
Parentage: Daisy Hill x Solarium
Other names: None
Other varieties: None
Year: 1936
Origin: Germany
Description: Vigorous, sprawling shrub with open habit, to 2.5 m (8 ft) high if given support, and 2 m (7 ft) wide. If unsupported, tends to be weighed down by many flowers which are deeply pink with many small, incurving petals. Flowers are also globular and lightly fragrant.
Flowering: Summer only
Cultivation: A hardy rose suitable for exposed positions, and an excellent low hedge, or recumbent specimen. Can also be trained as a scrambler or pillar rose. Remove dead flower heads during the summer, and in winter take out some older stems, and shorten others in order to promote new growth.

Raubritter

Redcoat

Robin Hood

Rosy Cushion

REDCOAT

Botanical grouping: Modern shrub
Parentage: Unnamed seedling x Golden Showers
Other names: Red Coat
Other varieties: None
Year: 1973
Origin: England
Description: This rose has a dense bushy growth, up to 1.5 m (5 ft) high. Its mid to dark green foliage is studded with small, simple blooms arranged in a shallow saucer-like fashion. The petals are scarlet and are complemented by a bright golden yellow centre.
Flowering: Freely over a lengthy period
Cultivation: A hardy shrub that is disease resistant and will thrive and flower well in harsh conditions.

ROBIN HOOD

Botanical grouping: Modern shrub
Parentage: Seedling x Miss Edith Cavell
Other names: None
Other varieties: None
Year: 1927
Origin: England
Description: Bears clusters of small cherry red flowers which deepen in colour as they age and are followed by tiny brown hips. The bush is a neat and vigorous grower, reaching 1.2 m (4 ft), with dark green leaves.
Flowering: Flowers very freely through a long season.
Cultivation: Healthy and resistant to weather extremes, this makes an attractive container plant or a colourful hedge.

ROSY CUSHION

Botanical grouping: Modern shrub
Parentage: Yesterday x seedling
Other names: Interall
Other varieties: None
Year: 1979
Origin: Holland
Description: Dense and wide shrub to 1 m (3 ft) high and 1.2 m (4 ft) wide, with dark and glossy leaves. Single flowers are blush pink on the edges, fading to cream in the centre, with prominent golden stamens, and good fragrance.
Flowering: Continuously throughout summer
Cultivation: Very hardy plant suitable for massed display as a border or hedge, or as a specimen. Remove dead flower heads during summer, and in winter take out some older stems, and shorten others to promote new growth.

Sadlers Wells

Scharlachglut

Schoener's Nutkana

SADLERS WELLS

Botanical grouping: Modern shrub
Parentage: Penelope x Rose Gaujard
Other names: None
Other varieties: None
Year: 1983
Origin: England
Description: Shiny, dark green foliage provides the backdrop for clusters of dainty, semi-double flowers with pale pink centres and striking cherry red edges. The effect is light and frilly. The flowers last well when cut and used in an arrangement. Grows to 1.2 m (4 ft) high.
Flowering: Free flowering right through summer, with a very good show in autumn.
Cultivation: This vigorous, robust plant flourishes even in some shade and mediocre soil.

SCHARLACHGLUT

Botanical grouping: Modern shrub
Parentage: Poinsettia x Alika
Other names: Scarlet Fire, Scarlet Glow
Other varieties: None
Year: 1952
Origin: Germany
Description: An extremely vigorous shrub growing to 3 m (10 ft) high and 2 m (7 ft) wide, with brown-purple stems and foliage and a few large thorns. The very large flowers are single and deep red, with prominent golden stamens. Ornamental hips are large, urn-shaped and bright orange.
Flowering: Early summer only
Cultivation: Tolerates poorer soils and light shade and is suited to planting in woodland where it can climb through the trees. Promote foliage and flowers by removing some old wood, and reducing new long canes by one-third, each year.

SCHOENER'S NUTKANA

Botanical grouping: Modern shrub
Parentage: *R. nutkana* x Paul Neyron
Other names: None

Sea Foam

Other varieties: None
Year: 1930
Origin: United States
Description: Large, single, cerise-pink, very fragrant flowers are produced on an arching shrub. Foliage is mid-green and almost thornless. Grows to 1.8 m (6 ft) high and 1 m (3 ft) wide.
Flowering: Summer only
Cultivation: A versatile rose that will tolerate poorer soils and shady areas. Suitable for hedging, if pruned hard in both summer and winter.

SEA FOAM

Botanical grouping: Modern shrub
Parentage: White Dawn x Pinocchio
Other names: None
Other varieties: None
Year: 1964
Origin: United States
Description: A trailing, semi-prostrate shrub with lightly scented, creamy white, pompon-like flowers. Has glossy green foliage. Spreads to 2 m (7 ft) wide.
Flowering: Continuously throughout summer
Cultivation: An ideal plant to use as a ground cover and can also be successfully grown as a climber. Prefers full sun and good growing conditions.

SIR CLOUGH

Botanical grouping: Modern shrub
Parentage: Chaucer x Conrad F. Meyer
Other names: None
Other varieties: None
Year: 1983
Origin: England
Description: This semi-double rose will grow up to 1.5 m (5 ft) high, with a thick covering of arrow-like dark green foliage. The slender stems are topped by large, saucer-shaped blooms that are a deep pink in hue.
Flowering: Continuously throughou summer
Cultivation: To achieve the most favourable results from this shrub, plant in a well-drained soil and keep the roots mulched continuously.

SIR WALTER RALEIGH

Botanical grouping: Modern shrub
Parentage: Lilian Austin x Chaucer
Other names: Ausspry
Other varieties: None
Year: 1985
Origin: England
Description: This shrub will grow up to 1.2 m (4 ft) high and features a dense, vigorous dark green foliage. The flowers are rich creamy pink, large and fragrant.
Flowering: Recurrent through summer
Cultivation: A relatively hardy shrub that will flower in many and varied conditions. It is best to keep the soil about the plant mulched and well-drained.

SUMA

Botanical grouping: Ground cover shrub
Parentage: Nozomi seedling
Other names: Harsuma
Other varieties: None
Year: 1989
Origin: Japan
Description: A true ground cover, spreading to 1 m (3 ft) and only reaching 45 cm (1½ ft) in height. The foliage is red-green, and the small red rosette flowers are borne

Sir Walter Raleigh

on clusters along the creeping stems. The foliage turns a deep bronze-crimson in autumn.
Flowering: Summer to autumn
Cultivation: Once established, the plant forms a small hummock in the centre. Mulch to keep weeds down. Suitable for a wide range of soils and conditions.

SURREY

Botanical grouping: Modern shrub
Parentage: The Fairy x unknown seedling
Other names: Korlanum, Sommerwind, Vent d'Eté
Other varieties: None
Year: 1985
Origin: Germany
Description: Dense, rounded and spreading shrub to 75 cm (2½ ft) high and 2 m (7 ft) wide. The small flowers are 6 cm (2½ in) across and pink, and tend to be spread evenly over the plant.
Flowering: Continuously throughout summer
Cultivation: Very hardy shrub which can be used as a border, low hedge, or groundcover Remove dead flower heads during the summer, and in winter take out some older stems, and shorten others in order to promote new growth.

SUSAN LOUISE

Botanical grouping: Modern shrub
Parentage: Belle Portugaise seedling
Other names: None
Other varieties: None
Year: 1929
Origin: United States
Description: Produces long pointed buds which open out into semi-double, clear, pink, fragrant flowers. Grows to 1.5 m (5 ft).
Flowering: Continuously throughout summer
Cultivation: Remove dead and spindly wood in winter. Full sun and good growing conditions are preferred.

Surrey

Suma

Susan Louise

Suzanne

The Reeve

The Miller

The Squire

SUZANNE

Botanical grouping: Modern shrub
Parentage: Second generation *R. laxa* x *R. spinosissima*
Other names: None
Other varieties: None
Year: 1949
Origin: United States
Description: Produces fragrant double flowers on an upright plant growing to 1.5 m (5 ft). Its attractive foliage changes colour in autumn.
Flowering: Repeats from early summer
Cultivation: Remove dead and spindly wood if necessary in winter. Plant in a warm, protected position.

THE MILLER

Botanical grouping: Modern shrub
Parentage: Baroness Rothschild x Chaucer
Other names: None
Other varieties: None
Year: 1970
Origin: England
Description: An 'old rose'-type bloom, having clear, almost translucent pink, slightly cupped, double blooms which are

borne in open sprays in rosette formation and are lightly perfumed. It will grow to 2 m (7 ft) but can be kept to 1.2 m (4 ft).
Flowering: Repeats throughout summer
Cultivation: This is a sturdy shrub or hedge rose which is very tolerant of adverse weather conditions, including pollution. It will thrive in full sun and fertile soil.

THE REEVE

Botanical grouping: Modern hybrid
Parentage: Lilian Austin x Chaucer
Other names: None
Other varieties: None
Year: 1979
Origin: England
Description: This shrub features spreading growth and thorny stems, reaching a height of 1.2 m (4 ft) at the most. Its shining dark green foliage provides a good backdrop for the large bowl-shaped flowers with delicate, papery petals. These are a dusky-pink colour and strongly scented.
Flowering: Continuously throughout summer
Cultivation: Plant in full sun in rich, well-drained soil. Dead-head after flowering, and mulch around the base of the plant to suppress weed growth.

THE SQUIRE

Botanical grouping: Modern shrub
Parentage: The Knight x Château de Clos Vougeot
Other names: None
Other varieties: None
Year: 1977
Origin: England
Description: A vigorous shrub, growing to 1 m (3 ft) with a rather sparse habit. The flowers are rich crimson, fully petalled and

cup-shaped, with a strong fragrance. Not a prolific producer of blooms.

Flowering: Summer to autumn
Cultivation: Subject to black spot. Likes full sun, a well-drained moderately rich soil and a light winter pruning to encourage more compact growth.

THE WIFE OF BATH

Botanical grouping: Modern hybrid
Parentage: Mme Caroline Testout x (Ma Perkins x Constance Spry)
Other names: None
Other varieties: None
Year: 1969
Origin: England
Description: This delicate rose will grow up to 1 m (3 ft) high. It has thin stems and light green foliage, and pink fully double flowers. The flowers have a light, sweet fragrance and are densely clustered on the bush.
Flowering: Repeat flowering throughout summer
Cultivation: This rose must be carefully treated. A sheltered position is preferred, and mulching the roots will prevent the soil surface drying out.

THISBE

Botanical grouping: Modern shrub
Parentage: Marie Jeanne x Perle des Jardins
Other names: None
Other varieties: None
Year: 1918
Origin: England
Description: A bushy shrub, growing to 1.2 m (4 ft) with slender pointed foliage and masses of richly fragrant, semi-double, creamy yellow flowers borne in clusters. The buds are a much deeper yellow.
Flowering: Summer through to autumn
Cultivation: Prefers a sunny but sheltered situation and well-drained soil. Keep the base free from weeds to avoid black spot.

TIGRIS

Botanical grouping: Modern shrub
Parentage: *R. persica* x Trier
Other names: Harprier
Other varieties: None
Year: 1985
Origin: England
Description: Low growing, thorny bush to 50 cm (1½ ft) with abundant stems and foliage. The flowers are in the *R. persica* mould, yellow with a red spot at the base; however, unlike the species parent this bloom is multi-petalled, resembling a powder puff.
Flowering: Summer only
Cultivation: Unlike *R. persica*, this is a

The Wife of Bath   *Thisbe*

Thisbe   *Trier*

hardy and healthy rose which enjoys an open sunny position but which can tolerate poorer soils. Useful as a border plant or for small spaces.

TRIER

Botanical grouping: Modern shrub
Parentage: Perhaps a seedling of Aglaia x Mrs R.G. Sharman Crawford
Other names: None
Other varieties: None
Year: 1904
Origin: Germany
Description: This is a vigorous bush, reaching as high as 1.8 m (6 ft). It bears

Troilus

Vanity

Warwick Castle

Wenlock

Other varieties: None
Year: 1983
Origin: England
Description: A robust rose, growing to 1.2 m (4 ft) high. The dark green, matt foliage contrasts well with the large and showy creamy apricot blooms. Fragrance is sweet and honey-scented.
Flowering: Continuously throughout summer
Cultivation: A hardy shrub that can be cultivated under a wide range of conditions. Full sun and moderately rich, well-drained soil is preferred.

VANITY

Botanical grouping: Modern shrub
Parentage: Château de Clos Vougeot x seedling
Other names: None
Other varieties: None
Year: 1920
Origin: England
Description: A slightly leggy but vigorous plant which freely bears many sprays of large cerise-pink nearly single flowers and has a pleasing open habit of growth, spreading to 1.5 m (5 ft). Fairly sparse foliage and fruit. Will reach 1.8 m (6 ft).
Flowering: Virtually continuous flowering over a long season.
Cultivation: Give this plant plenty of room and it will reward with a bright, long-lasting display.

WARWICK CASTLE

Botanical grouping: Modern shrub
Parentage: Seedling of Lilian Austin
Other names: None
Other varieties: None
Year: 1986
Origin: England
Description: A small shrub, only growing up to 75 cm (2½ ft) in height, yet quite sturdy. It has mid-green foliage and large, saucer-shaped blooms, the petals of which are a warm pink with a faint cream centre. It has a delicate, sweet scent.
Flowering: Continuously throughout summer
Cultivation: This is an extremely hardy and disease-resistant shrub that can be grown in a wide range of soils and conditions.

WENLOCK

Botanical grouping: Modern shrub
Parentage: The Knight x Glastonbury
Other names: Auswen
Other varieties: None
Year: 1984
Origin: England
Description: A vigorous grower, reaching up to 1.2 m (4 ft) in height. It has slender

masses of delightful, small, semi-double, fragrant flowers of creamy white followed by a substantial crop of fruit. The foliage is medium green and plentiful.
Flowering: Flowers reliably over a long season
Cultivation: This plant is particuarly suited to growing on a wall or at the rear of a large border.

TROILUS

Botanical grouping: Modern shrub
Parentage: Seedling crosses
Other names: None

stems and shiny dark green foliage, plus masses of medium-sized, rounded flowers that are a deep scarlet colour, and sweetly fragrant.
Flowering: Continuously throughout summer
Cultivation: Quite hardy, this shrub will grow in a wide range of soils and conditions. Prune back in winter to maintain shrubby growth and encourage flowering the following season.

WILL SCARLET

Botanical grouping: Modern shrub
Parentage: Wilhelm sport
Other names: None
Other varieties: None
Year: 1948
Origin: England
Description: Bright crimson, nearly single flowers with a slight fragrance are carried in profusion on a healthy, vigorous bush growing to 1.5 m (5 ft). The red hips are particularly attractive.
Flowering: Flowers consistently through summer into autumn.
Cultivation: A hardy plant which will flourish in some shade and indifferent soil.

WILLIAM SHAKESPEARE

Botanical grouping: Modern shrub
Parentage: The Squire x Mary Rose
Other names: Ausroyal
Other varieties: None
Year: 1987
Origin: England
Description: An upright shrub, reaching 1.2 m (4 ft) in height with mid-green foliage and outstanding cupped flowers that are rich crimson, darkening to purple. The flowers have a delightful old-fashioned appearance.
Flowering: Summer to autumn
Cultivation: Suitable for cultivation in a wide range of soils and conditions, preferring full sun and some shelter from prevailing winds. Prune in winter to maintain the shape of the plant.

WISE PORTIA

Botanical grouping: Modern shrub
Parentage: The Knight x seedling
Other names: Ausport
Other varieties: None
Year: 1982
Origin: England
Description: A vigorous shrub growing to 1 m (3 ft) with rather sparse stems of mid-green foliage and medium-sized, cup-shaped flowers of rich mauve-pink. The flowers are strongly scented.
Flowering: Summer through to autumn
Cultivation: Plant in an open, sunny position in well-drained soil, and mulch well

Will Scarlet

William Shakespeare

Wise Portia

Yesterday

with organic matter to encourage flowering. Prune lightly in winter.

YESTERDAY

Botanical grouping: Modern shrub
Parentage: (Phyllis Bide x Shepherd's Delight) x Ballerina
Other names: Tapis d'Orient
Other varieties: None
Year: 1974
Origin: England
Description: A compact and bushy plant with small, dark green foliage growing to 1.2 m (4 ft) high and wide. Produces very large clusters of small, semi-double, lilac-pink flowers with golden stamens. Fragrance is soft.
Flowering: Continuously throughout summer
Cultivation: Good for bedding or planting in groups. Can also be used for hedging and growing in containers.

Miniature and Dwarf Roses

This group contains those roses bred to be grown in small spaces, or as container specimens. The early examples were pleasing from a distance, but the flowers did not really stand up to closer inspection and as they were only available in a limited range of colours, their acceptance was short-lived. In the early 1920s from Switzerland came an outstanding miniature named Rouletii, and from that time they have steadily gained popularity. More recently, miniatures and dwarfs have been bred with even more showy and colourful blooms, and they have become established as an important group in their own right, with many hundreds of new varieties being raised and introduced.

Baby Masquerade

ANNA FORD

Botanical grouping: Dwarf cluster-flowered patio
Parentage: Southampton x Darling Flame
Other names: Harpiccolo

Anna Ford

Baby Darling

Other varieties: None
Year: 1980
Origin: England
Description: Dense and low spreading shrub to 50 cm (1½ ft) high and wide, with shiny dark foliage. Clusters of small-petalled flowers are red with yellow centres.
Flowering: Continuously throughout summer
Cultivation: Needs good soil, but will tolerate light shade. Useful as a container plant. Dead-head spent flowers through the summer. In winter remove all dead and diseased wood, and cut back thinner canes.

APRICOT SUNBLAZE

Botanical grouping: Dwarf cluster-flowered patio
Parentage: Sheri Anne x Glenfiddich
Other names: Mark One, Savamark
Other varieties: None
Year: 1982
Origin: United States
Description: Neat, dense and glossy-foliaged bush to 40 cm (1¼ ft) high. Fragrant flowers are orange-red, prolific and carried in small and compact trusses.
Flowering: Continuously throughout summer
Cultivation: Needs good soil and full sun, useful as a bedding or container plant. Remove dead flower heads during the summer, and in winter take out some older stems, and shorten others in order to promote new growth.

BABY DARLING

Botanical grouping: Miniature
Parentage: Little Darling x Magic Wand
Other names: None

Other varieties: Climbing sport from United States, 1972
Year: 1964
Origin: United States
Description: A dwarf, upright and bushy plant to 30 cm (1 ft) high. Double flowers are lightly fragrant and salmon-apricot, and occur in medium-sized clusters.
Flowering: Continuously throughout summer
Cultivation: Needs good soil and full sun. Makes a good bedding or container plant, as well as a cut flower. Inclined to resist mildew. Remove dead flower heads during the summer, and in winter take out some older stems, and shorten others in order to promote new growth.

BABY MASQUERADE

Botanical grouping: Miniature
Parentage: Peon x Masquerade
Other names: Baby Carnaval, Tanbakede, Tanba
Other varieties: None
Year: 1956
Origin: Germany
Description: Upright, dense shrub with tiny leaves, to 50 cm (1½ ft) high, taller if unpruned. Double and yellow to pinky red flowers are tiny but this is one of the most floriferous cultivars.
Flowering: Continuously from summer to autumn
Cultivation: Tolerates poor soil, but needs full sun. Can be used as a bedding or container plant, and for cut flowers. Sometimes grafted onto a standard. Remove dead flower heads during the summer, and in winter take out some older stems, and shorten others in order to promote new growth.

Benson and Hedges Special

BABY SUNRISE

Botanical grouping: Miniature
Parentage: Benson and Hedges Special x Moana
Other names: Macparlez
Other varieties: None
Year: 1984
Origin: New Zealand
Description: Bushy shrub to 30 cm (1 ft) high with slightly shiny foliage. Semi-double flowers are carried in large trusses, and are small, apricot and handsome.
Flowering: Continuously throughout summer
Cultivation: Needs good soil and full sun. Useful as a container plant. May be difficult to obtain. Remove dead flower heads during the summer, and in winter take out some older stems, and shorten others in order to promote new growth.

BENSON AND HEDGES SPECIAL

Botanical grouping: Miniature
Parentage: Darling Flame x Mabella
Other names: Dorola, Macshana
Other varieties: None
Year: 1982
Origin: New Zealand
Description: Dense, upright shrub to 30 cm (1 ft) high with shiny foliage. Handsome, full double flowers are carried in large trusses and are a deep yellow.
Flowering: Continuously throughout summer
Cultivation: Needs good soil and full sun, and can be used as a container plant. Remove dead flower heads during the summer, and in winter take out some older stems, and shorten others in order to promote new growth.

BIANCO

Botanical grouping: Dwarf cluster-flowered patio
Parentage: Darling Flame x Jack Frost
Other names: Cocblanco

Other varieties: None
Year: 1983
Origin: Scotland
Description: Wide, dense shrub to 50 cm (1½ ft) high with coarse, semi-glossy foliage. Lightly scented flowers are pure white and fully double and are carried in clusters.
Flowering: Continuously throughout summer
Cultivation: Needs good soil and full sun. Useful as a ground cover, and as a container plant. Availability may be limited. Remove dead flower heads during the summer, and in winter take out some older stems, and shorten others in order to promote new growth.

BLUE PETER

Botanical grouping: Miniature
Parentage: Little Flirt x seedling
Other names: Azulabria, Bluenette, Ruiblun
Other varieties: None
Year: 1983
Origin: The Netherlands
Description: Small shrub to 30 cm (1 ft) high with small, light and shiny foliage. Unusual flowers are lavender-purple, double, and about 5 cm (2 in) across with a light fragrance.
Flowering: Continuously throughout summer

Cultivation: Needs better soils and full sun, but is a curiosity suitable for container planting or for small spaces. Remove dead flower heads during the summer, and in winter take out some older stems, and shorten others in order to promote new growth.

BOYS' BRIGADE

Botanical grouping: Dwarf cluster-flowered patio
Parentage: (Darling Flame x Saint Alban) x (Little Flirt x Marlena)
Other names: Cocdinkum
Other varieties: None
Year: 1984
Origin: Scotland
Description: Dense, low shrub to 50 cm (1½ ft) high with even, semi-glossy foliage. Small clusters of carmine to crimson flowers have creamy centres and are prolific.
Flowering: Continuously throughout summer
Cultivation: This rose tolerates poorer soil, but needs full sun. Use as a bedding or hedge plant, in a container or in a small space. May be difficult to obtain. Remove dead flower heads during the summer, and in winter take out some older stems, and shorten others in order to promote new growth.

Boys' Brigade

Carnival Parade

Clarissa

Buttons 'n' Bows

Cider Cup

Cultivation: This is an ideal miniature rose for planting in window boxes, in pots or tubs on balconies or patios or massed in garden borders. It will thrive in full sun and fertile soil. Mulch and water well, especially if grown in containers.

CARNIVAL PARADE

Botanical grouping: Miniature
Parentage: Starburst x Over The Rainbow
Other names: None
Other varieties: None
Year: 1978
Origin: United States
Description: A delightful miniature growing to 45 cm (1½ ft) with glossy, mid-green foliage and comparatively large blooms on short, sturdy stems. The flowers are a fully double, warm yellow edged with rosy pink, giving a 'multi-coloured' appearance.
Flowering: Summer to autumn
Cultivation: Prefers full sun and moderately rich, well-drained soil. Cut out dead wood in winter, and prune to maintain a compact shape.

CIDER CUP

Botanical grouping: Dwarf cluster-flowered patio
Parentage: Seedling from Memento
Other names: Dicladida
Other varieties: None
Year: 1988
Origin: Northern Ireland
Description: Dense, wide shrub to 50 cm (1½ ft) high with dark, shiny foliage. The flowers are very prolific and provide a constant source of small, apricot, shapely flowers during its long flowering season.
Flowering: Continuously throughout summer
Cultivation: Hardy shrub if reasonable soil and full sun are provided. Excellent as a cut flower, container plant and for bedding and hedge. May be difficult to obtain. Remove dead flower heads during the summer, and in winter take out some older stems, and shorten others in order to promote new growth.

BUTTONS 'N' BOWS

Botanical grouping: Miniature
Parentage: Mini Poul x Harriet Poulsen
Other names: Teeny Weeny, Felicity II
Other varieties: None
Year: 1982
Origin: Denmark
Description: A dwarf compact shrub growing to a height of just 20 cm (8 in) with masses of deep pink, many petalled flowers set off by bright green foliage.
Flowering: Repeats prolifically throughout summer.

CLARISSA

Botanical grouping: Cluster-flowered patio
Parentage: Southampton x Darling Flame
Other names: Harprocrustes
Other varieties: None
Year: 1983
Origin: England
Description: Upright shrub to 75 cm (2½ ft) high with narrow habit, and small dark shiny leaves. Small flowers have high centres, are full double, and are carried in dense clusters very high above the foliage.
Flowering: Continuously throughout summer
Cultivation: Tolerates poorer soils, but

needs full sun. Excellent as a cut flower as the supply is endless during the season. Also useful as a bedding plant, low hedge and container specimen. Remove dead flower heads during the summer, and in winter take out some older stems, and shorten others in order to promote new growth.

CONSERVATION

Botanical grouping: Dwarf cluster-flowered patio
Parentage: [(Sabine x Circus) x Maxi] x Darling Flame
Other names: Cocdimple
Other varieties: None
Year: 1986
Origin: Scotland
Description: Neat, dense but wide shrub to 50 cm (1½ ft) high and wide, with small, glossy foliage. Semi-double flowers are apricot pink, with a neat crimp in the centre of each petal, clustered in short-stemmed trusses.
Flowering: Continuously throughout summer
Cultivation: Hardy and vigorous, but needs good soil and full sun. Useful for bedding, ground cover or as a container plant. May be difficult to obtain. Remove dead flower heads during the summer, and in winter take out some older stems, and shorten others in order to promote new growth.

DRESDEN DOLL

Botanical grouping: Moss Miniature
Parentage: Complex breeding involving both Golden Moss and William Lobb
Other names: None
Other varieties: None
Year: 1975
Origin: United States
Description: An exquisite miniature rose reaching not much more than 30 cm (1 ft) high. The double, cupped, fragrant blooms are of a delicate, pure shell pink revealing golden stamens, and open from heavily mossed buds. The foliage is lush and fresh.
Flowering: Repeat flowers throughout the season

Cultivation: A hardy little rose that is suited to small gardens, as a low border edge, in large pots and even in window-boxes provided regular watering is maintained.

DRUMMER BOY

Botanical grouping: Dwarf cluster-flowered patio
Parentage: Seedling x Red Sprite
Other names: Harvacity
Other varieties: None
Year: 1987
Origin: England
Description: Brilliant, deep red flowers in a delightful frilly shape, which hold their colour well. The flowers grow profusely on an attractive, low-growing plant, to 45 cm (1½ ft), with good foliage.
Flowering: Flowers reliably through summer into autumn.
Cultivation: Ideal for use as a border plant, this also looks charming in a container. A robust plant; will stand extremes of weather.

EASTER MORNING

Botanical grouping: Miniature
Parentage: Golden Glow x Zee
Other names: Easter Morn
Other varieties: None
Year: 1960
Origin: United States

Description: Vigorous, dense, upright shrub to 30 cm (1 ft) high with shiny leaves. Larger than average flowers begin as urn-shaped buds, and open to ivory white, neat, and very double flowers carried in clusters which contrast well with the foliage.
Flowering: Continuously throughout summer
Cultivation: Needs good soil and full sun. Useful as a container specimen or in a small space. Remove dead-heads during the summer, and in winter take out some older stems, and shorten others to promote new growth.

EMILY LOUISE

Botanical grouping: Dwarf cluster-flowered patio
Parentage: Judy Garland x Anna Ford
Other names: Harwilla
Other varieties: None
Year: 1990
Origin: England
Description: A most unusual patio or dwarf-clustered bush rose, growing to 45 cm (1½ ft) high, with deep purple-green foliage and brilliant yellow flowers that have only five petals, and prominent stamens. The flowers age to a pinkish-brown shade. The plant has rather a spreading habit.
Flowering: Summer through to autumn.
Cultivation: Useful for a bed, border or container, this charming small rose is quite hardy and resistant to pests and diseases. It also makes an excellent low hedging specimen.

Conservation

Drummer Boy

Dresden Doll

Easter Morning

Emily Louise

Fairy Changeling

Gentle Touch

Gold Coin

Gentle Touch

are double.

Flowering: Summer only

Cultivation: This widely available rose needs full sun and good soil. It is useful as a container plant. Remove dead flower heads during the summer, and in winter take out some older stems, and shorten others in order to promote new growth.

GENTLE TOUCH

Botanical grouping: Dwarf cluster-flowered patio
Parentage: Liverpool Echo x (Woman's Own x Mememto)
Other names: Diclulu
Other varieties: None
Year: 1986
Origin: Northern Ireland
Description: Dense, low and wide, this shrub reaches 30 cm (1 ft) high and has small scale, dark foliage. The lightly scented, double flowers are pale pink, begin as tiny urn-shaped buds, and are carried in trusses.
Flowering: Continuously throughout summer
Cultivation: Needs good soil and full sun, but is an excellent low hedge or ground cover, and can be used for cut flowers. It also makes a good container specimen. May be difficult to obtain. Remove dead flower heads during the summer, and in winter take out some older stems, and shorten others in order to promote new growth.

FAIRY CHANGELING

Botanical grouping: Dwarf cluster-flowered bush
Parentage: The Fairy x Yesterday
Other names: Harnumerous
Other varieties: None
Year: 1981
Origin: England
Description: An interesting small bush, reaching 45 cm (1½ ft) in height, with burnished red-green foliage and clusters of wonderful small blooms, varying in colour from blush to deep pink and magenta.
Flowering: Summer to autumn
Cultivation: Useful as a low bed or border plant, or as a container specimen. Quite hardy and easy to cultivate in most soils and climates, preferring full sun.

FASHION FLAME

Botanical grouping: Miniature
Parentage: Little Darling x Fire Princess
Other names: None
Other varieties: None
Year: 1977
Origin: United States
Description: Dense shrub to 30 cm (1 ft) high with handsome leathery green leaves. Trusses of orange-peach coloured flowers

GOLD COIN

Botanical grouping: Miniature
Parentage: Golden Glow x Magic Wand
Other names: None
Other varieties: None
Year: 1967
Origin: United States
Description: Dense, compact and upright, this rose grows to 30 cm (1 ft) high. Fragrant, semi-double flowers are intense butter yellow and are carried in trusses.

Flowering: Continuously throughout summer
Cultivation: Needs good soil and full sun, but this rose is an excellent tub specimen. May be difficult to obtain. Remove dead flower heads during the summer, and in winter take out some older stems, and shorten others in order to promote new growth.

GOLDEN ANGEL

Botanical grouping: Miniature
Parentage: Golden Glow x (Little Darling x seedling)
Other names: None
Other varieties: None
Year: 1975
Origin: United States
Description: Mid-green, bushy shrub to 30 cm (1 ft) high. Deep yellow flowers are relatively large, double, and very fragrant.
Flowering: Continuously throughout summer
Cultivation: This little rose needs good soil and full sun but makes an excellent container plant. May be difficult to obtain.

GUIDING SPIRIT

Botanical grouping: Dwarf cluster-flowered patio
Parentage: [Seedling x (seedling x *R. californica*)] x Little Prince
Other names: Harwolave
Other varieties: None
Year: 1989
Origin: England
Description: Bears dark pink flowers in profusion, which open to an unusual arrangement of elegant, curved petals around a cluster of gold stamens. The dark leaves provide a good backdrop to the flowers and the bush grows to 50cm (1½ ft).
Flowering: Flowers through summer and autumn.
Cultivation: A hardy, weatherproof plant which adapts well to most positions and is suitable for container cultivation.

Golden Angel

HAKUUN

Botanical grouping: Dwarf cluster-flowered patio
Parentage: Seedling x (Pinocchio selfed)
Other names: None
Other varieties: None
Year: 1962
Origin: Denmark
Description: This diminutive plant (40 cm/1¼ ft) makes up for its size by the profusion with which it bears the shapely, fragrant flowers, coloured buff yellow to cream, which cover the plant over a long season.
Flowering: Flowers over a long season, through summer and autumn.
Cultivation: A healthy, hardy plant requiring no special treatment.

HAPPY THOUGHT

Botanical grouping: Miniature
Parentage: (*R. wichuraiana* x Floradora) x Sheri Anne
Other names: None
Other varieties: None
Year: 1978
Origin: United States

Guiding Spirit

Description: Clusters of double flowers in shades of pink and gold are carried on a small bush (30 cm/1 ft) with medium green, shiny foliage. Slightly scented.
Flowering: Flowers reliably over a long period, into autumn.
Cultivation: An attractive rose for container cultivation.

HOLLIE ROFFEY

Botanical grouping: Miniature
Parentage: Seedling x Darling Flame
Other names: Harramin
Other varieties: None
Year: 1986
Origin: England
Description: A compact, small rose only reaching 30 cm (1 ft) in height, with masses of deep green leaves and a profusion of tiny clear pink flowers with many petals. The flowers are often used for small arrangements.
Flowering: Summer to autumn
Cultivation: Prefers full sun and a warm, sheltered position. Mulch around the base of the plant to keep weed growth down, and cut out dead wood in winter. Will grow in most soils.

Hollie Roffey

Hakuun

Happy Thought

Honeybunch

Hula Girl

International Herald Tribune

HOMBRE

Botanical grouping: Miniature
Parentage: Humdinger x Rise 'n' Shine
Other names: None
Other varieties: None
Year: 1982
Origin: United States
Description: Shapely double blooms with a slight fragrance are apricot pink with a lighter underside, and open flat with prominent centres. They grow in clusters on a small bush (30 cm/1 ft) with plentiful clear green foliage.
Flowering: Flowers through summer and autumn.
Cultivation: A robust plant useful in any position where space is a consideration.

HONEYBUNCH

Botanical grouping: Dwarf cluster-flowered bush
Parentage: Seedling x Bright Smile
Other names: Cocglen
Other varieties: None
Year: 1989
Origin: Scotland
Description: A beautiful small rose, growing to 45 cm (1½ ft) in height, with dark green foliage and clusters of yellow and salmon-pink flowers covering the plant for many months. The flowers have a good perfume.
Flowering: Summer to autumn
Cultivation: A hardy small rose, suitable for a wide range of soil types and climates. Can be grown in a container, or incorporated into a low bed or border.

HONEYFLOW

Botanical grouping: Miniature
Parentage: Spring Song x Gartendirektor O. Linne
Other names: None
Other varieties: None

Year: 1957
Origin: Australia
Description: A splendid rose that deserves to be better known. Highly fragrant masses of almost pure white single flowers, faintly blushed with pink on the outer petal edges, are borne on arching branches. This vigorous, compact bush grows to a height of 1.2 m (4 ft) with lush, pale green foliage.
Flowering: Repeats freely throughout summer
Cultivation: Very vigorous and free blooming, it can be grown as a standard rose in a garden bed or in a large pot in a sunny position. It also grows well on a wall.

HULA GIRL

Botanical grouping: Miniature
Parentage: Miss Hillcrest x Mabel Dot
Other names: None
Other varieties: None
Year: 1975
Origin: United States
Description: Quite tall for a miniature, growing up to 70 cm (2 ft), with neat, mid-green foliage and large, full blooms that are a soft orange-pink. The flowers have a strong, fruity fragrance.
Flowering: Summer to autumn
Cultivation: Useful for a low bed or border, or for cultivation in a container. Choose a sunny but sheltered position, and prune out dead wood in winter.

INTERNATIONAL HERALD TRIBUNE

Botanical grouping: Dwarf cluster-flowered floribunda bush
Parentage: Seedling x [(Orange Sensation x Allgold) x *R. californica*]
Other names: Harquantum, Violetta, Viorita
Other varieties: None
Year: 1985

Origin: England
Description: Named for the newspaper's tenth anniversary, this bush is a short and neat, growing to 40 cm (1¼ ft), with crisp, dark green leaves. The flowers are outstanding in a violet shade with purple overtones. The flowers have a pleasant fragrance.
Flowering: Summer to autumn
Cultivation: A hardy rose, suited to cultivation in most soils and climates. Can be grown in a container, or as a low hedge.

KIM

Botanical grouping: Dwarf cluster-flowered patio
Parentage: (Orange Sensation x Allgold) x Elizabeth of Glamis
Other names: None
Other varieties: None
Year: 1973
Origin: England
Description: Dwarf bush reaching only 50 cm (1½ ft) but bearing copious clusters of shapely canary yellow double flowers which are flushed reddish-pink, particularly in hot weather. The foliage is dark green, matt and dense and provides an attractive backdrop

Kim

to the flowers.

Flowering: Reliable continued flowering over a long period.

Cultivation: An ideal rose for a small space or to grow in a container. A hardy and robust specimen. Mulch well after pruning.

LAVENDER JEWEL

Botanical grouping: Miniature
Parentage: Little Chief x Angel Face
Other names: None
Other varieties: None
Year:1978
Origin: United States
Description: Elegant, lavender-coloured double blooms on a small plant (30 cm/1 ft) well covered with glossy dark green leaves. The blooms are slightly fragrant.
Flowering: Flowering through summer into autumn
Cultivation: This rose makes an unusual colour effect when planted in a container, or used as part of a low bed or border.

LILAC MINIMO

Botanical grouping: Miniature
Parentage: Unknown
Other names: None
Other varieties: None
Year: Unknown
Origin: Unknown
Description: This is a new class of rose. Masses of light lilac-shaded blooms with abundant mid-green foliage growing on a small bush up to 70 cm (2 ft). If grown in a pot it can be taken indoors for a week.
Flowering: Prolifically throughout summer
Cultivation: This is a miniature-style rose that can be grown in pots, 18 cm (7 in) across or more, and is equally effective when massed in a border. Requires full sun or partial shade.

Lilac Minimo

Lavender Jewel

Little Red Devil

LITTLE RED DEVIL

Botanical grouping: Miniature floribunda
Parentage: Gingersnap x Magic Carousel
Other names: None
Other varieties: None
Year: 1980
Origin: United States
Description: A vigorous and bushy miniature, growing to 60 cm (2 ft), with small, mid-green foliage. The small flowers start as pointed buds, and then open to fully double, fragrant blooms in a rich shade of cherry red.
Flowering: Recurrent throughout summer
Cultivation: Easy to grow; prefers a sunny, sheltered position and well-drained soil. Mulch to prevent soil drying out in summer. Dead-head often to encourage flowers. Will grow in pots.

Magic Carrousel

Meillandina

Little Buckaroo

Flowering: Reliable flowers through summer into autumn.
Cultivation: Tendency to black spot, against which the usual precautions should be taken.

MAGIC CARROUSEL

Botanical grouping: Miniature
Parentage: Little Darling x Westmont
Other names: Morrousel
Other varieties: None
Year: 1972
Origin: United States
Description: Multi-petalled blooms which grow in clusters are cream to yellow with dark pink edges and form a neat rosette shape. Slightly fragrant, the flowers can be cut and make a lovely effect in a vase. The bush bears small, clear green, glossy leaves and is compact and upright, reaching 40 cm (1¼ ft).
Flowering: Bears flowers most of the time during summer and into autumn.
Cultivation: Hardy and robust, will withstand extremes of weather and some shade. Excellent container specimen.

MEILLANDINA

Botanical grouping: Miniature
Parentage: Rumba x (Dany Robin x Fire King)
Other names: Meirov
Other varieties: None
Year: 1975
Origin: France
Description: Cup-shaped, densely packed blooms in deep red are set against dark green foliage on a bushy plant reaching 40 cm (1¼ ft).
Flowering: Bears flowers reliably through summer and into autumn.
Cultivation: This rose makes a striking display if planted in a group, or used as a container specimen. Because of its spreading habit, it is a useful ground covering plant.

MR BLUEBIRD

Botanical grouping: Miniature
Parentage: Old Blush x Old Blush
Other names: None
Other varieties: None
Year: 1960
Origin: United States
Description: The small, upright bush (to 30 cm/1 ft) produces prolific trusses of small buds opening to blue-mauve flowers, set against dark foliage.
Flowering: Flowers most of the time from summer through to autumn.
Cultivation: Makes an unusual colour effect if used as a container plant. Hardy, needs no special attention.

LITTLE BREEZE

Botanical grouping: Miniature
Parentage: Anytime x Elizabeth of Glamis
Other names: None
Other varieties: None
Year: 1981
Origin: Eire
Description: This small bush (30 cm/1 ft) bears shapely buds which open to reddish-orange flowers with pink flushes. Attractive and plentiful clear green foliage.
Flowering: Long flowering season
Cultivation: Healthy and hardy, this rose requires no special attention.

LITTLE BUCKAROO

Botanical grouping: Miniature
Parentage: (*R. wichuraiana* x Floradora) x (Oakington Ruby x Floradora)
Other names: None
Other varieties: None
Year: 1956
Origin: United States
Description: Clusters of clear red, loose, double blooms with a white centre are set against a background of shiny, copper-toned leaves. The bush is taller than the average miniature, reaching up to 40 cm (1¼ ft). The flowers can be cut for use in arrangements.

Mr Bluebird

Otago

Pallas

Orange Sunblaze

Orange Sunblaze

ORANGE SUNBLAZE

Botanical grouping: Miniature
Parentage: Parador x (Baby Bettina x Duchess of Windsor)
Other names: Orange Meillandina, Meijikatar, Sunblaze
Other varieties: Climbing variety, reaching 1.5 m (5 ft)
Year: 1981
Origin: France
Description: A multiplicity of tiny, rosette-shaped flowers of vivid orange-red are carried in clusters on a compact bush (30 cm/1 ft). Small, pointed, light green leaves provide an attractive counterpoint to the flowers. Slightly scented.
Flowering: Flowers reliably over a long period, summer to autumn.
Cultivation: A hardy plant which will stand poor soil and extremes of weather. Useful in a border or for container cultivation.

OTAGO

Botanical grouping: Miniature
Parentage: Anytime x Minuette
Other names: Macnecta
Other varieties: None

Year: 1978
Origin: New Zealand
Description: Salmon-orange, full double flowers with delicate pointed petals in a shape similar to a hybrid tea. Fragrant, long lasting and suitable for cutting. The plant is bushy with pretty, darkish leaves and grows to 30 cm (1 ft).
Flowering: Very free-flowering over a long period
Cultivation: Healthy and hardy, this plant can take some shade, though if planted in a shady position it requires well-drained soil.

PALLAS

Botanical grouping: Miniature
Parentage: Clarissa x New Penny
Other names: Harvestal
Other varieties: None
Year: 1989
Origin: England
Description: A petite grower, reaching only 25 cm (10 in), yet covered in a profusion of small apricot buff flowers that have many petals. The foliage is dark green and glossy.
Flowering: Summer to autumn

Pandemonium

Pandora

Peachy White

Cultivation: A useful rose for a very small space or for growing in a container. Choose a warm and sheltered, sunny position for the best results.

PANDEMONIUM

Botanical grouping: Dwarf cluster-flowered patio
Parentage: New Year x [(Anytime x Eyepaint) x Stars 'n' Stripes]
Other names: Claire Rayner, Macpandem
Other varieties: None
Year: 1988
Origin: New Zealand
Description: Reminiscent of old-fashioned, striped roses, this is a colourful rose, opening flat and streaked and flecked with vibrant orange and yellow. The light green foliage is plentiful on a healthy, robust bush growing to a height of 50 cm (1½ ft).
Flowering: Spring and summer
Cultivation: Prefers day-long sun in soil that is drained, fertile, well mulched and watered but will grow in conditions of light to filtered shade.

PANDORA

Botanical grouping: Miniature
Parentage: Clarissa x Darling Flame
Other names: Harwinner
Other varieties: None
Year: 1989
Origin: England
Description: This delightful rose is notable for its densely packed creamy white, rosette-shaped flowers, borne in profusion against a background of glossy dark green foliage. The bush is compact with a slightly spreading habit. Grows to 30 cm (1 ft) high and 40 cm (1¼ ft) wide.
Flowering: Bears flowers most of the time from summer through to autumn.
Cultivation: A hardy, healthy plant which will stand extremes of weather and is a useful addition to a border, small bed, or container.

Peek a Boo

PEACHY WHITE

Botanical grouping: Miniature
Parentage: Little Darling x Red Germain
Other names: None
Other varieties: None
Year: 1976
Origin: United States
Description: Delicious, white, semi-double, fragrant flowers with warm pink tinges are carried in clusters and are suitable for cutting. The small upright bush reaches 30 cm (1 ft), and is well-foliaged with matt leaves.
Flowering: Flowers reliably from summer into autumn.
Cultivation: When grown in a container, this rose makes a charming addition in any small garden or to fill a small space.

Penelope Keith

Petite Penny

PEEK A BOO

Botanical grouping: Dwarf cluster-flowered patio
Parentage: Memento x Nozomi
Other names: Brass Ring, Dicgrow
Other varieties: None
Year: 1981
Origin: Northern Ireland
Description: Shapely buds of rich apricot open flat into many-petalled flowers which turn pink as they mature and are carried in substantial clusters. The leaves are narrow, darkish and slightly glossy and provide excellent cover for the bush. Grows up to 50 cm (1½ ft) high.
Flowering: Flowers freely over a long period through summer and autumn.
Cultivation: The spreading habit of this plant makes it a useful rose for ground covering purposes or to fill a border. It is resistant to extremes of weather.

PENELOPE KEITH

Botanical grouping: Dwarf cluster-flowered patio
Parentage: Seaspray x Benson and Hedges Special
Other names: Freegold, Macfreego
Other varieties: None
Year: 1983
Origin: New Zealand
Description: Lightly scented flowers in bright yellow-gold with a darker reverse are carried on an upright, well-covered plant growing to 50 cm (1½ ft) high. Glossy clear green foliage. Very showy and suitable for cutting.
Flowering: Flowers well over a long season.
Cultivation: Makes a striking border or container plant.

PERLA DE MONSERRAT

Botanical grouping: Miniature
Parentage: Cécile Brunner x Rouletii

Other names: None
Other varieties: None
Year: 1945
Origin: Spain
Description: The origins of this rose are evident in its elegant sprays of soft pink blooms with a slightly darker centre, which make a lovely addition to any vase. The bush is well-covered with dark green leaves and is of upright habit. Grows to 23 cm (9 in) high.
Flowering: Flowers freely through summer into autumn.
Cultivation: This tiny gem looks particularly appealing when grown in an appropriate container.

PETITE PENNY

Botanical grouping: Dwarf cluster-flowered patio
Parentage: Unknown
Other names: Dresselhuys, Macjocel
Other varieties: None
Year: 1987
Origin: New Zealand
Description: The dense masses of eye-catching, semi-double, white flowers have reflexed petals and golden stamens and grow on a small bush which reaches 70 cm (2 ft). A pretty feature plant producing clusters that are attractive in a vase or garden.
Flowering: Freely from spring to autumn
Cultivation: Grow as a potted patio rose or massed in a border where it will give a good display for many months. Full or filtered sun suits it best and the soil should be fertile and mulched in warmer conditions. It can also be grown in a glasshouse.

PETIT FOUR

Botanical grouping: Compact Floribunda
Parentage: Marlena seedling x seedling
Other names: Interfour
Other varieties: None
Year: 1982
Origin: The Netherlands
Description: Clusters of small, loose, lightly

Phoenix

scented flowers, clear pink with white touches, grow in profusion against a backdop of plentiful bright green leaves. Very free-flowering, the bush grows to 40 cm (1¼ ft) and is thorny.
Flowering: Flowers continually over a long season, summer to autumn.
Cultivation: Because of its slightly spreading habit and its neat compact shape, this rose is an ideal addition to the foreground of a border or to a small garden bed.

PHOENIX

Botanical grouping: Miniature
Parentage: Clarissa x (Wee Man x seedling)
Other names: Harvee
Other varieties: None
Year: 1989
Origin: England
Description: Masses of rosette-shaped flowers, crimson with orange flushes, are borne in upright clusters among a profusion of tiny leaves. Compact growth to 40 cm (1¼ ft).
Flowering: Flowers well over a long season.
Cultivation: A striking plant when massed in a low border, this can also grace a container or brighten a small space. Hardy.

PINK SUNBLAZE

Botanical grouping: Miniature
Parentage: Sport of Orange Sunblaze
Other names: Pink Meillandina, Meijidoro
Other varieties: None
Year: 1983
Origin: France
Description: Apart from its clear pink

Pink Sunblaze

Red Pixie

Pretty Polly

Red Rascal

colour, this rose is in every respect the same as its parent Orange Sunblaze (qv). Light fragrance. Grows to 40 cm (1¼ ft).
Flowering: Reliable blooms through summer and autumn.
Cultivation: This plant will tolerate less than ideal soil conditions, and will grow well in a container. Looks good when massed in a group planting.

PRETTY POLLY

Botanical grouping: Dwarf cluster-flowered patio
Parentage: Coppélia '76 x Magic Carrousel
Other names: Meitonje
Other varieties: None
Year: 1988
Origin: France
Description: The combination of small, shapely, rose-pink blooms and a well-covered bush gives an altogether pleasing effect. Grows to 40 cm (1¼ ft) high.

Flowering: Free flowering over a long season
Cultivation: A hardy plant which will tolerate most positions and makes an attractive inclusion in a border, or may be grown in a container.

RED RASCAL

Botanical grouping: Dwarf cluster-flowered bush
Parentage: Seedling x seedling
Other names: Jacbed
Other varieties: None
Year: 1986
Origin: United States
Description: An attractive, leafy, spreading shrub to 40 cm (1¼ ft) with mid to deep green foliage and sprays of fully-double, cupped flowers with satiny red petals. The flowers have golden yellow stamens at their centres.
Flowering: Summer to autumn

Cultivation: A useful rose for a small space, for bed, border or container. The flowers are also good for small arrangements. Suitable for cultivation in a wide range of soils and climates.

RED PIXIE

Botanical grouping: Dwarf cluster-flowered patio
Parentage: (Satchmo x seedling) x (Messestadt Hannover x Hamburg)
Other names: Heinzelmännchen, Kornuma
Other varieties: None
Year: 1984
Origin: Germany
Description: A dwarf, cluster-type rose featuring bright, luminous red flowers borne in abundant, large clusters set amid very attractive foliage. Exceptionally free-flowering and suitable for cutting. The bush grows to about 70 cm (2 ft).
Flowering: Freely throughout summer
Cultivation: Mass in borders or companion plant with larger roses. This is a versatile rose that will grow equally well in a glass house or in pots on a patio or verandah. Plant in full sun or partial shade in fertile soil that is mulched.

RISE 'N' SHINE

Botanical grouping: Miniature
Parentage: Little Darling x Yellow Magic
Other names: Golden Sunblaze, Golden Meillandina
Other varieties: Climbing sport from United States, 1990
Year: 1977
Origin: United States
Description: This justly admired rose has upright sprays of elegant buds which open to deep yellow, hybrid-tea shaped small flowers. These keep their colour well and may be cut successfully. Attractive, light green foliage covers the bush, which grows

Robin Redbreast

up to 50 cm (1½ ft).
Flowering: Very free flowering through summer and autumn.
Cultivation: Use for a low hedge or border, or grow in a suitable container.

ROBIN REDBREAST

Botanical grouping: Dwarf cluster-flowered shrublet
Parentage: Seedling x Eyepaint
Other names: Interrob
Other varieties: None
Year: 1983
Origin: The Netherlands
Description: A dense, spreading shrub, reaching 45 cm (1½ ft) in height, with matt, mid-green foliage. The flowers are a striking currant-red, with whitish yellow eyes giving

Rise 'n' Shine

Rosy Future

the plant a dramatic appearance when in full flower.
Flowering: Summer to autumn
Cultivation: Cut the spent blooms immediately to encourage further flowering. Plant in a warm and sunny, sheltered position.

ROSY FUTURE

Botanical grouping: Dwarf floribunda
Parentage: Anna Ford x Radox Bouquet
Other names: Harwaderox
Other varieties: None
Year: 1991
Origin: England
Description: A beautiful small rose, reaching only 50 cm (1½ ft) in height, with lush dark green foliage and urn-shaped buds that open to warm rose-red flowers. The flowers are sweetly fragrant.
Flowering: Summer to autumn
Cultivation: A hardy rose for most soil types, preferring a warm, sheltered position in full sun. Can be grown in a container, or as part of a low-growing bed or border.

Salmon Rosa Mini

SALMON ROSA MINI

Botanical grouping: Miniature
Parentage: Unknown
Other names: Ruisalro
Other varieties: None
Year: Unknown
Origin: The Netherlands
Description: A new class of rose bred as a 'patio' or potted rose. Dense clusters of beautiful, small, deep salmon flowers abound on a well-foliated bush that grows to 70 cm (2 ft) which can be taken indoors for up to a week.
Flowering: Freely from spring to autumn
Cultivation: This miniature can be grown in a pot, 18 cm (7 in) across, or massed in garden beds as a border 70 cm (2 ft) apart. Plant in full sun and fertile soil that is drained, mulched and well watered, especially in pots.

SHERI ANNE

Botanical grouping: Miniature
Parentage: Little Darling x New Penny
Other names: Morsheri
Other varieties: None
Year: 1973
Origin: United States
Description: The semi-double flowers are an attractive colour combination of red-orange on yellow, and may be cut for use in arrangements. The plant is well covered with shiny, clear green leaves and is of upright habit growing to 30 cm (1 ft).
Flowering: Flowers well over a long season.
Cultivation: Because of its colour, this rose makes a particularly striking effect when grown in a container.

SILVER TIPS

Botanical grouping: Miniature
Parentage: (*R.wichuraiana* x Floradora) x Lilac Time

Sheri Anne

Other names: None
Other varieties: None
Year: 1961
Origin: United States
Description: This rose is aptly named, for its densely packed double flowers are tipped with silver on each pink petal, and the underside of the petals is silver, fading to light mauve with maturity. The well-covered bush grows to 30 cm (1 ft). The flowers are suitable for cutting.
Flowering: Flowers well over a long season, summer into autumn.
Cultivation: With its bushy growth and strikingly coloured flowers, this rose makes an attractive container plant.

SNOOKIE

Botanical grouping: Miniature
Parentage: Torchy x Orange Honey
Other names: Tinsnook
Other varieties: None
Year: 1984
Origin: United States
Description: This small (23 cm/9 in) well-foliaged plant bears double blooms of deep copper-orange which darken to red as they mature. The leaves are shiny and clear green.
Flowering: Bears flowers through most of summer and autumn.
Cultivation: Use for a bright effect in containers or in a very small space.

Snowball

Starina

Stars 'n' Stripes

SNOWBALL

Botanical grouping: Miniature
Parentage: Moana x Snow Carpet
Other names: Angelita, Macangel
Other varieties: None
Year: 1982
Origin: New Zealand
Description: This tiny rose (20 cm/8 in) has a slightly spreading habit to 30 cm (1 ft), and bears many double white pompon-like flowers in clusters. Plentiful, small, clear green leaves.
Flowering: Reliable flowers over a long season through summer and autumn.
Cultivation: A hardy rose that can be used to good effect in a container or small space.

STARINA

Botanical grouping: Miniature
Parentage: (Dany Robin x Fire King) x Perla de Montserrat
Other names: Meigabi

Other varieties: None
Year: 1965
Origin: France
Description: Elegant, hybrid-tea style blooms in bright scarlet orange are carried on a compact, well-formed bush with shiny mid-green leaves. The blooms are very showy and may be used to great effect in an arrangement. Grows to 35 cm (1¼ ft).
Flowering: Long flowering period, into autumn.
Cultivation: A useful plant for a container or low border, or to fill a small space. Healthy and tolerant of weather extremes, it will also stand light shade.

STARS 'N' STRIPES

Botanical grouping: Miniature
Parentage: Little Chief x (Little Darling x Ferdinand Pichard)
Other names: None
Other varieties: None
Year: 1975

Origin: United States
Description: This miniature is striking for the unusual colour of its blooms—splashy red stripes on a white base. The flowers are quite large relative to the size of the plant (30 cm/1 ft) and are slightly, though not unattractively, ragged in appearance. They grow in clusters on a bushy plant, and may be cut.
Flowering: Flowers most of the time from summer into autumn.
Cultivation: A striking inclusion in a container, bed or border because of its colour. This plant is unaffected by harsh weather.

SWEET DREAM

Botanical grouping: Dwarf cluster-flowered bush
Parentage: Unknown
Other names: Fryminicot
Other varieties: None
Year: 1988
Origin: England
Description: A pretty dwarf rose, reaching 45 cm (1½ ft) in height, with neat upright growth and dark green, matt foliage. The plant is covered in clusters of double peachy-apricot flowers, packed with petals and sometimes quartered.
Flowering: Summer to autumn
Cultivation: Quite a versatile small rose, suited to most soil types, but preferring full sun. Can be grown in a low bed or border, or cultivated in a container.

SWEET MAGIC

Botanical grouping: Dwarf cluster-flowered patio
Parentage: Peek a Boo x Bright Smile
Other names: Dicmagic
Other varieties: None
Year: 1987
Origin: Northern Ireland
Description: A free-flowering rose bearing many clusters of elegant, semi-double, light

Sweet Dream

Sweet Magic

Tear Drop

Top Gear

orange flowers with a slight scent. The plant is covered in mid-green, shiny foliage and slightly spreading in habit, reaching a height of 45 cm (1½ ft).

Flowering: Flowers reliably over a long period, summer to autumn.

Cultivation: This rose can be used to make a delightful low hedge, or included effectively in a border.

TEAR DROP

Botanical grouping: Dwarf cluster-flowered patio
Parentage: Unknown
Other names: Dicomo
Other varieties: None
Year: 1989
Origin: Northern Ireland
Description: This tiny, rounded bush, 40 cm (1¼ ft) high and wide, bears many small white flowers which open into flat, gold-centred rosettes.
Flowering: Long flowering period.
Cultivation: Planted in groups, these will make a delightful effect in a low border or small bed, or in matching containers. Hardy and robust.

TOP GEAR

Botanical grouping: Dwarf cluster-flowered patio
Parentage: Eyepaint x Ko's Yellow
Other names: Little Artist, Macmanly
Other varieties: None
Year: 1982
Origin: New Zealand
Description: A densely clustered miniature rose producing flowers that are red with yellowish-white markings at the base and on the petal reverse They are scentless but are suitable for cutting. The small bush grows to 50 cm (1½ ft).
Flowering: Prolifically from spring to autumn

Yellow Doll

Cultivation: A fine border rose which is also suitable for potting as a patio plant. It has a long stem and is a good feature rose, requiring little more than full sun, fertile soil and adequate watering, especially if grown in pots.

YELLOW DOLL

Botanical grouping: Miniature
Parentage: Golden Glow x Zee
Other names: None
Other varieties: None
Year: 1962
Origin: United States
Description: The small, delicate, mildly scented flowers are densely packed with bright yellow petals and make a charming display in an arrangement, lasting well and paling slightly as they mature. The bush is a strong grower, reaching 30 cm (1 ft), and is well covered with glossy, clear green, shapely leaves.
Flowering: Flowers well over a long season, summer into autumn.
Cultivation: An ideal plant to fill a small space or container, it can withstand extremes of weather.

Glossary

Alternate: single leaves emerging from a node, on either side of a stem

Anther: the pollen-bearing part of the plant, generally carried on a filament

Apex: the tip of a leaf or shoot

Bloom: flower or blossom

Bract: leaf-like structures at the base of a flower, sometimes colourful

Bud: embryonic flowers or leaves

Climber: roses that require support or climb on other plants

Cutting: a length of stem that has been removed for the purpose of propagation

Dead-heading: removal of spent flowers to encourage future flowering

Disbud: removal of excess flower buds to encourage larger flowers

Dormant: period when no growth occurs

Espalier: trained against a wall in a stylised arrangement

Eye: the centre of the flower

Filament: the stalk which holds the anther

Flush: appearance of flowers

Friable: soil with a texture that is easy to cultivate

Fruit: the seed-bearing part of the plant, i.e. rosehip

Grafting: propagation by uniting a section of one plant to the rootstock of another

Hardy: capable of withstanding cold conditions and frosts

Inflorescence: clusters of flowers

Lateral: side growth from a shoot

Leggy: loose, open growth habit

Loam: a soil that has a balanced texture; well-drained but capable of holding moisture

Mulch: organic matter layered on the soil surface to suppress weeds and maintain soil moisture

Node: the point on the stem from which the leaf arises

Procumbent: ground-covering habit

Raceme: unbranched flower cluster

Recurrent: flowering more than once in a season

Repeat flowering: recurrent flowering

Rootstock: a healthy root and main stem used for grafting

Shoots: aerial part of a plant; bearing leaves

Sport: an accidental mutation that bears different characteristics from the parent plant

Stamen: the filament and the anther

Standard: a rose with a tall length of stem below the lowest branches

Acknowledgements

Warm thanks are extended to Valerie Swane, Miriam Hannay, Muriel Moody and Sarah Kants.

Photography Credits

The first number indicates the page number, the second number (1,2,3) indicates the column number and the letters (A,B,C,D) indicate the position in the column from the top down.

Richard Balfour 140:3, 143:2, 152:3, 231:1, 248:1B

Bear Creek Direct 158:1, 233:2A, 262:1

Cants of Colchester 106:3A, 177:2B, 181:3B, 212:2, 221:1, 222:2, 225:3, 226:1B, 237:1, 249:3, 253:3B

Derek Fell 10:3, 30:3, 33:1, 33:3, 34:1A, 34:1B, 43:2B, 63:3A, 67:2A, 94:1B, 102:1B, 117:3, 134:1, 147:1B, 157:2B, 178:1, 178:3, 205:2A, 205:3, 213:2, 227:3B, 228:1A, 234:1B, 259:1, 260:1B, 265:2A, 273:1B, 286:3

Dickson Nurseries 122:3B, 181:1, 218:1B, 221:2, 225:2, 227:3A, 232:1A, 235:3, 237:3B, 243:2B, 247:3B, 253:2A, 284:1C, 292:2B

Michael Gibson 26:2, 27:1, 34:3A, 35:3, 37:2A, 42:3B, 43:3, 45:2A, 48:2B, 54:1, 60:2A, 61:3C, 62:2, 71:3, 73:2B, 77:1B, 83:3C, 92:2, 93:3A, 100:3, 105:3, 121:1, 122:2A, 124:3A, 138:1, 146:3B, 156:3, 161:2B, 161:3, 168:2, 172:2, 187:3A, 200:1B, 256:1A, 256:2B, 267:3A, 272:3A, 273:1A, 291:1A

Betty Harkness 143:1A, 162:3A, 248:2A, 285:2A

Peter Harkness 24:3, 25:1, 29:1B, 31:3, 36:1A, 36:1B, 40:1, 40:2A, 40:2B, 44:1B, 47:3, 48:1B, 49:2A, 49:2C, 50:1, 51:2B, 53:3, 54:2A, 58:3A, 59:2A, 59:2B, 59:3A, 59:3B, 65:3, 66:3A, 76:2, 76:3A, 83:1, 83:3B, 84:1A, 84:1B, 85:3, 89:1, 90:3B, 93:3B, 95:2A, 97:2A, 98:1B, 98:2, 99:1, 107:3, 115:3A, 118:1, 118:2, 120:3B, 124:2B, 125:3D, 127:3, 144:3, 145:3A, 145:3B, 146:3A, 148:1A, 150:1C, 152:2C, 153:3B, 156:2A, 159:1A, 162:3B, 165:1A, 165:1B, 166:2, 167:2A, 168:1, 169:2B, 169:3, 170:1A, 170:1B, 173:2B, 174:2A, 178:2, 179:2B, 179:3, 180:2B, 181:2B, 183:2A, 183:2B, 186:3A, 187:2A, 187:3B, 195:2A, 196:2, 198:2, 206:1A, 208:1B, 208:1C, 208:2, 208:3, 209:1, 209:3A, 209:3B, 210:1B, 210:2, 211:2A,211:3B, 213:3A, 215:2A, 216:2A, 217:2, 218:3, 219:3, 222:1B, 224:2, 224:3, 225:1, 229:2B, 230:1A, 230:3, 231:3B, 236:1A, 236:1B, 238:1A, 240:1B, 243:2A, 247:2A, 250:1B, 251:2B, 253:2B, 255:3A, 257:3A, 263:2A, 265:2C, 266:1, 267:2B, 269:2B, 272:2, 273:3, 274:2, 275:3C, 277:3A, 282:1A, 282:3, 287:2B, 288:1, 288:3A, 288:3B, 291:3, 294:2, 295:2, 298:1

Jerry Harpur 8:1, 10:1, 13:2

Kevin Hughes 28:2A, 30:1B, 39:1B, 39:1C, 47:1, 70:1A, 79:1, 80:1, 88:3, 92:1B, 97:2B, 101:2, 107:2A, 112:1B, 114:1B, 115:3B, 122:1, 137:2A, 140:1B, 141:2A, 143:1B, 149:2, 149:3A, 163:2B, 193:2A, 193:3A, 224:1A, 256:3, 267:3B, 268:1C, 272:3B, 275:3B, 280:2

Wilhem Kordes 159:3, 160:2, 179:1, 186:3B, 204:2A, 230:1B, 232:1B, 244:1B, 264:1A

E. Ulzega Doc. Meilland 154:1, 154:2, 171:2, 207:2B, 212:1B, 213:1B, 223:2A, 228:1B, 229:3, 238:1B, 247:3A, 268:1A, 287:3B, 290:2, 291:1B, 291:2B, 294:1A, 295:1B

Mary Moody 203:3A, 246:1A, 284:1B, 288:2

Dr Charles Nelson 41:3A

Vincent Page 28:1, 35:2, 36:2, 38:1B, 40:3, 44:2, 48:2A, 56:3, 64:1, 65:2A, 72:1B, 75:3, 81:3A, 82:3B, 85:2, 86:1, 86:2, 91:2B, 94:2, 101:3, 103:1A, 103:2A, 107:1, 109:2, 120:2B, 127:2, 129:3A, 131:3B, 133:3A, 133:3B, 139:2A, 139:2B, 139:2C, 139:3A, 141:1, 147:2, 148:1B, 148:2, 151:1, 152:1, 156:1A, 156:1B, 156:2B, 160:3, 161:1, 161:2A, 163:3A, 169:2A, 171:3, 173:1, 179:2A, 182:1B, 186:2A, 191:2, 195:3B, 196:1B, 197:1A, 200:1A, 200:1C, 206:1B, 207:1, 220:1C, 226:2, 229:1, 231:2A, 231:2B, 233:2B, 235:2A, 238:2, 239:1, 243:3, 247:2B, 253:3C, 254:1, 254:3B, 257:3B, 262:3B, 264:2C, 265:2B, 269:1, 270:1, 270:2B, 271:1, 276:2A, 279:2B, 281:2B, 281:3B, 284:2, 286:1A, 286:2, 287:3A, 289:2B, 295:1A, 297:1A, 297:1B, 297:3

Photos Horticultural 5:1A, 5:1B, 5:1C, 5:1D, 6, 9:1, 9:2, 9:3, 11:2, 12:1A, 12:1B, 12:1C, 12:2A, 12:2B, 13:1, 13:3, 16:1, 17:2, 18:1, 20:1, 21:2, 21:3A, 22:1B, 24:2, 25:2, 25:3, 26:3, 27:2, 27:3, 28:2B, 29:1A, 30:2, 32:1, 32:3, 33:2B, 34:3B, 35:1, 38:2, 39:3, 41:1, 46:1, 46:3, 47:2A, 51:2A, 52:1, 52:2, 52:3, 53:2, 54:2B, 55:1B, 56:2A, 56:2B, 57:1, 57:2, 58:3B, 60:2B, 63:1, 64:2, 66:3C, 67:2B, 68:3B, 69:2, 70:1B, 70:3, 71:2, 73:2A, 78:2, 80:3C, 87:2A, 88:1, 91:2A, 92:1A, 92:1C, 93:1A, 99:2A, 99:2B, 100:1, 102:1A, 102:2, 103:1B, 104:1A, 104:1C, 105:2, 106:1, 108:1A, 110:1, 117:2, 119:1, 119:2B, 121:2, 126:1, 126:3, 128:2B, 129:1, 130:1, 130:3B, 132:2, 133:1, 135:1B, 136:1, 136:3, 138:2A, 138:2B, 140:1A, 141:2B, 141:3, 142:2A, 144:1, 144:2A, 145:2, 146:1, 150:2, 150:3, 152:2A, 152:2B, 153:1, 153:3A, 154:3, 155:2A, 155:2B, 157:2A, 158:2A, 158:2B, 160:1, 162:1, 163:2A, 163:3B, 164:1, 165:2, 167:2B, 168:3A, 170:2, 173:2B, 174:3B, 175:2, 176:2A, 177:2A, 183:3A, 184:2, 194:2, 199:1, 201:1, 202:2, 205:2B, 210:1A, 214, 218:1A, 219:2, 220:1A, 222:3, 224:1B, 229:2A, 233:3, 234:1A, 239:2B, 239:3, 240:2, 240:3, 242:2B, 249:2B, 250:1A, 251:2B, 254:2, 257:2, 258:1, 258:3C, 259:2, 260:1A, 261:1, 261:2A, 263:1, 263:2B, 264:1B, 264:3, 266:2, 266:3A, 268:1B, 270:2A, 271:2, 271:3A, 273:2B, 274:1A, 275:1, 275:3A, 277:1, 278:2, 280:1B, 280:1C, 281:2A, 283:2, 285:2B, 286:1B, 290:1B, 292:3, 296:2, 298:2B

Poulsen Roser 153:2, 242:1

Rosen Tantau 184:1, 235:2B, 251:2A, 252:1A

Ross Roses 42:3C, 42:3D, 45:2B, 45:3B, 46:2, 48:3, 49:2B, 49:3, 50:3, 57:3, 67:3, 70:2, 74:2, 76:3B, 77:1A, 77:3, 78:3, 80:3B, 83:3A, 84:1D, 89:3, 90:1, 90:2, 90:3A, 91:1, 93:1B, 95:2B, 97:1, 97:3, 98:1A, 100:2, 101:1, 104:1B, 105:1, 106:2A, 106:2B, 108:1B, 109:3B, 110:3A, 110:3B, 111:3, 112:2, 113:2B, 114:1A, 114:2B, 114:3, 115:1, 116:1, 116:3, 119:2A, 120:2A, 121:3, 122:2B, 122:3A, 123:2, 124:2A, 125:3A, 129:3B, 130:3A, 131:3A, 132:1, 132:3, 135:1A, 135:2, 135:3, 137:3, 142:1, 142:2B, 143:3, 147:3, 148:3, 149:3B, 150:1A, 151:3, 167:3, 168:3B, 169:1, 170:3, 183:3B, 184:3, 196:1A, 213:3B, 223:2B, 226:1A, 236:3, 237:3A, 240:1A, 246:1B, 254:3A, 255:3B, 256:1B, 260:2, 269:2A, 271:3B, 276:1, 276:2B, 276:3, 277:3C, 278:1A, 279:3B, 280:1A, 285:1, 287:1, 294:1B

Royal National Rose Society 80:3A, 173:2A, 191:1, 193:2B, 215:2B, 215:3B, 227:2B, 235:1, 241:2, 264:2A, 265:3, 273:2A

Sequoia Nurseries 68:1, 289:1

Swanes Nursery 289: 2B

Bill Shaw 175:3B, 189:1A

Joan Waddington 272:1

Weldon Publishing/Richard Hersey Title page, Endpapers, Back cover, 4, 19, 30:1A, 32:2, 33:2A, 37:3, 41:3B, 42:3A, 44:1A, 50:2A, 55:2, 61:3A, 61:3B, 62:1, 63:3B, 74:1B, 75:2A, 77:2, 79:2, 81:3B, 81:3C, 82:1, 82:2, 84:1C, 86:3, 87:2B, 87:3, 94:1A, 96:3, 103:2B, 104:2, 107:2B, 108:3, 109:3A, 111:1A, 111:1B, 112:1A, 113:1, 113:2A, 114:2A, 120:3A, 123:1, 124:2C, 124:3B, 125:3B, 125:3C, 128:1, 128:2A, 131:2A, 131:2B, 133:2, 137:1, 137:2B, 139:3B, 144:2B, 147:1A, 150:1B, 151:2, 155:3, 159:1B, 159:2, 163:1, 163:3C, 164:3, 165:3, 166:1A, 166:1B, 171:1, 172:1A, 172:1B, 173:3, 174:1, 174:2B, 174:3A, 175:3A, 176:1, 176:2B, 176:3, 177:1, 177:3, 180:1, 180:2A, 181:2A, 181:3A, 182:3, 185:1, 185:2A, 185:2B, 185:3, 186:1, 186:2B, 187:2B, 187:3C, 188:1, 188:2, 189:1B, 189:2A, 189:2B, 189:3, 190:2, 190:3, 191:3, 192:1A, 192:1B, 192:2, 193:1, 193:3B, 194:1, 194:3, 195:2B, 195:3A, 196:1C, 197:1B, 197:2, 198:1A, 198:1B, 198:3A, 198:3B, 199:2, 199:3A, 199:3B, 199:3C, 201:2A, 201:2B, 201:3, 202:1, 203:1, 203:2, 203:3B, 204:1A, 204:1B, 204:2B, 204:3, 205:1, 206:2A, 206:2B, 207:2A, 207:3, 208:1A, 210:3, 211:2B, 211:3A, 212:1A, 213:1A, 215:2A, 215:2B, 215:3A, 216:1A, 216:1B, 216:2B, 217:1, 217:3, 220:1B, 220:3, 221:3A, 221:3B, 221:3C, 222:1A, 223:3, 227:1, 227:2A, 228:2, 230:2, 231:3A, 232:1C, 232:2A, 232:2B, 234:2, 236:2, 237:2, 238:3, 239:2A, 241:1, 242:2A, 243:1, 244:1A, 244:2, 244:3, 245:2A, 245:2B, 245:3, 246:2, 246:3, 247:1, 248:1A, 248:2B, 249:1, 249:2A, 250:1C, 250:2, 251:1, 251:3, 252:1B, 252:2, 253:3A, 255:2A, 255:2B, 256:2A, 258:3A, 258:3B, 259:3, 261:2B, 261:3A, 261:3B, 262:3A, 263:3, 266:3B, 267:2A, 268:2, 269:3, 270:3, 274:1B, 277:3B, 278:1B, 278:3, 279:2A, 279:3A, 281:3A, 282:1B, 283:1, 284:1A, 285:3A, 285:3B, 287:2A, 289:2A, 290:1A, 291:2A, 292:1, 292:2A, 293:1, 293:2, 293:3, 294:3, 296:1, 297:2, 298:2A, 298:3

Colin West 20:3, 21:1, 21:3B, 22:1A, 26:1, 29:2, 31:1, 37:1, 37:2B, 38:1A, 39:1A, 43:2A, 45:3A, 47:2B, 48:1A, 50:2B, 54:3, 55:1A, 55:3, 58:1, 60:1, 65:2B, 66:3B, 68:2, 68:3A, 69:3, 72:1A, 73:3, 74:1A, 75:2B, 95:3, 96:1, 106:3B, 111:2, 257:1, 264:2B

Front cover (Weldon edition)
Weldon Publishing/Richard Hersey (Clockwise from top left: Grenada, Gold Marie, Chicago Peace, Iceberg, Konrad, Jessika, Limelight, Chicago Peace, Cherry Gold, Blue Moon, Gold Medal, Fragrant Charm, Wise Portia, Diamond Jubilee, Heritage, Old Timer, Red Cedar, Charles Austin)

Front cover (Headline edition)
top left: Weldon Publishing/Richard Hersey (Peace)
middle left: Photos Horticultural (Silver Jubilee)
bottom left: Photos Horticultural (Rosy Cushion)
centre: Photos Horticultural (Parade)
top right: Weldon Publishing/Richard Hersey (Mr Lincoln)
middle right: Weldon Publishing/Richard Hersey (Woburn Abbey)
bottom right: Photos Horticultural (Elegance)
Page 1: Weldon Publishing/ Richard Hersey (Grande Amore)
Page 2: E. Ulzega Doc. Meilland (Colorama)